NEW JERSEY

BIOGRAPHICAL and GENEALOGICAL NOTES

FROM THE VOLUMES OF THE

NEW JERSEY ARCHIVES

WITH ADDITIONS AND
SUPPLEMENTS

BY THE LATE

WILLIAM NELSON

Corresponding Secretary New Jersey Historical Society

GENEALOGICAL PUBLISHING CO., INC.
BALTIMORE   1973

Originally Published As
Collections of the New Jersey Historical Society
Volume **IX**
Newark, 1916

Reprinted
Genealogical Publishing Co., Inc.
Baltimore, 1973

Library of Congress Catalogue Card Number 73-7838
International Standard Book Number 0-8063-0562-2

Prefatory Note

THE COLLECTION of "New Jersey Biographical and Genealogical Notes" embraced in this volume consists of the more important biographical footnotes appearing in the various volumes of the "New Jersey Archives," with the corrections and extensive additions made by the late Mr. William Nelson, Corresponding Secretary of the New Jersey Historical Society. The work of extending these notes was begun by Mr. Nelson about eighteen years ago, and much of it was then put in type. From time to time he added to it, and, at his death, August 10, 1914, the matter was nearly ready for publication. It is evident, from various marginal notes made by Mr. Nelson, that he had not fully completed some additions to the proofs, but the work is now published by the New Jersey Historical Society just as prepared and left by him. No attempt has been made to verify the innumerable dates and references, as, indeed, that would be an almost insurmountable task.

It is believed that this volume will prove extremely useful to those who are making biographical or genealogical researches.

The work of seeing the matter through the press has devolved upon the present Corresponding Secretary.

A. VAN DOREN HONEYMAN,

Corresponding Secretary.

Dated June, 1916.

346915

NEW JERSEY

BIOGRAPHICAL AND GENEALOGICAL NOTES.

JOHN ADAMS, of Salem.

John Adams was from Reading, in Berkshire, England. He married Elizabeth, dau. of John Fenwick, and came out with him in the ship *Griffin*, Robert Griffith, master, which arrived off the present Salem, on the Delaware, probably about the first of October, 1675. He brought with him his wife, and three children—Elizabeth, eleven years old; Fenwick, a lad of nine, and Mary, aged four years. Adams is described in the records first as a "weaver" or "clothier," indicating his occupation in England, but after his arrival here he is designated as "planter;" by 1686 he is on the border line, "yeoman alias gentleman," and in 1689 is a full-fledged "gentleman." On March 24, 1674-5, Fenwick gave him and his wife a patent for 2,000 acres of land in the proposed "Fenwick's Colony," afterwards "Salem Tenth," and ultimately Salem. He was among the signers, 25th of 4th mo. (June), 1676, of the agreement for apportioning and settling the town of New Salem, affixing his mark to that important instrument. On July 14, 1676, he received from Fenwick a warrant for the survey of 500 acres, which tract was deeded to him Sept. 12, 1676. On Oct. 18, 1676, a tract of 1,468 acres was surveyed for him. He had a decided predilection for affixing his mark instead of signing his name to documents of all kinds. He and his wife incurred the displeasure of the local court on Sept. 13, 1680, but frankly acknowledged their fault and promised better behavior in the future. It is doubtful if they kept the promise. John Fenwick, in his will, dated Aug. 7, 1683, indicates his lack of confidence in his son-in-law, Adams. The latter does not seem to have exerted much influence in the new community. He was a member of the West Jersey House of Representatives for several years, it is understood. He lived at Penn's Neck, Salem, his tract being known as Sapaney. His house, built at Ivy Point, near Market street, Salem, stood until about 1825. No record of any will by John Adams or by his wife has been found, nor is it certainly known when they died. They are not mentioned in the will of their son Fenwick, in 1689, and may have died before that. Issue:

      i. Elizabeth, b. in England in 1664. Her grandfather, John Fenwick, in his will, dated Aug. 7, 1683 (when she was only nineteen), proved April 16, 1684, provides: "I doe Except against Elizabeth Adams of haveing any the least pte of my Estate & her heirs for ever, Except the Lord open her eyes to See her abominable Transgression against him, & me her poore father by giveing her true repentance & fersakeing yt Black yt hath been the ruine of her and becoming penitent for her sins," etc. Col. R. G. Johnson, in his "Historical Account of the First Settlement of Salem," says: "From that illicit connection hath sprung the families of the Goulds, at a little settlement called Gouldtown, in Cumberland county."

2.   ii. Fenwick, b. in England in 1666. John Fenwick, in his will, appoints William Penn guardian of this grandson.

     iii. Mary, b. in England in 1671.

     iv. Walter, b. in Salem.

     vi. Ann, b. in Salem; m. Samuel Hedge.

2. Fenwick[2] John[1] Adams prob. m. Ann Watkin, Aug. 18, 1687.—*Salem Wills,* 2:11, reversed side. The will of Fenwick Adams, of Fenwick's Grove, Salem county, gentleman, dated June 7, 1689, was recorded August 26, 1689. He makes his wife Ann sole heiress and executrix of his "worldly" estate. His personal estate was appraised at £75. 17. 10, including a tankard of 66 lbs. of pewter at twelvepence per lb. If he was in the habit of draining that huge tankard often it would account for his presumably untimely death.[1] Issue: Sarah, m. Robert Pickman. She and her husband, by deed Aug. 23, 1718, quitclaimed to John Champneys, grandson of John Fenwick, all her rights in the estate of her great-grandfather, John Fenwick, and in the estate of her father, Fenwick Adams, but not in the estate of her grandfather, John Adams.—*Salem Deeds,* 1715-1797, p. 64.

There was another Fenwick Adams in Salem county about this time. In 1676, Sept. 4, he was appointed by John Fenwick to the office of Register of Salem Colony.—*Salem Surveys,* 1676, p. 35. He signed four deeds as a witness in that same year.—*Salem No. 1,* p. 148; *Salem Deeds,* Liber B., pp. 1, 2, 4. By 1680 he witnessed several more deeds. He is charged with assisting Fenwick actively in his resistance to the claims of the Governor of New York, on the trial of Fenwick, at New York, Jan. 12, 1676-7. No other mention of him has been found in the records. The writer was disposed to assume that he was the grandson of John Fenwick, but Mr. Edson Salisbury Jones, of Port Chester, New York, has called attention to the foregoing data, which appear to preclude that assumption.

By an error in N. J. Archives, 23: 3, the account of the estate of Esther Adams immediately follows the will of Fenwick Adams, whereas it should precede it, following Esther's will.

———

[1]Here is a fac-simile of part of the inventory (recorded in Salem Wills, Liber A. f. 33), including the pewter tankard in question. From the total valuation put on these items it is evident that the tankard weighed but 66 oz., instead of as many pounds.

REV. JOHN ALLEN of Woodbridge.

The people of Woodbridge, founded in 1665, made repeated efforts to secure a settled pastor, but during the first fifteen years of the new town enjoyed only nine months of religious services, with the brief pastorate of the Rev. Ezekiel Fogg, in 1674. On July 15, 1679, they commissioned Captain Andrew Bound, on a voyage to England, to treat for a minister, at £50 per year, with the use of 200 acres of parsonage land, and probably a residence, and to bring him over at the expense of the town, in case he was unable to pay his own passage. They also sent by the Captain two letters, one to Dr. Ovin and one to the famous Richard Baxter, setting forth the needs of the Woodbridge congregation. The results of this mission are not known, but in September, 1680, John Allen became the settled preacher in the town. On November 16, 1680, the inhabitants agreed to a voluntary subscription toward his salary, instead of the usual custom of a town rate for the purpose. On January 1, 1681, it was resolved in town meeting:

"We the freeholders and inhabitants of Woodbridge having sent to England to have an honest, able, godly minister to Come over to vs to preach the word of God sinserly and faithfully—and Mr John Alin by the providence of God being for that End Come amongst vs, and we having had Sum Experience of his good Abilities: are willing and doe hereby make Choise of him to be our Minister and desire to put ourselfe under his ministry According to the Rules of the gospel."

In February it was voted in town meeting that if Mr. Allen would consent to remain in the place as its clergyman he should be made a freeholder. He consented, and on November 15 ensuing it was voted to present him with a house-lot of ten acres. In pursuance of this resolution and agreement, John Dennis, carpenter, deeded to John Allen, clerice, both of Woodbridge, January 26, 1681-2, "a messuage there on the road from the Meeting House to the Common Court House and Prison, nineteen acres and a half, bounded on the north by Elisha Parker, on the west by Daniel Greasy, now Thomas Leonard, on the south by Samuel Moore, with said road between." Also seven and a half acres of meadow, bounded on the east by a small creek dividing it from Elisha Parker, on the south by Crane Neck Creek, on the west by Samuel Moore, and on the north by the first lot.

On September 26, 1682, the townsmen petitioned the Governor and Council to induct Mr. Allen formally as their minister, and the message was sent by Capt. Pike. We have no account of the result of this application. Of course, this was entirely unnecessary, but the people were probably so proud of their new pastor that they wished to have him honored by the most public official recognition.

Unhappily, they were destined to have his ministrations for only a little more than three years. On January 2, 1683-4, John Dennes, of Woodbridge, planter, was appointed administrator of John Allen, late of Woodbridge, Clerk; Nathaniel Fitzrandolph, of Woodbridge, and William Looker, of Elizabeth Town, planter, going on his bond. It is not unlikely that in this proceeding Mr. Dennis was acting for the town. It does not appear that he ever filed an inventory or any account.

There is nothing to indicate that Mr. Allen had wife or children in America. If a widow had survived him here she would most naturally have applied for letters of administration on his estate. Had there been minor children a guardian would have been appointed. It seems, however, that the minister left behind him in England a son, John Allen. The news of his father's death drifted slowly across the ocean, and it was fifteen months later, or on April 15, 1685, that he applied for letters of administration, which were granted to him (in Latin), by the Archbishop of Canterbury, by virtue of his prerogative to exercise jurisdiction over estates lying in more than one Diocese, or over the seas. These letters were "on the estate of John Allen, senior, of the Island of New Jersey." The Archbishop's knowledge of his prerogative was better than his geography. The administrator did not act himself, but immediately (May 1, 1685) executed a power of attorney to Daniel Allen, of Boston, New England, for the collection of debts, and for managing the land business of his (John's) father. This Daniel Allen was perhaps either a brother or a younger son of the deceased clergyman. He does not appear to have acted, and nothing further was done in the matter for ten years, when the older son, now designated as "John Allin, late of London, England, now of Boston, New England, son and sole heir of John Allen of New Jersey, deceased," gave a power of attorney, dated September 9, 1695, to Captain Samuel Walker, of Boston, as his land agent in New Jersey. Next, we find on record a deed, dated February 21, 1695-6, from "John Allin, late of London, now of Boston, son of John Allin, Clerk, by Captain Samuel Walker, late of Boston, New England, now of Piscataqua, Middlesex county, New Jersey, his attorney," to William Ellison, of Woodbridge, tanner, for the messuage of nineteen and a half acres, and the meadow of seven and a half acres adjoining, conveyed to John Allin, Clerk, by John Dennis, January 26, 1681.—*Dally's History of Woodbridge and Vicinity*, 81-84; *N. J. Archives*, XXI., 56, 78, 223, 226, 237-8; XXIII., 9.

In addition to the Rev. John Allen, of Woodbridge, there appear to have been two other John Allens, contemporaries of his. Dally, in his excellent History of Woodbridge, has confounded them or one of them with the clergyman, assuming that the latter retired from the ministry, but continued to reside in Woodbridge, where he married a wife, Deliverance, and that he was chosen by the townspeople to various local offices, which he held for several years. As shown above, the clergyman was retired by death, probably in December, 1683.

In this connection it will not be out of place to give a few particulars. not in Dally's History, regarding the

OTHER JOHN ALLENS, OF WOODBRIDGE.

In a deed dated May 2, 1685, from William Camptone, of Woodbridge, to Richard Powell, of the same place, for a homelot of ten acres there, the tract is described as bounded on the south by lands formerly "of John Smith, now John Allan."—*N. J. Archives*, XXI., 120. This John Allen doubtless married a daughter of Thomas Alger, of Woodbridge, who in his will, dated January 4, 1687-8, names "grandchild John, son of John Allen of Woodbridge."—*Ib.*, 108. When William Brown, of Woodbridge, died, the inventory of his personal estate was made by John Allen, January 10, 1698-9.—*Ib.*, XXIII., 66. John Allen, of Middlesex, made his will on January 4, 1702-3, naming son John, and daughters (names not given), under age. He left real and personal estate. His executors were John Fitzrandolph and Nathaniel Fitzrandolph, junior, both of Woodbridge. His personal estate was inventoried and appraised at £45, 14, 1. The will was proved the same month, January 28, 1702-3, indicating that it was made on his death-bed. No wife is mentioned, she having doubtless predeceased her husband.—*Ib.*, 10.

John Allen, of Woodbridge, cooper, doubtless son of the last-named, made his will January 16, 1715-16. He names wife Deliverance, and children Samuel, John, Ursula and a younger daughter, whose name is not given. He devises lands bought of Moses Rolf, and other lands inherited from his father, John Allen. The executors named were his wife, and his brother-in-law (? John Heard). The will was witnessed by Daniel Britten, John Thomson and Adam Hude, and was proved before James Smith, Secretary of the Province, in due course. The inventory of the personal estate was appraised at £103. 3s., including a great bible valued at £1, 10s., and a small one at 6 shillings.—*N. J. Archives*, XXIII., 10.

From sundry passages in Dally's History it would appear that these John Allens were Quakers.

ALLINSON FAMILY.

The progenitor of the Allinson family in New Jersey was Joseph Allinson (son of Peter, son of Bryan), who came to this country in May, 1718, and settled in Burlington county. He was a grandson of Bryan Allinson, of York, England, and Elizabeth Walker, his wife; he d. 1679; she d. 1663. Their only son was Peter Allinson, who m. Margaret Wrighton, dau. of Michael and Elizabeth (Brinks) Wrighton. Peter's son Joseph on coming to New Jersey was received into Burlington Friends' Meeting, 11 mo. 8, 1718, his certificate describing him as "from Great Britain, at Raby in Durham." He m. 2d mo. 20, 1721, the record describing the parties as "Joseph Allinson late of Yorkshire, Great Britain, but now of Burlington county, and Elizabeth Scattergood, dau. of Thomas Scattergood, of Mancefield township, said county." His wife's mother was Phebe, dau. of Christopher Wetherell. Mr. Allinson was probably a native of Yorkshire, and later resided at Raby, in Durham, taking his certificate from the latter place when he came to America. He d. at Burlington, 6th mo. 23, 1756. His will, dated May 6, 1755, proved July 28, 1756, designates him as of Burlington City, and devises to wife Elizabeth a house and lot on High street (Burlington), "which I bought of Francis Smith;" to son Peter, £10 "and my riding mare;" to sons Joseph and Jacob, minors. meadow land bought of Francis Smith, to be equally divided between them; to son Samuel, house and lot in Pearl street (Burlington), "that I bought of Richard Wheat," etc.; it also leaves bequests to Mary, wife of James Clothier, and to grandchildren, Elizabeth and Mary, children of son Thomas, deceased, when 18; remainder of estate to wife Elizabeth, to bring up son Samuel. Executrix—wife Elizabeth. Witnesses—John Saunders, John Hoskins, William Hewlings.—*Liber No. 8 of Wills*, f. 311. His wid., b. 1st mo. 14, 1688-9, d. at Burlington, August 22, 1768. Says a newspaper of the day: "She was possessed of many good qualities, that endeared her to her family and Friends." Her daughter-in-law, wife of Samuel Allinson, died a few hours before her. "As she had always lived in great Harmony with, and much esteemed her Daughter, the Sorrow her Illness gave her, affords Reason to believe it was a Means of hastening the Mother's End. They were carried to their Graves together, attended by a great Number of Relations, and Friends of all Denominations." The will of Elizabeth Allinson, of the city and county of Burlington, bears date 1st mo. 3d, 1765, and was proved Sept. 12, 1768. It gives to sons Peter, Joseph and Jacob each £50, "but Jacob is absent and it is not known whether he is dead or alive;" mentions daughters-in-law Elinor Allinson and Mary Clothier; grandchildren Elizabeth Allinson and Mary Allinson, children of son Thomas, deceased; "children" of son Peter; £5 to Mary Holmes; to son Samuel "all the rest of my estate." Executors—brother Thomas Scattergood, son Samuel Allinson. Witnesses—John Hoskins, Mary Holmes. The will was made, she says, "as my Husband's Executrix."—*Liber No. 13 of Wills*, f. 429. Of the sons of Joseph Allinson, the most distinguished was Samuel Allinson, the prominent lawyer named below.

Joseph Allinson and Elizabeth, his wife, had issue:

ALLINSON

2.   i.   Thomas², b. 11 mo. 29, 1721-2; m. Mary Shinn (b. 10 m. 23, 1727, dau. of Thomas Shinn and Martha Earl, m. in 1718); they were passed the second time in Burlington Friends' Meeting, 4 mo. 3, 1745; he. d. Jan. 12, 1754. Thomas Allinson, blacksmith, of Bridgetown (now Mt. Holly), Burlington county, made his will March 21, 1752, proved March 18, 1755, in which he names wife Mary, daughter Elizabeth, an expected child, and brothers Peter, Jacob, Joseph and Samuel Allinson. Executors—friend Thos. Atkinson, miller, wife Mary Allinson. Witnesses—Henry Paxson, Benj. Bispham, Thos. Laurence.—*Liber No. 8 of Wills*, f. 39. His wid. m., 2d, James Clothier or Cloather.

    ii.   Mary², b. 10 m. 30, 1723; d. 11 mo. 12, 1728.

3.   iii.   Peter², b. 11 mo. 26, 1725-6; m. Eleanor or Ellen, dau. of John and Mary West. Peter Allinson, joiner, of Mt. Holly, d. intestate, and administration on his estate was granted January 10, 1782, to Thomas Allinson (doubtless his son), tanner; bondsman, George West, saddler, of Mt. Holly. The inventory, taken 1st mo. 1st, 1782, was appraised by Solomon Gaskill and Aaron Smith at £110. 5s. 6d.—*Lib. H of Wills*, f. 215.

    iv.   Mary², b. 1 mo. 9, 1728-9; d. 8 mo. 12, 1730.

    v.   Elizabeth², b. 11 mo. 14, 1730-1; d. 7 mo. 20, 1732.

    vi.   Joseph², b. 2 mo. 1, 1734; d. 2 mo. 18, 1800. His brother Samuel refers to him in his will as "my poor brother Joseph."

    vii.   Jacob², b. ———; he is referred to in the will of his brother Thomas, in 1752. In his mother's will, dated 1st mo. 3d, 1765, £50 is left to Jacob, but it is stated that "he is absent and it is not known whether he is dead or alive." There is no further trace of him.

4.   viii.   Samuel², b. 6 mo. 26, 1739; m. 4 mo. 25, 1765, Elizabeth Smith (b. 11 mo. 26, 1738-9; d. Aug. 21, 1768); 2d, Martha Cooper, Jan. 29, 1773.

Third Generation.

2. Thomas² Joseph¹ Allinson and Mary Shinn had issue:

    i.   Elizabeth²; Elizabeth Allinson, of Mt. Holly, m. William Chew, of Gloucester, mar. lic. dated April 21, 1774.

    ii.   Mary³; Mary Allinson, of Burlington, probably the dau. of Thomas, m. George Githens, of the county of Gloucester, Oct. 30, 1774, as appears by a certificate of the Rev. Robert Blackwell, of Old Coles Church. Mr. Githens paid the equivalent of $6 for the marriage fee.

3. Peter² Joseph¹ Allinson and Ellen West had issue:

5.   i.   Thomas³, b. 1 mo. 7, 1754; prob. m. Sarah ———, who d. 6 mo. 7, 1806; he d. 1828.

    ii.   Mary³, b. 2 mo. 26, 1756; m. 11 m. 12, 1783, William Atkinson, son of Thomas and Susannah (dau. of Peter and Ellen ———, deceased, of same place) Atkinson, of Mt. Holly, at Mt. Holly Meeting house; d. 1787.

    iii.   Elizabeth³, b. 1 mo. 30, 1759; m. Samuel Clark, of Mt. Holly. Children: 1. Joseph Allinson; 2. Thomas Allinson.

iv.   Samuel, b. 6 mo. 24, 1761. He appears to have removed
to Virginia, from which State he was appointed ensign
of the second sub-legion of the U. S. army, June 2,
1794; transferred to the second infantry Nov. 1, 1796;
commissioned first lieutenant March 3, 1799. He d. at
St. Mary's, Camden county, Ga., Nov. 2, 1799. His
will was made at that place June 17, 1799; it was
proved by the affidavits of the witnesses—E. Hebbard
and Will Mowbray—taken at St. Mary's, Nov. 25,
1799, before a notary public. The testator gives all
his estate to his only daughter, Frances Barber Allinson, a minor, and in case of her death without issue,
then to his sister, Sarah Allinson. He mentions sisters—Mary Atkinson and Elizabeth Clarke—and appoints his brother-in-law, Samuel Clarke, turner and
chair maker, of Mt. Holly, guardian of his daughter.
Executors—Samuel Clarke and Capt. A. Y. Nicoll, of
1st U. S. Regiment of Artillerists and Engineers.
Samuel Clarke alone qualified, March 27, 1800, when
the will was admitted to probate. The inventory of
the personal estate, taken March 27, 1800, was appraised by John Dobbins and John Perry at $2,620.28.
—*W. J. Wills,* Liber No. 39, f. 59. His dau. Frances d.
young.

v.   Joseph West[3], b. 9 mo. 2, 1764.

vi.   Sarah[3], b. 9 mo. 17, 1766; living and unm. in 1799; subsequently m. William Widdifield, of Philadelphia.

4.   Samuel[2] Joseph[1] Allinson was a member of the Society of Friends.
He was licensed as an attorney and counsellor-at-law of New Jersey,
November 9, 1760, and was commissioned one of the Surrogates of New
Jersey, March 22, 1762. He was clerk of the corporation of Burlington
in 1764. In the same year he was also clerk of "The Lower Sluice Company in the city of Burlington," formed to bank the meadows on both
sides of the creek surrounding the Island of Burlington. In 1765-6 he
advertised for the heirs of a deceased client in Maryland, for whom he
had collected a claim. He also advertised a large number of deeds
which had come into his hands, and which he thought the grantees
ought to come and get, for the security of their estates. In 1769 numerous petitions were presented to the Legislature, complaining of many
lawyers, for exacting extortionate fees. Among those accused was Samuel Allinson, but he produced certificates, signed by the Justices of the
Supreme Court, and three of the most distinguished members of the
New Jersey bar—Messrs. Richard Stockton, James Kinsey and John
Lawrence—to the effect that they had carefully inspected the bills of
costs complained of, and found them to be in every particular correct
The Assembly thereupon dismissed the complaint. On October 25, 1769,
James Kinsey and Samuel Allinson were permitted to appear before the
Assembly and address that body in behalf of their fellow members of the
bar, who had been so generally accused, and with so little justice, when
Allinson turned the tables on one of his prosecutors by showing that
the people's grievances were mainly due to the excessive charges of
the Sheriffs, one of whom—Samuel Tucker—was then a member of
the House, and particularly vigorous in his denunciation of the lawyers. In 1773 Allinson was designated by the Legislature to prepare a
new edition of the laws of New Jersey, for which purpose the Council
gave him permission to peruse the first three volumes of their minutes.
His work was so far completed on January 14, 1775, that the Legislature appointed a committee to inspect the laws as prepared by him for

the press. His compilation, known as Allinson's Laws, was printed in 1776 by Isaac Collins, at Burlington, in a handsome folio of pp. 493, 6, and index, pp. 15. Samuel Allinson was one of the overseers of the Burlington school in 1774. He was Clerk of the Burlington Friends' Preparative Meeting in 1779, and was by that meeting in that year appointed one of the first trustees of the Friends' School in Burlington. Samuel Allinson was of course precluded by his principles as a member of the Society of Friends from taking an active part in the Revolution, and his name does not appear conspicuously in that connection. He married, 1st, Elizabeth, dau. of Robert Smith, junior, and Elizabeth Bacon, of Burlington; she d. Aug. 21, 1768, after a short illness. For an interesting sketch of her character, see N. J. Archives, XXVI., 262. Mr. Allinson m. 2d (in 1773), Martha, daughter of David Cooper, of Woodbury, and Sybil (dau. of Timothy and Martha) Matlack. She d. 3 mo. 9, 1823, aged 76 years. He died 6 mo. 2, 1791. He left him surviving his second wife and two children by his first wife, and seven by his second wife—four sons and three daughters. Seven of his nine children lived to be seventy-five years of age. The will of Samuel Allinson, of Waterford, dated 12 mo. 30, 1784, proved at Woodbury, June 21, 1791, mentions his wife Martha and eight children, to whom he bequeaths £500 to each of his four sons, and £300 to each daughter; also commends "my poor brother Joseph to the kind care of my wife and my son William." Executors—"my wife," "my father," brother (in-law) David (Cooper), son William, Amos Cooper. Guardians of minor children—"my father" (in-law), "my brother." A codicil, 8 mo. 30, 1787, provides for son John Cooper, born since date of the will. —*W. J. Wills*, Lib. No. 32, f. 203. Issue:

By his first wife:

 i. William³, b. 4 mo. 1766; d. 10 mo. 1, 1841, unm. He was a trustee of Friends' burying ground in Burlington, 1810-1837. In 1796 he was appointed by Burlington Meeting to receive subscriptions for a boarding school under charge of Philadelphia Yearly Meeting—the Westtown school fund. The will of William Allinson, of the City of Burlington, dated 10 mo. 1, 1841, was proved Oct. 14, 1841. He names brothers David, Samuel and John C.; sisters Mary Allinson, Elizabeth Allinson, Sibyl Allinson, Margaret Parker, Bernice Allinson (i. e., sister-in-law, widow of his deceased brother James); sister-in-law Beulah, wife of brother David Allinson; nieces—Martha Allinson, dau. of brother Samuel, Esther Hughes "and all her children;" nephews—George Boyd Allinson, Samuel Allinson (to whom is devised "my place at Locust Hill where he lives"), John C. Allinson, William J. Allinson (to whom is devised "my house where I live corner of High and Union streets, Burlington city"), Cooper Allinson, Joseph Allinson (to whom is devised "my lot in Juliustown"). Executors—nephews Samuel Allinson, Jr., William I. Allinson, Cooper Allinson and John Allinson, sons of brother David. Witnesses— Thos. Collins, Wm. W. King, Wm. Bishop. Thos. Dugdale to take charge to bring estate to final close.

 ii. Mary³, b. 2 mo. 16 (elsewhere in the record the date is 2 mo. 3), 1768; d. 9 mo. 10, 1859, in her 92d year. She was an elder in Burlington Friends' Meeting, and one of the first clerks of the Women's Meetings, the minutes of which date back to 1800. She never married.

By his second wife:

6.   iii.   David³, b. 1 mo. 14, 1774; m. Beulah Zane, dau. of Jonathan and Elizabeth Zane; d. 9 mo. 14, 1858, in his 85th year. "David Allinson an adult" was baptized in St. Mary's P. E. church, Burlington, June 20. 1819. Was this the same person? David³ Samuel² Joseph¹ Allinson began printing at Burlington in 1803, and during a period of twenty years or more published many volumes highly creditable to his press. In 1810 he published a weekly paper, the *Rural Visitor*, useful and entertaining in character. The will of David Allinson of Pemberton township, is not dated; it was proved Sept. 2, 1858. In it he mentions wife Beulah, children Joseph, John C. and David Cooper Allinson; nephew Wm. I. Allinson; sisters Mary and Bernice; brother Samuel Allinson, "nieces and nephews." Executors—sons David Cooper Allinson and John C. Allinson. Witnesses—Wm. E. Page, Joseph Griffith.—*Original Will.*

   iv.   Elizabeth³, b. 7 mo. 26, 1775; d. 8 mo. 11, 1856, in her 82d year, unm. She was blind from birth.

7.   v.   James³, b. 1 mo. 27, 1778; m. June 6, 1806, Bernice, b. March 4, 1781, dau. of James and Rebecca Chattin; her father was an officer in the American Revolution. During her minority, through conviction she became a member of Friends' Meeting. On her marriage to James Allinson she removed to New York, where he was then in business. He subsequently located at Yardville, a few miles from Trenton. He d. aged 33 years; she d. 11 mo. 12, 1858, in her 78th year. See Memoir of Bernice Allinson in *Friends' Review*, 3 mo. 19, 1859, p. 433. The will of Bernice Allinson, of Mercer county, N. J., dated 1 mo. 9, 1858, was proved Jan. 1, 1859. It names sons Samuel Allinson, jun., and William James Allinson, who are also appointed executors, and are empowered to sell her property in Philadelphia, "late 218 now 480 North 4th street." Witnesses—Saml. P. Nicholson, John H. Broadbent and George D. Leaver.—*Original Will.*

   vi.   Sybil³, b. 12 mo. 26, 1779; d. 8 mo. 28, 1855, in her 76th year, unm.

   vii.   Margaret³, b. Dec. 2, 1781; m. 3 mo. 24, 1831, Benjamin Parker, of Shrewsbury, Monmouth county, son of Peter Parker and Lydia ———, deceased. She was recommended by the Burlington Monthly Meeting in 1808 as a minister among Friends. She d. in 1857.

8.   viii.   Samuel³, b. 8 mo. 7, 1784.

   ix.   John Cooper³, b. 7 mo. 23, 1786; d. 8 mo. 22, 1812, in his 27th year, unm.

Fourth Generation.

5.   Thomas³ Peter² Joseph¹ Allinson, b. 1 mo. 7, 1754, made his will 5 mo. 8, 1828, and it was proved Nov. 15, 1828. He mentions son John and grandchildren Samuel Allinson and Sarah Allinson, children of John; refers to John's wife, without naming her, and leaves £100 to be divided among his brothers' and sisters' children. Executors—nephews Joseph A. Clark and Thomas A. Clark. Witnesses—Saml.

Clark, Clayton Monrow, John Neale. In this will he speaks of himself as "aged but of sound mind."—*Original Will.* Issue:

    9.   i. John[4], m. ——— Boyd.

6. David[3] Samuel[2] Joseph[1] Allinson and Beulah (Zane) Allinson had issue:

    i. Ann[4], b. April —, 1825; d. Aug. —, 1825.

    ii. Joseph[4], b. Jan. 24, 1826; d. Oct. 2, 1862.

    iii. David Cooper[4], b. April 29, 1827.

    iv. John Cooper[4], b. Oct. 30, 1828; m. Lucy Ann Leaver, dau. of William and Hannah, at Burlington Meeting House, 10 mo. 23, 1856. Witnesses—Beulah D., D. Cooper, Mary, Bernice, Samuel, Ann, William J. and James Allinson, and others. Children: 1. Helen Margaret; 2. William; 3. Lucy, d. young; 4. Charles; 5. Emily.

7. James[3] Samuel[2] Joseph[1] Allinson and Bernice (Chattin) Allinson had issue:

    i. Rebecca, b. Aug. 27, 1807; d. April 1, 1829.

10.   ii. Samuel[4], b. 12 mo. 20, 1808, at Yardville; d. there, 12 mo. 5, 1883. He was a distinguished philanthropist, and was influential in the cause of prison reform in New Jersey and elsewhere. For a memoir of his life and work, see 2 N. J. Hist. Soc. Proceedings, VIII., 72. He m. 1st, June 6, 1839, Elizabeth Alsop, who d. June 11, 1850. He m. 2d, April 11, 1855, Ann Tatum, dau. of Josiah and Rachel Tatum. The will of Samuel Allinson, of Locust Hill, bears date 7th mo. 13th, 1880, and was proved at Trenton, Dec. 18, 1883. He bequeaths certain shares of stock to wife Ann, and mentions children—James Allinson (a lawyer, of Trenton, who d. intestate, in 1887), Rachel Elizabeth Allinson, Bernice Allinson, Josiah Tatem Allinson, Caroline Allinson; gives $30 to "sister-cousin" Georgeanna E. Nicholson; to Richard Cadberry, "Treasurer of Friends' Freedman Association, of Philadelphia," $100 for their schools in Virginia and North Carolina; to Children's Home in city of Trenton, $100; to nieces Anne F. and Elizabeth F. Baily, $100 for cause of total abstinence; $30 to nieces Martha Allen, Anna Bernice Lewis and Gertrude Allinson, and nephews Edward P. Allinson and Francis G. Allinson, children of brother and sister W. J. and Rebecca W. Allinson, to be shared equally between them, "to buy some memento of my affection." In a paper dated 1 mo. 7th, 1879, he mentions death of brother, and of his own daughter Mary. Executors—Ann Allinson, sons James and Josiah T. Allinson. Witnesses—D. Cooper Allinson, Joseph De Cow.—*Original Will.* Rachel and Josiah resided in 1905 at the old home at Yardville.

11.   iii. William J.[4], m. Rebecca W. Hinchman, dau. of John and Elizabeth Hinchman, Aug. 18, 1839. He established himself in Burlington as a druggist, but subsequently devoted himself to literary pursuits, compiled one or more school books, and for a number of years was editor of the *Friends' Review*, since changed to the *American Review*, published in Philadelphia. He

and his brother Samuel were among the trustees of Friends' burial ground, Burlington, named in deed of 6 mo. 21, 1837. He lived on the corner of High and Union streets, Burlington, in a house having the date 1731 on the gable end. His will, dated 5 mo. 2, 1872, was proved June 22, 1874. He mentions his wife, Rebecca W. Allinson, and "children," without naming them. Executors—wife Rebecca W. Allinson, and brother Samuel Allinson. Witnesses—J. Howard Pugh, Rowland J. Dutton, Wm. R. Bishop.—*Original Will.* In the Autobiography of the Rev. Dr. Theodore L. Cuyler, of Brooklyn, published in 1904, are related some pleasing reminiscences of William J. Allinson.

Concerning the last two brothers, the writer has received the following interesting letter from Henry S. Haines, of Burlington, the Surveyor-General of West Jersey:

"Samuel Allinson, the Philanthropist, and William J., his brother, characterized by the Rev. T. L. Cuyler, D. D., as the Charles Lamb-like editor of the *Friends' Review*, were warm personal friends of my father, who was associated with them in works deemed philanthropic by them. Their prominence in temperance and anti-slavery movements brought them and others in Burlington, notably Samuel Allinson, under the ban of the then existing general public sentiment regarding those measures of reform; and I can distinctly remember, although less than three years of age, that the front door of our house was violently forced open by the mob, and the violent indignities heaped upon it and its inmates on account of their avowed opinion in these matters. *O tempora! O mores!* Now, how changed! The aged aunts of Samuel and William, whose names appear in your memoir, were venerated and beloved friends of my earliest youth, and it was my privilege at that period to meet occasionally the poet, John G. Whittier, at that home of piety and refinement."

8. Samuel[3] Samuel[2] Joseph[1] Allinson, b. 8 mo. 7, 1784; m. 1st, April 14, 1814, Susannah Dillwyn Smith, b. March 5, 1792, dau. of James Smith, of Philadelphia (b. Oct. 15, 1750, son of the Hon. John Smith, of Franklin Park, Burlington, and Hannah, dau. of James Logan), and Esther (dau. of William) Hewlings; she d. 7 mo. 2, 1816. He m. 2d, May —, 1821, Eliza Welsh. Samuel Allinson and Susannah Dillwyn Smith had issue:

      i. Esther[4], b. Dec. —, 1814; m. Henry Pearse Hughes, of "The Priory," Walthamstow, Essex, England. Children: 1. Hetty Elizabeth, m. Albrecht G. Eggers; 2. Annie Margaret; 3. Mary Strother, m. John S. Cousens; 4. Henry Pearse, m. Emma S. Cousens; 5. Emma Martha; 6. Georgina Allinson, m. G. E. Hignett; 7. Willie F., m. Edith Cousens; 8. Alice Emily, m. Henry Layton; 9. Susan Dillwyn; 10. John Arthur.

      ii. Martha[4], b. Dec. —, 1814; mentioned in the will of her uncle, William Allinson, in 1841.

Fifth Generation.

9. John[4] Thomas[3] Peter[2] Joseph[1] Allinson and ——— Boyd, his wife, had issue:

      i. Samuel[5], m. Mary Ann Foster, dau. of Joshua and Ann (Robbins) Foster. The will of Samuel Allinson, of Springfield township, Burlington county, dated April

11

5, 1870, proved Feb. 4, 1871, mentions son, Thomas B. Allinson, and sister-in-law Abigail B. Foster. Executors—son Thomas B. Allinson and friend Thos. H. Sutton. Witnesses—Nathl. W. Fenimore, Isaac A. King. Inventory, Feb. 3, 1871, $850.50. Children: 1. Anne, d. aged 18 yrs.; 2. Albert, d. young; 3. Edward, d. young; Thomas B., who in 1905 resided about three miles from Burlington.

ii. Sarah[5], mentioned in the will of her grandfather, Thomas, in 1828.

iii. (prob.) George Boyd[5]. George Boyd Allinson, an infant, was bap. in St. Mary's Church, Burlington, March 28, 1824. Joseph Allinson, an infant, was bap. in the same church May 7, 1826. Were they children of John Allinson and ——— Boyd?

10. Samuel[4] James[3] Samuel[2] Joseph[1] Allinson had issue:
By his first wife, Elizabeth Alsop:

i. Mary Eliot, b. March 8, 1840; d. unm.

ii. James, b. Sept. 23, 1841; d. 1887.

iii. Rebecca, d. in inf.

iv. Rachel Elizabeth, b. Jan 6, 1847.

v. Samuel E., d. in inf.

By his second wife, Ann Tatum:

vi. Bernice, b. Feb. 12, 1856.

vii. Josiah Tatum, b. March 19, 1858.

viii. Caroline, b. Aug. 2, 1859.

In 1905 Rachel and Josiah resided in the old homestead at Yardville.

11. William J.[4] James[3] Samuel[2] Joseph[1] Allinson and Rebecca W., his wife, had issue (b. at Burlington):

i. Martha, b. 6 mo. 28, 1840; m. Charles Milton Allen, son of Francis (dec'd) and Mary Allen, of Beverly, 5 mo. 11, 1871, at Burlington Meeting House. Witnesses—William J., Rebecca W., Anna B., Mary E., Edward P., Francis G., Martha, Samuel, Ann and Rachel E. Allinson.

ii. Anna Bernice, b. 8 mo. 6, 1846; m. Gifford Vernon Lewis.

iii. William, b. 9 mo. 25, 1848; d. same day.

iv. Edward P., b. 11 mo. 21, 1852; he was a lawyer, and lived in Philadelphia, where he d. about 1902 or 1903.

v. Frances Greenleaf, b. 12 mo. 16, 1856.

vi. Gertrude, b. 9 mo. 16, 1862.

—*Supreme Court Records*, passim; *N. J. Archives*, IX., 359; XVIII., **395**, 482; XXIII., 4; XXIV., 439, 446; XXV., 4-5; XXVI., 262; *Friends in Burlington*; *Field's Provincial Courts*, 167-8; 2 *N. J. Hist. Soc. Proceedings*, VIII., 72; *Penna. Magazine of Hist. and Biog.*, X., 33; XVI., 467; *The Burlington Smiths*, 115; 2d *N. J. Archives*, I., 63; *Records Burlington Monthly Meeting*; *Records St. Mary's Church, Burlington*.

ANOTHER ALLISON FAMILY.

Richard Allison came from Long Island and settled in Burlington county in 1695 or earlier. In a volume entitled "Burlington Records 1680," in the Burlington County Clerk's office, at Mt. Holly, is an entry, p. 13, without date: "Richard Allison his Hoggs Eare Marke a hole in Right Eare a Slit in ye Left thus ——" followed by drawings of each. By deed dated Dec. 9, 1695, John Snowden, of Bucks county, Pa., yeoman, and wife Anne, conveyed to Richard Allison, "late of Long Island, yeoman," a plantation of 210 acres on the Delaware river, called White

Hill, above Sepassings Island, including six acres of meadow on Cross-wicks creek, and four acres near that meadow.—*N. J. Archives*, XXI., 495. By deed dated Feb. 20, 1698-9, Richard Allison, of Mansfield township, Burlington county, yeoman, conveyed to Thomas Black, of the same place, yeoman, 112 acres, being half of above plantation, between John Snoden and John Hooton, and surveyed for said Snoden, as in Liber A, p. 57.—*N. J. Archives*, XXI., 514. Richard Allison, senior, was baptized in St. Mary's church, Burlington, in March, 1714, perhaps during a dangerous illness. He was one of the appraisers of the estate of Henry Tuckneys, of Burlington, Nov. 29, 1714, and a witness to the will of Samuel Territt, smith, of Burlington, Nov. 24, 1714.—*N. J. Archives*, XXIII., 456, 473. During the strenuous administration of Gov. Robert Hunter, Col. Daniel Coxe wrote to "Capt. Rich. Allison, at Burlington," urging him to aid him in getting up evidence against the Governor, that he might take the same to England, whither he was about to sail. The letter, dated July 7, 1716, was written from Philadelphia, where Coxe had prudently taken refuge from the Governor's wrath. It subsequently (probably after Allison's death) fell into the hands of the Governor.—*N. J. Archives*, IV., 266, 274. Allison was one of the signers of a representation to the King, severely arraigning Governor Hunter, and asking to have their charges investigated.—*N. J. Archives*, IV., 306; XIV., 71. Administration was granted on the estate of Richard Allison, of Burlington, to his widow, Elishep, Dec. 27, 1716. —*N. J. Archives*, XXIII., 12. Issue:

2.   i.   Richard[2], b. in England, 3d mo. 20, 1695-6.

        ii.   Elizabeth[2], m. Thomas Shreve, son of Caleb (? Thomas), of Mancefield township, 5th mo. 26, 1711, at Burlington Friends' Meeting House. Witnesses—Elizabeth Allison (the mother?), Hannah, Richard and Sarah Allison, and twenty-four others.

        iii.   Mary[2], m. Isaac Hutchinson, son of John, late of Hopewell township, Burlington county, 7th mo. 12, 1728, at Burlington Friends' Meeting House. Witnessses— Elisha and Richard Allison.

        iv.   Sarah[2], m. Rowland Ellis, April 17, 1715, in St. Mary's church, Burlington. Child: Richard, bap. Aug. 26, 1718.

        v.   (?) Elisha[2].

        vi.   Hannah[2].

2.   Richard[2] Richard[1] Allison, b. in England, 3d mo. 20, 1695-6; m. Anne (b. 11 mo. 14, 1696), dau. of Capt. John Harrison, of Perth Amboy, July 6, 1721, the Rev. Charles Smith officiating. The will of John Harrison, gentleman, of Perth Amboy, dated March 2, 1723-4, names her and her husband. Mr. Allison was one of the appraisers of the estate of Francis Collings, of Burlington, April 28, 1728. The will of Richd Allison, of Burlington, Sadler, being weak, is dated Feb. 19, 1730-31, and was proved Aug. 2, 1731. He gives to wife Ann "my plate," slaves and "rest of real and personal estate." To child Richard "my dwelling house in Burlington," etc. To daughters Elizabeth and Ann each £20 when 18 or married. He also mentions "my tracts of lands in the Jerseys and elsewhere in America." Executors—wife Ann and brother (i. e., brother-in-law) Rowland Ellis. Witnesses—Joseph Heulings, Benja Marriott, Dinah Bard.—*West Jersey Wills*, Lib. No. 3, f. 295. Richard Allison and Anne, his wife, had issue:

        i.   Elizabeth[3], b. 1722.

3.   ii.   Richard[3], b. 10 mo. 18, 1725.

        iii.   Anne[3], b. 1729.

ALLISON

3. Richard[3] Richard[2] Richard[1] Allison, b. 10 mo. 18, 1725; m. Ruth (b. 1 mo. 18, 1729), dau. of Burgiss Hall, a mariner, of Bordentown, 1 mo. 9, 1751; he d. June —, 1766; she d. 2 mo. 4, 1802. He was a saddler, like his father. Richard Allison, probably the same person, was received by letter from Middletown into the Hopewell Baptist church, Nov. 25, 1764, as appears by the MS. records of the latter church, Vol. I., p. 24. In 1764, being then of Hopewell, he advertised for sale "A Good two Story Brick House in Bordentown, with four Rooms on a Floor below, and two above, with good Cellars, and a Well at the Door, and a good Garden. Also a good Shop, suitable for a Tradesman, fronting the Street with a Stable, Chair-house, and a Cow-shed."—*N. J. Archives*, XXIV., 456. It is not unlikely that he occupied this property before removing to Hopewell. His will, dated June 3, 1766, when he was "sick and weak," and evidently on his deathbed, was proved two weeks later, or June 17, 1766. In it he devises to wife Ruth, after payment of debts, the rest of the estate, to bring up the children, and then one-half of two-thirds in fee; to son Burgis Hall, when 21, one-third of the estate; to daughter Anna, when 18, one-half of the remaining two-thirds. Signed, "Rd Allison." Executors—son Burgis Hall, friends Saftey McGee and John Butler, Jr. Witnesses—Saml. Mulladay, Stephen Burrowes, Josiah Ellis. Safety Meghee qualified as executor, June 17, 1766; the others did not qualify; the son, of course, was under age.—*West Jersey Wills*, Lib. No. 12, f. 389. On August 14, 1766, Safety Meghee, Executor, advertised for sale, by public vendue, on September 1, ensuing, "The plantation of Richard Allison, late of Hopewell, deceased, containing 54 acres of land, with two dwelling-houses, a barn, and stable, with other out-houses, a bearing orchard, a good piece of watered meadow before the door, a good new convenient tanyard, all in excellent order, with leather in the vatts, which may be sold with or without the place, as may best suit the purchaser. The place is remarkably pleasant, situate on the great road leading through the country to Hacket's, from whence a great quantity of hides may be had yearly; it is about seven miles from Trenton, and one from Pennington. Likewise will be sold, on Thursday following, the fifth day of September, by way of public vendue, on the premises, a brick dwelling-house, two stories high, with a kitchen back, a good shop, will suit any tradesman, a good hay-house and stable, a yard and large garden, a well at the door, it being pleasantly situate in Bordentown, about half way along the main street. Likewise a lot of land, lying on Bank-street, containing one quarter of an acre, with a young bearing orchard on the same, being also the property of the said Richard Allison, deceased."—*N. J. Archives*, XXV., 187. The will of Ruth Allison, of Bordentown, presumably his widow, dated June 26, 1795, she being weak at the time, was proved March 6, 1802. She mentions only one child, Ann Allison, to whom she gives all her household goods, etc. Executor—friend Wm. Snowden. Witnesses—Wm. D. Nixon, Deborah Snowden, James Butler.—*West Jersey Wills*, Lib. No. 39, f. 510. Issue:

      i. Richard[4], b. 1751; d. 1753.

4.   ii. Burgess Hall[4], b. August 17, 1753, at Bordentown.

      iii. Anna[4], not 18 at date of her father's will, 1766. Apparently not married at date of her mother's will, 1795. She d. 1837.

4. Burgess-Hall[4] Richard[3] Richard[2] Richard[1] Allison, b. Aug. 17, 1753; m. Rhoda, dau. of Nathaniel Stout, and wid. of Zephaniah Stout; she d. June 3, 1798, and is buried in Hopewell Baptist churchyard. He was "a teacher, preacher, inventor, and a sterling patriot during the Revolution." In connection with Samuel Morey he built at Bordentown a

sidewheel steamboat that ran to Philadelphia and back, at least once. This is said to have been "probably before Fulton ran the Clermont," or prior to 1807. He finished his education at Pennepeck, under the Rev. Dr. Jones, and was ordained by him, June 10, 1781. Soon after the organization of the Baptist church at Jacobstown, Oct. 19, 1785, he became its pastor, preaching also at Bordentown, where, perhaps, he had filled the pulpit previously. He served both churches for many years. He started a school at Bordentown in 1778, which drew pupils from all over the United States, as also from France, Spain, the West Indies and South America. He discontinued this school in 1796, but resumed it in 1801. He was one of five clergymen called on in 1780 to supply the pulpit of the Hopewell Baptist church. On Aug. 18, 1787, his wife, by her father, Deacon Nathaniel Stout, asked the Hopewell Baptist church for a letter of dismissal to the church at Jacobstown, and it was granted four days later. Mr. Allison was still preaching at Jacobstown as late as 1813. In 1815 he published "The American Standard of Orthography and Pronunciation, and Improved Dictionary of the English Language, abridged for the use of Schools." He d. at Trenton, Feb. 20, 1827. His tombstone says:

> While tears bedew thy silent clay,
> And Zion mourns her absent son,
> We hail with hopes that joyful day
> When parting scenes shall all be done.

Morgan Edwards says of him, in 1789: "Mr. Allison is a slender built man, and neither tall, nor of firm constitution; yet approaches towards an universal genius beyond any of my acquaintance." He constructed many pieces of apparatus for his academy, was "an adept in music, drawing, painting, katoptrics, &c.," and was a skilled artisan. He had issue:

    i. Richard[5].
    ii. Charity[5].
    iii. Nathaniel Stout[5].
    iv. Ann[5], m. James L. Edwards, 11 mo. 21, 1821.

Miscellaneous.

James Alleson, of New Brunswick, m. Anne Wells, of New Brunswick, m. lic. Mar. 11, 1739.

John Allison, of Oxford township, Sussex county. Inventory of the personal estate of, £522. 2. 6, incl. bills, bonds, book debts, and cash £331. 3. 2., a negro £20, a bible and other books, 5s. Made by Edward Hunt and James Stinson, May 30, 1759. Bond of widow, Sarah Allison, as administratrix, Sept. 1, 1759; Edward Hunt fellow bondsman, both of Oxford.—*West Jersey Wills*, Lib. No. 9, f. 393.

John Allison, of Burlington county. Bond (not executed) of Joseph Allison as administrator, May 2, 1761; John Allison fellow-bondsman, both of said county. The original is in the office of the Secretary of State, at Trenton.

John Allison, of Washington township, Burlington county, died intestate. William Braddock and Caleb Shreve, administrators, took an inventory of his personal estate, March 31, 1829, appraised by Israel Small and John Taylor at $239.32, and affirmed to by the administrators, April 2, 1829.—*Burlington Wills*, 1829.

Mary Alleson, of Elizabethtown, made her will Oct. 24, 1770; proved April 13, 1772. She gives to her sister, Hephzibath Allisson, "one half of my Dwelling house lott &c. where I live, bought of Mr. John Halstead;" to sister Thankful, wife of Henry Spencer, the rents of the other half of said property; also mentions sister. Louisa Allison, and nephew. William Spencer. Executors—Rev. James Caldwell, Benj. Spinning, Oliver Spencer. Witnesses—Jacob Croes, Daniel Sayre, John Chetwood.—*E. J. Wills*, Lib. K, f. 416.

Mrs. Mary Ann Allison, widow of Richard Allison, died Aug. 8, 1829, aged 50 yrs., and is buried in St. Michael's churchyard, Trenton. She was perhaps the wid. of Richard, son of Burgess-Hall Allison.

ANDERSONS of Bergen County.

The progenitor of this family was John (styled Jan in the Dutch church records) Anderson, a native of Scotland, who came to this country early in the eighteenth century, and settled at or near Hackensack, Bergen county. The family tradition, however, is that he was a native of Ireland, but came to America via Scotland. He m. Elizabeth De Marest, spinster, living in the precincts of the Hackensack church, January 23, 1736. Issue:

Second Generation.

    i. Margrietjin², bap. Nov. 14, 1736; d. in inf.

    ii. Margrietje², bap. Aug. 9, 1741; m. Samuel Peek, and with him joined the Schraalenburgh Dutch church on confession, Nov. 17, 1763. Children: 1. Jacobes, b. March 2, 1763; 2. Elesebeth, bap. April 28, 1765; 3. Sara, bap. March 12, 1771.

2.   iii. Johannes², bap. Oct. 30, 1743; m. Rebecca Demarest, spinster, b. and living on the Flats, Jan. 27, 1766; he was b. at Hackensack (i. e., in the bounds of the Hackensack church), but lived at Schraalenburgh (i. e., in the bounds of the Schraalenburgh church) at the time of his marriage.

3.   iv. David², m. Jane Stuart, m. l. March 5, 1768.

    v. Sara², b. Jan. 19, 1747; m. David Peek. Children: 1. Elisabet, bap. Oct. 9, 1768; 2. Marya, b. Aug. 18, 1773; 3. Jacobes, b. Sept. 20, 1777; 4. Daniel, b. Aug. 3, 1782; 5. Sara, b. Jan. 10, 1785.

    vi. Maria², bap. Dec. 11, 1748; m. Christiaen Van Hoorn, widr., March 18, 1768. Children: 1. Cornelius, b. Sept. 5, 1769; m. Catharina Haring; 2. Johannes, b. Sept. 24, 1774; m. Jannetje Losier; 3. Altie, b. Feb. 19, 1776; m. John Lozier; 4. David, b. Jan. 7, 1779; 5. Maria, b. Sept. 4, 1781; 6. Liesabeth, bap. Jan. 9, 1785; 7. Marigrieta, b. May 24, 1787; 8. Jacobus, b. Oct. 16, 1791.

    vii. Annaatje², b. March 24, 1751; prob. m. Jan Quackenbos. Children: 1. Johannes, b. Oct. 16, 1776; 2. David, b. Oct. 6, 1781; 3. Elisabeth, b. Aug. 22, 1784; 4. Davidt, b. March 8, 1788; 5. Abraham, b. Sept. 13, 1791.

    viii. Jacobes², b. April 15, 1753.

    ix. Lidea², b. March 6, 1756.

Third Generation.

2. Johannes² Jan¹ Anderson and Rebecca Demarest had children:

    i.   i. Johannes³, bap. Jan. 18, 1767; m. Maria (Polly) Bogert, Sept. 20, 1792. The family record says that he and his wife were active members in the Schraalenburgh church, until the True Reformed ("Seceder") church was organized, when they identified themselves with that movement. They were buried in the graveyard of the North Reformed Dutch church, at Schraalenburgh.

5. ii. Jacobus[3], bap. Oct. 22, 1769; m. Merjery Wortendyke.
6. iii. David[3], bap. April 25, 1771; m. Geertje Nagel, spinster, of Tappan, Oct. 14, 1792. He removed to St. Louis, Mo.
   iv. Daniel[3], bap. Dec. 18, 1774.
   v. Pieter[3], bap. May 28, 1780.
   vi. Safya[3], bap. June 23, 1782.
3. David[2] Jan[1] Anderson and Antje Demarest (?) had children:
7. i. Johannes[3], b. Nov. 30, 1769; m. Catherine, dau. of Christian Zabriskie, of Param is. He built up an extensive mercantile and shipping business at Hackensack, which he carried on for many years.
   ii. Elizabet[3], b. July 7, 1774; m. Andries Zabriskie, July 21, 1793.
   iii. David[3], bap. Nov. 28, 1779.

Fourth Generation.

4. Johannes[3] Johannes[2] Jan[1] Anderson and Maria Bogert had issue:
   i. John[4], b. Feb. 14, 1794.
   ii. Sara[4], b. April 23, 1797.
   iii. Matthew[4], b. Oct. 18, 1800; m. ———. Children: 1. Ann Maria; 2. Garret; 3. John; 4. Elizabeth; 5. James; 6. Cornelius.
   iv. James[4], b. Oct. 8, 1804.
   v. Albert[4], b. Aug. 21, 1811.
   vi. Eliza[4], b. Aug. 8, 1824.
5. Jacobus[3] Johannes[2] Jan[1] Anderson and Merjery Wortendyke had issue:
   i. Johannes[4], b. Dec. 11, 1791; d. in inf.
   ii. Johannes[4], b. June 25, 1795.
   iii. Friedrikus[4], bap. Aug. 20, 1797.
6. David[3] Johannes[2] Jan[1] Anderson and Geertje Nagel had issue:
   i. John[4], b. Jan. 25, 1794.
   ii. Gerritt[4], b. Aug. 16, 1795.
7. Johannes[3] David[2] Jan[1] Anderson and Catherine Zabriskie had issue:
8. i. David[4], b. Nov. —, 1792; m. Anna Strong, of New York; d. 1873. He was called David I. Anderson. He succeeded to his father's business, which he greatly enlarged and extended. In 1848 he removed from Hackensack to Acquackanonk Landing (now Passaic), where he carried on the lumber business many years.
   ii. John Christian Zabriskie[4]. He was a merchant at Hackensack in partnership with his brother David. He m. Harriet, dau. of Garret Myer; d. in 1836. She was b. June, 1803; she m. 2d, Sept. 2, 1841, Capt. Robert Colfax Avery Ward, of Hackensack; she d. Oct. 23, 1873.
   iii. Maria[4], m. Abram Berry.
   iv. Jane[4], m. Andrew Parsons, the first Cashier of the Paterson Bank.

Fifth Generation.

8. David[4] Johannes[3] David[2] Jan[1] Anderson and Anne Strong had children:

ANDERSON: ANTILL

    i. Helen[5], m. —— Price.
    ii. John[5].
    iii. Catherine[5], m. John B. Aycrigg, of Passaic.
    iv. William S.[5], b. 1827, at Hackensack; m. 1st, Clarissa, dau. of John Adrian Post, of Acquackanonk; she d. in 1872; he m. 2d, Sarah, dau. of Richard Terhune, of Lodi. Children (by his first wife): 1. John; 2. William S.; 3. Kate; (by his second wife): 4. Richard; 5. Sarah.

JAMES ANDERSON.

No record has been found of the license of James Anderson as an attorney at law. He is mentioned in the records as early as April 19, 1763, when Altia Durlandt, widow of John Durlandt, of Milstone, Somerset county, appoints James Anderson, of the same place, her attorney.—*East Jersey Deeds*, A 3, page 56. Two years later he appears to have been of Sussex county. On September 11, 1765, James Anderson, attorney at law, of Sussex county, is appointed administrator of Anna Reed, of Milstone.—*East Jersey Wills*, Liber H, page 530. By deed dated October 28, 1765, Samuel Ford, of Morris Town, Morris county, and his wife Grace, convey to James Anderson, of Newton township, Sussex county, attorney at law, several tracts of land in Pequanack township, Morris county, about a mile and a half above John Johnson's iron works.—*East Jersey Deeds*, D 3, page 42. He seems to have returned to Somerset county soon after this, for on September 24, 1766, administration was granted on the estate of James Anderson, of Somerset county, to John Anderson and Kenneth Anderson, father and brother of the deceased.—*East Jersey Wills*, Liber I., page 5; *N. J. Archives*, XXV., 261. He was a son of Capt. John Anderson, of Freehold, and Anna (Reid) Anderson. He was bap. July 6, 1740; d. Sept. 15, 1766, in his 27th year, and was buried in the Tennent Presbyterian church.

ANTILL FAMILY.

In 1899 the writer published a paper on "Edward Antill, a New York Merchant of the Seventeenth Century, and his Descendants," in Proceedings of the New Jersey Historical Society, and also in a separate pamphlet. Since then he has received from Robert Henry Antill, Jarvisfield, Picton, New South Wales, Australia, the additional information that Edward Antill, 1st, was born in Richmond, Surrey, England, March 20, 1659, and bap. April 4, 1659, son of John Antill, of that place. Edward Antill, 1st, acquired large tracts of land at Piscataqua, near New Brunswick, Middlesex county, New Jersey, whereon his son, Edward Antill, 2d, settled, whose second wife was Anne Morris, dau. of Gov. Lewis Morris, of New Jersey; he d. Aug. 16, 1770. A full account of him is given in the pamphlet referred to. The sketch given by the writer of Major John Antill, fourth child of Edward Antill, 2d, and of his descendants, is very fully and interestingly supplemented by his Australian offshoot.

John[4] Edward[3] Edward[2] John[1] Antill, b. 1744; m. 1st, Margaret Colden, dau. of Alexander Colden, of Coldenham, Dutchess county, N. Y.; 2d, Jane, dau. of same. He was Major of the Second Battalion, New Jersey Volunteers (Loyalists); d. in Canada in 1816. Issue:

Fifth Generation.

By his first wife (Margaret):
    i. John Collins[5]; Major 76th Regiment of Foot; d. in Ceylon, without issue.

2. ii. Henry Colden[5], b. 1779; left America at an early age, and served in the army in India, receiving a medal for courage shown at the Battle of Seringapatun. He returned to England, where he spent a few months, and then went to New South Wales, as aide-de-camp to Governor John Macquarie, of that Colony. He eventually settled there, married Eliza Wills, in 1818, and d. in 1852 on his estate at Jarvisfield (so called by him after Gov. Macquarie's estate in Scotland), Picton, N. S. W. Part of this estate is called Coldenham.

    iii. Eliza Hope[5], m. Cadwallader Colden, a cousin. Children: 1. Thomas, a physician, d. s. p.; 2. Margaret, m. J—— Trimble, and had a number of children; many of her descendants live at Newburgh, N. Y.

By his second wife (Jane):

    iv. Edward[5], d. s. p., in America. He was an invalid, suffering from epileptic fits.

    v. Alexander Colden[5], d. s. p., in America.

Sixth Generation.

2. Henry Colden[5] John[4] Edward[3] Edward[2] John[1] Antill and Eliza Wills had issue:

3. i. John Macquarie[6], b. Liverpool, N. S. W.; named after his father's friend, Governor Macquarie; m. Jessie Hassall Campbell; d. June 4, 1900.

    ii. Alice[6], m. Henry Moggridge. Children: 1. John Antill, Major South Lancashire Regiment (82d); 2. M. Moggridge, m. Lieut. Keppel Foote, R. N.

    iii. Henry Colden[6] m. and had issue.

    iv. William Redfern[6], m. and had issue.

    v. Thomas Wills[6], m. and had issue.

    vi. Edward Spencer[6], m. and had issue.

    vii. James Alexander[6], m. and had issue.

    viii. Selina E.[6], m. Capt. R. F. Pockley, and had issue.

Seventh Generation.

3. John Macquarie[6] Henry Colden[5] John[4] Edward[3] Edward[2] John[1] Antill and Jessie H. Campbell had issue:

    i. Margaret Campbell[7], m. N. Wade Brown, and has issue.

    ii. Robert Henry[7], b. 1849, unm. Resides on the estate, "Jarvisfield," acquired by his father, which he owns. So far as known he is the senior male descendant living of Edward Antill, 1st.

    iii. Celia Farrington[7].

    iv. Selina Johnston[7].

    v. John Macquarie[7], b. 1855; m. A. M. Wills Allen, and has issue. He fought in the British army in the war with the Boers, greatly distinguishing himself, winning seven medals, and on the recommendation of Lord Roberts was made a Companion of the Bath, and was enrolled in Burke's Peerage, being the only man with the low rank of Captain who up to that time had obtained such a distinction. He went to South Africa as an Australian soldier, and returned at the conclusion of the war. He is now Major John Macquarie Antill, C. B., and upholds the honor of the family of Edward Antill, 1st.

ANTILL

        He also served in the Boer War, as Captain of the
        Royal Australian Artillery, which he commanded.
        (Three other Antills, first cousins, and two others and
        a brother-in-law—Pockley, Macpherson and Colonel
        Lansetter—served in the same war, indicating that
        the fighting instinct of the three sons of Edward An-
        till, 2d, persists even to the seventh generation.)
   vii. Guy Forrest[7].
  viii. Elizabeth Ann[7], m. Col. H. B. Lansetter, C. B., and has
        issue.

At the auction sale of the genealogical library of the late Dr. Samuel
S. Purple, at Boston, in February, 1909, the writer purchased a family
Bible published at Charlestown, Mass., in 1803. On the reverse of the
last page of the Old Testament is a neatly-printed card, with the
printed words: "This Bible is the property of," followed by this inscription in manuscript: "Alice Antill the Gift of her Grandmother
Elizabeth Colden." This entry, and all the other entries except the
last, hereinafter given, are in the chirography apparently of Alice,
daughter of Dr. Lewis Antill. Most of them were evidently copied
from another Bible. The family record is at the end of the book of
Revelation. From it the following entries are gleaned:

Cadwallader Colden, eldest son of Lieutenant-Governor Colden, b.
June 6, 1724; m. Elizabeth Ellison in May, 1744; he d. Feb. 18, 1797;
she was b. November 16, 1726; d. July 10, 1815.

Dr. Lewis[1] Edward[3] Edward[2] John[1] Antill, b. Dec. 10, 1746 (this date
of birth is taken from a note by Dr. Purple); m. in 1771, Alice, dau. of
Cadwallader and Elizabeth Colden; she was b. Feb. 22, 1745; ("he died
at sea"—marginal note, date not given); she d. Feb. 22, 1776, about
five weeks after giving birth to a daughter. Writing to a friend in
Scotland, in 1796, giving a detailed account of the Colden family, Cadwallader Colden 2d says of this match: "Our eldest daughter, Alice,
married young, not much to our satisfaction. Both she and her husband, Dr. Antill, died soon after the commencement of the American
war, leaving nothing behind them but two dear little infants, both
girls, whom we took to our own bosom (one of them was but six
weeks old), and they knew no other father or mother. One of them is
married to a clergyman and has made us great grand parents. Her
sister is a fine handsome girl of about twenty years of age."—*Eager's
Hist. Orange County*, Newburgh, 1846-7, p. 247. Issue:
    i. Edward, b. January 1, 1772; died in infancy.
   ii. Elizabeth Colden, b. May 9, 1774; m. Rev. Frederick
       Van Horne, May 27, 1793; d. June 3, 1835; he d. May
       31, 1835, only three days before her. (This marriage
       is announced in the *New York Magazine*, June, 1793,
       as having taken place at Coldenham, N. Y.) "Mr.
       Van Horne, a candidate for the ministry, was, on
       the recommendation of Bishop Moore, called to the
       ministry of St. Andrew's church, in the village of
       Wallkill, Ulster county, N. Y., which at the time was,
       or was about to be, vacant. He accepted the call,
       and on the receipt of holy orders, entered upon the
       duties of the Rectorship, Dec. 10, 1793." (The List
       of Deacons of the P. E. Church, published in 1875,
       states that Mr. Van Horne was ordained a Deacon
       by Bishop Provoost, in 1794.) "He continued Rector

of the parish until 1805, when he removed to Balls-ton."—*Eager's Hist. Orange County*, Newburgh, 1846-7, p. 317. He was inducted into Christ's Church at Balltown, and into St. Paul's Church at Charlton, August 8-9, 1805, both churches in Saratoga county, N. Y. He retired from the active ministry a few years later, and took up his residence at Coldenham. He d. at Poughkeepsie, May 31, 1835, after a short illness, in his 64th year.

iii. Alice, b. January 17, 1776; m. William Davies, April 18, 1818. He was b. March 21, 1763, at New Milford, Conn., the only son of the Rev. Thomas Davies (rector of the Episcopal church at New Milford, at the time) and Mary Hervey, his wife. At an early age William removed to Amenia, Dutchess county, New York, where he was engaged in mercantile business many years. He there m. 1st, Polly Leach, Jan. 23, 1787; she d. July 23, 1814. He removed about this time or earlier to Poughkeepsie, in the same county, where he lived for sixty years. He m. 2d, Mrs. Maria Foote, of Poughkeepsie, Dec. 31, 1814; she d. Nov. 18, 1815. He m. 3d, Alice Antill, as above stated. She d. June 25, 1870, without issue. He d. Feb. 7, 1857. By his first wife, Polly Leach, he had issue: 1. Thomas Leach; 2. William Augustus, b. at Pough-keepsie, May 10, 1808; 3. Charlotte Davies. Both sons, and perhaps the daughter, survived him. William Augustus m. 1st, Sarah, dau. of Hubert Van Wagoner, June 15, 1842; she d. s. p. He m. 2d, Frances, dau. of Joseph Barrett, June 4, 1861, by whom he had one son, Augustus, b. August 15, 1867, and living in 1909 at Poughkeepsie, an architect by profession.

There is another entry, in a different hand:

"Augustus Davies was born Aug. 15/67—son of William A. & Frances Davies."

The following additional notes are gleaned from the records and files of the Supreme Court, at Trenton:

John Bell, of the city of New York, house carpenter, brought suit in the Supreme Court of New Jersey, against William Antill, of the city of New Brunswick, merchant, on a bond, dated Perth Amboy, October 23, 1740, conditioned for the payment of £106.8.8, current money of New York.

A summons was issued March 20, 1741, at the suit of Mary Bickley, on a note made by William Antill at Burlington, September 23, 1740, for £14.19.11, Joseph Ross being her attorney. An inquisition was taken at the order of Thomas Hunloke, High Sheriff of Burlington, at the Sign of the Angell, Bridge Town (Mount Holly), October 2, 1742, when the Sheriff and a jury of twelve men awarded her £16.11.6 damages, and sixpence for costs and charges. She brought suit, also, November 2, 1742, against Edward Antill, for £28.3.1, proclamation money. The summons was returned "non est inventus," by the Sheriff of Middlesex, to whom it had been issued. On November 8, a ca. sa. was issued to the Sheriff of Somerset, "it being on the part of said Mary sufficiently testified that the said William lyes hid and skulketh in the old country."

ARNOLD: ARTHUR

James Alexander wrote to Edward Antill, January 12, 1743-4, referring to matters proposed between Mrs. Gordon and the representative of Antill's father and mother, and encloses two copies of a document in pursuance thereof, each to be executed by Antill and his brother, "and then one sent to Mrs. Callender to be executed by her at Boston and returned to you, and the other to be executed by your sister Gallop and her husband and her daughter."—*Alexander Papers, N. J. Hist. Society.*

COLONEL JACOB ARNOLD.

Col. Jacob Arnold was a son of Samuel Arnold, who came from Connecticut in 1730, and settled in Washington Valley, three miles northwest of Morristown, where he bought 300 acres of lands of William and Richard Penn. He m. Phebe Ford, Oct. 16, 1748. His son Jacob was born Dec. 14, 1749; he m. 1st, Elizabeth Tuthill, of Morris county, Oct. 1, 1770; she d. May 9, 1803; he m. 2d, Sarah H. Nixon, Dec. 26, 1807; she was b. Oct. 1, 1783; d. July 29, 1846. He d. March 1, 1827. He was associated in partnership with Thomas Kinney, at one time Sheriff of Morris county, a large land owner, and landlord of a tavern on the north side of the public Green in Morristown. Arnold, Kenney & Co. advertised in the *New Jersey Gazette*, on Feb. 10, 1779, that they had opened a store "next door to Col. Remsen's, in Morris-Town," for the sale of all sorts of merchandise, from broadcloth to frying-pans, "for cash or country produce, and by wholesale and retail." In the *New Jersey Journal* (Chatham), June 8, 1779, the partnership is advertised as dissolved and creditors and debtors are requested to settle.—*N. J. Archives*, 2d Series, 3: 59, 414. Arnold was captain of a troop of Light Horse at the beginning of the Revolution, and likewise succeeded Kinney in the proprietorship of the tavern mentioned, which for many years was known in local history as Arnold's tavern. A horse was advertised as "strayed or stolen from the house of Capt. Jacob Arnold in Morristown, August 9, 1778." The confiscated estates of Morris county tories were to be sold at his house March 30, 1779. In the same month he advertised to be let for one year "that valuable farm whereon the subscriber lately lived, lying on the road between Mendom and Morris-Town, three miles from the said town," having two dwelling houses and barn and two orchards on the premises.—*Ibid.*, 2: 360; 3: 92, 133. It was in that building that Washington had his headquarters during the winter of 1776-7, after the battles of Trenton and Princeton. In 1886 it was about to be demolished, to make way for a modern building, but was bought by Mrs. Julia Keese Colles, who thought it a pity to sacrifice such a relic of the Revolution, and she had it removed to the Colles estate, on Mt. Kemble avenue, where it has been remodeled for All Souls Hospital. The rooms occupied by Washington are preserved intact. See "History of the Arnold Tavern, Morristown, N. J.," by Philip H. Hoffman, Morristown, 1903.

REV. THOMAS ARTHUR.

Thomas Arthur was graduated from Yale in 1743, and preached for a time at Stratfield, Conn. He was ordained and installed pastor at New Brunswick in 1746. He was one of the original Trustees of Princeton College. His sermon at the ordination of Thane, in August, 1750, was printed, and the trustees of the New York church requested for publication a copy of his sermon at the ordination of the Rev. Alexander Cumming as their pastor in October, 1750.—*Webster's Hist. Pres. Church*, 504.

WILLIAM AYNESLEY.

Very little is known of Chief Justice William Aynesley. William Smith, the historian of New York, who hesitated not to say what he Jersey had been mortified by the arrival of one Ainsley, who was raised to be chief justice from the low station of treasurer to a turnpike in the North of Ireland"—which is improbable.—*History of New York*, 1830, Vol. II., 347. This statement, however, was made in a letter written from Perth Amboy, December 16, 1761, and published in the *Pennsylvania Journal* of January 7, 1762. The writer, after referring to Robert Hunter Morris the former Chief Justice, says: "What glorious Successors; *the Treasurer of a Turnpike, and a Newgate Solicitor!*" —*N. J. Archives*, XXIV., 2. He was said to have been recommended to the Earl of Halifax by Lord Ravensworth.—*Ib.*, 348, note. His appointment was ordered by the King in Council, Feb. 16, 1757.—*N. J. Archives*, IX., 232; XVII., 136; *N. J. Hist. Soc. Coll.*, V., 338-9. He seems to have been very deliberate about coming to America to enter upon his new duties, for it was not until the March Term, 1758, that he took his seat on the bench of the Supreme Court. He went on Circuit in April.— *N. J. Archives*, IX., 214, 217, 232. By his order, notice was published in the *New York Mercury* of April 3, 1758, that the Circuit Courts would be held for Cumberland and Cape May Counties on Friday, April 21, 1758; in Salem, April 25, in Hunterdon on the first Tuesday of May, and for Gloucester on the third Tuesday in May, 1758.—*N. J. Archives*, XX., 186. On May 22, 1758, the Governor signed a warrant "To William Aynsley Esqr Chief Justice of the Province of New Jersey for Holding of Four Courts of Oyer & Terminer and General Goal Delivery in the following Counties Vizt In the County of Cumberland on the 21st day of April Last In the County of Salem on the 25th day of the same Month In the County of Hunterdon on the 2d Instant And for the County of Gloucester on the 16th day of this Instant £40."—*N. J. Archives*, XVII., 172. His death at New Brunswick, on July 6, 1758, after so short a sojourn in New Jersey, was a shock to the community. Gov. Bernard wrote that his sudden demise "was occasioned by his drinking milk and water when he was Very hot on Wednesday last & he died the next day."—*N. J. Archives*, IX., 124. His widow, Mrs. Elizabeth Aynsley, was appointed administratrix of his estate, July 11, 1758.—*E. J. Wills*, F, 531. On August 12, 1758, the Governor signed a warrant: "To Mrs. Elizabeth Aynsley Widow of the Honble William Aynsley Esqr late Chief Justice of this Province deceased for Services done by the late Chief Justice, £70."—*N. J. Archives*, XVII., 199. A correspondent (perhaps the Rev. Robert McKean), writing over the pseudonym "Philaretes," from New Brunswick, under date of July 10, 1758, to Mr. Bradford, the Philadelphia printer, gives the following handsome panegyric on the deceased Chief Justice, which was published in the *Pennsylvania Journal* of July 20, 1758, and is reproduced in N. J. Archives, XX., 230:

"Thursday last in the Afternoon died here, of a sudden Indisposition, supposed to be occasioned by the Intense heat, the Honourable WILLIAM AYNESLEY, Esq; late Chief-Justice of this Province. His Lady had been arrived only a month from *England*, when they were thus fatally Parted.——

"An Eulogium of him to those that had the happiness of his Acquaintance, would be impertinent——His virtues were too conspicuous to escape the Notice of the slightest Observer——But a Character so well supported in the important Post he filled, and in every branch of social Life, certainly claim a public Tribute————His ready discernments of the Merits of a cause, the wise Regulations he was about to introduce in the Courts, over which he presided, his earnestness in Expediting, and his Justice in determining Suits, all which he shewed even in his short Administration, were too sufficient Testimonies of his Knowledge in the Law, and his capacity for Executing the high *Trust* committed in him.—·——

"As a *Man*, he appeared to be a perfect lover of the human Race; Friendly, Affable, and good Natured; a Temper universally Serene, and Unruffled, and a certain Complacency ever dwelling on his Countenance, shewed a Mind of ease, at the same Time that it secured the Affection of every Beholder.————In his Family, he was loved, respected, and happy: Proofs of his amiable Conduct there.————In short his good sense and agreeable Conversation was such as rendered him the delight of all his Acquaintance.—·——For he was not only Loved, but Esteemed.————

"But in another point of View, he shone still with a brighter Lustre. ————Religion ever influenced his Mind; his Morals were unblamable; and *Christ*, his Doctrines, and Institutions, he was never *ashamed to Confess before Men*, such was his Life.————His Death no doubt was Similar, and Crowned with the just Consequence.————His worthy and much afflicted Relict, his Friends, and *New-Jersey*, indeed, feel the loss, but he the Gain.————

"Weep, mortals weep, the worthy *Aynesley's* gone!
If human woes, and cares, affect alone.
But if thoughts, superior far, take place,
Let joy and gladness smile in ev'ry face."

JONATHAN BALDWIN.

Jonathan Baldwin was a son of Nathaniel Baldwin, who d. at Newark, Aug. 10, 1750, aged 50 years. He was b. at Newark in 1731, and graduated from the College of New Jersey in 1755. He m. Sarah Sergeant, and removed to Princeton, where he served the College as Steward for a number of years, beginning as early as 1762. In 1764 he had tickets for sale at Princeton in the College lottery. He engaged in an animated controversy with a butcher who sold mutton to the College, in 1768. He d. Nov. 28, 1816, aged 85 years. Issue: 1. Charles, a lawyer; 2. William; 3. Susan; 4. Elizabeth Davidson; and four other sons, unm. at his decease.

COLONEL FRANCIS BARBER.

Francis Barber was born in Princeton in 1751, a son of Patrick Barber, an Irishman, who came to America and settled in New York a year or two before his son was born, and after a short stay in that city took up his residence in Princeton, where he remained fifteen or sixteen years, when he removed to Orange county, New York.—*Hageman's Hist. of Princeton*, 1: 90. Francis graduated from the College at Princeton in 1767, and then engaged in teaching at Hackensack. After a brief experience there, he took charge, Nov. 1, 1771, of an Academy at Elizabethtown, New Jersey. The school soon became distinguished. Alexander Hamilton was prepared for college under Mr. Barber. At the commencement of the Revolution he offered his services to the country, and on the 9th of February, 1776, he was appointed, by the Legislature, Major of the Third Battalion, New Jersey troops, and on November 8th was promoted to the rank of Lieutenant-Colonel of the Third Regiment, and on January 1st, 1777, he received his commission from Congress. Soon after this he was appointed Assistant In-spector-General under Baron Steuben. Colonel Barber was in constant service during the whole war. Although a strict and rigid disciplin-arian, always scrupulously performing his own duty, and requiring it from all under his command, yet so bland were his manners, and his whole conduct so tempered with justice and strict propriety, that he was the favorite of all the officers and men, and highly valued by Washington. He served in the Northern army under General Schuy-ler; was at the battles of Trenton, Princeton, Brandywine, German-town and Monmouth, and in the latter was severely wounded. In 1779 he served as Adjutant-General with General Sullivan in his memorable expedition against the Indians, where he distinguished himself and was again wounded. In 1780 he was conspicuously en-gaged with the army in New Jersey, and was at the battle of Spring-field. In 1781 he accompanied the Jersey Line to Virginia, and was at the investment and capture of the British at Yorktown. The day on which the Commander-in-Chief intended to communicate the intelli-gence of peace to the army, a number of the officers, with their fami-lies, were invited to dine with him, and among others Colonel Barber and his wife. He was acting at the time as officer of the day in place of a friend. While on duty, and passing by the edge of a wood where some soldiers were cutting down a tree, it fell on him, and both rider and horse were instantly crushed to death. Thus was ended, January 11, 1783, the career of this brilliant and gallant young soldier, who was but thirty-two years old when he met with this cruel and un-timely death. He was buried at Neelytown, N. Y., beside his father's vault. Col. Barber m. 1st, Mary Ogden (b. Sept. 18, 1752, dau. of Robert Ogden 2d, and Phebe (Hatfield) Ogden); she d. Oct. 7, 1773, s. p.; he m. 2d, March 24, 1778, Anne ("Nancy," he always called her, affectionately, in his letters) Ogden—"a Lady of beauty and merit," said a newspaper of the day, in announcing the marriage—a cousin of his first wife; she was b. April 18, 1758, dau. of Moses Ogden and Mary (Cozzens) Ogden; d. July 17, 1825. In the summer of 1910 some per-son in Elizabeth proposed to have the remains of Major Barber re-moved to and reinterred in that city on October 19, the anniversary of the surrender of Cornwallis at Yorktown, but the authorities of Good-vill Cemetery, at Montgomery, N. Y., where the body lies, refused to consent to the removal. Francis Barber had issue:

      i. George Clinton, b. Dec. 27, 1778; m. Mary Chetwood Ogden, dau. of Gov. Aaron Ogden; d. Oct. 29, 1825.

      ii. Mary, b. Nov. 1, 1780; m. William Chetwood; d. April 18, 1873.

      iii. Frances Barber, b. Sept. 20, 1782; d. July 26, 1799.

See Alexander's Princeton College in the 18th Century; Hatfield's Hist. Elizabeth; Eager's Hist. Orange County, 302; N. J. Archives, passim; The Ogden Family, 141. A very affectionate "Elogy" (Eulogy) on Col. Barber's death was delivered by his companion in arms, Dr. Ebenezer Elmer, and was printed at Chatham. The only copy known is in the author's collection.

SAMUEL BARD.

Samuel Bard was a son of Peter Bard, 2d, who was the second son of Peter Bard, 1st, a Huguenot, who came from Montpellier, France, about 1700, and settled in Burlington, where he carried on business as a merchant until 1723, and then engaged in buying and selling land, building and operating mills, &c., until his death, in 1734.—*N. J. Archives*, XII., 667, note. Peter Bard, 2d, was a merchant in Philadelphia, until 1734; within a few years after that date he removed to Mount Holly, where he was living in 1750. He took up several hundred acres of land in Burlington county, but sold the same in 1764. He died at Mount Holly November 30, 1769. Samuel Bard, his son, was born in 1740, and was admitted to the New Jersey Bar November 3, 1761. In 1765 he removed to Bristol, Penn., where he continued practising, until his death, December 14, 1769. His will, dated Nov. 27, 1768, was proved Dec. 20, 1769, and is recorded in the Secretary of State's office, Trenton, Liber No. 14, p. 135. He appoints his father, Peter Bard, and Zachariah Rossell, executors, and directs them to sell all his land and property, consisting of a brick house at Mount Holly, and a tract of land adjoining the iron works he bought of his father; also all his real estate, and after payment of his debts the remainder to go to his wife Mary, in fee. He probably had no children, as none are mentioned in his will. He was a cousin of Dr. Samuel Bard, one of the most eminent physicians in the eighteenth century, the first President of the College of Physicians and Surgeons, in New York.

THOMAS BARTOW, 1st and 2d.

Thomas Bartow was the eldest son of Rev. John Bartow, the first rector of St. Peter's church, Westchester, New York, his mother being a Miss Reid, probably a sister of John Reid, of Perth Amboy. His parents were married in 1705. His grandfather was Gen. Bertaut, a French Protestant, who fled from France to England in 1685. Thomas Bartow was a merchant at Perth Amboy, and dealt largely in real estate. He held various public offices in the Province, being one of the recruiting officers in 1740; Clerk of the Assembly, 1745-1752; Clerk in Chancery, in 1746; Register of the East Jersey Proprietors, in 1747; and in 1756 was appointed Deputy Surveyor for East Jersey, by William Alexander. He was Register so late as 1765. He lived in a house standing on the southeast corner of Market street and the Square, in Perth Amboy, and was very fond of his books, they and a man-servant being his only companions.

His son, Thomas Bartow, jun., born at Perth Amboy, Jan. 27, 1737, was employed in a store in Bethlehem, Penn., in 1755; he joined the Moravians there, and married Sarah, daughter of Daniel and Elizabeth (North) Benezet, June 23, 1768. He was a prominent merchant of Philadelphia many years, but at the beginning of the Revolution went to Bethlehem, where he arrived May 7, 1776, with his wife and five children, and remained there more than three years. During the troublous times of the Revolution his father took refuge with him, and died about 1780, at Bethlehem. Thomas Bartow, jun., d. Jan. 26, 1793.—*Whitehead's Perth Amboy*, 138; *N. J. Archives*, passim; *Pa. Mag.*, 12: 388.

REV. ABRAHAM BEACH.

The Rev. Abraham Beach was b. in Cheshire, Conn., in 1740, and graduated at Yale in 1757. He went to England in 1767 for ordination, and was appointed missionary at New Brunswick and Piscataqua, N. J., arriving there the latter part of September in that year. In July, 1776, declining to omit the prayers for the King and the royal family, he was obliged to close the churches, but continued during the war to "dispense spiritual consolation alike to Whigs and Tories." In 1783 he was appointed temporary missionary at Perth Amboy. In 1784 he removed to New York, having been appointed assistant minister of Trinity church in that city. In 1813 he resigned, on a pension of $1,500 for life, voted him by the church. He retired to a farm on the Raritan, where he d. in 1828. His wife, Ann, was the daughter and sole heiress of Evart Van Winkle, one of the early Dutch settlers on the Raritan; she d. in 1808.

BEAKES FAMILY.

The will of William Beaks, of Nottingham, Burlington county, dated March 24, 1710-11, names sons William, Edmond, Stacey, Nathan, daughter Sarah, and wife Ruth, who is called the mother-in-law of son Edmond.—*W. J. Wills*, Liber No. 1, f. 313. ("Mother-in-law" was formerly used in the sense of stepmother.) It was doubtless this William Beaks who is stated (in 1711) to have been received as a witness in a capital case in the court of oyer and terminer against one Thomas Bates, who was condemned on his testimony.—*Smith's Hist. N. J.*, 392; *N. J. Archives*, IV., 42.

Edmund Beakes (son of William) and Ann, his wife, daughter of Thomas Gilberthorpe, of Burlington county, by deed dated Dec. 2, 1719, conveyed to Mahlon Stacy a plantation of 300 acres in Nottingham township, on Crosweeks creek. On Dec. 4, 1719, Stacy reconveyed the same premises to Edmund Beaks and wife Ann.—*W. J. Deeds*, BB, ff. 226, 228. Edmund Beaks was a shopkeeper in Trenton in 1751; he sold a saw-mill to William Morris. He was still of Trenton in 1755.—*N. J. Archives*, VII., 637; XIX., 489.

Nathan Beakes (son of William) was of Chester township, Burlington county, in 1734, but in 1749 seems to have been of Philadelphia.—*N. J. Archives*, XI., 401; XII., 525. He married Lydia, daughter of William (son of Griffith) and Hannah Morgan, and had one child, Morgan Beaks.— *Clement's First Settlers of Newton*, 212, 310, 311.

Thomas Potts, the ancestor of that family in New Jersey and Pennsylvania, married Sarah Beakes, about 1700.—*Cooley's Early Settlers of Trenton and Ewing*, 192.

Stacy Beaks (probably a grandson of William Beaks) and Mary, his mother, sold a plot of land on Hanover street, Trenton, for a parsonage for the Presbyterian church, May 3, 1762.—*Hall's Hist. Pres. Church in Trenton*, 176.

Abraham Beaks was of Crosswicks in 1764.—*N. J. Archives*, XXIV., 335.

Mary Trent, granddaughter of Chief Justice William Trent, of New Jersey, was born Dec. 3, 1762; she married Nathan Beakes (probably a son of Morgan Beakes), and had children: 1. Morgan, who m. Hannah, dau. of George Miller, of Trenton; 2. Lydia, m. Gen. Zachariah Rossell.— *Cooley*, ut supra, 290. Mrs. Mary Trent Beakes died Dec. 20, 1840, in Trenton, "the last person that had borne the name of Trent," said a local newspaper of the day.

REV. CHARLES BEATTY.

Charles Beatty was born in the County Antrim, Ireland, about 1712-1715, and was brought to this country by his uncle, Charles Clinton, in 1729, arriving in October at Cape Cod, Mass., where they remained until 1731, when they removed to Ulster county, N. Y. Young Beatty engaged in trade, traveling about the country with a pack. He had studied Latin, and the story goes that once, stopping at Log College, he offered his wares to the Rev. William Tennent, the master of that famous school, in Latin, with the result that Tennent was greatly drawn to him and persuaded him to prepare for the ministry. He was licensed by the New Brunswick Presbytery, Oct. 13, 1742, and was sent to Nottingham. He was called to the Forks of Neshaminy, May 26, 1743, and was ordained Dec. 14 of that year. He was sent to Virginia and North Carolina in 1754, and he served as chaplain in the forces sent out to defend the frontiers during the next two or three years. In 1766 he was sent by the Synod on a missionary tour among the Indians, as far as one hundred and thirty miles beyond Fort Pitt. His account of this trip, published in 1768, is valuable and interesting. He was a warm friend of David Brainerd, the missionary to the New Jersey Indians. In 1760 and 1761 he was very successful in raising funds in Great Britain for the Presbyterian Widows' Fund. Being greatly interested in the College of New Jersey, he sailed for the West Indies to solicit funds in its behalf, but d. Aug. 13, 1772, soon after reaching Bridgetown, in Barbadoes. He m., June 24, 1746 (mar. lic. Jan. 13, 1746), Ann, dau. of John Reading, sometime President of the Council of New Jersey; she was bap. July 21, 1723, in Old Amwell township, Hunterdon county; d. 1768, at Greenock, Scotland, whither he had taken her to secure the aid of eminent surgeons.—*Webster's Hist. Pres. Ch.*, 478.

JOHN BEATTY.

John Beatty, a son of the Rev. Charles Beatty, the noted missionary, after studying medicine with Dr. Benjamin Rush, entered the American army as a private soldier, reaching, by degrees, the rank of Lieutenant-Colonel. In 1776 he was captured at Fort Washington, and suffered a long and rigorous imprisonment. In 1779 he succeeded Elias Boudinot as Commissary-General of prisoners. After the war he settled at Princeton, where he practiced medicine. He was in 1789 a member of the Legislature from Middlesex, and the Speaker of the Assembly. He represented Burlington county in the Council, 1810-13. From 1795 to 1805 he was Secretary of State of New Jersey. In 1783 and 1784 he was a member of Congress. From May, 1815, until his death, April 30, 1826, he was President of the Trenton Banking Company. He was also an elder in the Trenton Presbyterian church.

BERRIEN FAMILY.

The Berriens are believed to have been of French origin. The progenitor of the American family bore the very Dutch name of Cornelis Jansen Berrien. He was in Flatbush, L. I., as early as 1669, and there m. Jannetie, dau. of Jan Stryker. Among her children was Peter, b. 1672, m. (1706) Elizabeth, dau. of Samuel Edsall, a member of the Council of East Jersey. Peter had several children, one of whom was John Berrien, b. Nov. 19, 1711; removed to Rocky Hill, Somerset county, N. J., and there m. Margaret, dau. of Thomas Eaton, of Eatontown. He was a merchant, highly esteemed; Trustee of Princeton College, 1763 until his death; Justice of the Supreme Court, 1764 until his death; member of the Assembly, 1768-1772. In 1766 he wrote to the Society for Promoting Arts, etc., in New York, enclosing samples of home manufactured stuffs, which were received with much interest. In the same year he was one of the managers of the lottery to raise money for running straight roads between New York and Philadelphia. He d. April 22, 1772, and is buried at Princeton.

His son, John Berrien, jun., was one of the commissioners appointed by act of the Legislature in 1764 to partition the Bergen common lands. He removed to Georgia in 1775, and took an active part in the Revolution. At the close of the war he m. Margaret, dau. of Capt. John Macpherson, of Philadelphia; he d. at Savannah, Ga., in 1815. His son, John Macpherson Berrien, b. at Rocky Hill, Aug. 23, 1781, was a Judge of the Georgia State Courts ten years; U. S. Senator, 1825-1829; U. S.

BLACKWELL: BLAIR: BLANCHARD

Attorney General, 1829-31, and again U. S. Senator, 1840-1852. Washington wrote his farewell address to his army at the Berrien homestead at Rocky Hill.

ROBERT BLACKWELL.

Robert Blackwell, son of Jacob Francis Blackwell, of Long Island, New York, was born May 6, 1748, and entered Princeton College, from which he graduated in 1770. After his graduation he studied for the ministry, and on June 11, 1772, he was ordained a Deacon in the chapel of Fulham Palace, near London, by Bishop Richard Terrick, and subsequently to the order of the priesthood. Returning to America, he was stationed in the southern part of New Jersey as a missionary of the Society for the Propagation of the Gospel in Foreign Parts, officiating at Gloucester and Waterford, and at Greenwich. In the war of the Revolution he served as Chaplain to the First Pennsylvania Brigade, and Surgeon to one of the regiments in the year 1778. In 1781 he was called to be one of the assistant ministers of Christ church and St. Peter's, Philadelphia, where he served until 1811. He died Feb. 12, 1831.

REV. SAMUEL BLAIR.

Samuel Blair was a son of the Rev. Samuel Blair, of Faggs' Manor, Penn. He graduated from Princeton College, 1760, and was a tutor in the College, 1761-1764. In 1764 he received the degree of Master of Arts from Princeton. He was pastor of Old South, Boston, 1766-67, when his health gave way. He then retired to Germantown, Penn., where he died in 1818.

BLANCHARD FAMILY.

The progenitor of this family was Jean or John Blanchard, who is first mentioned in our records under date of October 2, 1687, when he was a witness to the baptism at Kingston, N. Y., of Anna, child of Jan David and Esther Vincent. The other witness was Anne Valleau. Appended to the record is the note: "They are French people." The next mention of him is on the occasion of the baptism of his own child, Anna, at the same place, April 7, 1689, the witnesses being the parents, Anna Mahoult being the mother, and Marie Mahoult one of the witnesses. "French Reformed" notes the record. Upon the accession of William and Mary to the throne of England, the residents of Ulster county, N. Y., were called upon, in common with the other settlers in the English colonies, to take the oath of allegiance, which they did under date of September 1, 1689. John Blanchard's name is enrolled among them. He m. 1st, Anna Mahoult, probably in 1688 or earlier; 2d, with license, in the N Y. Dutch church, June 30, 1695, Jeanne Gaulthier. He is described as the widower of Anna Mahoult, and his residence as New Castle (on the Delaware). His wife, Jeanne Gaulthier, was a spinster, living at New York. They had one child, Jeanne, b. January 20. 1696-7, and baptized March 21 following, in the French Church at New York. On the ensuing October 27, 1697, Jean Blanssard, living at "newcastel en painsiluanie," married Susanne Rezeau, in the French Church at New York. She was a dau. of Rene Rezeau, of Staten Island, and Anne Coursier, his wife. Jean Blanchard evidently d. before April, 1730. His wife d. before 1720, as she is not mentioned in the will of her father, dated Feb 18. 1719-20, proved October 3, 1720, that instrument naming only her children. Blanch-

BLANCHARD

ard must have settled soon after his third marriage, at Elizabethtown, New Jersey, and perhaps before, as he was carrying on a country store at that place as early as 1700, which was carried on by him, and afterwards by his son, John, for many years. The following debit appears against him in the ledger of the Rev. John Harriman: "1703, May 17th, a house &c sold you this day at 80 lb is £80,00,00." (This house was sold by John Mills.) He took a mortgage, Oct. 27, 1701, on two tracts in Elizabethtown, from William Darby and wife; in this instrument Blanchard is described as "trader."—*N. J. Archives*, 21: 151 In 1711 he was one of the justices of the peace, and in 1720 a member of the town committee.—*Hatfield's Hist. of Elizabeth*, 251, 265, 306. At a meeting of the inhabitants and freeholders of Elizabethtown, August 2, 1720, Blanchard was chosen one of a committee of seven to defend the rights of the purchasers under the Nicolls grant, against the East Jersey Proprietors.—*Ib.*, 310. Administration was granted in his estate, April 6, 1730, to John Blanchard, doubtless his son, of Elizabethtown. As his wife is not mentioned in the will of her father, Feb. 18, 1719-20, she had probably d. before that date Jean Blanchard had issue:

By his first wife. Anna Mahoult:

    i. Anna, bap. April 7, 1689, at Kingston, N. Y. She doubtless m. William Dixon, of Elizabethtown, but was left a widow when only twenty-six years of age. Her husband's will, dated Sept. 16, 1715, was proved October 10, 1715, indicating that it was a death bed will. He mentions only one child, Anne.

By his second wife, Jeanne Gaulthier:

    ii. Jeanne, b. January 20, 1696-7; bap. at the French Church, N. Y., March 21, 1697. According to her family Bible, in her own handwriting, she was b. January 7, 1696-7, a difference of thirteen days from the church record. She m. Dec. 16, 1725, Dirck or Derrick Dey, bap. at New York March 27, 1687; she d. in New York, and was buried there August 14, 1756; he d. there also, and was buried May 11, 1764. His will, dated August 4, 1761, was proved May 29, 1764. He settled early in life at Lower Preakness, near Paterson, N. J., and there erected, about 1740, the handsome stone mansion, still standing, which was occupied by Washington as his headquarters during October and November, 1780. Children (according to the family Bible): 1. Theunis, b. October 18, 1726. m (marriage license dated Dec. 12, 1749), Hester Schuyler; she d. Sept. 30, 1784; he was a Colonel in the Revolution: d. June 10, 1787; 2. Jane, b. January 18, 1728; m. John Varick, June 15, 1749; both are buried in the Hackensack Dutch church yard; 3. John. b. Nov. 27, 1729; d. about 1753, unm.; 4. Derrick, b. May 4, 1732; d. young; 5. Anna, b. Aug. 12, 1735; m. William McAdam, Dec. 12, 1764; he d. about 1779; 6. Sarah, b. April 1, 173-(the record is torn here); d. young; 7. Mary, b. Aug. 18, 1741; m. David Shaw, Nov. 24, 1761; he is buried in the Hackensack Dutch church yard.

30

By his third wife, Suzanne Rezeau:

2. iv. Jean, b. Oct. 3, 1699; bap. Nov. 5, 1699, in the French Church in New York.

3. v. Isaac, b. Sept. 14, 1701; bap. October 12, 1701, in the French Church in New York.

4. vi. Peter, prob. bap. in one of the French churches then in existence on Staten Island.

vii. Susannah, prob. bap. in one of the French churches then in existence on Staten Island; she was still living Feb. 18, 1719, as she is mentioned in the will of her grandfather, Rene Rezeau, of that date. She m. John Halstead, of Elizabeth. He left a will, dated Aug. 28, 1785, in and by which he appointed his wife Susanna sole executrix, and gave her all his estate, real and personal. Witnesses—Daniel Marsh, Abraham Terrill, Amos Morss, junior.—N. J. Wills, Liber No. 28, f. 378. This will was proved July 19, 1786. But his wife had died before that date, without executing the will, probably dying immediately after her husband, and accordingly, on the same date that his will was proved John Halstead, of Perth Amboy, was appointed administrator, Mathias Halstead, of the same place, going on his bond. N. J. Archives, 23:42; and will of John Blanchard, Jun., Liber E of Wills, f. 188.

viii. Elizabeth, prob. bap. on Staten Island, in one of the French churches there. She is mentioned in the will of her grandfather, Feb. 18, 1719.

ix. Marian, Maritie, Marie, Maria, Mary; although she is named in the above order in her grandfather's will, she was prob. the third child of Jean Blanchard by his third wife, as she was m. and had at least one child as early as 1724. She m. John Mead, son of John Pieterse Meet and Margrietje Mandeville, bap. at New York March 25, 1691; will dated Aug. 12, 1762; proved June 15, 1769, names wife Mary and the following children: 1. Peter, m. Nov. 18, 1753, Janneke Van Winkle; 2. Johannes, b. January 31, 1724, bap. at Hackensack; m. January 15, 1753, Maria Cadmus; 3. Jacob, b. May 11, 1728; bap. at Acquackanonk June 10, 1728; m. March 14, 1756, at Acquackanonk, Maria Derjee; 4. Isaac, b. Sept. 13, 1730; bap. at Acquackanonk, Oct. 11, 1730; 5. Jillis. There was another child bap. at Acquackanonk, January 11, 1730-31, which prob. d. in inf.

2. Jean² Jean¹ Blanchard, b. Oct. 3, 1699; m. Mary ———; will proved 1749. He is named as one of the executors of the will of Cornelis Bryant, of Elizabethtown, Oct. 2, 1720.—N. J. Archives, 23: 69. He was granted administration, as principal creditor, on the estate of Thomas Garring, of Whippany, Feb. 12, 1724-5.—Ib., 181. The same day and for the same reason, he was appointed administrator of John Johnston, of Whippany.—Ib., 266. He wittnessed the will, May 5, 1721, of William Stiles, of Elizabethtown.—Ib., 442. His brother Isaac named him as executor of his will, April 4, 1727.—Ib., 42. He signed an agreement, Nov. 18, 1729, in reference to the records and convey-

ances in the old Town Book of Elizabethtown.—*Hatfield's Hist. of Elizabeth*, 312. On June 18, 1739, he was named first on a committee of five to collect money from the inhabitants to defray the expense of running out the lines of the Elizabethtown purchase; and the same day was appointed on a committee to agree with the Newark people upon the division line between the two towns.—*Ib.*, 318, 319. He was one of the petitioners, about the same time, for the incorporation of the Borough of Elizabethtown, and in the charter granted by Governor Lewis Morris, Feb. 8, 1739-40, Mr. Blanchard was appointed Recorder of the Borough.—*Ib.*, 320-321. He was usually called John Blanchard, junior. He appears to have carried on his father's mercantile business most of his life. By deed dated March 27, 1746, John Schuyler, Peter Schuyler and Adoniah Schuyler conveyed to William Chetwood, John Halsted and John Blanchard "One certain Parcell or Tract of Land Situate lying and being within the Bounds of Elizabeth Town by Raway Brook on the East side thereof containing Nine hundred Acres be the same more or less;" by an indenture dated June 19, 1747, the grantees declared and agreed that "no right or benefit of Survivorship shall be had or claimed by the survivor of them," but that their heirs should take the shares to which their respective ancestors would be entitled if living.—*Original Unrecorded Deed, Nelson MSS.* On June 20, 1747, "being sick in body but of a perfect memory," he made his will. He directs all his estate to be sold and converted into ready money, and his debts paid, and gives the rest and residue to his wife Mary in fee simple. He appoints his wife and his brother-in-law John Halsted, junior, executors. The will was proved May 1, 1749. The executors renounced, and Jonathan Hampton, of Elizabeth Town, principal creditor, was appointed administrator with will annexed.—*Liber E of Wills*, f. 188.

3. Isaac[2] John[1] Blanchard was one of the witnesses to the will of John Frazee, of Elizabethtown, Jan. 26, 1723-4.—*N. J. Archives*, 23:172. The will of Isaac Blanchard, of Elizabethtown, yeoman, dated April 4, 1727, was proved May 16, 1727. He names wife Jane, daughter Jane (under 18), and expected child.—*Ib.*, 42. Executors—wife Jane and brother John Blanchard.

4. Of Peter[2] John[1] Blanchard, we have no data.

One Peter Blanchard, of the city of New York, "sea faring man," made his will January 24, 1757, in which he directs that after the payment of his debts all his personal estate shall go to his "loving mother Mrs. Mary Giffard," of the city of New York; also "all the landed and real estate which I have or by right ought to have or might claim in the province of New Jersey or elsewhere," to have and to hold the same during her natural life, with remainder to his half-sister, Mary Giffard, in fee simple. His mother is appointed executrix. The will was proved in New Jersey, June 22, 1759, and his mother qualified as executrix —*Liber G of Wills*, f. 84. It has been conjectured that this Peter was a son of John[2] John[1] Blanchard and Mary ——, his wife; that John's widow married a Giffard after his death, and had a child Mary by her second husband. This child, of course, would not be the "half-sister" of Peter.

BLOOMFIELD FAMILY.

In a copy of the English Bible, brought from Amsterdam, in 1715, there is a family record of the Bloomfields, copied from an older record, by Dr. Moses Bloomfield, father of Gov. Joseph Bloomfield, of

New Jersey. The history is given in the language of the original for several generations. Additions are here given from other sources.

1. "Thomas Bloomfield.—A major in Cromwell's army. Upon ye restoration of Charles ye II emigrated from Woodbridge, Suffolk, England, with his five children, Ezekiel, John, Thomas, Nathaniel and Mary. He first took up lands where ye town of Newbury now stands in Massachusetts and on ye 21st May 1666 with his associates purchased of ye proprietors of East Jersey ye township of Woodbridge— so named for their home in England—It includes Perth Amboy and Piscataiway—And were among ye first settlers of ye town." (Woodbridge never included the other two towns named.)

2. "Ezekiel Bloomfield.—Eldest son of Thomas Bloomfield. Married Hope Fitzrandolph, whose father came in ye same vessel from England. Their children were Joseph, Timothy, Ezekiel, Jeremiah, Benjamin and Mary.

3. "Joseph Bloomfield.—Eldest son of Ezekiel. Was born March 3, 1695. September 5, 1721, he married his cousin Eunice, daughter of David Dunham and ye first above named Mary. Eunice died November 30, 1760, in her 59th year. Joseph her husband died May 23, 1782." Issue:

      i. Hannah,[4] b. Nov. 17, 1722; d. Feb. 12, 1724.
      ii. Hannah. 2d, b. June 12, 1724; m. Jonathan Allston.
      iii. Martha, b. July 26, 1726; d. April 10, 1731.
4. iv. Moses, b. Dec. 4, 1729; d. Aug. 12, 1791.
      v. Asa, b. Aug. 25, 1733; d. aged 2 yrs. 9 mos.
5. vi. Jonathan, b. Aug. 25. 1735.
      vii. Esther, b. 1737; d. in inf.
    viii. Esther, 2d, b. 1740; d. in inf.
      ix. Samuel, b. 1743; d. in inf.
6. i. Joseph,[5] b. October 18, 1753.
      ii. Samuel, b. March 10, 1755; d. aged ten days.
7. iii. Samuel, 2d, b. Feb. 14, 1756.
      iv. Isaac, b. May 20, 1759; d. in his fourth year.
      v. Nancy, b. Dec. 3, 1761; d. Sept. 5, 1764.
      vi. Hannah, b. January 13. 1763; m. May 23, 1784, James Giles; d. Dec. 20, 182?; he was b. March 8, 1760; d. ———. Children:—1. Mary McIlvain, b. Aug. 10, 1785; m. Abraham H. Inskeep, Oct. 1, 1803; (children —a. Sarah H., b. July 23, 1804; b. Phoebe Giles, b. Sept. 7, 1808; c. Mary Bloomfield, b. July 4, 1811; d. Nancy Hampton, b. Sept. 20, 1818); 2. Phoebe Holmes, b. Aug. 10, 1785: twin with Mary McIlvain; d. August 7, 1803; 3. Frances Giles, b. May, 1788; d. Oct. 20, 1793; 4. Nancy Bloomfield, b. April 26, 1795; d. Sept. 17, 1800; 5. James Bradford, b. July 6, 1801; 6. Sarah Ogden, b. March 5, 1804; d. August 10, 1805.
      vii. Nancy, 2d, b. June 16, 1766; m. October 28, 1787, Dr. John Garet Wall; he was b. Dec. 15, 1759; d. January 14, 1798. Issue: Moses Bloomfield, b. August 3, 1792; d. Sept. 5, 1823. It would appear from a legacy in the will of Joseph Bloomfield that his sister Ann (?Nancy) m. 2d, James Paton.

4. Moses[4] Joseph[3] Ezekiel[2] Thomas[1] Bloomfield, b. at Woodbridge, Dec. 4, 1729; m. 1st, Nov. 27, 1752, Sarah, b. March 17, 1733-4, dau. of Robert and Phebe (Baldwin) Ogden; she d. Oct. 25, 1773; he m. 2d. the

iii

BLOOMFIELD

widow of Dr. Samuel Ward. "His first wife was a granddaughter of Jonathan Ogden, whose mother's maiden name was Harrison, (a daughter of) one of the original proprietors of Elizabethtown, New Jersey, her father, John likewise migrated with him and his two brothers, from England, after ye restoration in 1666." Moses was educated for a physician in the best manner, finishing his studies in Edinburgh. Upon his return to this country he soon achieved a reputation for skill in his profession. He was one of the original members of the New Jersey Medical Society, organized July 23, 1766, and his name as secretary is appended to notices of meetings of the Society, October 4, 1767, and March 23, 1768. He was prominent and influential in promoting the welfare of the Society. He was named as a trustee in the charter of the First Presbyterian Church in the Township of Woodbridge, granted by Governor Jonathan Belcher, September 8, 1756. The "Meeting House Green" was surveyed, at his request, Aug. 8, 1784. In the charter of the Free Schools in the Town of Woodbridge, granted by Governor Franklin, June 24, 1769, Moses Bloomfield is named as one of the trustees. In the charter granted by Governor Franklin, December 22, 1773, for incorporating "The New Jersey Society for the better support of the widows and education of the children of deceased Presbyterian ministers in communion with the present Established Church of Scotland," Moses Bloomfield was named as one of the incorporators. His name is appended to a set of resolutions adopted by the "Freeholders and Freemen" of Woodbridge, July 23, 1770, affirming allegiance to King George, but declaring their adherence to the Non-Importation Agreement, until the British ministry should make "ample Confession of their Crime" in infringing upon the "natural Privileges of our happy Constitution," previously enjoyed by the Colonists. Nevertheless, when there appeared in the same paper that published these resolves, and immediately following them, an advertisement plainly threatening the merchants who violated the agreement with tar and feathers, he wrote to the paper disclaiming for the Sons of Liberty of Woodbridge all responsibility for said advertisement, and declared that the "respectable Freeholders and Freemen of Woodbridge (acting as a Body) never did, nor ever will do, or cause to be done, any Thing inconsistent with Law or Liberty." He was appointed a Justice of the Peace and Judge of Middlesex County, September 19, 1776, and was again appointed Justice of the Peace of the County, June 5, 1787. He was clerk of the Board of Chosen Freeholders of the County, 1773-1784, and frequently served as moderator of the town meetings. His name is signed as secretary, to a letter sent by the Woodbridge committee, May 1, 1775, to the several patriotic committees of Massachusetts, thanking them for the "noble stand" they had made. Among the deputies elected by Middlesex county to the Convention of New Jersey, which met at Burlington, June 10, 1776, and which adopted the first constitution of the State, July 2, 1776, was Moses Bloomfield, but his name seldom appears in the minutes, indicating that for some reason he was not regular in attendance—probably because of service in the field, for on August 21, 1776, he was appointed one of a committee of four members to audit bills approved by the Convention, and on the same day that body ordered paid "to Dr. Moses Bloomfield five Pounds eleven Shillings and five Pence, in full of his account of medicines and attendance on Capt. Neal's Artillery Company," which was encamped at Perth Amboy during the summer. On May 14, 1777, he was commissioned Hospital Surgeon of the Continental Army, and Hospital

Physician and Surgeon, October 6, 1780. He was at the hospital in Princeton, in October, 1778. He resigned December 13, 1780. The *New Jersey Journal*, published at Chatham, in its issue for August 9, 1780, states that he was carried off by a party from Staten Island, the week previous. His capture is also reported in the *New Jersey Gazette*, Trenton, of August 16, 1780. He was exchanged within a month, for Dr. de Bass, a Hessian Surgeon. He was elected a member of the Assembly from Middlesex county in 1784. He died at Woodbridge, August 14, 1791, and his tombstone stands in the Presbyterian church-yard in that town. In an obituary notice of his death, in the *New Jersey Journal*, August 31, 1791, a correspondent writes: "He main-tained an eminent character as a scholar, a physician, a gentleman and a Christian. In the early part of his life, he became acquainted with men as well as books. When his assistance as a physician was called for by the public, he cheerfully stepped forward and served with faith-fulness and reputation as senior physician and surgeon until near the close of the war, when he retired to private life of his own accord. As a physician he was skilful, attentive and successful; easy and familiar in his manners and address; he was benevolent and liberal to the poor without ostentation, religious without bigotry, never ashamed to own in any company that he was a Christian; nor would he neglect his duty to God or to his fellow-men on any account whatever. His last illness, which lasted more than two years, he bore with an uncommon Chris-tian patience and fortitude. In his death the State has lost a worthy citizen, and the Presbyterian Church an important member." Dr. Wickes says "he was a man of fine appearance and of more than or-dinary culture and ability, and was considered one of the best phy-sicians of his day." His residence is thought to have been the old Bloomfield homestead, which in 1873 was occupied by George C. Hance. The will of Moses Bloomfield, "late practitioner of Physic and Surgery," dated Dec. 20, 1790, devises to daughter Hannah, now wife of James Giles, Esq., and her heirs, "a lot of land beginning at the Southeast corner of a certain lot of land, heretofore conveyed by me to my son-in-law Dr. John G. Wall"; to grandson Moses Bloomfield, son of Dr. Samuel Bloomfield, and his heirs, land between the said daughter Hannah and the parsonage belonging to the eldest Presby-terian Society in Woodbridge; in case of his death before coming of age, then to his father; to sons Joseph and Samuel all the residue of real estate equally, as tenants in common, and to be estimated in the division at £2,000 specie; to wife Phebe £40 specie, "together with the labor and service of my negro Festus until the first of October, 1798, on which day the said negro shall be manumitted"; has advanced £444 to son Samuel, and £170 to daughter Hannah, and £170 to daughter Nancy, etc. Executors—sons Joseph and Samuel. Witnesses—Jarvis Bloomfield, Samuel Herriott, John Mersereau, of the town of Woodbridge, merchant. Proved Aug. 20, 1791. Dr. Samuel Bloomfield renounced and Joseph Bloomfield qualified as executor.—*N. J. Wills*, Liber 31, f. 53. In the Newark (N. J.) *Eagle*, sometime in 1840, there was published an account of a meeting held at Woodbridge, July 4, 1783, whereat Dr. Bloomfield ascended the platform with fourteen slaves, and after a patriotic speech setting forth his belief in the principles of the Declaration of Independence, formally declared all his slaves free. Moses Bloomfield had issue (all by his first wife).

5. Jonathan[4] Joseph[3] Ezekiel[2] Thomas[1] Bloomfield, b. Aug. 25, 1735; m. January 12, 1758, Elizabeth, dau. of John Wood, of Huntington, Long Island; she d. Aug. 22, 1776. His farm lying on the direct road

between New York and the South, he was greatly harassed by the movements of the troops back and forth. On one occasion he, and Dr. Moses Bloomfield, and others were captured by the British and carried off to New York, where they were lodged in the sugar house, but they were exchanged within a few weeks. Issue:

       i. Jarvis,[5] m. ———. Child: Anna, b. about 1792; m. ——— Bernard of Constantia, N. Y. He was a lieutenant in the Revolution, but on account of straitened circumstances withdrew from the army in 1781, and engaged on board a privateer, commanded by Captain Truxton. The vessel on her first expedition was captured, and Jarvis thrown into the prison ship at New York. In the summer of 1782 he was exchanged, and returned home, much weakened by sickness caused by his long confinement. As soon as he recovered he formed a company of volunteers and fitted out several large boats with which he made trips from the mouth of Woodbridge creek around Staten Island, and cut several merchant ships. After the war he engaged in the lumber trade between New York and Virginia. In returning to New York in the sloop which he commanded, in 1794, he was thrown overboard by a sudden turn of the boom as he came on deck. He was ill at the time, and closely bound up in his overcoat, and before assistance could reach him he was drowned.

8. ii. John Wood.
    iii. Eunice, m. Jonathan Bloomfield.
    iv. Betsey, m. Nathan Bloomfield; d. s. p.
    v. Martha, m. Richard Marsh.
    vi. Phebe, m. Timothy Jervis.
    vii. Mary, d. 1773.
    viii. Sarah, d. 1780.
    ix. Mary, 2d, m. Richard Carman.

JOSEPH BLOOMFIELD.

6. Joseph[5] Moses[4] Joseph[3] Ezekiel[2] Thomas[1] Bloomfield, born at Woodbridge, October 18th, 1753; m. 1st, December 17, 1778, Mary, dau. of Dr. William McIlvaine. of Philadelphia; she d. in 1818; m. 2d, Isabella ———, who survived him. He d. October 3, 1823. There is an unsupported tradition that in the second year of his marriage to Miss McIlvaine, they had a child, who lived only ten days. Joseph studied law with Cortlandt Skinner, at Perth Amboy, and was licensed as an attorney and counsellor November 12th, 1774; in November, 1792, he was called up to be serveant-at-law. On the breaking out of the war he volunteered, and was commissioned a Captain in 1775. He served in the unfortunate expedition against Quebec. On his return to New Jersey he was obliged to arrest his old preceptor. In 1777 he was a Major. After the war he was appointed Register of Admiralty, 1783. and Attorney-General of New Jersey, 1783-1792; was Brigadier-General in the brief expedition to suppress the Whiskey Rebellion, in 1794; Mayor of Burlington (where he had taken up his residence soon after the war), 1795-1800; and member of the Board of Chosen Freeholders of Burlington county. The New Jersey Legislature elected him Governor of the State, annually,

1801-1312, except in 1802, when there was a tie vote and the State went without a Governor for a year. In 1811 he published a compilation of the Laws from 1799. He was a Brigadier-General in the War of 1812. In 1817 he was elected to Congress, and again in 1819, serving four years. He died October 3d, 1823, and was buried two days later in St. Mary's churchyard, Burlington. He was a man of decidedly literary tastes, accumulating a fine library. In politics he was an ardent Republican, and a friend of Thomas Jefferson. He was also a warm friend of Aaron Burr, and while Governor urged the Prosecutor of the Pleas of Bergen county to enter a nolle prosequi in the case of the indictment of the Vice-President for shooting Alexander Hamilton, in the duel in July, 1804, at Weehawken, in that county. The indictment was accordingly nolled. He was a man of excellent qualities, kindly in his intercourse with his fellows, a little whimsical or even eccentric at times, but always highly respected by those who knew him. See 2 Proceedings New Jersey Historical Society, IX., 12; 2 N. J. Archives, I., 341. His will, dated Dec. 30, 1823, proved Nov. 10, 1823, names as executors wife Isabella, sister Hannah, wife of James Giles, James Giles and Samuel Wetherill Price, of the city of Philadelphia, they to sell and convey real and personal estate, and to pay sister Ann Paton $300 semi-annually during life; the income from remainder of estate to wife Isabella, and so much of the principal as she may need for her support, with power to bequeath one-half of residue of estate remaining at her decease; the other half to sister Hannah Giles, or in case of her prior death, to her children. Witnesses—A. Griffith, Mary B. Griffith, Wm. S. Coxe. The inventory of the estate was made Dec. 31, 1823. Furniture, $888.52. Notes from David E. Paten and Joseph B. Wiggins ("desperate"); bonds of Isaac Humphreys, Moses Bloomfield, Patrick Ford; shares in the Burlington Aqueduct Co.; bond of Joseph Ellis Bloomfield, dated Oct. 26, 1822, payable Aug. 9, 1827, doubtful. Total of notes, etc., $6,322.46. Sworn to May 31, 1825.—*Original Wills*, etc. It might be added that Joseph Bloomfield was chosen by the Legislature of New Jersey to be Presidential elector in 1792; he was vice-president of the Society of the Cincinnati of New Jersey, July, 1794, until his election as president of the Society, July, 1808 When the village of Bloomfield assumed that name the Governor wrote a graceful letter of acknowledgment, and sent a check for a substantial amount to the Presbyterian congregation of the place.

7. Samuel, 2d,[5] Moses[4] Joseph[3] Ezekiel[2] Thomas[1] Bloomfield, b. Feb. 14, 1756; m. Abigail Ellis. dau. of Joseph Ellis, of Gloucester, N. J.; d. November 25, 1806; she was b. January 7, 1761; she survived her husband. He studied medicine with his father, and was otherwise well educated. He settled and practised for many years at Colestown, Gloucester county. He served in the Revolutionary army as surgeon. His will, dated April 24, 1801, proved April 20, 1807, gives to wife Abigail all his estate for his maintenance and the maintenance and support of her children, with remainder equally to sons—Joseph Ellis, Moses and Samuel. Executors—wife Abigail, and brother Joseph Bloomfield. Witnesses—Mary Ann McIlvaine, Rachel McIlvaine, Sally Reading.—*Gloucester Wills*, 1807. Issue:

  i.   Sarah Ogden,[6] b. Sept. 23, 1781; d. Aug. 28, 1794.
9. ii.   Joseph Ellis, b. Dec. 16, 1787.
  iii. Moses Ogden, b. Aug. 23, 1790. He was a lieutenant in the U. S. army which invaded Canada in the War of 1812-15, and served with that portion of the army which was at Sackett's Harbor. He was with Gen.

Zebulon Montgomery Pike, at the storming of York (now Toronto). His division carried the heights and captured the colors. He was the first to seize the flag, and was shot dead in the act. His recovered body was wrapped in the flag he had so gallantly captured until buried, after which the ensign long remained in the family of his oldest brother, Joseph Ellis Bloomfield.

iv. Samuel-Giles, b. April 14, 1796; d. Sept. 17, 1814. He entered the army during the War of 1812-15, and was commissioned a lieutenant of artillery, U. S. A. He was killed in a duel with a superior officer at Fort Stanwix, Oneida county, N. Y. (Another account gives the locality as Greenbush, opposite Albany.) His brother, Joseph-Ellis Bloomfield, was wont to say that "at the time it was termed an almost deliberate murder. Giles Bloomfield, a mere inexperienced youth of eighteen, was upon more than one occasion twitted in some way by an officer more than twice his age. It is said he had a sort of grudge against Giles, who was a favorite with everybody else. When again receiving some taunt, the mere boy, with all the proud spirit of the Bloomfields in him, and brave courage, too, challenged the officer, who was an experienced duellist, it was afterwards learned. At the very first fire he killed Giles. It was pronounced at once by all who witnessed the occurrence, a cruel and almost deliberate murder. The officer had to resign, or leave the company. His name was never mentioned, but with scorn." It is not given in any account of the duel that has come to the writer's notice.

9. Joseph-Ellis[6] Samuel[5] Moses[4] Joseph[3] Ezekiel[2] Thomas[1] Bloomfield, b. at Woodbridge, Dec. 16, 1787; m. Mary Frances Barbarous, Sept. 24, 1819; d. at Oswego, N. J., June 29, 1872. She was b. at Burlington, May 30, 1801; d. at Oswego, Dec. 3, 1881. (Her father was Jean Andre Barbaroux, a native of Au Valour Marseilles, France. He became a coffee planter in the Isle of Martinique, according to one account, but according to another, he settled in the island of San Domingo, where he owned several large coffee plantations. He m., in the West Indies, Jeanne Marie Amarinthe De Vaucelles. During the insurrection of 1791 he and his wife were obliged to flee for their lives, taking only their personal property with them. They came to Burlington, where they ended their days. He was buried in St. Mary's church yard, May 7, 1825; she was buried in the same church yard March 31, 1826. They had two children—Mary Frances, m. Joseph-Ellis Bloomfield, as mentioned above; and Jane Eliza, m. Dr. William S. Coxe, of Burlington.) Joseph-Ellis Bloomfield entered into mercantile life at an early age, and in the course of time represented a Philadelphia mercantile house at Cadiz, Spain. At one time he served under a U. S. consular appointment in the same city. While in Europe he traveled quite extensively. After his return to this country he resided in New Jersey and New York, and interested himself in the canal improvements of the day, writing and corresponding much on the subject. Subsequently, he removed to Oneida county, N. Y., where he had large landed interests. Part of the time he made

his home in Utica, where he carried on milling. He also resided for a time at Taberg, N. Y. He became deeply interested in the subject of railroads, which were just making their way into public notice, and wrote a great deal in relation thereto, corresponding extensively with the leading railroad builders and managers of the day, urging the importance of easy grades and direct routes, that would avoid crooked lines and local interests.

8. John-Wood,[5] Jonathan[4] Joseph[3] Ezekiel[2] Thomas[1] Bloomfield, b. ———, 1765; m. in 1789, Ann Ellis. wid. of Joseph Ellis, and dau. of Samuel Bullus; d. ———, 1849, at Rome, N. Y., and was buried there. From an autobiographical memoir which he prepared in 1844, many of the incidents of the lives of his father, brothers and sisters have been extracted, as well as the particulars of his own life. (This memoir was published in the Rome Daily Sentinel, June 2, 1887.) At the close of the Revolutionary war he continued to assist his father in carrying on his farm at Woodbridge, until 1786. Then, through the influence of Joseph Bloomfield (afterwards Governor), he went to Burlington and became interested with him and one John Little, in the manufacture of iron. In 1788 this partnership was dissolved, and another formed with Joseph Bloomfield and William Coxe. In 1791 this partnership was dissolved, having lost much money, John's share being between $1,500 and $2,000, for which he was in debt to Joseph Bloomfield. He continued the manufacture of iron alone, until the fall of 1792. Mr. McIlvaine, of Burlington, had bought of Joseph Bloomfield a tract of 1,600 acres in the present town of Lee, New York. The terms of the grant to Bloomfield stipulated that a certain number of settlers should be located on the land within a given time. This period had nearly expired. In the spring of 1793 Bloomfield, as the agent of Mr. McIlvaine, went from Burlington on horseback to Oneida county, and caused the lands to be surveyed. In company with three others he bought from George Scriba 4,000 acres of land as a private speculation. He got back to Burlington about July 10. He returned to Oneida county the next year, and settled at Annsville, which was named for his wife. In 1804 he took up his residence at Rome, N. Y. At one time he had charge of the iron works at Constantia, and was also interested in the iron works at Taberg, N. Y.

      i. Mary Frances.[7] b. in Burlington, Oct. 11, 1820; m. April 20, 1852, at Mexico, N. Y., George Monizette Chapman, b. April 24, 1827, son of Levi and Permela (Colburn) Chapman; d. in Chattanooga, Tenn., March 25, 1901; he d. March 4, 1908. Children:—1. Josephine Kirby, b. in Oswego, N. Y., Sept. 4, 1853; living (1910) in Chattanooga, Tenn., unm.; 2. Julia Bloomfield, b. in Brooklyn, N. Y., March 19, 1855; d. Feb. 15. 1900; 3. Levi Colburn, b. in Chicago, Ill., Dec. 3, 1858; d. May 28, 1861.

     ii. Julia Ann, b. in Taberg, Oneida county, N. Y., Sept. 23, 1822; d. March 18. 1824.

    iii. Francis Ogden, b. in Taberg, Oneida county, N. Y., Aug. 17, 1824; d. in Oswego, N. Y., Sept. 9, 1837.

    iv. Elizabeth Barbarroux, b. in Burlington, Aug. ———, 1826; d. in Oswego, April 29, 1899, unm.

     v. James Andre, b. in New York city, March 4, 1828; d. near Watab, Minn., March 17, 1852, unm.

    vi. Julia Keen, b. in New York city, July 27, 1829; living at Oswego, in 1910. Although a confirmed invalid for many years, confined to her bed most of the time, she was in the possession of a remarkably vigorous intellect, and in 1909 produced a most elaborate and admirable History of Oneida County, N. Y., giving an especially full account of the Indian Nation from whom the county is named.

vii. William Russell, b. in Utica, N. Y., Oct. 20, 1833; m. ———, of Philadelphia; d. in Kansas, 1906, s. p. He served as an officer of a Wisconsin regiment during the war of the rebellion.

10. viii. Ogden, b. in New York city, January 16, 1843.

·10. Ogden[7] Joseph-Ellis[6] Samuel[5] Moses[4] Joseph[3] Ezekiel[2] Thomas[1] Bloomfield, b in New York city January 16, 1843; m. at Utica, N. Y., October 9, 1857, Elizabeth Spencer, of Ohio; d. in New York, April 4, 1891; she was b. in Ohio Aug. 6, 1848; d. in Fair Haven, Cayuga county, N. Y., Dec. 22, 1879. He was a physician. He served in an Oswego regiment in the war of the rebellion, when but nineteen. Issue:

    i. Frederick-Ellis[8] b. at Oswego, Sept. 2, 1869; d. at Berne, Ohio, Sept. 11, 1870.

    ii. Frances Barbarroux, b at Berne, Ohio, January 8, 1871; d. at Berne. March 6, 1873.

    iii. Edward Russell, b. at Fair Haven, Cayuga county, N. Y., April 2, 1874; d. in Phoenix, Arizona, March 26, 1904, unm.

    iv. Mary Elizabeth, b. in Fair Haven, N. Y., August 6, 1877; living (1909) at home, in Oswego, unm.

    v. France Ogden, b. in Fair Haven, N. Y., June 9, 1879; d. at that place Sept. 26, 1879.

From the foregoing, it seems that the name Bloomfield has become extinct in the lines above given.

BORDEN FAMILY.

Richard Borden baptized Feb. 22, 1595-6, married Sept. 28, 1625, Jane Fowle, born Feb. 15, 1604. He was admitted an inhabitant of Aquidneck, R. I., in 1638, and on May 20 was allotted five acres. On March 16, 1641, he became a freeman. In 1665 he and Benjamin Borden (his son, then a minor), James Grover and others, all of Gravesend, L. I., bought considerable tracts of land at Neversink, Narumson and Portupick, in Monmouth county, N. J., for which he contributed £9, and was allotted three shares. Richard was a Deputy to the General Court in 1667-70, indicating that he had returned from Long Island, if, indeed, he ever removed from Rhode Island. He died May 25, 1671, and was buried in "the burying place that Robert Dennis gave Friends in Portsmouth," R. I. His (nuncupative) will was proved May 31, 1671, by the Town Council, on testimony concerning the wishes of the deceased. By its provisions land in New Jersey was left to his son Francis. His personal estate was inventoried at £1572 8s. 9d. His widow, Joan Fowle, d. July 16, 1688.—*Genealogical Dictionary of Rhode Island*, by John Osborne Austin, 1887, 23-24; *Monmouth County Deeds*, AAC; *Hist. Burlington and Mercer Counties*, 454; *Old Times in Old Monmouth*, 207; *Borden Genealogy*. His children were:

Second Generation.

    i. Thomas[2], m. Mary Harris, Jan. 20, 1664; d. Nov. 25, 1676; she d. March 22, 1718. He lived at Portsmouth, N. H.

2.   ii.   Francis[2], b. in England; m. Jane Vicars, 12th of 4th
               mo., 1677; d. 19th 1st mo., 1704-5. His will is dated
               May 24, 1703; codicil, Feb. 18, 1705.
        iii. Matthew[2], born May 16, 1638; married Sarah Clayton,
               March 4, 1674; died July 5, 1708; she died April 19,
               1735, aged 82. He lived at Portsmouth, R. I. He was
               "the first English child born on Rhode Island," say
               Friends' records. He owned land on Cooper's creek,
               Gloucester county, in 1685. A patent was issued to
               him for 400 acres on Crosswicks creek and John Tom-
               linson's Run, 4th mo. 1695.—N. J. Archives, XXI., 377,
               651.
        iv.   John[2], born September, 1640; married Mary Earle, Dec.
               25, 1670; she was born 1655, and d. June 4, 1716; d.
               June, 1734. He lived at Portsmouth, R. I. He de-
               vised to his daughters, Hope and Mary Borden, all his
               lands in Shrewsbury, N. J., and certain lands in Penn-
               sylvania. He owned land in Monmouth county as
               early as 1687. See N. J. Archives, XXI., 99.
        v.   Joseph[2], born July 3, 1643; married Hope ———. He
               lived at Portsmouth, R. I., and at Barbadoes, W. I.
               Joseph Borden, of Chester county, Pa., cordwainer,
               bought a tract of 356 acres of land at Oneanickon,
               alias Carmell, Springfield township, Burlington county,
               Dec. 1, 1701.—N. J. Archives, XXI., 531.
        vi.   Sarah[2], born May, 1644; married Jonathan Holmes, b.
               cir. 1637, son of Obadiah and Catherine Holmes; she
               died about 1705; he died in 1713. She had 9 children.
        vii. Samuel[2], born July, 1645; married Elizabeth Crosse,
               June 1, 1679. On Feb. 10, 1672, he sold Lewis Mattox,
               of Portsmouth, R. I., a share of land in Monmouth,
               N. J. He is said to have removed to Westchester,
               N. Y., prior to his marriage, but was afterwards at
               Philadelphia, where he died. He was a member of
               the West Jersey Assembly in 1682, says Smith's Hist.
               of N. J., 151. There was surveyed for Samuel Borden
               a tract of 200 acres "at Hatt's Plantation on the
               northwest side of the road from Burlington to Shrows-
               burry," Feb. 21, 1681-2.—N. J. Archives, XXI., 350.
               This tract was conveyed by his administrators about
               1694.—Ib., 372. Administration on the estate in West
               Jersey of Samuel Borden was granted Feb. 8, 1692-3,
               to Francis Rawle, of Philadelphia, merchant, princi-
               pal creditor of the deceased; Thomas Budd, of Phila-
               delphia, and John Budd, of Burlington, were bonds-
               men for the administrator.—Burlington Records, p. 19;
               N. J. Archives, XXIV., 46. Francis Rawle, adminis-
               trator of the estate of Samuel Borden, of Pennsyl-
               vania, dec'd, and Thomas Woodroof, of Salem, late of
               London, conveyed to James Antram, of Mansfield,
               Burlington, yeoman, one twenty-fourth of a share of
               the Province, bought by Woodroof of Borden.—Ib.,
               454. Was this the same person?
3.   viii. Benjamin[2], born May, 1649; died 1718; married Abigail
               Grover, Sept. 22, 1670.
        ix.   Amey[2], b. Feb., 1654; d. Feb. 5, 1684; married William
               Richardson, of Flushing, L. I. She had three sons.

BORDEN

x. Mary[2], b. April —, 1656; married John Cook, son of Thomas, of Providence, R. I., and died before 1691.

Third Generation.

2. Francis[2] Borden was a freeman of Portsmouth in 1655. He removed to Shrewsbury, N. J., in 1665, or soon after. The first Friends' meeting in New Jersey is said to have been held at his house, in 1672. The court was held at his house, Sept. 3, 1678. He married Jane Vicars, 12th of 4th mo., 1677. He d. in Shrewsbury, 19th 1st mo., 1704-5. His will, dated May 24, 1703, describes him as of Shrewsbury, yeoman. In it he devises lands patented March 25, 1687, and other tracts bought May 4, 1696, and of his brother, John Borden, April 7, 1700; also property in the Parish of Gouderhst (Goldhurst), Kent, England, inherited from Francis Fowle, of Cranbrook, county of Kent, by his will of October 8, 1632. This is suggestive of the origin of the Borden family, although Fowle was probably a connection or an ancestor in the maternal line. Francis Borden appointed his wife and his son Francis executors of his will. His personal estate was inventoried at £106, 11, 6.—*East Jersey Wills,* Lib. 1, p. 151. The "Jean Borden" who in 1707 was induced to contribute £3 toward a fund said to be for the purpose of bribing Lord Cornbury, then Governor, to do justice to the people, was probably the widow of Francis Borden.— *Austin,* as cited; *Hist. Burlington and Mercer Counties,* 454; *N. J. Archives,* III., 214; *Shrewsbury Friends' Records.* He made a codicil to his will, dated Feb. 18, 1705, and the will and codicil were proved May 9, 1706. Many references to Francis Borden are to be found in *N. J. Archives,* XXI. In the early records this name usually appears as Burden or Burdein.

The children of Francis Borden and Jane Vicars were (all b. at Shrewsbury):

4.   i.   Richard[3], b. 11th of 2d mo., 16—; m. Mary ——; d. April 6, 1759, at Shrewsbury.

5.   ii.   Francis[3], b. 1st of 9th mo., 1680; m. Mary ——; d. at Evesham, Burlington county. His will was proved April 6, 1759.

       iii.   Joyce[3], b. 4th of 4th mo., 1682; m. John Hance, junior, b. 11th 3d mo., 1683; d. Feb. 26, 1728-9; she d. Feb. 4, 1722-3. She and her husband were buried in the old Rumson burying ground, their gravestones being perfectly preserved, although the oldest in the yard. Issue: 1. Joseph; 2. John, named in the will of Francis Borden; 3. Joyce, who married Zebulon Dickason; and perhaps others.

6.   iv.   Thomas[3], b. 4th of 12th mo., 1684; d. Sept. 28, 1764; m Margaret ——.

3. Benjamin[2] Borden married Abigail Grover (dau. of James Grover, senior, of Middletown), Sept. 22, 1670; she d. Jan. 8, 1720, aged 66 years. He probably removed from Portsmouth, R. I., soon after making the purchase of lands in Shrewsbury, in 1665, and settled at the latter place, being allotted Lot No. 29 of "the lotts of Middleton," Dec. 30, 1667, and the next day Lot No. 23, in "the lotts that are in the Poplar feild and the mountany feild."— *Town Book of Old Middletown,* 1. He was allowed, April 9, 1670, to take up nine acres elsewhere in lieu of Lot No. 23, "considering the badnes of it being throwne up to make good some other lotts."—*Ib.,* 10. He was admitted, July 8, 1670, as one of the associate patentees. He contributed £6 toward the purchase, and was allotted one share. The court was held at his house in Shrewsbury, in 1676. He was a Justice

of the Peace in 1685. In 1692 and 1694 he was elected to the Assembly from Middletown, and in 1695 and 1698 as one of the six members from Monmouth county. In 1693 he was appointed by act of the Assembly to be one of the Road Commissioners for Monmouth County, a position he still held in 1711. He was one of three men "legally Chosen (Jan. 1, 1695-6) to meet the men of the other towns of the County to Assess . . . . the tax or Rate that is to be Raised for the Support of the Government," to which office (corresponding with the "chosen freeholder" of to-day) he was re-elected in 1697-8.—*Town Book*, 32-33. The records of conveyances show that he was a large landholder; some of his purchases were as follows: Oct. 21, 1676—return of survey for tract in the allotment of Cohanzick; 1677-8, Feb. 28—patent for same, 300 acres; he was then a weaver, of Middletown; June 20, 1677—patent for 351 acres at Middletown; Jan. 22, 1687—patent for 150 acres in Monmouth county; March 28, 1688—he was the owner of 1-20th of 1-48th of East Jersey; May 1, 1695—patent for 240 acres at Crosswicks, and 30 acres at Barnegat; Oct. 5, 1696—deed for 560 acres in Monmouth county.—*N. J. Archives*, XXI., 27, 113, 116, 235, 297, 542, 556, 566. In 1716 he appears to have been of Evesham, Burlington county, when he conveyed lands to his son Joseph, of Freehold. In 1718, being then of Auchweas, Burlington county, he conveyed lands to his son James.—*Austin*, as cited; *Old Times in Old Monmouth*, 170, 171, 207, 208, 249; *N. J. Archives*, XXI., 158-61. His children were:

    i. Richard[3], b. Jan. 9, 1672; married Mary Worthley, April 7, 1695. Probably on account of some of the political troubles of the day, the Attorney General was directed in 1734 to file an information against him. In 1739 he was of Chester, Burlington county. In 1750 he resided at Evesham, Burlington county. He had a suit in chancery against Richard Stout, but his solicitor, John Coxe, threw up the case in a huff, saying that he could not get justice from Gov. Belcher, the Chancellor ex-officio.—*N. J. Archives*. XIV., 505; XI., 580; VII., 542-3, 547.

    ii. Benjamin[3], b. April 6, 1675. He settled at Middletown, Monmouth county. He bought, Jan. 8, 1700, of Anthony Woodward, a tract of 1,000 acres of the great Dockwra patent, south of Arneytown.—*Hist. Burlington and Mercer Counties*, 454. When the court of sessions at Middletown, on March 25, 1701, arraigned Moses Butterworth for piracy, and he confessed that he had sailed with Capt. William Kidd on his last voyage, Benjamin Borden and his brother Richard were conspicuous among the thirty or forty men who dashed into the court room to rescue the prisoner. The two Bordens were arrested by the constables, but a hundred men quickly rallied, and they were rescued from the officers' grasp, though wounded in the melée, and the rioters turned the tables by imprisoning the Governor (Col. Andrew Hamilton), the Court, the Attorney General and the court officers for four days, in token of their contempt for the waning authority of the Proprietary Government.—*Monmouth County Records*, *Book of Minutes* No. 1, quoted in "Old Times in Old Monmouth," 263; *N. J. Archives*, II., 362-3. Benjamin Borden and James Borden were among the petitioners in 1701 for a Royal instead of a Proprietary Governor.—*N. J. Archives*, II., 396. He was the agent for the receipt of the Monmouth county taxes in 1705 and 1706.—*Ib.*, III., 351-2. Administration on the estate of Benjamin Borden, of Evesham township, Burlington county, yeoman, was granted June 6, 1728, to Susannah Borden, his widow. The inventory of his personal estate amounted to £222, 10, 10½.—*East Jersey Wills*, Liber 2, p. 532.

7.   iii.   James³, b. Sept. 6, 1677; m. Mary ———. The will of James Borden, of Freehold township, Monmouth county, is dated Dec. 23, 1727, and was proved Feb. 22, 1730-31. His personal estate was inventoried at £115, 16, 10.

       iv.   Rebecca³, b. June 8, 1680; d. young.

       v.   Safety³, b. Sept. 6, 1682; m. Martha ———.

       vi.   Amey³, b. March 4, 1684.

8.   vii.   Joseph³, b. May 12, 1687; m. his cousin, Susannah Grover; he is said to have also m. Ann Conover; he d. Sept. 22, 1765.

     viii.   Jorathan³, b. April 14, 1690. He was living at Chester, Burlington county, in 1739.

       ix.   David³, b. March 8, 1692; d. young.

       x.   Samuel³, b. April 8, 1696.

Fourth Generation.

4. Richard³ Francis² Richard¹ Borden, b. 11th of 2nd mo., 16—; m. Mary ———; d. April 6, 1759, at Shrewsbury. Issue:

       i.   Francis⁴, b. Aug. 5, 1717; m. Mary ———, Oct. 29, 1740; d. Sept. 11, 1782, at Mansfield.

5. Francis³ Francis² Richard¹ Borden, b. Nov. 1, 1680; m. Mary ———; his will was signed Feb. 3, 1753; proved April 6, 1759; d. 1759, at Evesham, Burlington County. Issue (b. in Shrewsbury):

       i.   Elizabeth⁴, b. 6th mo. 5th, 1707; m. Thomas White, 1724-5.

       ii.   Jane⁴, b. 6th of 7th mo., 1708; m. Amos White.

9.   iii.   Francis⁴, b. 24th of 12th mo., 1709-10; m. Lydia (b. 11th mo. 1714-15, dau. of Thomas and Patience Tucker) Wooley, 4th 3d mo., 1732; his will, dated March 12, 1784, proved October 21, 1784, describes him as of Nottingham, Burlington county.

       iv.   John⁴, b. 23d of 11th mo., 1710-11; m. Elizabeth ———, 1736; d. 1772.

       v.   Amey⁴, b. 6th of 12th mo., 1714; m. Samuel Scott, 14th 2d mo., 1736.

       vi.   Mary⁴, b. 21st of 6th mo., 1717; m. William Bills, 22d 3d mo., 1735.

10.   vii.   Thomas⁴, b. 27th of 4th mo., 1719; m. Mary, dau. of Philip and Catharine (Webley) Edwards, 29th 5th mo., 1742; his will, dated July 25, 1788, was proved Sept. 6, 1788.

     viii.   Jeoms⁴, b. 4th of 8th mo., 1722. He advertised a farm for sale at Evesham, Burlington county, adjoining his own, in March, 1766.—*N. J. Archives*, XXV., 55. A vendue of his farm stock was advertised by his executors for October 28, 1771.—*Ib.*, 27: 610.

6. Thomas³ Francis² Richard¹ Borden, b. 4th of 12th mo., 1684; d. Sept. 28, 1764; m. Margaret ———. Issue:

11.   i.   Jeremiah⁴, b. July 1, 1711; d. 8 mo., 5th, 1754; m. Esther Tilton (b. 10th of 3rd mo., 1722), dau. of Thomas and

Faith (Lawrence) Tilton, 7th of 5th mo., 1746; she m.
2d, Amos White, 17th of 12th mo., 1761, and d. Aug.
11, 1777.

    ii. Joseph[4], m. Hannah (? Bennett, m. l. Jan. 25, 1757).

12.   iii. Richard[4], m. Hannah Tilton (b. 24th of 4th mo., 1726).
June 22, 1758. His will, dated March 25, 1791, was
proved Oct. 3, 1803.

    iv. Benjamin[4], m., Dec. 29, 1757, Rebecca Tilton (b. 4th of
5th mo., 1720). D. s. p.

    v. Samuel[4].

It will be observed that Jeremiah, Richard and Benja
min, three brothers, married three sisters.

7. James[3] Benjamin[2] Richard[1] Borden, b. Sept. 6, 1677; m. Mary ———.
In his will he names children:

    i. Richard[4].

    ii. Innocent[4], m. John Bozworth, of Burlington county,
marriage license dated July 13, 1734.

    iii. Joseph[4].

    iv. Phebe[4], prob. m. Benjamin Gardiner, of Burlington
county, marriage license dated May 18, 1737.

    v. Rebeckah[4].

    vi. Abigaill[4].

    vii. Mary[4].

    viii. Hellen[4].

    ix. Ann[4].

8. Joseph[3] Benjamin[2] Richard[1] Borden, born May 12, 1687; m. Susannah Grover in 1717; she d. March 11, 1744, in her 58th year. He
d. Sept. 22, 1765. Sailing in a coasting vessel (probably his own) from
Shrewsbury, he came to Farnsworth's Landing, Burlington county, in
1719, and determined to locate there. On March 3, 1724, he bought from
Samuel Farnsworth a tract of 105 acres of land on the Delaware, to which
he added by subsequent purchases until he owned nearly the whole site
of the future Bordentown. As early as 1722 he had become interested in
the erection of a bloomary forge on Black's Creek, Burlington county.
In 1724 his place on the Delaware was known as "Burden's Landing,"
but by 1739 it was called "Burden's Town," whence the transition to
"Burdentown" and "Bordentown" was easy. Joseph Borden was
appointed one of the Quorum Justices for Burlington county in 1739.
In 1740 he started a "Stage Wagon to carry Passengers or Goods, between Perth-Amboy and Bordens-Town," in order to develop the latter place and make it an important point on the route from Philadelphia to New York. This stage route was kept up by him and his
son Joseph for twenty years or more. He gave the site for the
Friends' meeting house in 1740, and Aug. 5, 1751, conveyed to the Baptists, for a nominal consideration (£5), the site for a church and
burying ground. He opened a store, and carried on a general mercantile trade many years; laid out streets, erected what was then considered a splendid mansion, and on other ways manifested a most enter-
prising spirit, and a confidence in the future of Bordentown. "As he
was esteemed for his public, so he also was for his private Worth, he
being a kind Neighbour, and a sincere Friend; a tender Husband, and
an affectionate Parent," says the newspaper which announced his
death.—*Hist. Burlington and Mercer Counties*, 456, 458-9; *History of Iron
in All Ages*, by J. M. Swank, 2d ed., 1892, 157; *N. J. Archives*, XI., 342.
586, note, 587; XII., 22, note, 171; XV., 98; XXIV., 651.

His children were:

    i. Anna[4], m. the Rev. Joshua Potts, pastor of the Baptist
church at South Hampton, Bucks county, Pa.

BORDEN

13.   ii. Joseph[4], b. Aug. 1, 1719; m. Elizabeth Rogers; d. April 8, 1791, in his 72d year.

iii. Rebecca[4], m. Joseph Brown, perhaps a physician near Bordentown, at whose inn Benjamin Franklin stopped in 1723 when on his journey from Boston to Philadelphia.

iv. Hannah[4], m. John Lawrence, of Monmouth, marriage license dated April 26, 1731; m. 2d, James Seabrook. See affirmation of Silvanus Grover, of Middletown, a Quaker, in Liber D., p. 154, of records at Perth Amboy.

v. Elizabeth[4], m. Thomas Douglass, of Monmouth, marriage license dated Jan. 9, 1734.

vii. Amey[4], m. Thomas Potts, who bought the iron works on Black's Creek, Feb. 1, 1725.

viii. Abigail[4], m. 1st, ———— Clayton; 2d, Micajah How, son of Micajah and Martha How; he was Sheriff of Hunterdon county, and one of the judges of the Court of Common Pleas of that county.

Fifth Generation.

9. Francis[4] Francis[3] Francis[2] Richard[1] Borden, of Nottingham, Burlington county, b. 24th of 12th mo., 1709-10; m. Lydia Woolley. Issue:

i. Joseph[5] m. Rebecca Middleton, of Nottingham, in Chesterfield Monthly Meeting, 15th of 2d mo., 1759.

ii. Thomas[5].

iii. Francis[5], b. 1743; m. 24th of 2d mo., 1763, Elizabeth (b. 14th of 11th mo., 1745), dau. of Josiah and Margaret (Woolley) Parker; she d. 27th of 2d mo., 1788. His will, dated March 5, 1799, was proved March 10, 1802. He lived at Allentown, Monmouth county. Children: 1. Margaret, b. Nov. 9, 1763; m. Samuel Allen; 2. Lydia, b. Jan. 7, 1765; m. ———— Pew; 3. William, b. July 15, 1767; m. Lucy Harrison; 4. Josiah, b. Nov. 10, 1769; m. Mary (b. Feb. 13, 1779, dau. of Aaron) Robbins; d. March 2, 1826; she d. Sept. 1, 1861; 5. Daniel, b. Nov. 17, 1771; m. Rhoda Stout; 6. Asher, b. Aug. 7, 1773; m. Mrs. Ann Mellon; 7. Sarah, b. Nov. 5, 1775; m. Thomas Black; 8. Elizabeth, b. Feb. 4, 1778; m. Thomas Tooley; 9. Francis, b. March 20, 1779; m. 1st, Mary Erwin, and 2d, Letitia Erwin; 10. Edward, b. March 23, 1784; d. unm.; 11. Samuel, b. April 28, 1785; m. and had children, John, James, Asher, Thomas; 12. (by a second wife), Morris Johnson Woolley, b. Aug. 20, 1794.

iv. James[5], m. Susan Robbins. He lived in Salem county. She was b. June 12, 1754; d. Oct. 5, 1823. Children: 1. Patience, b. Aug. 14, 1775; m. John (son of Williams and Ann Levis) Lloyd; d. 1817; 2. Ann, b. June 14, 1778; m. John Hance (b. Aug. 20, 1762), Dec. 15, 1800; d. May 28, 1856; he d. Aug. 13, 1827; 3. Lydia, b. Jan. 14, 1781; m. ———— Woolley; 4. Ruth, b. Aug. 19, 1785; m. ———— Tiler; 5. Asher, b. Sept. 19, 1790; 6. James, b. April 10, 1794; 7. John, b. April 9, 1797.

v. Rhoda[5], m. ———— Robbins.

vi. Mary[5], m. James Lawrie, 15th of 11th mo., 1759.

vii. Lydia[5], m. James Ford.

viii. Hannah[5], m. John Hawkins.

46

10. Thomas⁴ Francis³ Francis² Richard¹ Borden, b. 27th of 4th mo., 1719; m. Mary Edwards, 29th of 5th mo., 1742. Issue:

  i. Amos⁵, m., 1st mo. 8th, 1768, Rachel Woolley, dau. of Rachel White (dau. of Amos White and Jane Borden) and Thomas Woolley. She survived her husband and m. 2d, James Parker. Children: 1. Mary, m. Aug. 28, 1802, Hugh Boude; 2. Aaron; 3. Thomas; 4. Amos.

  ii. Philip⁵.

  iii. Thomas⁵, prob. m. Hannah Woolley, marriage license dated Jan. 12, 1780. He and his wife Hannah signed a deed April 18, 1796.

11. Jeremiah⁴ Thomas³ Francis² Richard¹ Borden, b. July 1, 1711; m. Esther Tilton (b. 10th of 3rd mo., 1722), 7th of 5th mo., 1746; d. 8 mo., 5th, 1754; she d. Aug. 11, 1777. Issue:

  ii. Rebecca⁵, b. March 22, 1749; m., 10th mo. 14th, 1767, John Woolley, of Shrewsbury. Children: 1. Jeremiah; 2. Robert; 3. Rachel, m. Thomas Hance; 4. Esther, m. Ebenezer Hance.

  iii. Hester⁵, b. Oct. 9, 1754; m. 3d mo. 4th, 1770, Capt. Richard Lippincott (b. 1745, d. 1826). Child: Esther, m. George Taylor Dennison.

  iv. Jeremiah⁵, b. Dec. 30, 1750; d. Sept. 7, 1777.

  v. Samuel⁵, b. Nov. 10, 1752; d. Sept. 11, 1777; m. ———. Children: 1. Elizabeth, m. Feb. 5, 1797, Josiah Parker; 2. Esther.

12. Richard⁴ Thomas³ Francis² Richard¹ Borden and Hannah Tilton had issue:

  i. Sarah⁵, b. April 11, 1759; m. John De Bow.

  ii. Thomas⁵, b. Nov. 6, 1760; d. Sept. 17, 1848, s. p.

  iii. Rachel⁵, b. Feb. 16, 1763; m. Thomas Cook, of Point Pleasant; d. March 7, 1811.

  iv. Benjamin⁵, b. Dec. 22, 1766; m. Mary, dau. of Williams and Ann (Levis) Lloyd; d. March 18, 1849.

13. Joseph⁴ Joseph³ Benjamin² Richard¹ Borden, junior, b. Aug. 1, 1719; m. Elizabeth, dau. of Samuel and Mary Rogers, of Allentown, New Jersey; died at Bordentown, April 8, 1791. She was b. July 10, 1725; d. Nov. 2, 1807. He was actively engaged from early manhood in his father's extensive business enterprises, especially the stage boat and stage wagon from Philadelphia to Perth Amboy, via Bordentown, until his advancing years caused him to retire from active life, in 1788. In 1748 tickets for a lottery for the benefit of St. Mary's Church, Burlington, were to be had from him. He was appointed a Justice of the Peace in 1749, and a Judge in 1757 and again in 1767. In 1761 he was elected to the Assembly as one of the two members for Burlington county, and served until 1769, evidently occupying a conspicuous position among his colleagues. In 1765 the Assembly elected him as one of the three deputies to represent New Jersey in the Stamp Act Congress, at New York, and he and Hendrick Fisher signed the appeal of that Congress to the King and Parliament, urging the repeal of the Act. The Assembly heartily approved of their conduct. He was chosen as one of the members of the first Provincial Congress, which met at New Brunswick, July 2, 1774, to send delegates to the Continental Congress. In the ensuing February he was selected by his fellow citizens as one of the Committee of Observation for Burlington County, and later as a member of the Provincial Congress held at Trenton in May, June and August, 1775. This body appointed him one of the Committee of Safety, which was vested with executive power during the recess of

BORDEN

the Provincial Congress. Early in 1776 he was commissioned Colonel of the First Regiment of Burlington County militia, but he resigned, Sept. 28, 1776, when he was appointed Quartermaster, for which position his business experience and abilities rendered him peculiarly well qualified. He was appointed Judge of the Common Pleas, Sept. 11, 1776, and again Sept. 28, 1781. He was one of the promoters of the episode made famous by Francis Hopkinson in his poem on the "Battle of the Kegs," when it was designed to blow up the British vessels in the Delaware near Bordentown by a rude sort of torpedoes made of kegs filled with powder, which were sent floating down the river shortly before daylight on Jan. 7, 1778, and were expected to explode on coming in contact with the war vessels, having certain mechanical attachments to ensure such result. Unfortunately for the success of the enterprise, the vessels were hauled into their docks the night before the kegs were set loose. The British soon after raided Bordentown, and Judge Borden's handsome residence was laid waste by fire, May 10, 1778. He was liberally educated, had a fine presence, and was highly influential in the community. In 1762-3 he ran a line of stageboats between Bordentown and Philadelphia. It may be noted here that in some works it is stated that Joseph Borden m. in 1750 Elizabeth, daughter of Marmaduke Watson, a widow. But the will of Elizabeth Borden, wid. of Joseph Borden, dated September 15, 1798, proved November 5, 1807, names her dau. Ann Hopkinson and her three daus.: Elizabeth, "dau. of my brother Isaac Rogers, lately deceased," and grandson, Joseph Hopkinson.—*Hist. Burlington and Mercer Counties*, 467;; *N. J. Archives*, XII., 442; XVI., 89; XVII., 137, 455; XXIV., 89, 210, 654-5, 683; XXV., 103; *N. Y. Public Library Bulletin*, I., 104; *Gordon's Hist. N. J.*, 140; *Penn. Mag. of Hist. and Biog.*, IX., 435. Issue:

    i. Mary[5], b. July 21, 1744; m. Thomas McKean, of Newcastle, Del., marriage license dated July 21, 1763; d. March 12, 1773, in her 29th year. Thomas McKean was one of the Delaware Signers of the Declaration of Independence. He was elected Governor of Pennsylvania in 1799, 1802 and 1805, serving nine stormy years. He d. June 24, 1817, aged 83 yrs., 2 mos. and 25 days.

    ii. Ann[5], b. Jan. 24, 1745-6; d. June 9, 1746.

    iii. Ann[5] ("Nancy"), b. May 9, 1747; married Francis Hopkinson (afterwards one of the Signers of the Declaration of Independence), Sept. 1, 1768. For the announcement of the marriage, in the flowery language of the day, see *N. J. Archives*, X., 427, note and hereinafter, in the sketch of Francis Hopkinson.

    iv. Amey[5], b. Oct. 30, 1749; bap. in Christ church, Shrewsbury, April 8, 1750, "at the age of 5 months," says the record; d. Aug. 31, 1751.

    v. Letitia[5], b. July 29, 1751; d. June 30, 1753.

    vi. Joseph[5], born June 23, 1755. He was an ardent patriot during the Revolution, being Captain of a troop of light-horse, which he raised in Burlington county. He was wounded at the battle of Germantown, in 1777, but although his injury inconvenienced him the rest of his life, he repeatedly volunteered for active service when he felt he could be of use to the cause. He was a United States loan officer, and was appointed one of the commissioners to sell lands confiscated to the State for treason. He married, Nov. 26, 1778,

Mary, daughter of Langhorne Biles, of Bucks county, Pa. He died Oct. 16, 1788, leaving one child, Elizabeth Borden, who married Azariah Hunt, of Hopewell, N. J. Mr. Borden was appointed by the Legislature a Continental Loan Officer for New Jersey, Feb. 7, 1777; and a Judge and Justice of the Peace for Burlington county, Sept. 28, 1781.

Many of the dates given above are from a Borden Family Record, entered in a Concordance of the Holy Scriptures, the property (1901) of Benjamin Borden, and printed in 1706. For these dates the writer is indebted to John P. Hutchinson, Esq., of Bordentown. The Rev. William White Hance, of Palenville, N. Y., has also revised and corrected the proofs of the above sketch of the Borden family, and has furnished many data.

WILLIAM BOTT.

In an advertisement of "Newark races," to be run October 29, 1771, it was announced that the horses were "to be shewn and entered the day before running, with William Bott," from which it may be inferred that he then kept a public house at or near Newark.—*N. J. Arhives*, 27: 628. William Livingston wrote from Elizabethtown to the Provincial Congress, July 8, 1776: "If you have not appointed an Adjutant General I should beg leave to recommend to the choice of the Congress Mr. William Bott of Springfield as a Person who would execute that office as well as anyone I can think of, he has been in the Navy understands the Business and is extremely active & punctual." The Congress replied July 12, 1776: "You have enclosed a commission for Mr. Bott as Adjutant General."—*Originals*, in *Nelson MSS*. He continued in office until June 4, 1793, when he resigned.—*Records, Adjutant General's Office*. No will of William Bott has been found on record in New Jersey, nor any letters of administration upon his estate. It is not unlikely that he removed from the State about the time of his resignation, perhaps with the settlers then flocking to the "Genessee country" in Central New York, or to Ohio.

ELIAS BOUDINOT.

Elias Boudinot, a prominent merchant at Princeton, born Aug. 3, 1706, died July 4, 1770. He married, in Antigua, Catherine Williams, daughter of a Welsh planter. The house occupied by him in 1756 was advertised at the time to be sold by the Rev. Aaron Burr. He was Postmaster at Princeton in 1757. He removed from Princeton in 1760, or later, to Elizabethtown, where he and his wife are both buried. Of his sisters, Mary Boudinot married John Chetwood, of Elizabethtown, afterwards a Justice of the Supreme Court of New Jersey; Jane Boudinot married the Rev. Thomas Bradbury Chandler; Suzanne married Pierre Vergereau, of New York, one of whose daughters, Suzanne, born Dec. 21, 1743, married the Rev. William Tennent, Jr., of Charleston, S. C. Elias Boudinot was the father of Elias, member of Congress, etc.; of Elisha, Justice of the Supreme Court of New Jersey, and of other well-known children.

WILLIAM BRADFORD.

William Bradford, a grandson of William Bradford, the celebrated printer of Philadelphia, and son of Colonel William Bradford of the Revolutionary Army, was born in Philadelphia, September 14, 1755. He graduated at Princeton in 1772, and remained a year, studying theology with Dr. Witherspoon. On returning to his home, he read law in the office of Edward Shippen; but the Revolution commencing, he joined the army, and rose to the rank of Colonel, which he was compelled to resign in April, 1779, on account of ill health. Returning to the study of law, he was admitted to the Bar in the same year, and settled in Yorktown, Pennsylvania. His marked ability soon attracted attention, and in 1780, when but twenty-three years of age, he was appointed Attorney-General of the State. He held this position for eleven years, when, on the 22d of August, 1791, he was elevated to the Supreme Bench of Pennsylvania. This office he filled until 1794, when he was appointed by Washington Attorney-General of the United States, in which office he remained until his death, which occurred August 23, 1795, at Rose Hill, near Philadelphia. Judge Bradford married in 1782 Susanne Vergereau, daughter of Elias Boudinot; she was b. Dec. 21, 1764; d. Nov. 30, 1854. Both are buried in St. Mary's churchyard, Burlington.

FRANCIS BRAISIER.

Francis Braisier was probably a merchant at the Upper Landing on the Raritan, near New Brunswick. He was a vestryman of St. Peter's Church, Perth Amboy, in 1744-5.—*Whitehead's Perth Amboy*, 239. He was authorized to receive subscriptions for Nevill's Laws, Vol. I., in 1750, and was one of the distributors of the volume when printed, in 1752.—*N. J. Archives*, XII., 589; XIX., 10, 28. In 1759 he was one of the managers of a lottery for the benefit of Christ Church, New Brunswick. He married Elizabeth Beekman (born Aug. 30, 1725), daughter of Marten Beekman and Elizabeth Waldron. She survived him, dying Nov. 9, 1810, and was buried in Christ Church yard, New Brunswick. The will of Francis Brasier, of Somerset county, dated June 15, 1781, was proved May 10, 1784, at New Brunswick. He devises to wife Elizabeth "my farm where I now live called New Aperfield." He names sisters—Mary Brasier, Sarah Hay and Frances Legrange; nephew Mead Brasier; niece Mary Hay; friend Henry Beekman; Francis Brasier Beekman son of Henry Beekman. Executors—wife Elizabeth, Rev. Abraham Beach, Samuel Beekman. Witnesses—Henry Beekman, William Vanduyn, John Bice.—*N. J. Wills*, Liber No. 26, p. 537.

CORNELIS BREYANT.

Cornelis Breyant appears to have been of Bergen before 1680, and in 1687, of Hackensack, or within the parish of the Hackensack Dutch church. Children:

    i. Pieter, m. Hendriktie Arents. Child: Lysbeth, bap. in the Hackensack church, 1686.

    ii. Antie, m. Nicasius Kip, received into the Hackensack church upon confession of faith, Sept. 22, 1694, with her husband. She m. 2d, Oct. 10, 1715, Isaack Van Gijsse, widr. of Hillegond Kuyper, both being residents of the parish of Hackensack. Children (all by her first husband): 1. Isack, bap. 1697; 2. Cornelis, bap. Jan. 1, 1700; 3. Jacob, bap. Dec. 14, 1702; 4. Annatie, bap. Jan. 3, 1706; 5. Catrina, bap. Sept. 12, 1708; 6. Elizabeth, bap. March 11, 1711.

    iii. Geertruy; received into the Hackensack church on

confession of faith, Sept. 22, 1694; Geertruyt Breyhandt, y. d. m. Oct. 26, 1695, in the Hackensack
church, Roelof Bongaert, y. m., he from Vlacke
Bosch (Flatbush). and she from Bergen. He m. 2d,
Elisabeth Bertholf, wid. of Jan Terhune, Aug. 23.
1718, in the Hackensack church. Children: 1. Hen-
drickie, bap. Sept. 29. 1700; 2. Marretie, bap. same
day; 3. Jan. bap. January 21, 1705.

2.   iv. Cornelis.

      v. Elisabet Breyandt, y. d., b. Ackinsack, m. April 12,
1707, at Hackensack, Egbert Ackerman, y. m., b. at
Bergen in East N. Jersey; both were living in the
Hackensack church parish at the time of their mar-
riage. Children: 1. Louwerens, bap. January 18,
1708; 2. Petrus, bap. Dec. 7, 1709; 3. Geertie, bap.
Feb. 15, 1712; 4. Geertie, bap. May 2, 1714; 5.
Louwerens, bap. Aug. 15, 1716; 6. Hendriktie, bap.
Sept. 29, 1717; 7. Annatie, bap. Aug. 14, 1720; 8.
Louwerens, bap. March 3, 1723; 9. Cornelis, bap.
April 17, 1726; 10. Cornelia, bap. April 4, 1731.

2. Cornelis Cornelis Breyandt was received into the Hackensack
church upon confession of faith. July 10, 1698; Cornelis Breyhandt, y.
m., m. in the same church, Dec. 7, 1700, Margrita Simese Van
Winckel, wid. of Marte Winne; both were b. at Bergen. (Maerten
Winne. m. b. at Albany, m. Margrita Simese Van Winckel, y. d. b. at
Asemes, Oct. 30, 1697, in the Hackensack church. Peter Winne, com-
missary or magistrate of Bethlehem, Albany county, N. Y., b. at
Ghent, Flanders, made a will July 6, 1684, in which he names wife
Jannetie Adams, b. in the city of Leuwaerden, Friesland, and son
Marten, one of thirteen children.—*Albany County Wills*, Liber I., f. 44.)
Cornelis Breyandt was a witness at the baptism in the Hackensack
church, Jan. 23, 1715, which is the last mention of him in the Hackensack records. He appears to have removed about this time to the
neighborhood of Elizabethtown, where he made his will, in which he
is described as yeoman, Oct. 2, 1720, proved Dec. 19, 1720. He gives
to wife Margarett "that part of my new dwelling place in Springfield
lying on the south side of the road," for life, with remainder to his
two youngest sons, Simon and Andris; to son Johannis, his riding
horse, etc.; to dau. Hannah, negro Harry when he is 21; to son-in-
law (stepson) Peter Winne, son of my wife Margarett, and son
Johannis, "my land in Springfield on the north side of the road and
all buildings thereon." Executors—wife and John Kewman (Coey-
man), of Newark, and John Blanchard, junior, of Elizabeth Town.
Witnesses—John Blanchard, Cornelis Vanderoif, Peter Rutan.—*Liber
A of Wills*, f. 196. Margaret. wid. of Cornelis Bryant, of Elizabeth
Town, Essex county, made her will Nov. 8, 1729, and it was proved a
few weeks later, or January 13, 1729-30. She gives to son Peter
Wenem 20 shillings; to her three sons Johannis Simeon and Ansri
Bryant, "all those two tracts of land bought of John Blanchard,
junior," to be equally divided between them; to dau. Hannah, wife of
Cornelius Westerveld, 5 shillings; to granddau. Elizabeth Carl. dau.
of Jonah Carle and my dear dau. Hendriekie, £20 when 18 or married;
to dau. Rachel Bryant, £40 when 18 or married. Executors—Johannis Kewman, of Newark, and Egbert Ackerman, of Bergen county
Witnesses—Benjamon Bonnel, Henery Demoney, Rachel Kewman.—
Liber B of Wills, f. 148. Issue:

BREYANT: BROUGHTON: BROWN:
BRYANT FAMILY

    i.   Annetie. bap. June 28, 1702; m. Cornelis Westervelt, y. m., Sept. 14, 1723, in the Hackensack church; both are said in the record to have been' b. at Ackinsack, where Westervelt was living, while she is described as living at New Britain, a region lying west of Elizabethtown. Child:—Cornelis, bap. Sept. 27, 1724, and perhaps others.

   ii.   Johannis, bap. Aug. 27, 1704.

  iii.   Hendriktie, bap. April 24, 1709; m. John Carl (?Earl).

   iv.   Simeon. bap. April 22, 1711.

    v.   Andries bap. January 3, 1714.

   vi.   Rachel, (Or was this a granddaughter?)

JOHN BROUGHTON.

John Broughton lived in the town of Raritan, Somerset county, about twelve miles from New Brunswick. He was manager of the New Brunswick lottery in 1748. He advertised in 1752 and again in 1758 for a schoolmaster for his neighborhood.—*N. J. Archives*, XII., 472, 518; XIX., 344, 524. John Broughton, of Raritan, Somerset county, merchant, conveyed to Jonathan Runyan, of Cranberry, Middlesex county, mason, by deed dated Nov. 16, 1761, for the consideration of 800 (pounds), a tract of forty-one acres on the north side of Raritan river, being the west half of one-fifth of one-fourth of a certain lot which formerly belonged to James Graham, bounded on the upper side by land late of Andries Coleman and on the lower side by lot now or late of Cornelius Middah.—*N. J. Deeds*, I 2, p. 435.

REV. ISAAC BROWN.

The Rev. Isaac Brown was a descendant of John Brown, one of the first settlers of Newark in 1666. He graduated at Yale College in 1729, and in 1733 was appointed rector of the Episcopal Church at Setauket, town of Brookhaven, L. I., where he remained for fourteen years, acquiring the reputation of being "a man of talents and education." In 1747 he became rector of Trinity Church, Newark. He practiced medicine in Newark, and when he sent his bills to members of his congregation for medical advice, some of them thought it should have been included in his spiritual ministrations, and there was some friction in consequence. At the beginning of the Revolution he was an outspoken Loyalist, and in consequence of his zeal was confined in the Morris County jail early in 1777, only to be released in order that he and his family might be sent to the enemy in New York. In 1784 he went to Annapolis, Nova Scotia, where he died in 1787. Mr. Brown had a daughter who married Isaac Ogden, a prominent Newark lawyer, a Loyalist in the Revolution; she died March 15, 1772, aged 26 years.

BRYANT FAMILY.

[1]Nothing has been found throwing light on the ancestry or place of origin of Capt. William Bryant. The fact that two of his children were named Joshua and Ebenezer suggests the possibility that he was akin to the Bryants of Huntington, Suffolk county, Long Island, where Bryants of those names were to be found. Family tradition says he had a brother in London, from which an English nativity might be inferred. He was b. in 1688 or 1689, but the earliest mention that has been found of him in the records is on April 4, 1729, when he witnessed the will

of Ann Johnston, of New York, widow. Eleven days later—April 15, 1729—he was enrolled as a freeman of New York. On Nov. 30, 1739, Lieut. Gov. Colden, of New York, wrote that Capt. Bryant was soon to sail for England with old guns, etc.; he was "commander of a constant trading vessel to London," at that time. He seems to have been held in high esteem in New York and London, for we find him repeatedly appointed administrator, in London, on the estates of deceased sailors, as attorney for their "relicts" residing in New York, between 1743 and 1749. "Capt. William Bryant, mariner, of New York," was named as one of the executors of the will of Edith Feavor, of New York, spinster, April 29, 1747. William Bryant was appointed, June 30, 1749, administrator upon the estate of his son, John Bryant, deceased, but it is not clear that this was the Captain. So, too, it may have been another William Bryant, and not the Captain, who was appointed administrator on the estate of his brother, Dennis Bryant, of New York, Aug. 30, 1753. Bishop Spangenburg, the famous Moravian missionary, came to America from London with Capt. Bryant, in 1751. In November, 1752, John Penn, grandson of William Penn, came from London to New York in the ship *Joseph*, commanded by Capt. Bryant. A shipment of arms was dispatched from New York for London, by the same vessel, William Bryant, master, in March, 1754. Part of the time he was a merchant as well as a mariner.—*Early Long Island Wills*, 215; *N. Y. Hist. Soc. Coll.*, 1885, 215; *Ib.*, 1895, 5, 223, 265, 485; *Ib.*, 1896, 229, 431; *N. Y. Gen. and Biog. Rec.*, 10: 97; 34: 289, 290; 35: 122; 36: 25; *N. Y. Col. Docs.*, 6: 151, 158; *N. J. Archives*, 19: 201, 202, 206; *N. Y. Hist. MSS.*, 2: 614; *Pa. Mag.*, 21: 338; 22: 78. Just when Captain Bryant took up his residence at Perth Amboy has not been ascertained, but he was living there early in 1761, when George Willocks Leslie, of Reading Town, Somerset county, gentleman, and his wife, Mary, executed a deed to William Bryant, of Perth Amboy, Middlesex county, merchant, on April 2, 1761, which deed, for the consideration of £300, conveyed "all that certain dwelling house and lott of land Scituate, in the City of Perth Amboy. Beginning at the southwest corner of land lately conveyed by said Leslie to John Wattson, said corner is two chains and thirty-seven links from Market Street, and on the east side of Water Street, thence along Water Street south twenty-six degrees and fifteen minutes west two chains and sixty-three links; thence at right Angles with said Water Street to Low Water Mark; thence along Low Water Mark to the southeast corner of John Watson's said Lot; thence along Wattson's line to the Beginning. Bounded on the east by the Sound; on the north by the said Watson's Lott; and on the west by Water Street; it being two chains and sixty-three links in front along Water Street; and in length (both sides at Right Angles with Water Street) to low water Mark, together with all fences," etc. This deed was witnessed by P. Kearny, Ravaud Kearny and Alexander Wattson. —*N. J. Deeds*, I², p. 439. He and his wife Eleanor conveyed this property by the same description, to Alexander Watson, of Perth Amboy, gent., by deed dated May 30, 1768. In this deed Bryant is described as "of Westfield, Essex county, gent." Witnesses—Sophia Waterhouse, Jona. Deare.—*E. J. Deeds*, Liber E², f. 218. It was probably with a view to removing to Elizabethtown that he advertised in *The New York Journal* of August 20, 1767, the sale at public vendue, at Perth Amboy, on September 3 following, of "A Convenient Brick House, with 8 Fire-Flaces, very pleasantly situated on the Bank, (with a good Water Lot) a Stable and Barn, and a large Garden, which contains a Variety of the best Fruits: Likewise sundry household Furniture," etc.—*N. J. Archives*, 25: 435. This advertisement gives a very good idea of the comfortable sort of residence the

BRYANT FAMILY

old Captain must have enjoyed in Perth Amboy. He was probably residing with his daughter. Mrs. William Peartree Smith, when he made his will, October 21, 1769, in which he is described sa "William Bryant, of the Borough of Elizabeth, Essex county, mariner," and as being "weak." This will was proved July 9, 1772, and letters testamentary were granted thereon July 29, 1772. In this instrument he gives to his wife Eleanor, after the payment of his debts, all the rest of his estate for her life, the same to be at her disposal; if she should die intestate, then the same to go to his daughter, Elizabeth Woodruff, to whom he also gives 20s.; to each of his five other surviving children he gives 5s. Executrix—wife Eleanor. Witnesses—Nathaniel Baker, John Scudder, Jr., David Baker.—*N. J. Wills*, Liber K. 466. Although he was living at Elizabeth in 1769, he was buried in St. Peter's churchyard, Perth Amboy, where the inscription on his tombstone relates about all that we know of his career: "Sacred to the Memory of William Bryant, who, in 55 Voyages, in the Merchant Service, between the Ports of New York and London, approved himself a faithful and fortunate Commander. Of Integrity and Benevolence to Man he lived a Singular Example. Of Piety and Resignation to God he died an Amiable Pattern 14 July, A. C. 1772, ætatis 83." The upper part of the headstone was broken off by a cannon ball from a British armed vessel, during the Revolution. Below the inscription is this somewhat abbreviated Latin sentence, showing that the stone was doubtless erected by Dr. William Bryant, the Captain's son: "Sax. inornat. pat. sui. dignum. memoriæ. sacrum. fil. amor. posuit." His widow d. in February, 1776, at Perth Amboy, and probably was buried beside her husband.—*Whitehead's Perth Amboy*, 145; *Alden's Epitaphs*, 1044. Issue (bap. in the First Presbyterian church, New York):

2. i. Mary, bap. October 14, 1722.

   ii. Martha, b. January 24 and bap. January 31, 1725-6; m. the Rev. Lorens Thorstansen Nyberg, a Lutheran clergyman, who came from Sweden to take charge of the Swedish Lutheran church at Lancaster, Pa., in 1744. About a year later he joined the Moravians. His conduct seems to have caused much comment and disturbance, and a few years later he went to England. He is said to have been "historiographer to the King of Sweden; she d. a widow, at Fulneck, a Moravian establishment near Leeds, England. Their portraits are in this country."—*N. Y. Gen. and Biog. Record*, 10: 96. Martha Nyberg, of Fulneck, Parish of Calverly, Yorkshire, Great Britain, widow, "before my marriage called Martha Bryant, one of the four sisters of William Bryant, late of the City of New York in North America, deceased, and a devisee in his last will and testament," executed June 24, 1799, a power of attorney to William Peartree Smith, of Newark, N. J. (her nephew), empowering him to sell one undivided fourth part of land in Trenton and elsewhere in North America, relating to the estate of said William Bryant, deceased.—*N. J. Deeds*, AT, f. 519.

   iii. Rebecca, b. Feb. 18 and bap. Feb. 26, 1728-9; m. Capt. Le Chevalier Dean, who, in 1750, lived in Wall street, New York, but subsequently settled in Charleston, S. C.—*N. Y. Gen. and Biog. Record*, 10: 96. Children: 1. A. son; 2. Mary; 3. William

3. iv. William, b. Jan. 3 and bap. Jan. 11, 1730-31.
4. v. Joshua, b. Feb. 7 and bap. Feb. 15, 1732.
   vi. Elizabeth, b. Sept. 4 and bap. Sept. 10, 1734; m. (as his 2d wife) the Rev. Benjamin Woodruff, pastor of the Presbyterian church at Westfield, in the spring of 1763; he d. April 3, 1803, aged 70 yrs.; she d. in N. Y., March 17, 1805. Children: 1. William Bryant, bap. March 21, 1764; 2. Elizabeth, bap. July 17, 1766; 3. Bryant, bap. Nov. 4, 1767; 4. Charlotte Bryant, bap. Sept. 3, 1769; 5. William, bap. Sept. 15, 1771.—*Hatfield's Hist. Elizabeth*, 583.
   vii. Ebenezer, b. July 15 and bap. July 23, 1736; admitted to the N. J. Bar, March 25, 1758; d. 1761. He not unlikely studied law with his brother-in-law, William Peartree Smith, who was executor of his estate. He died before he was twenty-five. The will of Ebenezer Bryant, of Elizabethtown, attorney at law, being "sick and weak" at the time, dated July 10, 1760, was proved Feb. 5, 1761. He gives to wife Elizabeth the money arising from some sales, etc.; to Trustees of the Presbyterian church of Elizabethtown, £50 for the use of Church; to the College of New Jersey, £50 for the purchase of apparatus for experiments in philosophy—or physics, as we would say today; to brother Joshua, "a debt of £30 he owes me is to be canceled." Executor—"my brother in law William Peartree Smith." Witnesses—Andrew Whitehead, William Bryant, Elizabeth Bryant.—*N. J. Wills*, Liber G, f. 450. And see N. J. Archives, 20: 571, for advertisement by the executor.

2. Mary² (William¹) Bryant, bap. October 14, 1722; she went to England with her father, when quite young, and enjoyed the friendship and counsels of the famous Rev. Isaac Watts. She m. William Peartree Smith, May 12, 1745. He was then of New York, the "heir to an ample fortune, and devoted himself to no particular calling," though he studied law with an eminent attorney. He was a trustee of the College of New Jersey, 1746-1793. He was associated with William Livingston in the patriotic movements of his time. Removing to Elizabethtown, he was appointed Mayor of that borough. He took an active part in the Revolution, serving on the Committee of Safety. He d. at Newark, Nov. 20, 1801, aet. 78; his wid. d. there Aug. 16, 1811, in her 92d year, says her tombstone. Issue:

   i. Eliza, b. July 17, 1746; d. Sept. 10, 1747.
   ii. Ebenezer, b. Feb. 20, 1747; d. July 12, 1750.
   iii. William Peartree, b. Feb. 20, 1748; d. Aug. 14, 1748.
   iv. Catharine, b. Dec. 16, 1749; m. Oct. 14, 1778, Elisha Boudinot, of Newark; d. Aug. 30, 1797.
   v. Mary, b. June 26, 1751; d. Aug. 18, 1751.
   vi. William Peartree, b. July 25, 1752; d. Aug. 12, 1752.
   vii. William Peartree, b. Sept. 23, 1755; d. July 17, 1756.
   viii. Belcher Peartree, b. Oct. 25, 1756; graduated at Princeton College, 1773; was taken prisoner at his father's house, at Elizabethtown, by the British, Jan. 25, 1780; d. May 10, 1787.
   ix. Ann Frances, b. May 10, 1758; d. March 10, 1759.
   x. William Pitt, b. June 7, 1760; professor of Materia Medica in Columbia College, in 1792; m. Mary Holliday, June, 1781; d. Jan. —, 1796; she d. Nov. 26, 1805.—*N. Y. Gen.*

BRYANT FAMILY

and Biog. Record. 9: 32. In the *Centinel of Freedom*, Newark, October 11. 1814, is this announcement: "In the late gale on Lake Ontario, Mr. William P. Smith, formerly of this town, master's mate of the Schooner 'Conquest,' was instantly precipitated to a watery grave, in the 24th year of his age." Was this a son of the above named Prof. William Pitt Smith?

3.   William, b. January 3, 1730-31. After his father's death he ministered to his mother's wants until her death. Studying medicine, he settled in New York, where he practised a few years, or until 1769, when he purchased a residence in Trenton, whither he doubtless removed about that time. By deed dated Oct. 28, 1769, Robert Lettis Hooper, of Kingsbury, Nottingham township, Burlington county, Esqr., conveyed to William Bryant, junr., of the city of New York, Doctor of Physick, for the consideration of £2,800, a plantation in Kingsbury: Beginning at a white oak tree on the south side of Assunpink creek, and from thence running south twenty-five degrees thirty minutes east twenty-nine chains and twenty-eight links to Dr. Cadwallader's corner in the line of said Robert Lettis Hooper's land, called the Ferry tract or Ruth Beaks's: thence along the same south seventy-five degrees west forty-eight chains and fifty-five links to the centre or middle of Broad street; thence along the same north thirty-four degrees and thirty minutes west two chains and sixty-eight links to the centre of the street that leads to the ferry; thence along the same south forty-nine degrees and fifty minutes west nine chains and eighty-one links to a stake in the centre of said street; thence north twenty-one degrees and fifteen minutes west two chains and fifty-eight links to a post; thnce south seventy-four degrees west thirteen chains and sixty-nine links, etc., etc.—*N. J. Deeds*, Liber AE, f. 291. By deed dated Feb. 5, 1771, Philip Kearny, of Perth Amboy, attorney at law, quitclaimed to William Bryant, junior, all his right, title, claim, etc., to the lands and premises just described. Witnesses—Anthony White, Fras. Kearney,—*N. J. Deeds*, Liber AE, f. 295. (Dr. Bryant subsequently—Oct. 28, 1778—conveyed said premises to John Cox, of Burlington county, Esqr., his wife Mary joining in the deed.—*N. J. Deeds*, Liber AN, f. 457.) Samuel Tucker, of Hunterdon county, and Elizabeth his wife, conveyed to William Bryant, of Kingsbury, esquire, May 4, 1773, for the consideration of £219, 1sh. 3d., a tract of 175¼ acres in Nottingham township, "beginning at a black oak corner of land surveyed to Thomas Lambert in a line of lands of John Watson," adjoining Abraham Lobb's land, etc.—*N. J. Deeds*, Liber AF, f. 6. In Trenton he speedily acquired a reputation as a successful physician. He appears to have been recognized as a man of scholarly tastes, being elected a member of the American Philosophical Society, January 21, 1774; and read a paper before that society, an "Account of an Electrical Eel or Torpedo from Surinam," which is published in the Transactions of the Society, Vol. II, 166 (Old Series). In September, 1778, he presented Peter du Simitiere with copies of the almanacs compiled by Daniel Leeds, and printed at New York by William Bradford, for the years 1694, 1695, 1696, 1697, 1698 and part of 1700. —*Memorial Hist. of N. Y.*, I., 592. What would not a modern collector be willing to give for those priceless bits of seventeenth century printing, now carefully preserved by the Library Company of Philadelphia! His residence was at Kingsbury—a suburb of Trenton, south of the Assunpink creek—and at the time of the battle of Trenton he was temporarily occupying a house on the Bloomsbury Farm, on the present South Broad street, south of that creek. On Dec. 23, 1776, he informed

Col. Rall, commander of the Hessian regiment, that "he had just heard from a negro who had crossed the river (Delaware) that the rebels had drawn rations for several days, and were about to attack Trenton," but Rall regarded the information as "old women's talk."—*Stryker's Battles of Trenton and Princeton*, 91, 110. Notwithstanding this apparent friendliness with the Hessian commander, Dr. Bryant continued to reside in Trenton, undisturbed by his neighbors, and from time to time rendered medical service to the American soldiers. Either on account of ill health, or because he wished to be relieved from the excessive burdens of his practice and enjoy a life of more leisure, he took Dr. Nicholas Belleville (b. in Metz, France, 1753) into partnership before he had himself rounded out half a century. On Oct. 7, 1780, the Legislature appropriated £4 1s. 3d. to Drs. Bryant and Belleville, "for medical attendance on Enoch Anderson, taken sick in the service, June, 1780."—*Assembly Minutes.* In a deed dated Oct. 24, 1780, from Dr. William Bryant, of Trenton, Hunterdon county, to Rachel Stille, of the same place, it is recited that William Plaskett, of Trenton, deceased, was seized of several houses and lots of land in and about Trenton, and by his will, dated May 14, 1748, bequeathed to his son, William Plaskett, a certain house and lot in Trenton; said William Plaskett and wife Elizabeth conveyed the same, July 9, 1779, to Joseph Clunn, who on April 4, 1780, conveyed the same to William Bryant, and he, for £200, conveys it to Rachel Stille; said "house and lot are situated on the east side of Kings street in Trenton, beginning at the corner of the (St. Michael's) church lot, thence along said street northwest to a stone for a corner thirteen feet south from the corner of a brick building belonging to John Flasket; thence square off from the street eastward to the line of land late Enoch Anderson's; thence along said Anderson's line southward to the church lot aforesaid; thence along the church lot to the street and place of beginning, being one-eighth of an acre more or less. Witnesses—Isaac De Cow, Elizabeth Hooten. Instead of joining in the deed, Mary Bryant, his wife, executed a separate release, Feb. 8, 1781, "of all my Right and Title of Dower of and in a certain house and lot near the Church sold by my husband William Bryant to Rachel Stille." Witnesses—Elizabeth Hooten, Mary Hooten, Isaac De Cow.—*N. J. Deeds*, Liber AT, f. 198. This separate instrument, executed more than three months after the deed of her husband, hints at a domestic disagreement, if not a separation. Three days after the date of the above deed, or on Oct. 27, 1780, William Bryant, Esqr., of Trenton, practitioner of Physick, bought another tract of land in Trenton, from James Cummins, of Trenton, yeoman, and Margaret his wife, for the consideration of £336 in gold and silver, at the rate of 35 shillings to an English guinea, and 7sh. 6d. the Spanish dollar. The deed recites that Ralph Hunt, of Hopewell, and Elizabeth his wife, executors of the will of Mary Snow, for £100 sold a tract of one-eighth of an acre by deed dated Nov. 8, 1749, to James Cummins, of Trenton, peruke maker; said James Cumins by his will dated Feb. 27, 1769, bequeathed all his estate to his wife Jane for life, with remainder to be equally divided among James, William, Samuel and Joseph Cumins, sons of William Cumins, of Nottingham, Chester county, Pa.; it further recites that Jane Cumins, wife of testator, is deceased; also William, Samuel and Joseph, sons of William Cumins, without issue, whereby James Cumins became vested in the tract in question, which begins: at the corner of David Pinkerton's lot (late Joseph Paxton's), on the east side of King street, and from thence runs along the east side of said street north and by east two rods to

George Ely's land (formerly the widow Pidgeons) and thence runs
along said Ely's land east by south ten rods, and from thence south
two rods to said Pinkerton's corner, and thence along said Pinkerton's
line west and by north ten rods to the place of beginning, containing
one-eighth of an acre.—*N. J. Deeds*, Liber AL, f. 336. Being still of
Trenton he purchased of Lambert Cadwalader, of that place, for £70,
a tract of five acres in Trenton: beginning at a corner of Abraham
Hunt's lot, on the north side of a two-rod road and running from
thence along said Hunt and in a line with his meadow fence northwest thirty-two degrees seven chains and eighty-seven links to
Maidenhead road; then along same southwest fifty-two degrees seven
chains fourteen links to a post on the south side of Maidenhead road,
thence from said road in a line with the fence on the west of the Rev.
Mr. Spencer's meadow southeast thirty-two degrees seven chains and
twenty links to the above mentioned two-rod road; and thence to the
place of beginning, containing five acres one quarter and four perch,
strict measure.—*N. J. Deeds*, Liber AL, f. 342. His final purchase of
land, as far as the records show, was by deed dated Dec. 17, 1783, from
John Dixon, of Trenton, and Mary his wife, to Dr. William Bryant of
the same place, for the consideration of £1,100, for a certain house
and lot in Trenton on the east side of King's street: beginning at a
corner of a lot of land late Benjamin Robeson's now Dr. Bryant's, on
the east side of King street, and thence runs along said Robeson's
line east and by south 165 ft. to William Morris's line, now Benjamin
Smith's; thence along said Morris's line south 60 ft. to the corner of
land which said Morris bought of Joseph Green to lay out an alley
from one street to another; thence along the line of said land west and
north to King street; and from thence along said street north and east
60 feet to the beginning, containing one quarter of an acre.—*N. J.
Deeds*, Liber AN, f. 4. Dr. Bryant's will, without date, was proved
June 2, 1786. In it he describes himself as of Trenton, "practitioner of
Physic." He gives to his wife Mary the house where he lives and
£900 of a bond for £1650 owing by the Hon. John Cox, Esqr., and
other property, including "all my negro slaves except the boy William
and the girl Peggy upon the express condition that none of them shall
be sent off or sold in the West Indies contrary to their own will and
consent;" to natural son, William Bryant, by Charity Murrow, £600,
when 21, etc.; to sister, Rebecca Deane, £150, and the interest on
£600 to be invested for her, during her life; to nephew Belcher P.
Smith, "my gold watch and cases," etc.; to nephew William Pitt
Smith, £100; his books to the foregoing two nephews; to William
B. Duffield, eldest son of Dr. Samuel Duffield, of Philadelphia, £50; to
nephew William Deane, second son of sister Rebecca Deane, £100 and
one-half the value "of my house at my wife's death;" to Mary Deane,
dau. of sister Rebecca Deane, £50 and half the £600 left to her mother,
at the latter's death. He also gives to the children of Samuel and Mary
Duffield, of Philadelphia; of Benjamin and Elizabeth Woodruff, of
Westfield, N. J.; of Elisha and Catharine Boudinot, "now of Hanover;"
and of William Pitt Smith, "now of Albany," the property left to his
natural son, in case of his death. Executors—"my friend and brother-
in-law," William P. Smith, and nephew Belcher P. Smith. Witnesses
—John Singer, William Plasket, John Dixon.—*N. J. Wills*, Lib. 28, p. 232.

4. Joshua Bryant, b. February 7, 1732-3, was also a physician. He
seems to have practiced in the West Indies, possibly having settled
there on account of his health, and apparently had his residence in
the Caronago, near the town of St. Georges, in the Island of Grenada.
Apparently realizing that his end was near, he returned to New Jersey,

BRYANT FAMILY: BRYANT: BRAIANT: BRIANT: BRYAN: ETC.

probably taking up his abode with his sister, Mrs. Rebecca Deane, who was now a widow, residing in Elizabeth, and there he made his will, February 18, 1774, in which he describes himself as "Dr. Joshua Bryant now of Elizabethtown, Essex County, late of the Island of Grenada, West Indies, Doctor of Physic," and as being "weak in body." The will was proved just one week later, and on the same day letters of administration with will annexed were granted to Mrs. Deane, her bondsman being William Peartree Smith. In this instrument he devises to his sister, Mrs. Rebecca Deane, of Elizabethtown, widow, all his estate, except what is hereafter excepted, to bring up her three children, "the rest of my relations being in good circumstances." He refers particularly to his house and lot in the Caronago, near the town of St. Georges, Island of Grenada; he leaves £100 to Penelope Parkinson, alias Wilson, his housekeeper in Grenada; he refers to his brother. Dr. William Bryant, of Kingsbury, near Trenton, and to his brother, Ebenezer Bryant, deceased, and provides that his brother-in-law, William Peartree Smith, the executor of Ebenezer's estate, shall be paid for any loss incurred in settling said estate. He states that "Mr. John Wharton, my old partner, owes me £100, which is to be collected by my executors. Philip Obin owes me £130. He used to sail from the Island." He refers to his friend, Dr. Samuel Duffield, of Philadelphia. Executors- "my friends, Mr. James Cox and Mr. George Fitzgerald, Merchant, at St. George, Island of Grenada." Witnesses—Elias Boudinot, William Livingston, Belcher P. Smith.—*N. J. Wills*, Lib. K, p. 490.

BRYANT, BRAIANT, BRIANT, BRIAN, etc.

Aaron Bryan and wife narrowly escaped drowning, in December, 1765, by the upsetting of a shallop, on the way from Philadelphia to Mount Holly.—*N. J. Archives*, XXIV., 679.

Aaron Bryant, of Northampton township, Burlington county, was one of the borrowers from the New Jersey Loan Commissioners, Dec. 5, 1786.

Abraham Bryan, of Burlington county, advertises a runaway servant man, June 14, 1739.—*N. J. Archives*, XI., 570.

Alexander Bryant lived about fourteen miles from Reading Town (Hunterdon county ?), in 1766.—*N. J. Archives*, XXV., 192.

Anthony Braiant was witness to an Indian deed, July 20, 1666, for lands on the south side of the Delaware river, over against New Castle, and on West creek, Salem county.—*N. J. Archives*, XXI., 4. An Indian deed, October 4, 1665, conveys to Fop Jansen Outhout the Hoppemanse tract between two creeks, over against Anthony Breyant.—*N. J. Archives*, XXI., 7. Anthony Bryant was witness to an Indian deed, Feb. 8, 1673-4, at Finns' creek, Salem county.—*N. J. Archives*, I., 111, 528-9, 538.

Cornelius Bryan, living on Raccoon Creek, in Greenwich township, Gloucester county, advertises a runaway Irish servant man, June 20, 1765.—*N. J. Archives*, XXIV., 558.

Isaac Bryant is mentioned as a landowner in Monmouth county, adjoining Gawen Lawrie's 1,000 acres, June 20, 1699.—*N. J. Archives*, XXI., 309.

Jacob Brian was a landowner in Mt. Holly, in 1761.—*N. J. Archives*, XX., 530. He advertised two plantations at Upper Freehold, and a tract of woodland on South River, Middlesex county, in 1763.—*Ib.*, XXIV., 134.

Thomas Bryant bought 200 acres, apparently in Burlington county, Nov. 10, 1688.—*N. J. Archives*, XXI., 471. He had a survey made for

him for 300 acres along Ancokus creek, Salem county, 4th mo. 1689.—
Ib., XXI., 366. He is mentioned as a landowner in the same county in
1692.—*Ib.*, 389. He acquired 400 acres of land on Rancokus creek, by
deed May 10, 1694; in the deed he is described as a planter, of Northampton, Burlington county. This deed is from Thomas Raper, of
Burlington, Smith, and Abigail his wife, and includes 300 acres being
part of one-thirtieth part of a property given said Abigail by her
father, William Perkins, by deed dated Oct. 27, 1677, recorded Aug.
11, 1682, near and adjoining Rancokus or Northampton river.—*Ib.*, 470.
By deed dated 5 mo. (July) 3, 1689, he bought from Samuel Jenings,
cf Greenhill, Burlington county, yeoman, for £10, a tract of 100 acres
to be taken up in West Jersey, as part of the property of said Jenings.—*N. J. Deeds*, Liber B, Part 2, f. 499.

Thomas Brian (Briant) was a witness before the Governor and
Council, Feb. 24, 1713, in relation to certain surveys by Daniel Leeds.—
N. J. Archives, XIII., 526. William Budd, of Northampton township,
Burlington county, conveyed to Thomas Brian, of the same township,
April 1, 1698, for £40, a tract of 25 acres of meadow joining Restore
Lippincott.—*N. J. Deeds*, Liber B, Part 2, f. 615.

Thomas Brian, of Northampton township, husbandman, conveyed to
Thomas Hains 300 acres in the fork of Northampton river; the same
day he received from Hains a tract of 200 acres in Springfield township. By deed Feb. 5, 1697-8, he acquired 1-32 of a share in West Jersey.—*N. J. Archives*, XXI., 502. By deed April 1, 1698, Thomas Brian
and William Budd, both of Northampton, Burlington county, yeomen,
exchanged two small tracts (30 acres and 25 acres) in Burlington
county.—*Ib.*, 504. From a deed May 21, 1698, Thomas Bryan appears
to have owned land (and probably resided) near Mt. Holly.—*Ib.*, 507.
He conveyed 150 acres by deed dated Feb. 7, 1697-8, being described
as of Northampton township, husbandman.—*Ib.*, 528. Thomas Bryant
is mentioned in a deed of Jan. 13, 1699-1700.—*Ib.*, 529. Thomas Brian
is one of the signers of a petition to Lord Cornbury, about 1707.—*N. J.
Archives*, III., 164. He was a member of the Assembly for the Western
Division, in 1705.—*Smith's Hist. N. J.*, 284 n.

Valentine Bryant, of Hopewell, Hunterdon county, advertises a run
away servant man. in 1761.—*N. J. Archives*, XX., 550.

In 1722 William Briant, of "Stone bruk," was assessed on three hundred acres of land.

REV. THOMAS BUDD.

Rev. Thomas Budd, rector of the parish of Martock, Somersetshire,
England, became a minister among Friends about 1657. In 1661 he
was called upon by the authorities to take the "oath of obedience"
prescribed by the statute 1st James I., passed "for the better dis-
covering of papist recusants." He declared that he was willing to
affirm, but to take an oath was contrary to his religious principles.
He was arrested, convicted, and receiving the sentence of praemu-
nire, was sent to the Ilchester jail. where he remained nine years. or
until his death, June 22, 1670. In his last moments he "rejoiced and
praised God that his children did walk in the way of the Lord."—
Besse's Sufferings of the Quakers, 1: 580, 609. Issue:

    2.   i.   Thomas[2], b. in England about 1640, probably.

    3.   ii. William, b. in England.

        iii. John, b. in England. He was of Burlington, Feb. 8,
           1692-3; d. in Philadelphia, in 1704, s. p.

4. iv. James, b. in England.
    v. Ann, m. ――― Bingham.
    vi. Susannah. m. Samuel Woolston. Child: John, bap. May
        11, 1712. (Samuel Woolston and *Elizabeth*, his wife,
        had child Samuel bap. July 26, 1719.)

Third Generation.

2. Thomas[2] Thomas[1] Budd, b. in England, perhaps about 1640; m. in
England, Susannah ―――: d. in Philadelphia, Feb. 15, 1697-8; she d.
in Philadelphia, and was buried in that city Feb. 4, 1707-8.—*Penn. Mag.*
10: 490. The records of Burlington Monthly Meeting of Friends fail
to state when, if ever, Thomas Budd presented his letters and was
admitted to the Meeting, but he is mentioned as a witness at several
marriages. He certainly was one of the most prominent and influential of the first settlers of Burlington, and for many years exercised
a large influence in the Province. And yet information concerning his
personal history and characteristics, his appearance and habits, is
almost entirely lacking. In a paper read by Franklin W. Earl before
the Surveyors' Association of West Jersey, August 13, 1867, it is
stated that "Thomas Budd arrived at Burlington, N. J., in the year
1668, and after remaining in the country for a few years returned to
London for his family, with which he came again to Burlington in
1678, and came also with him his brothers, William, John and James,
with their families."—*Proceedings West Jersey Surveyors' Association,*
36-42. The statement that Budd arrived at Burlington in 1668 is evidently incorrect, careful and accurate as Mr. Earl usually is. There
was no settlement at Burlington earlier than 1678, if then. Budd is
first mentioned in the records as the grantee, by deed dated March
1-2, 1676-7, from William Penn, Gawen Laurie, Nicholas Lucas and
Edward Billing, of one share or one ninetieth of the ninety equal and
undivided parts of West Jersey.—*N. J. Archives,* 21: 395-6. Having
thus become one of the Proprietors of the Province, he signed with
others the Concessions and Agreements for the government of West
Jersey, dated the same month.—*N. J. Archives,* 1: 268; *Leaming and
Spicer,* 410. The first mention of his coming to New Jersey is in
a letter from John Crips, to his brother and sister, dated "Burlington,
in New Jersey, upon the River Delaware, the 19th of the 4th Moneth,
call'd June 1678," in which the writer says: "Thomas Budd, and his
Family are arrived. The ship Lieth before this Town that brought
them. I wish you have not cause to repent that you came not along
with them. They had a very good Passage, and so had the London
ship. They are both in the River at this time. I understand by
Thomas Budd that he did satisfie you as near as he could, of the
Truth of things here, and you had as much reason to believe him, as
that other person, and more too; for Thomas had far more Experience of this Place, than he (I say) could have in the short time he
was among us."—"*An Abstract or Abbreviation of some Few of the Many
(Later & Former) Testimonys from the Inhabitants of New-Jersey And
other Eminent Persons Who have Wrote particularly concerning that Place,*
London, Printed by Thomas Milbourn, in the year 1681." This is one
of the rarest tracts relating to New Jersey; it is a small quarto, of
32 pp.; the extract given appears on page 15. Appended to the letter
is this note: "To the Truth of the Contents of these things we sub-
scribe our Names—Daniel Wills, Thomas Olive, Thomas Harding,
Thomas Budd, William Peachy." In the same pamphlet appears a
letter from Thomas Budd, dated Weymouth, 28th 6th Month (August),
1678, to "Gawen Lawry in George-Yard, in Lombard Street, Mer-

chant, ' in which he says: "I am safely come from New Jersey, where I left Friends in Health. . . . I suppose I have Travelled more in New Jersey than any other Person that came lately, which I did at my own proper Charge, that I might be able to satisfie my Self, and Acquaintance concerning the Country. I intend to be shortly in London." He gives some account of the country, and states that "Many houses are being built on Chygoe's Island." From these letters it would appear that Budd had been some time in New Jersey and had returned to England, before the date of the letter of John Crips; that he returned to Burlington, with his family, arriving in June, 1678, and that two months later he was again in England. How long he remained absent from West Jersey this time it is impossible to tell, but on September 24, 1680, a survey was returned for him of 109 acres along the Salem town line and adjoining Edm. Stuart, and on October 9-10, 1680, we have a memorandum of a deed from Budd to John Long, for half an acre in Burlington. A survey was returned March 30, 1681, for 50 acres along the town bounds (Burlington), adjoining John Cripps, in exchange with Thomas Budd, of 450 acres along the town bounds, the "old head" line of Rankokus lots and the partition line between the two Tenths. He bought of John Kinsey, Dec. 22-23, 1681, one-third of a share in West Jersey, which he sold a week later. A survey was returned to him Feb. 15, 1681-2, for 500 acres, in exchange with Samuel Jenings. On Aug. 4, 1682, a return was made of a survey for Hance Monsiur, of 500 acres, bought of Thomas Budd and Thomas Gardner on public account. John Yeo and wife of Maryland sold to Thomas Budd 500 acres, being part of one-sixth of a share, and 66 acres in Burlington township, with his wharf lot. On Nov. 10, 1682, a return was made to Thomas Budd of Burlington, of 500 acres in Salem Tenth. Under date of 29th 9th mo. (November), 1682, Elianor Huffe, widow, by her attorney in fact, sold to Thomas Budd, of Burlington, merchant, 500 acres in Salem Tenth. There is a memorandum of a deed of trust, dated April 5, 1683, Edward Searson, late of the White Leay, Derbyshire, England, now of Maryland, to Samuel Jenings, Thomas Budd and Elias Farre, the consideration having been paid by Thomas Ellis, of Burlington, deceased, on behalf of his daughter, for one sixty-fourth of the First Tenth. In a letter from James Nevill to Governor Penn, dated Salem, ye 23d 3d mo. (May), 1683, he gives a list of lands sold, etc., by John Fenwick since his conveyance made to John Eldridge and Edmond Warner, among them being one to Thomas Budd, 500 acres, on Salem creek. Henry Stacy deeded, 15th 8th mo. (October) 1683, to John Gosling, 100 acres in the Yorkshire Tenth, to be equally divided between the grantee and Thomas Budd. Martin Hoult conveyed to Thomas Budd, 25th 10th mo. (Dec.) 1683, a house and lot in Burlington. He bought from George Porter, with the appointment of his guardians and feoffees, 300 acres in the First Tenth, with wharf lot and town lot in Burlington. A survey was returned to him for 216 acres, in March (1st mo.) 1684. On April 8, 1684, George Hutcheson sold him 100 acres at Lessa Point, Burlington, and the same day George Hutcheson and Thomas Gardner, commissioners for the raising of money towards the discharge of the public debt, sold Budd 600 acres, to be surveyed in the six Lower Tenths. Nov. 20, 1686, Godfrey Hancock, senior, conveyed to Thomas Budd, of Burlington, merchant, 50 acres or one-eighth of a share in the First Tenth. His next speculation was of a peculiarly interesting character; under date of May 25, 1687, Percifal Towle, Francis Collins and twenty-two others, Pro-

prietors of several undivided shares of West Jersey, conveyed to
Thomas Budd 15,000 acres of land, he to pay the Indians for their
rights. This land "was allotted said Budd by the Country for Satisfaction of a Debt of £1250 which they owed said Budd; it is said to
be the best Land in the Province."—*N. J. Archives*, 2: 99. Budd sold
this tract to Dr. Daniel Coxe, who sold it in turn to the Proprietors
of West Jersey, some time prior to December 24, 1692.—*Ib.* It was
then valued by Dr. Coxe at £10 per hundred acres, but they were
willing to sacrifice it at £5 per hundred acres. Hitherto, Budd appears to have been a resident of Burlington, where he was a "merchant" or "trades." But in the next conveyance, dated October 20,
1687, he is designated as of Philadelphia, merchant, he and his wife
Susanna deeding certain lands to Samuel Harriot, of Burlington.
Samuel Groome, of London, merchant, conveyed to Thomas Budd, of
Philadelphia, merchant, Feb. 11, 1689-90, two eights of a share of
West Jersey, and on February 5, of the same year, he acquired half
a share in West Jersey from James Wasse, of London. His activities
in dealings in real estate now relaxed, his next transaction being in
1693, when he located a tract "where the present road crosses the
main north branch of Rancocus creek at Pemberton, running north
almost as far as Juliustown, embracing all the land from the main
street in Pemberton, easterly for a mile and three quarters up said
creek."—(*Proc. W. J. Surveyors Assoc.*, 38.) In September, 1699,
Susanna Budd, by her deputy, resurveyed the above tract, on the east
side of Pemberton, and found it to contain 2,000 acres; on July 11,
1701, she sold it. John Chamnis having mortgaged a tract of 200
acres of land in Burlington county to Thomas Budd, and failing to
observe the obligations he had incurred, Budd foreclosed the mortgage and the property was sold to him and Susanna his wife, by
James Hill, sheriff of Burlington county, August 8, 1693. A return
was made of a survey of 2,000 acres of land at Mount Pisgah, for
Budd, in April, 1694 Henry Grubb, of Burlington, innholder, conveyed
to Thomas Budd, of Philadelphia, merchant, 4th d. 7th mo. (Sept.)
1695, a tract of 50 acres. November 2, 1695, Jonathan Beere made an
assignment to Budd. John Reading conveyed to Budd Dec. 3, 1695,
a tract of 200 acres called Mount Eagle, on the coast near Great Egg
Harbour. Jonathan Beere, Esquire, and Burgess of Salem Town, conveyed to Budd four 12-acre lots in Salem Town marsh, by deed dated
May 25, 1696, and on August 22 following Budd acquired two more
lots in Salem Town marsh, one of 17 and the other of 8 acres, the
grantor being William Hall, of Salem Town. In an Indian deed, May
8, 1699, from Hugnon and Lumoseecon, Sachems, to John Harrison,
the tract is described as lying between Cranberry Brook and Milston
river, Yorkroad and Thomas Budd, showing that Budd had acquired
lands much north of his original purchases. The foregoing list of
conveyances, probably by no means complete, has been taken from
N. J. Archives, 21. They show the remarkable activity and enterprise of the man. Having bought so extensively in West Jersey, he
found quite a number of Swedes already settled upon his lands. At
his request, they produced proofs of their titles, and Budd thereupon
gave them deeds from himself, confirming them in the ownership of
their homes.—*Penn. Mag.*, 17: 85. While he was thus engaged in real
estate investments or speculations, he was by no means neglectful of
public affairs. In 1681, he was appointed by the West Jersey Assembly one of the receivers general to collect £200 for the purpose of de-
fraying the debts of the Province. In May, 1682, he was chosen one

of the commissioners for "settling and regulation of lands," a member of the governor's council, and one of the regulators of weights and measures. In September, 1682, he was appointed a justice of the peace for Burlington; he was elected to the Assembly, and rechosen land commissioner, and to serve on the governor's council; in May, 1682, he was appointed one of the commissioners to raise Provincial moneys in the Second Tenth, and in the six Lower Tenths, and was appointed special Provincial treasurer. He was a member of the Assembly, 3d mo. 1685, and also a member of the governor's council; land commissioner for the Second Tenth, Indian land commissioner, and Provincial treasurer. Budd and Francis Collins were voted, in 1683, each 1,000 acres, "parts of lands to be purchased of the Indians above the falls," the present site of Trenton, in consideration and discharge for building a market and court house at Burlington. At the session of the Assembly in May, 1683, Budd was selected to write to members of the Society of Friends in London relative to the state of the case of the Proprietors with Edward Byllinge. In 9th mo. 1683 he was designated to write to Edward Byllinge on the same subject. In March, 1684, he was appointed with Samuel Jenings to represent the claims of the freeholders to the government, as opposed to Edward Byllinge's pretence to the same, and also to demand that Byllinge confirm what he had sold. The Assembly voted the commissioners 1500 acres above the falls as their security for £100 sterling. Soon after, in 1684, Budd sailed for England upon his mission. While abroad he rendered to the country his most distinguished service, in the publication of a small book on conditions in the Provinces controlled by Friends, entitled "Good Order Established in Pennsylvania and New Jersey," which appears to have been given to the printers October 25, 1685. This undoubtedly gave a great stimulus to emigration to West Jersey. In 1685 he was chosen to the Assembly, and became one of the chief promoters in the erection of the new Meeting House at Burlington. 17th 9th mo. in the same year he petitioned the Provincial Council of Pennsylvania for a special court to decide a difference between Philip Th: Lehman and himself. He and others petitioned the same body, 7th of 12th mo. 1688-9, for encouragement in setting up a bank for money. He went to England again in 1689, returning to Philadelphia the following year. August 6, 1690. he bought the Blue Anchor tavern and adjacent property on the west side of Front street, Philadelphia, and extending toward Walnut street; he gradually demolished the old buildings, and erected a row of timber and brick houses called in the old times "Budd's Long Row"; into the southernmost house of the row the Blue Anchor tavern was moved, so that it stood at the foot of Delaware and Front streets and Dock creek: two of the houses he sold to Anthony Morris, 4, 8, 1697.—*Penn. Mag.*, 20: 431. In 1691 took place the famuos schism among Friends, led by George Keith, who afterwards became connected with St. Mary's church, Burlington, when he wrote that magnificent hymn, which has been sung by countless thousands of Christions, "How firm a foundation, ye saints of the Lord." Budd was one of the signers of the confession of faith, or declaration, of Keith. Morgan Edwards says he afterwards became a Baptist, and was a preacher among them. No evidence of this has been found, however, and Edwards doubtless erred. Keith was formally disowned by Friends, 1692, and probably Budd likewise. In December, 1692, Keith and Budd were presented by the grand jury of Philadelphia, as the authors of an attack made by Keith upon Samuel Jenings and the

magistracy; they were tried, convicted and sentenced to pay a fine of
£5 each, but the penalty was never exacted.—*Proud's Hist. Penna.*,
1: 373; *Penn. Mag.*, 18. 425. Budd continued loyal to Keith, and accompanied him to England in 1694, to defend him before the Yearly
Meeting of Friends. His wife adhered to the Society of Friends,
among whom she was prominent. The will of Thomas Budd, of
Philadelphia, is signed February 8, 1697-8, and was proved March 25,
1698. The only real estate specified is that which he devised to his
son Thomas, and in which his son lived, "being the corner house
nearest the dock." He gives his daughters £100 each. There is no
residuary clause. His personal estate was inventoried at £457.—
Philadelphia Wills, Liber A, f. 384. There is much reason to believe,
however, that at the time of his death he still possessed much of the
vast estates acquired by him during his score of years in America.
In his will he names four children:

    i. Thomas[3].

    ii. Mary[3], b. 2d 7 mo. 1677, as recorded in Burlington
       Monthly Meeting Records of Births and Deaths,
       1677-1698, in Friends' Library, Philadelphia. The
       place of birth is not stated. It was not unusual to
       record in America births which had taken place in
       England She m 1st. Dr. John Gosling, of Burling-
       ton; 2, in 1686, Francis Collins; he was a bricklayer,
       in Gloucester, but on his marriage removed to Bur-
       lington; in 1690 he built the Burlington county court
       house, for which he received £100 and a tract of
       land.

    iii. Rose[3], b. 13th 1st mo. 1680-81, as recorded in the same
       volume as her sister Mary's birth.

5.   iv. John[3].

3. William[2] Thomas[1] Budd had issue (bap. in St. Mary's church, Burlington):

3. William[2] Thomas[1] Budd, b. 1680; m. Elizabeth ———. He was
known as William Budd, junior, to distinguish him from an uncle of
the same name. Edward Armstrong, in his interesting, accurate and
learned Introductory Note, to Gowans's reprint of "Good Order Established in Pennsylvania and New Jersey in America," says: "William, who died in 1723, at his farm in Northampton township, Burlington county, about four miles west of Mount Holly, and who by
his will left a benefaction to the Episcopal church of St. Mary's at
Burlington, of which he appears to have been a steadfast member,
and where he is buried, and also land in Northampton township, on
which to build a church. His descendants are very numerous in
Pennsylvania, and in southern New Jersey, and we believe that with
the exception of those of the name who trace their origin to Thomas
Budd, and who are comparatively few, all the rest in the regions referred to are descended from the first William." A return was made
2d mo. 1693, of a survey made by Symon Charles and Daniel Leeds,
for William Budd, for 500 acres of land with 15 acres highway allowance for other land, on the North branch of Rancokus river; and also
for 200 acres next to Budd. William Budd was appointed a justice of
the peace, June 5, 1705. Issue:

    i. Mary[3], bap. Sept. 9, 1704; prob. m. Joseph Shinn.
    ii. Susanna[3], bap. Sept. 6, 1706.
    iii. Thomas[3], bap. Dec. 3, 1708.
    iv. William[3], bap. Jan. 2, 1710 or 1711; d. 1723.

BUDD

    v.   David[3], bap. July 14, 1714.

    vi.   Abigail[3], bap. May 15, 1716.

   vii.   Sarah[3], bap. March 11, 1718.

  viii.   Rebecca[3].

   ix.   Elizabeth Ann[3].

4.   James[2] Thomas[1] Budd was elected to the West Jersey Assembly in 1685. and was appointed a justice of the peace the same year. He sold 500 acres of land on Northampton river to John Rodman, of Flushing, L. I. James was drowned at Burlington. His will, dated January 29, 1727-8, names four children:

    i.   William, under age, Jan. 29, 1727-8.

   ii.   James, m. ———. Ch., Samuel, bap. April 6, 1740.

   iii.   Joseph, under age, Jan. 29, 1727-8.

   iv.   Ann.

Fourth Generation.

5.   John[3] Thomas[2] Thomas[1] Budd m. Rebecca Sandiland, sister of James Sandiland, of Upland, who was sheriff of Philadelphia county 1706-7. In his will, dated June 1, 1710, he refers to kinsman Peter Baynton, b. 1696, d. 1723, m. his cousin Mary, dau. of John and Rebecca (Baynton) Budd.—*Penn. Mag*, 2: 448. (Prob. John[3] Thomas[2] Thomas[1], mentioned above as of Burlington, Feb. 8, 1692-3.) John settled in Morris county, where his father had located extensive tracts of land. He was probably the John Budd who sold to Jacob Corson, of Staten Island, lands described by the latter in his will dated Oct. 8, 1742, as "all my messuages and lands in Hunterdon county, New Jersey, at or near the township of Reading."—*N. Y. Hist. Soc. Coll.*, 1869, p. 120. His will, dated Sept. 6, 1749, proved May 16, 1754, names children:

    i.   John. He was a physician, and settled in Salem county, where he was Sheriff in 1758. In 1763, and again in 1764, being then of Salem, he advertised for sale a large new house, "just finished off in a handsome manner," near the court house, Morristown, and four other tracts of land in the vicinity.—*N. J. Archives*, XXIV., 188, 315, 373. He was again Sheriff of Salem county in 1764 and 1765.—*Ib.*, 346, 406, 517. He became financially embarrassed, placed his property in the hands of trustees for the benefit of his creditors, and made frequent appeals to his creditors for their support. He then removed to Long Island, New York. In 1769 he gave notice to his creditors that he feared they were not likely to get anything "if things remain in their present situation," and that he therefore proposed to apply to the Legislature for "a license to return and reside in the said province, five years free from arrest, to collect in the money due to me and pay my debts."—*N. J. Archives*, XXVI., 438. Nothing came of this. Some time after 1771 he removed to Charleston, S. C., where he d. in 1791. During the Revolution he served as Surgeon of a South Carolina Regiment of Artillery.

   ii.   Thomas, a physician. In 1767 he was living in Hanover, Morris county, and advertised for sale a plantation at that place, of 400 or 500 acres, joining the lands of William Kelly.—*N. J. Archives*, XXV., 434.

   iii.   Bern, a physician. "Dr. Bern Budd, of Hanover, in Morris county," advertises a runaway negro man, August 9, 1764.—*N. J. Archives*, XXIV., 399.

Miscellaneous: Jemima, "wife of Thomas Budd, senior," was buried at Mount Holly, Aug. 29, 1770. William Budd, senior, one of the vestrymen of St. Andrew's church, Mount Holly, was buried at Mount Holly, Aug. 29, 1770. Thomas Budd, a native of New Mills, Burlington county, b. Feb. 19, 1783, became a preacher in the M. E. church.

JOHN BUDD.

John Budd, b. in England, came from London about 1632, and was one of the planters of New Haven Colony, in 1639. He was appointed a deputy from Southold, L. I., in 1653 to the General Court, but had gone to England in the meantime. His appointment from Southold indicates that he was already settled there. He was lieutenant at Southold until 1660, when he resigned, he having removed or being about to remove to Rye, Westchester county, N. Y., where he was settled in 1661. He m. Katherine ———; d. 1670. By a declaration, dated October 15, 1669, he gave to son John his part of the mill on Blind brooke, and all lands otherwise undisposed of, and personal property, in consideration whereof John was to pay his father or his mother "thirty pounds a year in good pay that is to say wheat Twenty pounds porck one Barrell pease the rest. . . . that we may be freed from trouble." This instrument seems to have been recorded May 13, 1675, which was probably about the time of John's death. Issue:

   2.   i.   John².
   3.   ii.   Joseph.
       iii.   Judith, m. 1st, John Ogden; 2d, Francis Brown.
       iv.   Jane, m. Joseph Horton.

2. John² John¹ Budd m. Mary, 3d dau. of Barnabas Horton, of Southold; d. Nov. 5, 1684. After his father's death he returned to Southold, having apparently sold to his brother-in-law, Joseph Horton, the mill on Blind brook. The will of "John Budd of the Town of Southold, being at present weak in body," dated Oct. 27, 1684, proved November 12, 1684, provides for the comfortable maintenance of his wife, Mary, during widowhood, gives the bulk of his estate to eldest son John, and to son Joseph "all my right and interest in a neck of land in Westchester, which lieth between Blind Brook and Mamaroneck River, and an island of meadow belonging thereto (except 100 acres of upland and 4 acres of meadow), and all my housing and improvements on said land."—*N. Y. Hist. Soc. Coll.*, 1892, pp. 130-132. Issue:

       i.   John³.
       ii.   Joseph.
       iii.   Mary, m. 1st, ——— Niccols; 2d, Christopher Youngs.
       iv.   Hannah, m. Jonathan Hart.
       v.   Ann, m. Benjamin Horton.
       vi.   Sarah, under eighteen at the date of her father's will, Oct. 27, 1684; prob. m. Benjamin Conkling.

3. Joseph² John¹ Budd m. Sarah, dau. of Humphrey Underhill, of Rye; d. 1722. He "was known as 'Captain Budd' as early as 1700. He was prominent in town and county affairs, being townsman in 1701, justice of the peace in 1710, farmer of the excise 1714-21, and supervisor of the town, 1713-16, 1720-22. In 1720 he obtained a patent for a tract purchased by his father and known as 'Budd's Neck.' "—*Baird's Hist. of Rye*, 405. The will of "Joseph Budd of Rye in the county of Westchester, Esquire," is dated May 27, 1722, and was proved June 28, 1722. He devises many tracts of land and other property.—*N. Y. Hist. Soc. Coll.*, 1893, pp. 250-251. He names children:

BUDD: BURR

4.   i. **John³**, under 30 at the time of his father's will, May 27, 1722.

ii. Joseph, m Ann ———. His will bears date 1763.

iii. Elisha, b. 1705, m. Anne, dau. of Joseph Lyon; d. Sept 21, 1765; she d. Dec. 6, 1760.

iv. Underhill, b. April 29, 1708; m. Sarah, dau. of Capt. Henry Fowler, of Southold, Sept. 17, 1730; will proved May 31, 1755; she d. Aug. 19, 1798.

v. Gilbert.

vi. Hannah, m. ——— Palmer.

vii. Sarah.

viii. Annie.

ix. Tamar.

x. Mary.

4. John³ Joseph² John¹ Budd m. Mary Prudence, dau. of Daniel and Charlot Strang; d. ———. He inherited the estate on Budd's Neck, which he sold in 1745. Peter Jay being the chief purchaser. He removed about this time to Morris county, and bought a farm near Black River, in the present Chester township. In 1753, "John Budd, late of Rye, now of Roxboro, Morris county, New Jersey," sold a remaining parcel of land on Budd's Neck. Issue:

5.   i. Daniel⁴, b. July 27, 1722.

ii. Elijah, m. Ursula Sine.

iii. Joseph, m. ——— Budd.

iv. John, is said to have removed to Kentucky.

v. Underhill, d. unm.

vi. Gilbert, "was for thirty years a surgeon in the British navy. He returned to this country after the Revolution, and made his home with his cousin, Colonel Gilbert Budd, of Mamaroneck, until his death, October 14, 1805; he was 85 years old."—*Baird's Hist. Rye*, p. 405.

vii. Hannah, m. Hachaliah Purdy.

viii. Mary, m. Caleb Horton.

ix. Sarah, m. Thomas Sawyer.

x. Abigail.

5. Daniel⁴ John³ Joseph² John¹ Budd, b. July 27, 1722; m. ——— Purdy, d. Dec. 24, 1806. Issue:

i. John⁵.

ii. William.

iii. Elizabeth.

iv. Joseph.

v. Abigail.

vi. Daniel.

AARON BURR.

Aaron Burr was the son of President Burr, and the grandson of President Edwards. He was b. Feb. 6, 1756, in the parsonage of the old First Presbyterian church, of Newark, of which his father, Rev. Aaron Burr, was pastor, being at the same time President of the College of New Jersey, then located in Newark. The parsonage was on the west side of Broad street, a short distance north of William street. Young Burr graduated from the college, then at Princeton, in the class of 1772. In 1775 he joined the army at Cambridge, and accompanied Arnold in his expedition against Quebec. In 1779, with the rank of Lieutenant-Colonel, he retired from military life. In 1782 he commenced the practice of law at Albany, but soon removed to New York City. From 1791 to 1797 he was a member of the Senate of the United States. He and Jefferson had each seventy-three votes for President of the United States in 1800. On the thirty-sixth ballot in the House of Representatives Jefferson was elected, and Burr became Vice President. On the 11th of July, 1804, he mortally wounded Alexander Hamilton in a duel. In 1807 Mr. Burr was arrested for high treason, and was tried in Richmond and acquitted. Luther Martin, of the class of 1766, a personal friend, was one of his counsel. The remainder of Mr. Burr's life was passed principally in New York in comparative obscurity and neglect. He died September 14, 1836, and was buried at Princeton, near the grave of his father.

MAJOR THOMAS LANGHORNE BYLES.

Thomas Langhorne Byles (so he wrote the last name) was doubtless a grandson of Thomas Langhorne, who settled in Bucks County, Penn., in 1684, his daughter Sarah marrying William Biles.—*Penn. Mag. of Hist. and Biog.*, April, 1883, pp. 67-87. The Committee of Safety of Pennsylvania, on January 5, 1776, appointed him one of the Captains in the four new battalions of that Province.—*Penn. Col. Records*, X., 447. He was taken prisoner at the capture of Fort Washington, November 16, 1776, and was exchanged March 1, 1778. In the meantime, June 8, 1777, he had been promoted to Major. After being exchanged he joined his regiment (Colonel Lambert Cadwallader's Third Pennsylvania) at Valley Forge, July 3, 1778.—*Saffel's Records of the Revolutionary War*, 310-11; 2 *Penn. Archives*, X., 447. A letter dated April 17, 1780, gives this account of his death: "Yesterday morning, a detachment of 200 Continental troops, under the command of Major Byles, stationed at Paramus, was suddenly attacked by a party of the enemy, consisting of 200 horse and 400 foot. The attack commenced a little after sunrise. Major Byles, besides his usual patrols, had that morning sent out two parties, each with a commissioned officer, but such is the situation of that part of the country, intersected with roads, and inhabited chiefly by disaffected people, that all precautions failed. The sentinels, near the quarters, were the first that gave notice of the enemy's approach. He immediately made the best disposition the hurry of the movement would permit, and animated his men by his exhortations and example. The house he was in was surrounded. Some of the men began to cry for quarter; others, obeying the command of the officers, continued to fire from the windows. The enemy upbraided them for the perfidy of asking for quarter, and persisting in resistance. Major Byles denied, in a determined tone, that he called for quarter; but his resolution did not avail. A surrender took place, and, in the act, the Major received a mortal wound, with which he expired. . . . The enemy made their boast that, as Major Byles did not present the hilt of his sword in front when surrendering, they shot him."—2 *Penn. Archives*, X., 445-6.

REV. COLIN CAMPBELL.

The Rev. Colin Campbell was the tenth child of Colin Campbell, of Earnhill, Scotland, where he was born, Nov. 15, 1707. As a boy he attended school at Aberdeen and Inverness. He was appointed by the Society for the Propagation of the Gospel in Foreign Parts to the mission at St. Mary's, Burlington, where he arrived May 10, 1738, and was well received by the congregation. Although at first very bitter against the Friends ("What is the effect of Quakerism now in Pennsylvania but a nursery of Jesuits," he wrote in 1742), he soon became reconciled

CAMPBELL

to them, and in 1763 was able to report that he had lived among his people "these twenty five years in the greatest love harmony peace & quietness studying my own business and continuing in the esteem of our Quaker Neighbours." Two years later he declared: "We of this Province live peaceably with one another; as I do myself and congregations with all Dissenters whatsoever." Writing December 26, 1765, he says: "I have little or nothing by way of support from my Congregation; and a large Family of 6 Young Children to maintain, cloath & educate." He eked out the stipend allowed him by the Venerable Society, by teaching. In 1744 he advertised that he "proposed to teach young Men the classick Authors," and offered to board two or three boys at his house. His ministrations during his twenty-eight years of service were attended by a large increase in the several congregations under his care, and he seems to have gained the esteem of the entire community. He died Saturday, August 9, 1766, at Burlington, after a short illness, and was buried in St. Mary's Church, which he had served so long and faithfully. The Rev. Dr. William Smith, of Philadelphia, who preached the funeral sermon, said of him: "He endeavoured to be (what you will all allow he was) a Man of strict and severe Honesty; faithful in the Discharge of every Trust, and particularly of his most sacred Trust, a Minister of the Gospel of Jesus. He was a Lover of Peace, and rather willing to bear any Tolerable Wrong than ruffle the Serenity of his own Temper." His widow survived so late as 1796.—*Hills's Church at Burlington*, passim; *N. J. Archives*, XII., 229; XXV., 188; *N. Y. Marriage Licenses*; *Acadiensis*, III., 211; *Records of St. Mary's Church, Burlington*. Issue:

  i. Mary Ann, b. July 2, 1743; d. in inf.
 ii. Mary, b. Aug. 13, 1745.
iii. Hugh, bap. January —, 1747.
 iv. Rebecca, bap. March —, 1750; m. the Rev. William Frazer, of Amwell, and afterwards of Perth Amboy, July 13, 1768. Children: 1. Colin, b. May 24, 1769; 2. Elizabeth, d. Aug. 21, 1774, aged three months; and perhaps others.
  v. Colin, b. Dec. 15, 1751; m. Abigail Mumford Seabury, dau. of the Rev. Samuel Seabury, in New York, Dec. 26, 1781. He was licensed as an attorney at law of New Jersey, May 12, 1773. After the Revolution he was obliged to leave the country, and went to the Province of New Brunswick, where he settled at St. Andrews, being afterwards made Collector of Customs at that port. Subsequently he removed to Shelburne, and held the same office there, for forty years. He represented Shelburne county in the Assembly for one term of seven years. In his later life he removed to New Edinburgh, then in Annapolis, now in Digby county, and there died in 1834, leaving a widow, two daughters and a son. It was perhaps his son, Colin Campbell, who m. Mary, dau. of Lieut. James Campbell, of the 54th (British) Regiment, and whose son, John Campbell, was living in New Brunswick in 1878.
 vi. John, b. Feb. 24, 1754; m. Mary (b. October —, 1739), dau. of George Eyre, of Burlington, and had children: 1. Sarah, b. March 14, 1772; and two others.
vii. Jane, b. Nov. 6, 1755; d. Feb. 19, 1770.
viii. Archibald, b. Oct. 25, 1758.
 ix. Charles, bap. March 17, 1765.

ALEXANDER CHAMBERS.

John Chambers came from Antrim (famous for its round tower, one of the finest specimens of those ancient and mysterious structures), in the North of Ireland, about 1730, and settled in Trenton, where he died September 19, 1747, aged 70 years. He had two sons—David and Alexander—and five daughters. Alexander was born in Ireland in 1716. He lived at the corner of State and Willow streets, where his father had built a mud house, which he replaced by one of brick, and carried on the trade of turning, and making spinning-wheels and chairs. He was one of the managers of a lottery in 1753, for the purpose of raising funds to build a schoolhouse, to be "30 feet long, 20 feet wide and one story high, and built on the South-east corner of the [Presbyterian] Meeting-house yard" in Trenton. He was elected a director of this school in 1765. It was the forerunner of the Trenton Academy, founded in 1781. He was one of the trustees named in the charter of the Presbyterian Church of Trenton, Sept. 8, 1756, and continued in that office until his death, September 16, 1798, and the records show that he attended every meeting during the whole forty-two years. He was treasurer of the Board of Trustees, 1766-1796, and President from May 5, 1783, until his death. In the Trenton city charter of November 13, 1792, Alexander Chambers was named as one of the first two Aldermen of the city. He married Rose Crage, who was born 1720 at Ballintober ("town of the wells"), near Monaghan, Ireland; she died in Trenton, Nov. 23, 1780. Their children were: 1. John, born March 3, 1741; married Elizabeth Story, of Cranbury; he died in Trenton, Nov. 13, 1813. 2. David, a Colonel in the Revolution; married Ruth, daughter of Daniel Clark; he d. in 1842, aged 94; she d. in 1813, aged 58, having had nine children. 3. James. 4. Alexander, was one of the guides at the battle of Trenton; he was a prominent merchant in Trenton many years; he died in 1824. 5. Rose. 6. Margaret. 7. Elizabeth. 8. Mary.—*Hall's Hist. Pres. Church in Trenton*, 121, 158; *Cooley's Genealogy; N. J. Archives*, XIX., 245; *Joyce's Irish Gazetteer*, First Series, 4th ed., 451.

CAPTAIN JOHN CLUNN.

Captain John Clunn, a mariner, lived "below Trenton Landing, in Lamberton, now a part of the city of Trenton, in a house occupied ten or fifteen years ago by James Wooley."—*Stryker's "Trenton One Hundred Years Ago."* The will of John Clunn, senior, of Lamberton, Nottingham township, Burlington county, dated June 21, 1794, proved May 18, 1799, devises to wife Elizabeth, "the house and lot where I live during her life;" and names children—John, Amey, Margret and Elizabeth; also mentions house and lot occupied by David Snowden, and house and lot occupied by Hambleton Thompson; it also directs that the testator is to be "buried in the grounds of the (St. Michael's) Episcopal Church in Trenton." Executors—Wife and son John. Witnesses—David Snowden, James Mathis, junior, and Joseph Clunn.—*Liber 38 of Wills, in the Secretary of State's Office at Trenton*, p. 328. The widow of John Clunn, probably the mother of the Captain, died in August, 1781, aged 83 years, and was buried the same evening in St. Michael's churchyard.—*N. J. Gazette*, August, 1781. The minutes of St. Michael's church record the election of John Clunn as a vestryman on Saturday, April 2, 1785; again on April 29, 1786, and on Easter Monday in 1787, 1788, 1789 and 1790. Several Clunn tombstones are in St. Michael's churchyard, Trenton, as follows: John Clunn, Sr., d. November 27, 1798, in the 59th year of his age. Elizabeth Clunn, probably his wife, d. Dec. 5, 1823, aged 84 years. Margaret, dau. of John and Elizabeth Clunn, d. — 12, 1815. In the First Presbyterian church-yard, Trenton, is the tombstone of Amey Clunn, d. Dec. 12. —, aged 76 years.

DR. JOHN COCHRAN.

John Cochran, son of James Cochran, a native of the North of Ire-land, was born in Chester county, Pa., September 1st, 1730, studied medicine with Dr. Thompson, of Lancaster, and served in the war of 1758 (between England and France) as Surgeon's Mate in the hospital department. At the close of the war he settled in Albany, N. Y., where he married Gertrude, sister of General Schuyler. He soon after removed to New Brunswick, N. J., where he acquired a great reputa-tion. He was one of the founders of the New Jersey Medical Society, in 1766, and in 1769 was elected President. He was driven from his home by the British, who burned his house. He volunteered for hos-pital service, and on the strong recommendation of Washington to Congress, was, April 10th, 1777, commissioned Physician and Surgeon-General in the Middle Department, and in 1781 was commissioned Director-General of the Hospitals of the United States, being at-tached to headquarters, on Washington's staff. At the close of the war Washington gave him his headquarters furniture. He removed to New York, where he resumed his practice, until President Washington, re-taining "a cheerful recollection of his past services," appointed him Commissioner of Loans for the State of New York, an office he re-tained until disabled by a stroke of paralysis, when he resigned and removed to Schenectady, N. Y., where he died, April 6th, 1807. Wash-ington and Lafayette addressed him familiarly as "Dear Doctor Bones." —*Wickes*, 204-10; *Sparks's Washington*, VII., 192; *Irving's Washington*, III., 477; *American Historical Record*, III., 173, 289 (with portrait); 2 *N. J. Archives*, I., 147-8.

REV. NICHOLAS COLLIN.

The Rev. Nicholas Collin, of Upsal, Sweden, Theologiae Studiosus, was appointed by the Swedish Consistory, Curate to the Swedish church, May 19, 1769, and was sent to America by the Swedish gov-ernment, in 1770. In an account of the Swedish missions, entered by himself in the record of the ancient church at Swedesboro (formerly Racoon), New Jersey, he relates that he arrived here May 12, 1770, as minister extraordinary, and officiated throughout the mission, but es-pecially at Racoon and Penn's Neck, until the departure of Mr. Wic-sell, in the autumn of 1773. In 1775 Mr. Collin was Dean of the Swedish parishes in America. By letters to the Archbishop and Con-sistory of Upsal, dated July 8, 1778, he urgently solicited his recall. He had then officiated for about eight years in the mission, and was consequently entitled to preferment at home. Moreover, the disordered state of affairs here owing to the war, made it seem imperative that he should leave, and he threatened to return home in the following spring, without waiting for a recall. (During the year 1777 he was regarded by the Americans as a spy, and was threatened with death. —*Penn. Mag.*, 15:482. And for his account of events in 1778, see Penn. Mag., 14:218). Finally, the King of Sweden, on November 22, 1782, granted his recall. By this time, however, affairs had improved, with the end of the war, and he concluded to remain a short time. He was rector of the churches named from 1773 until July, 1788, and for seven years provost of the mission.—*Annals of the Swedes on the Delaware*, by the Rev. Jehu Curtis Clay, D. D., second edition, Philadelphia, 1858, pp. 122-125. His narrative, as entered in the Swedesboro Church records, December 10, 1791, is published in full in the Pennsylvania Magazine of History and Biography, 16: 349-358. "The Parish of Racoon," says the Rev. Israel Acrelius, writing in 1758, "lies upon the east side of the river Delaware, in the Province of New Jersey . . . Under the name of Racoon is understood the Swedish church and parish, which, extending the width of three Swedish miles, may be called the only one in the Province, with the exception of Pennsneck. Racoon is also the name of the navigable stream which empties into the Delaware, and upon which the church stands. The name comes from the river which the Indians called Memitraco and Naraticon; but the Swedes in former times, Araratcung, Ratcung, and now finally, Racoon; in Swedish orthography, Racuun."—*Acrelius, Hist. New Sweden*, 314. The site was bought for a church there, by deed dated September 1, 1703, and a church erected in 1704.—*Ib.*, 318. "The congregation of Pennsneck is in the Province of West New Jersey, in the Government of Burlington, Salem county, in the Townships of Upper and Lower Pennsneck, Pilesgrove and Mannington, on the east side of the Delaware, and along its strand." A site for a church was secured from Jean Jaquett, who gave two acres of land for the purpose, by deed dated January 8, 1715, in the middle of the Neck, on the highway. "The building of the church was immediately commenced, but it was not completed until March 31, 1717, when it was consecrated and called St. George's church. It is twenty-four feet square, built of logs, and weatherboarded."—*Acrelius, op. cit.*, 322-323. On August 10, 1785, Mr. Collin was appointed by the King of Sweden rector of Wicacoa and the churches in connection therewith. "The parish of Wicacoa," writes Acrelius, in 1758, "is in the Province of Pennsylvania, and its members live partly in the city of Philadelphia, and partly in various surrounding districts—Wicacoa, Moyamenzing, Passayungh, a district along the Schuylkill, Kingsesa, Bond's Island, and Pennypack, in Philadelphia county; Kalkonhook, Amasland, and Matzong in Chester county." A site was given for a church in 1697, and the church erected, being dedicated July 2, 1700, as "Gloria Dei."—*Hist. New Sweden*, 202-207. During the ensuing vacancy at Racoon and Penn's Neck, Mr. Collin says: "I gave the congregations every attention consistent with my distant situation and multiplicity of business. At Swedesboro I performed divine service every third Sunday during the summer and autumn of 1786, and at larger intervals the two following years. I likewise visited some worthy members in their sickness, and preached some funeral sermons. Besides, I made frequent journeys for settling the business of the new church. Penn's Neck could not possibly obtain the same share of service, yet I officiated a few times at that church, and also preached occasionally at houses on afternoons, after finishing the service at Racoon." In the meantime he sought to secure a settled minister to fill the vacancy. Ultimately (in 1790) the Rev. John Croes was engaged by the vestry, and continued to serve the church for many years. The church now ceased to be a mission, dependent on the bounty of the Swedish King, and became affiliated with the Episcopal church in America. Subsequently Mr. Croes was elected the first Bishop of New Jersey.—*Clay's "Annals,"* 129-130. "At the time Dr. Collin received his appointment as rector of these churches (at Wicaco, etc.) the Swedes began to feel the necessity, from the little knowledge of the Swedish language remaining among them, of having clergymen set over them, who had received their education in this country," and accordingly the vestry of the Wicaco church directed the wardens to notify the Archbishop of Upsal: "As the Rev. Mr. Collin has expressed a desire of returning to his native country shortly; whenever his majesty of Sweden shall think it proper to grant his recall, the mission to these congregations will undoubtedly cease." The relation which was then expected to be so brief, extended over nearly half a century. Dr. Collin "presided over these churches for a period of forty-five years: in which time he married 3375 couple, averaging about eighty-four couple a year. Dr. Collin, during the whole period of his ministry, was held in high esteem by his congregations. He possessed considerable learning, particularly in an acquaintance with languages. . . . He was a member, and for some time one of the vice presidents, of the American Philosophical Society, and was also one of the founders of the 'Society for the commemoration of the landing of William Penn.' "—*Clay's* "*Annals,*" as cited, pp. 126-127. In 1799 Dr. Collin translated a considerable portion of Acrelius's "History of the Swedes on the Delaware," for the use of the Rev. Dr. Samuel Miller, of Princeton, who was then engaged in preparing his "Church History." Dr. Miller appears to have turned this translation over to the American Philosophical Society, by whom it was transferred to the New York Historical Society (organized in 1804), which published the same in its Collections, New Series, 1841. Vol. I., pp. 401-448. Dr. Collin's unabated interest in the Swedesboro church, nearly twenty years after leaving it, is shown in an impassioned letter he wrote, April 30, 1804, to Dr. James Stratton, near Swedesboro, protesting against the proposed sale of a tract of land which had been devised to the old church.—*Penn. Mag.*, 14:211. Dr. Collin died at Wicaco, October 7, 1831, in his 87th year. His portrait, from a drawing evidently made in his extreme old age, by R. G. Morton, and engraved on stone by Neusam, is prefixed to Clay's "Annals," quoted above, 1st ed., 1835, and is inserted in the 2d ed. opposite p. 118. His wife, Hannah, died of yellow fever, in Philadelphia, Sept. 29, 1797, aged 48 years, two months, and is buried in the old Gloria Dei churchyard, in South Second Street.

COOK FAMILY.

The name Ellis Cook appears in the records of Morris county at a very early date. Mary, wife of Ellis Cooke (so the name is spelled on her tombstone in the Hanover graveyard), died April 19, 1754, aged thirty-eight years. Ellis Cook Esq'r "departed this life April 7th, 1797 In the 66th Year of his Age." Margret Griswould, wife of "Coll. Ellis Cooke," died March 15, 1777, aged forty-one years and three months. A tombstone was erected in the same graveyard in 1860, by their descendants, to the memory of "Ellis Cook, a Captain in the Revolutionary Army who died A. D. 1832, and of Isabella Cook, his wife who died A. D. 1825." According to local tradition, Ellis Cook was the "original blacksmith" of Whippanong township, whose shop occupied the site of the old Academy. In 1772, Ellis Cook kept a tavern in Hanover. The foregoing are evidently of three generations. During the Revolutionary period, Ellis Cook was very prominent in public affairs. He was elected a member of the Committee of Observation of Morris county, January 9, 1775, and on May 1 he was elected one of the delegates for said county, they being vested with power of legislation, and to raise men, money and arms for the common defense. He served as a member of the Provincial Congress in May, June, August and October, from Morris county, and was a member of the Committee of Safety which sat at New Brunswick from January 10 to March 2, 1776. At a meeting of the Committee of Safety on January 13, 1776, the Committee of Morris county applied to have Ellis Cook commissioned Lieutenant-Colonel of the Eastern Regiment of Militia in that county, and a commission was ordered to be issued to him accordingly. The Provincial Congress, which sat at New Brunswick in February and March of the same year, ordered that £1. 6s. 8d. be paid to Ellis Cook, Esquire, in full of his account for removing the records in the Surveyor-General's office at Perth Amboy to New Brunswick. He was a member of the Provincial Congress of New Jersey which met at Burlington June 10, 1776, and which adopted the Constitution of New Jersey, July 2, 1776. On July 18, 1776, he was appointed Lieutenant-Colonel of the battalion to be raised in Morris county. He was elected a member of the Assembly for Morris county in the years 1776, 1777, 1779, 1781-1792, and was appointed one of the Judges of the Morris county courts, 1793-1795.

The will of Ellis Cook, of Hanover, Morris county, yeoman, dated March 11, 1756, was proved Aug. 31, 1756. He devises to William and Ellis, his two eldest sons, "all my whole estate, Plantation and movable estate," to be equally shared; to his sons Jonathan, Epaphras and John, £10 each when 21. Executors—sons William and Ellis. Witnesses—Jonathan Squire, Thomas Bigelow and William Dixon.—*N. J. Wills*, Liber F., f. 404. No inventory is on file or of record at Trenton. It will be observed that he makes no mention of wife. Her tombstone in the Presbyterian churchyard at Hanover says: "Here lieth ye Body of Mary wife of Ellis Cooke Dec'd April ye 19 1754 Aged 38 Years." This Ellis Cook, b. 1703, was a son of Abiel[3] Abiel[2] Ellis[1], of Southampton, L. I. His mother was Martha Cooper. He m. Mary, dau. of John Williams. He removed about 1744-5, with his father-in-law, from Southampton to Hanover, Morris county. He seems to have had brothers Abiel, Samuel, Lemuel, Zebulon, Matthew, Abraham. He is said to have been killed at Fort Oswego, 1756. Issue:

      i.   William, b. 1734; m. Sarah Cocker, June 5, 1755. He was the father of Captain Ellis Cook, mentioned above, who d. in 1832. William Cook (was he the same, or of a later generation) m. Margaret Cooper, Feb. 12, 1778.

2.   ii. Ellis.

      iii. Jonathan, m. Margaret Tappan, Nov. 30, 1757.

      iv. Epaphras, m. Sarah Smith, Oct. 4, 1762. Epaphras Cook and Charlotte his wife were received into the Presbyterian church at Morristown, from the Hanover church, July 25, 1822, and were dismissed May 4, 1829, to New York. He was doubtless of a later generation.

      v.   John, m. Sarah Parrott. John Cook, of Pequannock, m. Jane Peer, of the same place, Oct. 14, 1772. Was this the son of Ellis?

2. Ellis[2] Ellis[1] Cook, b. 1732. m. Margaret Griswould Cocker, (b. Dec. 15, 1735), July 12, 1753; d April 7, 1797, in the 66th year of his age, according to his tombstone at Hanover; she d. March 15, 1777, aged 41 years and 3 months. Her tombstone sets forth that

      Here lies one bereav'd of Life,
      A Tender Mother and a Loving wife;
      Kind to Relations & a faithful friend
      Happy in her beginning, no doubt so in her end.

The very useful and distinguished career of Col. Cook has been narrater above. He m. 2d, Lucy (Ely) Perkins, who was received into

COOK FAMILY

membership in the Hanover church, Jan 12, 1791. His will, dated April 6, 1797, sets forth that he was at the time "infirm in body," which might be inferred from the fact that the instrument was proved on the 25th of the same month. In his will he provides that his wife Lucy should "furnish my son George Whitfield with clothing, &c., from her right of dower." He devises to son Jabez a tract of land "opposite my dwelling house, bounded by Mathew Kitchel, Samuel Merry, Passaick river and road, except a meadow; also my tract in Essex county joining Aaron Beach, Isaac Winans and others." Sons Zebulon, James and Ambrose "to share equally all the rest of my real estate, in Morris and Essex counties." To daughters Margaret Kitchel, Matilda Plumb and Rulatte Gregory, £10 each. "My son Ambrose to take my son George Whitfield and bring him up and instruct him in the Practice of Physic, and Ambrose to be paid £25 annually until George Whitfield is 21." Executors—Aaron Kitchell, Prudden Alling, James Cook. Witnesses—(Dr.) John Darcy, William Cook, Epaphrus Cook. The "Inventory of Coll. Ellis Cook Esqr," April 12, 1797, footed up £602, 14, 4, as appraised by Enoch Beach and David Bedford.—*N. J Wills*, Liber No. 37, p. 228. Issue:

 i. Jabez.

 ii. Zebulon, b. March 22, 1755; m. Mary Jones, Feb. 15, 1775; d. Dec. 12, 1810; she was b. May 20, 1758; d. April 14, 1830.

 iii. James, b. Mar. 25, 1760; m. 1st, Elizabeth P. Condit, Nov. 25, 1781; 2d, Ruth Pierson, Aug. 3, 1786; he d. March 26, 1836: he lived at Succasunna.

 iv. Ambrose. "Doctor Ambrose Cook and Miss Sally P. Wheeler" were married June 27, 1794. He d. in Monmouth county.

 v. Margaret, m. William Kitchell, of Hanover.

 vi. Matilda, m. David Plumb, Feb. 27, 1794. He was of Newark.

 vii. Rulatte (called Lotta), m. William O. Gregory, Sept. ---, 1792; he was of Newburgh, N. Y.

 viii. Elizabeth, d. Sept. 30, 1780, aged 1 yr. 4 mos. 2 days.

 ix. George Whitfield, bap. 1790 or 1791. In accordance with the terms of his father's will he was brought up a physician, and practiced in Hudson, N. Y.

Another Ellis Cook, of Bottle Hill (now Madison), m. Sarah Wortman, Sept. 28, 1789. He was of Hanover when he made his will, April 7, 1801, which was proved Aug. 5, 1807. In this instrument he gives to wife Sarah £60 in lieu of dower; to daughter Keziah Morris £70, New York money; to daughter Mary Miller, wife of John Miller, £70; to daughter Sarah Ward, wife of Israel Ward, £70; to grandson Ellis Morris, £30, when twenty-one years of age; to grandson Ellis Thompson, £30; to "grandson Benjamin Cook, son of my son Benjamin, in fee, all houses, lands and tenements in Morris County, if he shall live to twenty-one years, otherwise to be divided among surviving grandchildren allowing two shares of the whole to the daughters or daughter of my son Benjamin Cook, deceased, and the remainder in equal shares among the children of my three daughters Keziah Morris, Mary Miller and Sarah Ward, share and share alike;" to "daughter-in-law, Sarah Cook, widow of my son Benjamin Cook, deceased, all the use of the real estate herein devised to her son Benjamin Cook, and to bring up the children of my said son Benjamin, deceased, during her widowhood; in case of her marriage, his executors to take charge of the same;" residue of estate to be divided among surviving children as they shall arrive at the age of twenty-one years. Executors—Sons-in-law Luke Miller, John Morris and Israel Ward. Witnesses—John Donington, Jonathan Richards and John Blanchard. A codicil, dated August 5, 1807, gives to wife Sarah £100 additional. Witnesses—Archibald Sayre, John Blanchard.—*Morris County Wills*, Liber A, p. 236. According to the late Prof. George H. Cook, State Geologist of New Jersey, this Ellis Cook, of Bottle Hill, was a son of John Cook, of Southampton, and was 80 years old at the time of his death. He had a brother Obadiah, of Halseytown, Morris county, whose brother-in-law, Joel Halsey, was named as his executor in 1765.

All these Cooks were descendants of Ellis Cook, m. Martha, dau. of John Cooper, who was one of the "undertakers" or settlers of Southampton, L. I., 1640; d. 1679 at Southampton. Issue:

John, Ellis, Martha, Elizabeth, Mary, Abiel.

Abiel had children: Josiah, Frances, Abiel 2d.

Abiel 2d d. 1740 at Southampton, having had children: Abiel 3d; Samuel, d. at Shrewsbury, N. J., 1745; Ellis, b. 1703, d. 1756, who settled in Hanover, Morris county, as above stated; Phebe, Susannah, m. ⸺ Barton, and lived with nephew Abiel in N. J.; Matthew, d. in N. J.; Zebulon, settled at Freehold, N. J.; Lemuel, Abigail, Anna.

Abiel 3d m. ⸺ Leonard; he located in Monmouth county in 1720. Children: Abiel 4th; Sarah, m. Aaron Mattison, April, 1745; Nathaniel, m. ⸺ Robins; Frances, m. Samuel Mount, 1755; Susannah, m. ⸺ Imlay; Mary, m. Jonathan Lippincott, 1757; Phebe, m. Peter Dewitt, 1767; Abigail, m. ⸺ Strickland.

Abiel 4th, b. Nov. 15, 1723; m. Mary, dau. of Samuel Thompson, June, 1765; d. Jan. 24, 1797. Children: Sarah, William, Susannah, Samuel, Elizabeth, Nathaniel, Hannah, b. 1775, m. the Rev. Joseph Stephens, pastor of the Baptist church at Freehold, 1789-1793, d. 1817.

REV. SAMUEL COOKE.

The Rev. Samuel Cooke, a graduate of Caius College, Cambridge, was appointed by the Society for the Propagation of the Gospel in Foreign Parts to succeed the Rev. Thomas Thompson as missionary to the Episcopal churches in Monmouth county, and arrived there in September, 1751. He attended a Convention of the Episcopal clergy of Pennsylvania in 1760, and was recognized as an influential member of his denomination in New Jersey. He continued in charge of the Episcopal churches in Shrewsbury, Freehold and Middletown until the Revolution. He sailed with the Rev. Myles Cooper and the Rev. T. B. Chandler, on May 24, 1775, for Bristol, England. On his return he took up his residence in New York, where he became a deputy chaplain to the Guards. In 1785 he settled at Frederickton, New Brunswick, as the first Rector of the church at that place. In 1791 he was Commissary to the Bishop of Nova Scotia. He was drowned in crossing the river St. John, in a birch bark canoe, in 1795. His wife was Graham, daughter of Michael Kearny, of Perth Amboy; she d. at Shrewsbury, Sept. 23, 1771. His son perished with him. Lydia, his fifth daughter, died at Frederickton in 1846, aged 76; Isabella, bap. July 19, 1767, and the last survivor of the family, died at the same city in 1848. She was the widow of Col. Harris William Hales.

COTTNAM

ABRAHAM COTTNAM.

Abraham Cottnam was licensed as an attorney and counsellor-at-law of New Jersey at the November Term, 1746, of the Supreme Court. He married a daughter of Joseph Warrell, Attorney-General of the Province, 1733-1754, and in 1751 was deputed by him to prosecute the pleas of the Crown in Middlesex county. He married, second, by license dated June 11th, 1764, Elizabeth Ann Pearce. She was a daughter of Edward Pearce and Catharine, his wife, widow of Robert Talbot, and daughter of Jeremiah Basse, one of the last Governors of West Jersey. His residence was probably the place known as Doud's Dale, or "Downdale," near Trenton, on the Hopewell road," on the Pennington road, near Calhoun street, in the northern part of Trenton. By deed dated Nov. 6, 1766, Cottnam bought of Dr. Thomas Cadwalader, of Philadelphia, and wife Hannah, a tract of thirty-eight acres at Maidenhead, on the south side of Shabbacunk creek.—*Liber Y of Deeds, in office of Secretary of State*, fol. 270. In the latter part of his life he removed to what is now the northwest corner of Warren and Bank streets, Trenton, this property becoming, after his death, the inn of Rensselaer Williams. His sons continued in the house at "Doud's Dale," and purchased it from the executors, by deed dated April 20, 1779.—*Liber AL of Deeds*, f. 423. His will, dated December 16, 1775, proved February 12, 1776, appoints his wife Eliza Ann, the Honble Daniel Coxe, Esqre, his son-in-law Robert Hoops, and his son George Cottnam, executors, with Wm Pidgeon as advisor. His eldest son, Warrell Cottnam, is bequeathed £30, to be laid out for him by the executors, in "fitting him to go to sea or for any other rational purpose," at the discretion of the executors; "but I beg and entreat my other children, if in their power, that they will not see him want the common necessaries of life, but never to be security for him for any sum of money nor trust him with more money at a time, than will be sufficient for immediate subsistence." The will also mentions daughter Martha, wife of Robert Hoops, and niece Charity Lee. His son George receives "his mother's family pedigree roll by his mother's side being of the Bradshaw family." The wife is given all the books "that belonged to her mother, Mrs. Catherine Peirce," whose heiress-at-law she was. The will also devises the homestead, a meadow-lot of five acres, bought of Samuel Tucker at Sheriff's sale, and other land held on a long lease under a ground-rent of £3 per acre; also bequeaths personal estate: negro slaves, law books (at the house and also in the hands of Isaac Allen and Dr. John Coxe, claimed under will of Joseph Warrell, senior), pictures ("of my brother and of the Warrell family"), china, a gold watch, and a silver coffee pot. Witnesses—Wm. Pidgeon, Benj. Smith and R. L. Hooper.—*W. J. Wills*, Lib. 17, fol. 295. Abraham Cottnam had two sons, Warrell and George. It is to be inferred from his father's will that the older son was irregular in his habits. The younger was licensed as an attorney, May, 1780. A company of Hessian soldiers was quartered in the house of Warrell Cottnam previous to their capture by Washington on December 26, 1776. The two sons occupied the paternal residence until 1779, when they sold it to Captain (afterwards Chief Justice) David Brearley.—*Vroom's Supreme Court Rules*; *N. J. Archives*, VII., 613; *Ibid.*, XX., 248; *Ibid.*, XXII., 76; *Ibid.*, Second Series, I., 59, 79, 178, 382; *Hall's Hist. Pres. Church in Trenton*, 238; *Stryker's Trenton One Hundred Years Ago*, 6; *Stryker's Battles of Trenton and Princeton*, 119.

COWELL FAMILY.

The Cowell family of Trenton came from Dorchester, Mass., where was born (1704) David Cowell. He graduated at Harvard in 1732, and was installed, November 3, 1736, as the first pastor of the Presbyterian church of Trenton, where he continued until his death, at Trenton, December 1, 1760. He was prominent in the community and in the councils of his church, and appears to have been successful as a pastor. He left no issue. In his will, dated November 29, 1760, proved January 24, 1761, the Rev. David Cowell makes his brother, Ebenezer Cowell, of New England, his residuary legatee. He also mentions nephew, David Cowell, student at Nassau Hall; sisters Anna Fisher and Martha Blake; Margaret, widow of brother Joseph, and now wife of Richard Fisher; Samuel Cowell and Olive Haws, children of said brother.

Ebenezer Cowell, his residuary legatee, probably removed from New England to Trenton soon after this. Between 1765 and 1775 he acquired extensive tracts of land in West Jersey, including a share in a Propriety of that Division, most of which lands he disposed of in the same period. In 1765 he appears to have been living at Changewater, Hunterdon county. He was a Deputy Surveyor of West Jersey in 1774, and in 1782-1784 was of the Committee (Council?) of the West Jersey Proprietors. He is designated in the conveyances as a "yeoman," or "surveyor." From other circumstances he appears to have been a smith, working principally on guns, swords, locks and perhaps surveyors' instruments. In 1776 he advertised for gunsmiths, and offered to instruct others in the art of repairing guns for the American army. He was engaged in this work during the American occupancy of Trenton and vicinity, and employed many helpers, whom he paid out of his own pocket, often waiting many months before being reimbursed for his outlays, but did it gladly, for his love for the American cause. The British showed their resentment by ransacking his house when they entered Trenton after the famous battle at that place, December 26, 1776. In 1791 he was living in Philadelphia. He returned to Trenton, where he died May 4, 1799, his will, dated February 27, 1799, being proved May 11, 1799. In this will he devises house lot in Trenton, adjoining Doan's lot, a house and lot next to the preceding, lot on the south side of Market street, Trenton, an orchard lot of four acres in Trenton, house and lot in Springet lane, Philadelphia. Witnesses— Peter Gordon, A. Chambers, I. E. Spencer. His children were:

     i. David, graduated from Princeton in 1763; studied medicine in Philadelphia, and settled in Northampton, Bucks county, Penna. By deed, October 1, 1767, Ebenezer Cowell, yeoman, of Trenton, conveyed to him 503 acres in Knowlton township, Sussex county, West Jersey; on March 3, 1768, his father conveyed to him two houses and a lot in Trenton on the north side of Second street; also two other lots in or near Trenton, and a tract of 400 acres in Sussex county, on Paulin's Kiln. It is probable that soon after the last named conveyances Dr. David Cowell removed to Trenton, where he practiced until his death, of quinsy, Dec. 18, 1783. For two years he was senior physician and surgeon in military hospitals in the American army. In his will, dated Dec. 17, 1783, proved Dec. 30, 1783, he mentions children of his brother Joseph, and his sister Sally. He gives £100 to Congress, if they will settle at Lamberton (a suburb of Trenton), £100 to

COWELL FAMILY

the College of New Jersey, and £100 to the Grammar
School in Trenton. He was evidently unmarried.

ii. Ebenezer, of whom hereafter.

iii. John, studied medicine, and served as a Surgeon of
Militia in 1779. On the death of his brother David he
advertised in the *New Jersey Gazette* "that he had been
prevailed upon by the friends of his deceased brother
to establish himself as a physician in Trenton." He
died January 30, 1789, in his 30th year, according to
his tombstone, as cited by Dr. Hall, but his will, not
dated, was proved January 28, 1789, or two days before his death. The date on the tombstone is evidently incorrect. In the will he names wife Mary,
and children John and Mary, both under age. These
children are also mentioned in the will of their grandfather, Ebenezer Cowell. in 1799.

iv. Joseph, married Catherine Case, marriage license dated
January 19, 1769; died at Trenton, Sept. 30, 1808,
aged 63 years.

v.   Robert, died at Trenton, July 5, 1808.

vi. Eunice, died at Broadway, Warren county, N. J., July
30, 1829, unmarried. In her father's will she was
named as sole executrix. Over her grave, in the
Mansfield cemetery, near Washington, N. J., is a
large horizontal marble slab, inscribed with the date
of her death, and her age, 80 years.

vii. Lois, twin sister of Eunice. The tombstone over the
grave of Eunice states that it is in memory "also of
Lois, twin sister of Eunice Cowell, who departed this
life Septr. 9, 1793, whose remains were deposited in
the grounds of the 2d Presbyterian church in Arch
street, Philadelphia."

viii. Sarah, married Thomas Bowlby, doubtless a relative of
John Bowlby, of Sussex county, who by deed dated
July 12, 1765, conveyed to Ebenezer Cowell the right
to 500 acres of unappropriated land in West Jersey.
She d. April 16, 1826, in her 83d year. She is buried
beside her sister Eunice, in the Mansfield cemetery,
near Washington, Warren county. Her husband d.
Jan. 8, 1827, aged 82 yrs. 9 mos. 6 days; he was a
son of John[2] Thomas[1] Bowlby, and lived in Bethlehem
township, Hunterdon county.

Ebenezer Cowell, 2d, having graduated from Princeton College in
1766, studied law, probably with Abraham Cottnam, of Trenton, and
was licensed as an attorney November 30, 1769. The notices of him in
the records are scanty. On July 18, 1776, he presented a petition to the
Provincial Congress, complaining that John Barnes, Sheriff of Hunterdon county, had refused to receive and execute two writs issued under
the authority of the people of the State of New Jersey. Barnes admitted that he was unwilling to recognize the validity of the new government and was superseded. In joint meeting the Legislature on
Septemeb 7, 1773, appointed young Cowell clerk of Hunterdon county.
He died in Trenton, on the night of February 14-15, 1817. The following notice of his death. in the *Trenton Federalist*, of Feb. 17, 1817,
suggests a sad ending of a once promising career:

"Died. In this city on the night of the 14th inst. Ebenezer Cowell
Esq. formerly clerk of the pleas of Hunterdon Co. On the morning of

the 15th he was found dead in the house, where he resided, and probably perished in consequence of the severity of the weather."

He was probably about seventy years of age. As he died intestate, Samuel Bowlby and Abner Parke were appointed administrators of his estate. Their inventory and appraisement, taken March 5, 1817, indicates that Cowell had not prospered greatly in this world's goods. The following is the list and valuation of his personal property:

one Chest with Sundry Books and papers,	20 00
Six Iron pots and Cittles,	3 00
Three Jugs,	20
Two Pails and 1 Saddle,	50
Three Chairs,	1 00
Two Tables and 2 Boxes,	50
one Survayers Chair,	2 00
a Lot of oald Tin and Iron,	50
Half Barrel and Kug,	50
Two pairs of Saddle Bags and 1 Bed Stid,	1 00
Eight Volumes of the Statu of great Britain,	50 00
	77 10

The inventory actually foots up $79.20. No record has been found of the marriage of Mr. Cowell. On September 11, 1820, commissioners were appointed by the Supreme Court to divide the lands of Ebenezer Cowell, deceased, to wit: a tract conveyed Feb. 11, 1782, by Ebenezer Cowell the elder to Ebenezer Cowell junior: also a tract of land formerly known by the name of Doud's Dale, beginning at a corner by the road leading from Trenton to Hopewell, etc., containing ten acres; and a lot adjoining the last described, containing three and a quarter acres, conveyed by Elizabeth Ann Cottnam, executrix, and Robert Hoops Esquire and George Cottnam, executors of Abraham Cottnam, Esq., deceased, June 25, 1775, unto Ebenezer Cowell, junior, in fee simple. The lands were divided amongst John V. Cowell, Thomas Mitchell and Mary his wife, Sarah Bowlby, Eunice Cowell, the children of Dr. John Cowell, and the children and heirs of Joseph Cowell. John V. Cowell and Mary Mitchell were probably the children of Dr. John Cowell. Further genealogical details are supplied by a deed dated June 22, 1818, recorded in the Hunterdon County Clerk's office, Book 31, p. 100, from Thomas Bowlby and Sarah his wife; Eunice Cowell; John Cowell and Margaret his wife; Thomas Mitchell and Mariah his wife; Joshua Emlen and Catharine his wife; Robert Goodwin and Mary his wife, Samuel Cowell and Margaret his wife, John Cowell and Margare this wife, and Sarah Jones, heirs-at-law of Ebenezer Cowell, senior, deceased—to Joseph Cowell (wife's name Deborah), one of the heirs. —*West Jersey Wills, Liber* 10, p. 589; *Ibid.,* No. 27, p. 490; *Ibid.,* No. 32, p. 8; *Ibid.,* No. 33, p. 455; *Conveyances in Secretary of State's Office, Trenton;* Hall's *Hist. Pres. Church in Trenton,* passim; Wickes's *Hist. of Medical Men of N. J.,* 219, 220; 2 *N. J. Archives,* I., 543; *Cowell MSS.,* unpublished, in the collection of William Nelson; *Minutes Provincial Congress,* 513; *Minutes Supreme Court.*

DANIEL COXE, First, Second, Third, Fourth and Fifth.

The *first* Daniel Coxe of whom we have record was of Stoke Newington, England, and died in 1686.—*Penn. Hist. Mag.,* VII., 317.

He left a son, the *second* Daniel Coxe, born 1640 or 1641, died January 19, 1730, in his ninetieth year. The latter was one of the most eminent physicians of his day, a prolific writer on chemistry and medicine, and

DANIEL COXE—Second and Third

was physician to Charles II., and afterwards to Queen Anne. Although he never came to America, he acquired large possessions in New Jersey, and was at least nominally Governor of the Province, 1687-1691. By sundry deeds, 1686-1691, Dr. Coxe acquired from the heirs of Edward Byllinge all their interest in West Jersey, together with the right of government, and thus became the largest proprietor in that division, owning twenty-two shares of Propriety, estimated at more than 600,000 acres. He appointed Edward Hunloke to be Deputy Governor for him. Owing to various complications he conveyed, March 4, 1691, most of his West Jersey rights to a large number of citizens of London, who associated themselves together as "The West Jersey Society," which still exists, although its property has been long ago disposed of.— *Smith's Hist. N. J.*, 190; *Proceedings West Jersey Surveyors' Association*, 118-127; *N. J. Archives*, II., 10, 41-72; *Proceedings New Jersey Historical Society, Third Series*, VI., 129-135. Some of his published letters indicate that he was actuated by the highest motives in his conduct regarding the people of West Jersey.—*Smith's Hist. N. J.*, 190, note; *N. J. Archives*, II., 96. He also acquired title to a tract, imperial in its dimensions, lying between latitude 31 degrees and latitude 36 degrees, and extending from the Atlantic to the Pacific, which he spent a fortune in exploring, his vessels being the first to ascend the Mississippi from its mouth. This was called *Carolana*. He was a staunch Church of England man, interesting himself in establishing that church in West Jersey, near Cape May.—*Penn. Mag.*, V., 114; VII., 317-26.

The *third* Daniel Coxe was the Doctor's eldest son, and was baptized in London, August 31, 1673.—*Ib.*, VII., 326. Although he joined with other proprietors in recommending Andrew Hamilton for Governor (N. J. Archives, II., 376, 410), he seems to have been a favorite of Lord Cornbury, whom he probably accompanied to America in 1702, and by whom he was appointed Commander of the forces in West Jersey.— *N. J. Archives*, III., 35, 42, 44. He was thereafter known as "Colonel" Coxe. He doubtless returned to England after a very short stay here, for in 1704 he was in London, waging a vigorous defense against the attacks of some of the New Jersey Proprietaries.—*Ib.*, 35. His answer is far more dignified and admirable in tone than their criticisms He regrets that he had been proposed (entirely without his knowledge, he says) for the Council, and is entirely willing that someone else shall be appointed. He declares that his father asserts that he had not conveyed all his lands to the West Jersey Society, but had reserved large tracts.—*Ib.*, 39. He had been recommended in 1702 by the Earl of Nottingham and by the Earl of Clarendon for a seat in the new Governor's Council of New Jersey. —*N. J. Archives*, II., 486, 502. In 1705 he was again recommended by Lord Cornbury, and notwithstanding the hostility of the Quakers he was appointed in 1706, and soon after sailed for America, when Lord Cornbury appointed him one of the associate Judges of the Supreme Court of the Province.—*N. J. Archives*, III., 35, 78, 84, 125, 132; *Vroom's Supreme Court Rules*, 47. In the year following (1707), notwithstanding his hostility to Quakers in general, he made an exception in favor of Sarah, the presumably pretty daughter of John Eckley, a Quaker, of Philadelphia, with whom he eloped, being married to her by Lord Cornbury's chaplain, who most opportunely *happened* to be on hand, "between two and three o'clock in the morning, on the Jersey side, under a tree by fire light." The gallant bridegroom was then a "fine flaunting gentleman."—*Watson's Annals*, I., 50. Two days later (May 10, 1707) the young bride (she was but 17) was christened by the Rev. John Sharpe, the chaplain aforesaid.—*Penna. Magazine*, XXIII., 105. On the arrival of

DANIEL COXE—Third and Fourth

Lord Lovelace, in 1708, as Governor of New Jersey, Colonel Coxe was again named as one of the Council.—*N. J. Archives*, III., 316. He did not get along so well with Governor Hunter, at whose request he was removed from the Council in 1713.—*Ib.*, IV., 149, 182. He was elected to the Assembly in 1714, by the "Swedish vote" (N. Y. Col. Docs., V., 399, 404), and again in February, 1716, from the county of Gloucester and from the town of Salem, both, although Sheriff William Harrison, of Gloucester, was accused of having resorted to sharp practice to secure his defeat, by removing the polls several miles from the usual place. Colonel Coxe declared to serve for Gloucester, instead of Salem, and being chosen Speaker, April 4, complained of Sheriff Harrison on the 26th, and had the satisfaction of publicly reprimanding him, by order of the House. His triumph was short-lived, for Governor Hunter immediately prorogued the Assembly until May 7. The Governor's opponents in the House appear to have purposely staid away, in the hope of preventing a quorum, but by May 21 the Governor's friends got thirteen members together, and having a quorum they elected John Kinsey Speaker, in the absence of Colonel Coxe, and then coolly proceeded to expel the Colonel and the other anti-administration members for non-attendance, declaring them, moreover, ineligible to re-election, and when some of them were notwithstanding again returned, they were again expelled.—*MS. Minutes of Assembly in State Library, Trenton.* Colonel Coxe sailed the ensuing July for England, where he agitated vigorously during 1717 and 1718 for the removal of Governor Hunter, and appears to have had some idea of securing the succession for himself.—*N. Y. Col. Docs.*, V., 482; *N. J. Archives*, IV., 267, 299. While thus retired from official life, the Colonel directed his attention to literature, publishing in 1722 a description of "Carolana," which was republished in 1727 and 1741.—*Stevens's Historical Nuggets*, I., 199, 200. In this work he proposes a remarkably comprehensive plan for a Union of the British Colonies in America, much similar to that adopted 145 years later for the Dominion of Canada. Franklin commended it to the Albany convention of 1754. In 1725 he ran for the Assembly in Burlington, where the Sheriff adopted in his behalf the device of Sheriff Harrison some years before in Gloucester.—*N. Y. Col. Docs.*, V., 767. In 1730 he received a commission as Provincial Grand Master for New York, New Jersey and Pennsylvania, he being the first on the Continent to be thus honored.—*Hough's Historical Sketch of Free Masonry in New Jersey*, prefixed to Grand Lodge Proceedings, 1787-1857, VII. In 1734 he was again appointed, by Governor Cosby, to be third Judge of the Supreme Court, which office he held thereafter until his death.—*Vroom's Sup. Ct. Rules*, 47; *Lewis Morris Papers*, 48. He was a man of great business energy and enterprise. For several years prior to 1725 he was interested in the iron works on Black's creek, Burlington County.—*Swank's Iron in All Ages*, 2d ed., 1892, 157. The lands conveyed to him by his father occasioned him no little trouble, and when he asserted his ownership to the 30,000 acres and the 15,000 acres in Hopewell and Maidenhead, he was threatened with assassination.—*N. J. Archives*, XI., 400, 431. Most of his life in America had been spent at Burlington, but during his later years he lived at Trenton, where he died April 25, 1739, and was buried at St. Mary's Church, Burlington.—*Hills's Hist. of the Church in Burlington*, 255; *Dr. Hall's Hist. Pres. Church in Trenton*, 236. His wife died June 25, 1725, aged 35 years.

The *fourth* Daniel Coxe was the Colonel's eldest son. He appears to have led an uneventful life, but few notices of him appearing among contemporary records. In 1746 he was named as one of the Burgesses in the first charter of the borough and town of Trenton.—*Book AAA of*

DANIEL COXE—Fourth and Fifth

Commissions, in Secretary of State's Office, Trenton, fol. 266. During the rioting in 1747 he was naturally identified with the Proprietary party.—*N. Y. Col. Docs.,* VI., 345. His will, dated January 25, 1750, names his wife, Abigail, daughter, Grace Coxe, and son, Daniel Coxe, the latter being evidently a minor at this time. The will was proven January 21, 1758.—*Liber No. 8 of Wills, in Secretary of State's Office,* Trenton, fol. 536. His "acting Executors," Abigail Coxe, Grace Coxe and William Pidgeon, advertised in the *Pennsylvania Gazette,* of Feb. 2, 1760, for sale, his plantation, Bellemont, where he had lived, comprising 1,320 acres, on the Delaware River, about twelve miles from Trenton, with a fine mansion, with four rooms on a floor, and fire places. Also "two Negroes, a Man and Woman." He controlled a ferry and a fishery at the same place.—*N. J. Archives,* XX., 175. He had a great deal of trouble with the settlers of Hopewell, about their title, which they claimed under a deed from his grandfather, but which he disputed. There was much litigation, and he said his life was threatened by the tenants whom he ejected.

His son, the *fifth* Daniel Coxe, was probably born April 1, 1741. He studied law, and was licensed as an Attorney and Counsellor March 20, 1761, and as a Sergeant Nov. 15, 1772.—*Vroom's Sup. Ct. Rules,* 59, 54. In the fall of 1767 he sailed with his wife and his brother-in-law, John Tabor Kempe, Attorney-General of New York (who had married Grace Coxe), for England, where they managed to get their Carolana claims adjusted by accepting instead extensive grants of land in Western New York.—*Duer's Life of Lord Stirling,* 89; *Cal. N. Y. Land Papers,* 467 et seqq. In a letter dated Burlington, January 14, 1771, to the Earl of Hillsborough, Gov. William Franklin recommends for two vacant seats in the Council "two Gentlemen, who are in every respect the best qualified to serve His Majesty in that Capacity of any I am at Liberty to mention. One is Daniel Coxe Esqr. of Trenton. . . . He was lately in England, and had I hear the Honour of being personally known to your Lordship. . . . He is a member of the Church of England." He was appointed by order of the King in Council, May 1. 1771.—*N. J. Archives,* X., 225, 273, 275. He took his seat in the Council at Burlington, Nov. 21, 1771.—*Ib.,* XVIII., 259-260. The minutes of the Council show that after his appointment in 1771 he was regular and faithful in his attendance until the close of that body's existence in 1775.—*Ib.,* XVIII., passim. He was a zealous Tory, and in a letter dated July 4, 1775, viewed with prophetic foresight the cruel plight to which such as he would be reduced. "What then have men of Property not to fear and apprehend, and particularly those who happen and are known to differ in sentiment from the generality? They become a mark at once for popular Fury, and those who are esteemed Friends to Government devoted for Destruction.—They are not even allowed to preserve a neutrality, and passiveness becomes a Crime."—*Ib.,* X., 654. Even the burning of his handsome residence at Trenton by the British, during their pursuit of Washington in December, 1776 (5 American Archives, II., 1376), did not impair his attachment to the Royal cause, for in 1778 he went to New York, where he remained till the close of the war, serving as Chairman of an Association of Refugees. Christopher Sower maliciously says he "was appointed to the chair to deprive him of the opportunity of speaking, as he has the gift of saying little with many words."—*Sabine's Loyalists,* I., 339. In June, 1779, he wrote to Joseph Galloway that he was confident the end of the Rebellion would come that Summer.—*Hist. Mag.,* June, 1862, 181. He married, June 5, 1771, Sarah, daughter of Dr. John Redman, of Philadelphia.—*Records Christ Church, 2 Penn. Archives,* II., 68. Dr. Redman was a surgeon in the American Army during the Revolution, and appears to have kept his daughter and her children with him much if not most of the time during the war. She was evidently in Philadelphia when Coxe wrote to Galloway in 1779. In 1780 she was again with her father.—*Penn. Col. Records*, XII., 390. In December of that year Coxe was Secretary to the British Commissioners appointed to receive and pardon repentant rebels, an office which proved a sinecure.—*Moore's Diary of the Revolution*, II., 378. In his petition to the British government, dated March 13, 1784, for reimbursement for his losses sustained in the war, he says that "owing to his loyalty," on the advance of the British army into the Jerseys, in December. 1776, "he was obliged hastily to withdraw himself and family into Pennsylvania to avoid an intended apprehension and imprisonment of his person. He left his dwelling house and estates in Trenton, completely furnished, as was his wont when he removed his family to Philadelphia in the winter season.

His houses, offices and estate were seized upon as quarters for the Hessian troops, who broke open his rooms, closets, stores and cellars, and every species of furniture, china, glass, liquors, etc., plundered and destroyed, or taken away, and the most wanton desolation committed on his property and estate in and about the town, a great part of which was totally burned and destroyed." He remained in Philadelphia until the British took possession of the city, when he offered his services to Sir William Howe, under whose commission he soon afterwards acted as a magistrate of police, for which service he was allowed at the rate of £300 per annum, sterling. He also zealously aided in raising a corps of officers and men called "The West Jersey Volunteers," from the refugees. He remained in Philadelphia until the evacuation by the British in 1778, and accompanied the army to New York, where he remained thereafter until the close of the war. "His wife and four children remained in Philadelphia, supported by the bounty of their friends and what little he could spare from his own allowance," until the summer of 1780, when they were banished thence, and joined him in New York, "at great hazard and peril." He acted on the Board of Associated Loyalists, "and at his own expense procured and furnished to the commanders-in-chief a variety of useful intelligence." In June, 1781, he was appointed Assistant Secretary to the British commissioners for restoring peace to the Colonies, and in December following became a member, and as such remained on duty until the evacuation of New York, receiving a salary of 20s. sterling a day. "In April, 1783, at the desire of Sir Guy Carleton, he also acted as a member of the Board constituted by him for settling and adjusting matters of debt, &c., and in several other confidential trusts connected with the same Board, which existed to nearly the time he left New York." Scheduled in his losses were the mansion house, offices and lands in Trenton, about two acres, on Second (now State) street, £900 sterling; brick tenement, office and gardens in Lower or Water street, £300; another tenement, office and garden in Second street, £300; about four acres adjoining the town lots, £150; Busy Cottage, adjoining the above, 56 acres, £900; 26¾ acres on College road, about two miles from Trenton, £210; 20 acres wood and timber lot, on Maidenhead road, two miles from Trenton, £180; Belmont Farm, 507 acres, on the Delaware river, ten miles from Trenton, above the Falls, including ferry patent, £1800; 230 acres adjoining same, on Smith's Ford, £300; 495 acres, being his Trenton ferry estate and patent, Douglas farm and Lamberton, just below Trenton Falls, £4,800; also extensive tracts in Sussex and Burlington counties, and great tracts in Tryon county, New York, etc., etc. His annual rents he placed at £3320. 6. 01½; bonds, furniture and other personal effects, and property destroyed by the Hessians at Trenton, including what was afterwards sold by the New Jersey commissioners of forfeited estates, £1802. 9. 9½; loss of professional income as a lawyer, "calculated at £400 per annum on an average, from the usurpation of the King's Government there in 1776, to 1784," £1920. Total, £40,267. 11. 6. On arriving in England he was allowed £200 per year, from Jan. 5, 1784, to be increased to £300 on the arrival of his wife and family. At the close of the war he went to England, whither his wife and children followed him, probably in 1784, as in 1783 she and her father and her children were given passports from Philadelphia to New York.—*Penn. Col. Records*, XIII., 551. She returned in 1806, to comfort her aged father and dying mother.—*Sabine's Loyalists*, I., 340. The *Gentleman's Magazine* announces the death of Mr. Coxe thus: "March 10, 1826. In Upper Seymour-st., aged 87, Daniel Coxe, esq." In 1828 his widow brought suits in New Jersey for her dower rights in his property which had been confiscated, and recovered judgment therefor.—*N. J. Law Reports*—4 Halsted, 378; 5 Halsted, 328; 6 Halsted, 395. She died at Brighton, England, in 1843, aged ninety-one.—*Sabine*, I., 340.

Some Coxe Genealogical Details

Daniel[3] Daniel[2] Daniel[1] Coxe and Sarah Eckley had issue:

    i. John[4], named as one of the executors of his father's will, in 1739. He was admitted to the New Jersey bar as an attorney and counsellor at the March term, 1735, and the Supreme Court records indicate that he was a lawyer of much prominence, but evidently of a testy disposition, illustrated by the fact that he threw up a case in chancery once, because, as he asserted, Governor Belcher, the Chancellor, was not disposed to give him justice. He was an extensive land owner, largely from his father. Among the properties held by him were the following: 257 acres adjoining and surrounding Oxford Furnace, timber and wood, valued in 1784 at £308. 8s.; four lots adjoining the mansion house, at Trenton, one acre; a plot of two rods thirty-two perches adjoining, bought by him Sept. 9, 1743, of Temperance Harrow, Anthony and William Morris; a quarter of an acre adjoining, bought by him of John Patterson, March 3, 1745. The will of John Coxe of Trenton, dated April 8, 1753, proved Aug. 8, 1753, names brothers Daniel Coxe and William Coxe; nephew Daniel Coxe, and niece Grace Coxe, children of brother Daniel; mentions that his father was deceased; leaves a legacy to Charles, "commonly called Charles Coxe," and names as executor brother William Coxe and Robert Lettis Hooper. Witnesses— David Cowell, Joseph Reed and Moore Furman.-- *West Jersey Wills*, Liber No. 7, p. 343. As he makes no allusion to wife or children, he doubtless died without lawful issue, and probably unmarried. He was one of the counsel retained to defend the Rev.

William Tennent, on his indictment for perjury, in 1743. The *Philadelphia Repository*, of Feb. 14, 1801, announces the marriage of Richard Coxe, son of Charles Coxe, Esq., of Sidney, N. J., and Miss Henrietta Sayre, of Philadelphia. Was this the Charles Coxe said in John Coxe's will to be "commonly so called"?

2.   ii.   William, b. 1723.

       iii. Rebecca; prob. unm., as in the will of William Coxe, 1801, he speaks of "my sister Rebecca Coxe." In 1784 she was "upwards of sixty years of age."

3.   iv. Daniel, m. Abigail ———. His will, dated Jan. 25, 1750, proved Jan. 21, 1758, names wife Abigail, and children Grace and Daniel, the latter evidently a minor.— *Wills*, Lib. No. 8, p. 536. His widow removed to England at the close of the Revolution, and in 1784 was residing at Brixton Causey, Surrey, England.

2. William[4] Daniel[3] Daniel[2] Daniel[1] Coxe, b. 1723; m. Mary, dau. of Tench and Elizabeth (Turbutt) Francis; d. at Burlington, Oct. 11, 1801, aged 78 yrs.; she d. Aug. 27, 1800, aged 70 yrs. He was engaged in mercantile business in Philadelphia for some years, and resided there when he was appointed Stamp Distributor for New Jersey, for the stamps to be issued under the obnoxious Stamp Act of 1765, but promptly and prudently resigned when his resignation was demanded by popular clamor. He was a vestryman of Christ Church, Philadelphia, 1766-1768. The will of William Coxe, senior, of the City of Burlington, dated Dec. 27, 1800, proved Oct. 12, 1801, (the day after his death) speaks of "wife deceased," and children John D. (to whom "lands in Carolana, New York State," are devised), Daniel W., William, Tench (who had removed to Lancaster, Pa.), Mary; John Tabor Kempe and Grace his wife; Thomas Force and Susannah his wife; grand-daughter Rebecca C. McIlvaine, and sister Rebecca Coxe. Executors—sons John D., William and Daniel. Witnesses—Wm. Louden, George Aaronson and Charles Kinsey. In a codicil, Jan. 19, 1801, he states that his daughter (Mary) was infirm, and he appoints his executors to look after her affairs until she was well. In another codicil, April 10, 1801, he mentions nephew, Wm. Tilghman; Edward Burd, of Philadelphia, had advanced money to Daniel W. Coxe, of Philadelphia, merchant, son of testator, and he makes provision to secure said Burd against loss.—*N. J. Wills*, Lib. No. 39, f. 385. Issue:

       i. John D.[5], b. Sept. 29, 1752; m. 1st, Aug. 27, 1789, Grace Riche; 2nd, May 2, 1792, Mary Footman. (Elizabeth Coxe, dau. of John and Mary Coxe, d. Aug. 10, 1796, aged 1 yr. 6 mos. Was she a child of John D. Coxe?)

4.   ii. Tench, b. May 22, 1755.

       iii. Elizabeth, b. Dec. 9, 1756.

       iv. Ann, b. Jan. 9, 1758.

       v. Rebecca, b. Feb. 3, 1760; m. Samuel Witham Stockton; bap. May 20, 1818, prob. when supposed to be mortally ill.

       vi. Mary, d. Dec. 17, 1804, aged 43 yrs., unm.

5.   vii. William, b. May 3, 176?.

       viii. (?) Sarah, m. William Mannington, at Burlington, Feb. 14, 1772. She is not mentioned, however, in the will of William Coxe, sen.; if she was his daughter she may have d. without issue before him.

COXE GENEALOGICAL

  ix.-xii. Unknown.
  6. xiii. Daniel, "13th Child of William & Mary Coxe, was born
      at Philadelphia Septr 20th 1769, and baptized at
      Sunbury in Bucks County, Januy 9th 1771"—accord-
      ing to the records of St. Mary's church, Burlington.

  3. Daniel[4] Daniel[3] Daniel[2] Daniel[1] Coxe and Abigail his wife had
issue:

    i. Grace[5], m. John Tabor Kempe, of New York, Feb. 20,
      1766, by marriage license of Gov. Franklin; the mar-
      riage is recorded in Christ church, Shrewsbury; the
      bride is described as of Trenton. He was a native of
      England, and was the son of William Kempe,
      Attorney-General of New York, 1753-1759, and upon
      the death of the latter in July, 1759, was appointed
      to succeed him as Attorney-General, July 30, 1759,
      although he had been admitted to the bar of New
      York so recently as October 4, 1758. He was re-
      appointed Oct. 30, 1761, and May 27, 1768, retaining
      the office until the Revolution. Immediately on his
      appointment he went to England, with a view to
      obtaining a better establishment and support for his
      office. He became one of the proprietors of 100,000
      acres of land granted to Daniel, William and Rebecca
      Coxe, John Tabor Kempe and Grace his wife, in ex-
      change for the Province of Carolana, owned by Col.
      Daniel[3] Coxe. In November, 1775, he was on the
      British ship, the "Duchess of Gordon," in the harbor
      of New York. In February, 1776, he was on the ship
      of war, "Asia," in Raritan bay, and while there he
      wrote a poem of six stanzas, to greet Cortlandt
      Skinner, Attorney-General of New Jersey, who like
      himself had openly adhered to the British cause. He
      was attainted of treason in New York and New Jer-
      sey, and his property confiscated. His furniture was
      sold by him at auction, in New York, in June, 1783,
      doubtless preparatory to his removal to England. He
      had previously sent his family, consisting of eleven
      persons, besides servants, to that country. He was
      killed by being thrown from his carriage, sometime
      after 1791. His widow d. April 12, 1831, at Clifton,
      county Gloucestershire, England. He is said to have
      left several children, all of whom d. without issue.
      The Gentleman's Magazine, Vol. 61, p. 679, London,
      1791, contains this announcement: "July 12, 1791.
      At Stanstead, Herts, Capt. Stephen George Church,
      of the royal navy, to Miss Marie Kempe, eldest
      daughter of Jn. Tabor K. esq. of St. Margaret's
      place, in same co." His dau. Anne d. at Clifton, in
      1838.

  7. ii. Daniel[5], a minor at the date of his father's will, in
      1750. He came of age, April 1, 1762.

  4. Tench[5] William[4] Daniel[3] Daniel[2] Daniel[1] Coxe, b. May 22, 1755; m.
1st, Catharine McCall, who d. s. p., July 22, 1778; he m. 2d, Rebecca
Coxe, dau. of Charles Coxe, of New Jersey; she d. in Philadelphia in
1806; he d. in that city, July 17, 1824. He studied for a time in the
College of Philadelphia, and then entered the mercantile house of his

88

father, where he remained until his majority, when he became a partner. When the British army invaded Pennsylvania, he joined them,
and entered Philadelphia with them. For this he was charged with
treason, but surrendered himself, and was discharged. He was elected
by the Pennsylvania Legislature to the Convention which met at Annapolis, September 14, 1786, and in 1788 was elected to the Continental
Congress. In May, 1789, he was appointed by Washington to be
Assistant Treasurer of the United States; and in May, 1792, Commissioner of the Revenue, a position he held until the close of Washington's administration. He seems to have been regarded with disfavor
by Hamilton in 1795. In 1803 he was appointed by President Jefferson,
Purveyor of the Public Supplies of the United States, which office he
retained until it was abolished, in 1812. He was a close student of
economics, and was active and efficient in promoting the study and
patronage of domestic industries. At 20 years of age he became a
member of the United Company of Philadelphia for Promoting American Manufactures. He was also one of the founders of the Pennsylvania Society for the Encouragement of Arts and Domestic Manufactures, in 1787, of which he was President. He published at least
thirteen . essays on subjects allied with manufactures, political
economy, etc., and his "View of the United States of America" (pp.
513), the most valuable summary up to that time of the resources, the
manufactures, and the possibilities of the country's development, published in Philadelphia in 1794, was republished in London and Dublin
in 1795. He was a manager of the Pennsylvania Hospital, 1780-81; a
warden of Christ church, Philadelphia, 1786-1787; a delegate to the
General Conventions of the Protestant Episcopal church in the United
States, in 1789. He was the father of Charles Sidney Coxe, b. July,
1791; admitted to the bar in 1812; appointed a judge of the District
Court for the city and county of Philadelphia, 1826, and reappointed
in 1832. He m. Ann M. Brinton, in 1832, who died at a ripe age, having borne several children, the eldest being Brinton Coxe, b. in Philadelphia, Aug. 3, 1833; d. at Drifton, Luzerne county, Sept. 15, 1892,
and buried in St. Mary's churchyard, Burlington, where repose the remains of so many of his ancestors and kinsfolk. Mr. Brinton Coxe
was a distinguished scholar, and was for several years President of
the Historical Society of Pennsylvania.

5. William[5] William[4] Daniel[3] Daniel[2] Daniel[1] Coxe, b. May 3, 1762; m.
Rachael, dau. of Richard Smith, of Burlington; d. Feb. 25, 1831; she
was b. Feb. 22, 1773; d. July 7, 1832. He was "a worthy vestryman"
of St. Mary's church, Burlington. He is distinguished as the author
of the first work on American fruits, published in this country,
copiously illustrated. Its character and scope are fully set out in the
title, which follows, with the collation:

A view of the cultivation of fruit trees, and the Management of
Orchards and Cider; with accurate descriptions of the most estimable
varieties of native and foreign apples, pears, peaches, plums, and
cherries, cultivated in the middle states of America: illustrated by
Cuts of two hundred kinds of Fruits of the natural size; intended to
explain Some of the errors which exist relative to the origin, popular
names, and character of many of our fruits; to identify them by accurate descriptions of their properties, and correct delineations of the
full size and natural formation of each variety; and to exhibit a
system of practice adapted to our climate, in the successive stages of
a nursery, orchard, and cider establishment. By William Coxe, Esq.,
Of Burlington, New Jersey. Philadelphia: published by M. Carey and

COXE GENEALOGICAL

Son. Nov. 1, 1817. D. Allinson, Printer. Pp. i-iv., 5-253; 15 pp. of plates. 8°. Sheep.

The will of William Coxe, of Sunbury, Burlington township and county, dated January 15, 1822, was proved March 9, 1831. In it he mentions wife Rachel Coxe, and children William S. Coxe and Richard S. Coxe, and appoints his wife and said two children executors. Witnesses—Daniel Ellis, Chas. Stockton, Franklin Stockton. He says he had joined with William Griffith Esqr of the city of Burlington (a very prominent lawyer) in paying debts due from Edward Shippen and William McMurtrie, and the trustees of his wife's estate having advanced money, he (testator) to secure her from any loss, leaves her his entire estate.—*Original Wills*, Burlington Box, 1831. The will of Rachel Coxe, of Burlington, "at present wife of Wm. Coxe of the same place and only surviving child and heir at law of Richard Smith, deceased," bears date March 2, 1827, and was proved July 25, 1832. She seems to have had a better recollection of her children than her husband had, for besides the two sons mentioned by him in his will she names "my four unmarried daughters"—Maria, Margaret, Ann and Harriet, "not all of age,"—Emily McIlvaine (to whom she bequeaths $1,000), Elizabeth McMurtrie, and sons William S. and Richard S. Executors—husband William Coxe and sons William S. Coxe and Richard S. Coxe. Witnesses—Joseph Watson, Robert Thomas and William Bishop. By a codicil, March 31, 1831 (after her husband's death), she makes her two sons executors. Witnesses—Edward Rogers, William Bishop, Thomas Dutton. Issue:

       i.   Elizabeth[6]. m. William McMurtrie, June 1, 1811, in St. Mary's church, Burlington. Children (recorded in that church): William, buried Oct. 19, 1814; 2. Maria, bap. Feb. 22, 1818; 3. Rachel Coxe, bap. March 28, 1820; 4. William Henry, bap. Sept. 8, 1822; buried Aug. 2, 1824; 5. Emily, bap. April 24, 1825; Emily McMurtrie is named in her mother's will, 1827.

8.   ii. Richard Smith

9.   iii. William Smith.

      iv. Maria, b. Jan. 25, 1796; bap. Jan. 3, 1802; d. Aug. 1, 1831; unm. "She 'walked with God; and was not for God took' her." says her tombstone in St. Mary's churchyard.

      v. Emily, bap. Jan. 3, 1802, with Maria, both being infants. Emily was confirmed in St. Mary's church, June 23, 1819; she m. the Rev. Charles Pettit McIlvaine, Oct. 8, 1822; he was afterwards Bishop of Ohio, and d. March 12, 1873. She was bequeathed $1,000 in her mother's will, in 1827. Ch: Rebecca C(oxe), mentioned in the will of her grandfather, William Coxe, sen.

      vi. Margaret, bap. Aug 29, 1801; d. Aug. 30, 1801, aged 2 years, 11 mos., 20 days.

      vii. Margaret, bap. Feb. 10, 1805; confirmed June 23, 1819; mentioned as unmarried, in her mother's will, 1827.

    viii. Anne, bap. Jan. 1, 1807; d. Jan. 7, 1807, aged 15 mos.

      ix Ann, mentioned as unmarried, in her mother's will, 1827. Anne Coxe m. the Rev. Chauncy Colton, Oct. 15, 1832.

      x. Harriette, bap. Mar 20 (?30), 1812; confirmed May 27, 1828.

xi   Daniel James, bap. April 16, 1815; d. Sept. 15, 1815, aged 1 yr. 14 days. (So according to the church record, his tombstone says he d. Sept. 17.)

7. Daniel⁵ Daniel⁴ Daniel³ Daniel² Daniel¹ Coxe, b. April 1, 1741; m. Sarah, dau. of Dr. John Redman, of Philadelphia, June 5, 1771. His career to the close of the Revolution has been quite fully set forth above. He seems to have spent the last forty-three years of his life in England, in obscurity: d. March 10, 1826; his wid. d. at Brighton, England, in 1841. Dr. Redman, in his will, dated Nov. 9, 1807, proved March 24, 1808, mentions (Penn. Mag. 12: 375) the following children of his daughter Sarah, wife of Daniel Coxe:

    i.   John Redman⁶, b. at Trenton, 1773; m. 1st, Mar. 6, 1798, Sarah, dau. of Col. John Coxe, of Philadelphia; 2d, —— Potts, dau. of Robert Potts, son of Thomas Potts, some time Governor of British Honduras; d. at Philadelphia, 1864; his wid. long survived him, until 1890.

    ii.   Leonard Steel.

    iii.   George.

    iv.   Edward Plaisted.

    v.   Ann Philadelphia.

There may have been others.

8. Richard Smith⁶, William⁵ William⁴ Daniel³ Daniel² Daniel¹ Coxe, b. ——; m. June 23, 1816, Susan Bradford, dau. of Judge William Griffith, of Burlington; d. at Washington, D. C., July 28, 1865. He graduated from Princeton College in 1808; he read law, probably engaged in literary work after graduating, but finally settled down to the study of the law, doubtless with Judge William Griffith, and was admitted to the New Jersey bar as an attorney and counsellor at the May term, 1817. He had probably engaged in literary work after leaving college. His reading and studies took a wide range, especially in English literature. He was said to be the author of "A Dictionary of the English Language, by an American Gentleman." He may have assisted Burgess Allison in the preparation of his dictionary published at Burlington in 1811, and which was esteemed an authority of very high character for many years. He compiled the "United States Digest," in 1829. In 1830 he published the first of the series of New Jersey Equity Reports, which is known by his name, "Coxe's Reports," his material being largely obtained, it is stated in the preface, from his law-preceptor. He subsequently removed to Washington, D. C., and in the course of time was employed in more cases in the Supreme Court than any other lawyer in the United States. Many of his arguments and opinions were printed, as well as various occasional addresses, the latter especially being characterized by graceful and elegant diction. He delivered "An address the evening before the annual commencement of the College of New Jersey," Sept. 24, 1833, and an "Address before the Peithessophian and Philoclean Societies of Rutgers College," July 23, 1844. Kenyon College conferred upon him the degree of LL. D. in 1857. Issue:

Susan Bradford, bap. (at St. Mary's church), April 11, 1819.

There may have been other children.

9. William-Smith⁶ William⁵ William⁴ Daniel³ Daniel² Daniel¹ Coxe, b. at Burlington, April 16, 1790; m. November 3, 1825, Jane Eliza Barbaroux, dau. of Jean Andre and Jeanne Marie Amareuth (Devaucelles) Barbaroux, of Burlington; d. at Philadelphia, July 20, 1837; she d. ——. He was graduated from Princeton College in 1807, studied

medicine in Philadelphia, under Dr. Philip Syng Physick, and was graduated from the Medical School of the University of Philadelphia in 1811, after which he spent several years in the practise of his profession in Philadelphia. He returned to Burlington and practised there. He became a member of the Burlington County Medical Society (organized in 1829) in February, 1830, and was elected a delegate the same year to the New Jersey Medical Society. On the day of his election to membership in the former society he offered a resolution, which was adopted, urging compliance with the law regulating the practise of medicine and surgery in this State, and which provided for the prosecution of persons practising without a license. In 1830 he was elected by the State Society Censor of the Western District, and reported in that behalf at the meeting in May, 1831. In the latter year he submitted to the County society a series of resolutions declaring that the society deemed it its duty "to discountenance, by precept and example, the consumption of ardent spirits by men in health, and to abstain from their exhibition as medicine when less dangerous stimulants can be conveniently substituted, and may be expected to prove equally efficacious." In 1832 he served as Vice President from Burlington county. He acted on a committee of the county society in 1832 to revise its constitution. He returned to Philadelphia, in 1832, where he continued his practise, residing at No. 16 N. Tenth street. He connected himself with St. James church, Philadelphia. His will, dated Feb. 6, 1836, was proved July 26, 1837. He gives to wife, Jane Eliza Coxe, all his estate in stock, with all increase at time of his decease; also all books, plate, and household furniture; in general, all real estate, personal and mixed. He names his "dear wife Jane Eliza executrix, entreating her to implore divine direction and to seek the advice of judicious and pious friends that thus she may be assisted to manage her temporal concerns with prudence and to train up the dear children which have been entrusted to us in the nurture and admonition of the Lord." Witnesses—T. B. Wickersham, Uriah C. Vanhorn, David E. Wickersham.—*Philadelphia Wills*, Book 12, f. 552. The account of the executrix, filed Aug. 13, 1838, mentions, among other expenditures: July 23, 1837, paid Mr. Colton, for tuition of sons, $50; Sept. 28. St. James church, pew rent, $15.65. Dr. Joseph Parrish, in his History of the Burlington County Medical Society, speaks of him as "the courteous and cultured Wm. S. Coxe." Issue:

 i. Edward De Vaucelle, bap. at Burlington, May 9, 1830.
 ii. Mary Amarintha, bap. at Burlington, Oct. 30, 1831.
 iii. Richard Smith, b. July 23, 1833; bap. at St. James's church, Philadelphia, Nov. 16, 1834.

WILLIAM COXE.

William Coxe, appointed Stamp Distributor for New Jersey, under the obnoxious Stamp Act of 1765, was doubtless of Burlington, and hence probably owed the appointment to Gov. William Franklin, who resided there. Both belonged to St. Mary's Church, of that place. William Coxe was a son of Col. Daniel Coxe, 3d, who died at Trenton in 1739, and was buried at St. Mary's church, Burlington. The fact that the Stamp Distributor promptly resigned as soon as he perceived the temper of the people shows him to have been a man of excellent judgment, and apparently in sympathy with the American sentiment on the subject. He was probably the father of William Coxe, Jun., of Burlington, the author of a work on fruits, the first of the kind in America.

CRANE: CROLIUS FAMILY

BENJAMIN CRANE.

Benjamin Crane, 3d, was born Nov. 29, 1761, son of Benjamin Crane, 2d, and Phebe Halsey, his wife, dau. of Joseph Halsey, who lived between Elizabethtown and Rahway. Benjamin Crane, 2d, and his wife lived in Westfield, now in Union county. Benjamin Crane, 3d, m. Sarah, dau. of Hezekiah Thompson, and lived in Westfield. Issue: 1. John, m. Mary Clark, of Westfield; 2. Abigail, m. David Keyt; 3. Esther, d. at 18 or 20 yrs., unm.; 4. Hezekiah Thompson, m. Amanda Osborn; 5. Phoebe, m. 1st, Francis Randolph, son of Dr. Robert Randolph; 2d, George R. King, of Warren county; 6. Charlotte King, m. Hedges Baker; 7. Norris, removed to Cincinnati, O.; 8. Jacob Thompson, d. at Cincinnati, Ohio, aged 35 yrs., unm.; 9. Benjamin, 4th, m. 1st, Electa Baker, b. Sept. 28, 1804, dau. of Daniel Baker; she m. 1st, Aaron, son of Noah Woodruff; Mr. Crane m. 2d, Mary, dau. of William Baker, jun., of Madison; Mr. Crane was a marble cutter, of Paterson, where he was regarded as a most estimable citizen during a residence of sixty years or more; d. Dec. 3, 1889; 10. David Johnson, m. Ann Eliza, dau. of Isaac Roll; 11. Moses Thompson, m. Eliza Scudder. See Littell's Passaic Valley Genealogies.

CROLIUS FAMILY.

The Crolius family is descended from Johan Willem Crollius, who, being a bachelor, from Nieuw Wit (probably Neuwied, near Coblenz, on the Rhine), married Veronica Cortselius, spinster, also from Nieuw Wit, Jan. 30, 1724, in the Dutch Church, New York; both were from Germany, but were living within the jurisdiction of that church. He dropped his first name, and after his marriage appears in the records as Willem Crolius, though with many variations, according to the whims or the imperfect hearing of the clerks. William Crolyas, potter, was admitted as a freeman of New York City, March 18, 1728-9. He again had the freedom of the city granted him, Oct. 4, 1737. On the same day the burgher right was also granted to Peter Crolius, potter, probably his brother, of whom, however, we have no further account. Issue:

i. Johannes, bap. Dec. 23, 1733; m. Maria Clarkson. Children: 1. Willem, bap. Dec. 12, 1753; 2. Johannes, bap. Dec. 28, 1755; m. Jane Morgan; he carried on the potter's business left to him by his uncle; he was an Assistant Alderman, in New York, in 1799; 3. Maria, bap. May 7, 1758; m. Garret Van De Water; 4. Elizabet, bap. Oct. 10, 1762; 5. Feronica, bap. Oct. 1, 1764, m. William Sanford; 6. Ann, bap. Mar. 29, 1767; 7. George Clarkson, bap. Oct. 28, 1770; 8. Clarkzon, bap. Oct. 17, 1773; m. Elizabeth Meyers, Oct. 8, 1793; he was a potter; he was an Assistant Alderman, New York, 1802-3-4.

ii. Willem, bap. Sept. 26, 1731. He was a potter, in New York. He and his brother John were witnesses to the will of John Remmi, of New York, "Pot Baker," Jan. 26, 1762. He was admitted to the burgher right o f the city Sept. 1, 1770. He subsequently removed to Middle Brook, New Jersey, perhaps because his sympathies were with the Americans, rather than with the British, who were then in possession of New York city. He d. at Middle Brook, in 1779. William

Crolius, formerly of the City of New York, but now of Middle Brook, Somerset County, New Jersey, being "infirm," made his will January 26, 1778, which was proved January 22, 1779. He mentions no wife nor children. He devises to his nephew John, son of his brother John, the rest of the term of the lease of those four lots situate in the out-ward of the City of New York, leased of George Janeway, with dwelling houses, shops, etc., and all his tools, etc., of the potter's business; to his brothers, John, Peter and George, the proceeds of sale of his other house and ground in New York City, near the Moravian Meeting House, in Fare street, and his lot and house in Middle Brook, New Jersey, and the rest of his estate. With a proper recognition of the pending struggle of the American people to secure their own freedom, he provided that his slaves Tom and wife Venus and their children should be freed. He appoints as executors his friend George Janeway, and his brothers John and Peter. Witnesses—Robert Manely, Benjamin Harris, jun., and William Wilcocks.—*Liber No. 21 of N. J. Wills,* f. 53.

iii. Maria.

iv. Petrus, bap Feb. 11, 1736; m. by license, Feb. 11, 1736, Mary Chambers. In the record of the baptisms of their children, however, her name is given as Lack, Loch, or Lock. She was, perhaps, a widow when he married her. Peter Crolius, cordwainer, was granted the burgher right, Oct. 1, 1765. Children: 1. Willem, bap. Nov. 27, 1763 (the child's paternal grandparents both witnessed the baptism); 2. Elizabeth, bap. April 28, 1765; 3. Veronica, bap. June 22, 1766; 4. Mary, bap. Nov. 13, 1768; 5. Elizabet, bap. Oct. 7, 1770; 6. Peter, bap. Nov. 8, 1772; d. in inf.; 7. Pieter, bap. Oct. 30, 1774. Peter Crolius, son of Willem, and father of these children, joined the Reformed Dutch Church of New Brunswick, by certificate, in 1778.

v. Jurrie, bap. March 5, 1738; m. Catharina Coelbach, in 1763 or earlier. This is doubtless the brother 'George" mentioned in the will of William Crolius. As a matter of fact, "Jurrie" (pronounced Yury) is a contraction of Juriaan, the Dutch for Uriah. The Dutch equivalent of George is Joris, pronounced Yoris.

REV. ALEXANDER CUMMING.

Alexander Cumming was born at Freehold, N. J., in 1726, son of Robert Cumming, an immigrant from Montrose, Scotland, who was an Elder and Trustee in the old Presbyterian church in that vicinity, later known as the Old Tennent Church. He was educated under his maternal uncle, Samuel Blair, and studied theology with his pastor, William Tennent. He was licensed in 1746 or 1747, and spent some time in Augusta county, Va. He married Eunice, daughter of Col. Thomas Polk, of North Carolina. He was collegiate pastor with the Rev. Ebenezer Pemberton, of the Presbyterian church in New York, 1750-1753, after which he remained without a charge, partly on account of ill health, until 1761, when he was called to Old South, Boston, where he remained until his death, August 23, 1763.—*Webster's Hist. Pres. Church,* 614.

JOHN NOBLE CUMMING.

John Noble Cumming was born about 1752, son of Robert Cumming and Mary Noble. Robert Cumming was born in 1701 or 1702, in Montrose, Scotland, and came to this country at the age of eighteen years. He was the son of John Cumming, a lawyer of reputation. Robert lived in Newark about two years, and then removed to Freehold, Monmouth county, where in later years he held the office of High Sheriff. He married, first, Mary, daughter of Lawrence Van Hook, of Freehold; second, in 1746, Mary, daughter of John Noble (a merchant of Bristol, England, nephew of Sir John Stokes, of Stokes' Castle, Bristol), who came to New York about 1717, and married Catharine, daughter of Captain John Van Brugh. (Mrs. Catharine Van Brugh Noble married, second, the Reverend William Tennent, of Freehold, and died at Pittsgrove, N. J., in her eighty-second year.) Robert Cumming had children: By his first wife: (1) Alexander, pastor of the Presbyterian Church, in New York, and afterwards of the Old South Church, in Boston, where he died in 1763; (2) Lawrence, who lived and died in Freehold; (3) Mary, who, in October, 1758, married the Reverend Alexander Macwhorter, who had studied for the ministry at Freehold, and was afterwards pastor of the Presbyterian Church at Newark, 1759-1807. By his second wife: (4) Catharine, married the Reverend Philip Stockton, a native of Princeton, who settled in Sussex county; (5) Ann, married the Reverend William Schenck, of Huntington, L. I.; (6) John Noble; (7) Margaret, who died, aged 40 years, unmarried. Robert Cumming died at Freehold, April 15th, 1769, in his sixty·eighth year.—*Alden's Epitaphs*, 1039; *N. Y. Gen. and Biog. Record*. John Noble Cumming was graduated from Princeton in 1774.—*Princeton General Catalogue*. He was commissioned First Lieutenant in Captain Howell's Company, Second Battalion, First Establishment, November 29th, 1775; First Lieutenant, Captain Lawrie's Company, Second Battalion, Second Establishment, November 29th, 1776; Captain, Second Battalion, Second Establishment, to date November 30th, 1776; Captain, Second Regiment, Major, First Regiment, to date April 16th, 1780; Lieutenant-Colonel, Second Regiment, December 29th, 1781; Lieutenant-Colonel Commandant, Third Regiment, February 11th, 1783, and was discharged at the close of the war.—*Stryker's Revolutionary Roster*, p. 66. Soon after the war he appears to have settled in Newark, where, in 1787, he belonged to Newark Lodge, No. 2, of Free Masons. He had previously been a member of Lodge No. 19, Pennsylvania registry, probably at Freehold. In 1786 he was elected Grand Secretary of the Grand Lodge, which usually met at Trenton. He declined a re-election in 1791, owing to the inconvenience of getting there from Newark.—*Hough's Freemasonry in New Jersey*. In Newark he married Sarah, daughter of Justice Joseph Hedden, Jr., a prominent citizen, who was carried off by the British on the night of January 25th, 1780, and suffered such hardship in the New York sugar-house that he died from his ill-treatment September 27th, 1780. Cumming was a man of great business activity, and found plenty of enterprises to engage his attention. In 1793-4 he successfully executed a contract for the construction of the first raceways in Paterson, for conducting the water-power from above the Passaic Falls to the mills below. For many years his principal business was the management of extensive stage-lines and the carrying of the United States mails, between New York and Philadelphia, in connection with which he owned several wayside taverns along the route. He was elected one of the Trustees of the First Presbyterian Church, in

CUMMING: DAVENPORT: DEVENS: DE WITTE

Newark, in 1798, the pastor being his brother-in-law, but as he lived in the upper part of the town—corner of Broad and Lombardy streets—he took an active part in the organization of the Second Presbyterian Church, in 1809, being not only one of the first Trustees, but a generous contributor toward the erection of its house of worship. His son, the Rev. Hooper Cumming, was the first pastor of the church, 1811-15. Among the notices of Colonel Cumming in the official records of Newark, we find him elected Surveyor of the Highways, in 1787; Overseer of the Highways, in 1788; Appeal Commissioner, in 1790 and 1791; Vice-President of the Newark Fire Association at its organization, in 1797. He was deeply interested in the Newark Academy, and in 1793 was one of the managers of the lottery raised for the completion of the building. In 1795 he was elected a member of the first Board of Trustees, and served in that capacity for fifteen or twenty years, if not longer. He was one of the incorporators of the Newark Aqueduct Company, chartered in 1800, and was Vice-President and afterwards President of the company for a long time. In the act incorporating the Newark Banking and Insurance Company—Newark's first financial institution, and the first bank incorporated in New Jersey—in 1804 he was named as one of the commissioners to receive subscriptions to the stock, and he was one of the directors of the bank for many years—probably until his death. In 1811 he was a director of the Society for Establishing Useful Manufactures (at Paterson), of the Passaic and Hackensack Bridge Company, of the Steam Boat Ferry Company of New Jersey and New York, director of the Newark Turnpike Company (maintaining the road from Newark to Paulus Hook), and was connected with various other corporations of like character. In later years he was a General of Militia. He was Vice-President of the New Jersey Society of the Cincinnati from 1808 until his death. While at work about his farm on an intensely hot day, he was overcome by the heat, and died July 6th, 1821.—2 *N. J. Archives*, I., 346.

REV. JOHN DAVENPORT.

John Davenport was a son of the Rev. James Davenport, of Southold, Long Island. He was graduated from Princeton College in the class of 1769. He was ordained by the Presbytery of Suffolk, June 4, 1775, and served the Congregation in Southold, Long Island, for two years. On the 12th of August, 1795, he was settled at Deerfield, New Jersey, but resigned in 1805, on account of failing health. He died July 13, 1821.

RICHARD DEVENS.

Richard Devens was born at Charlestown, October 23, 1749. At his graduation at Princeton, in 1767, he stood at the head of his class. For three years he was engaged in teaching in various schools in New York and New Jersey. In 1770 he was appointed tutor in the College, where he remained until 1774, when, in consequence of too close and intense application to his studies he became insane, and, so far as known, he never recovered his reason.

REV. PETER DE WITT.

Peter Dewitt studied theology under the Rev. Dr. John H. Livingston, and was licensed as a preacher by the General Meeting of Ministers and Elders of the Reformed Dutch Church, in 1778. From 1787 to 1798 he was pastor of the Reformed Dutch churches of Rhinebeck, Rhinebeck Flats and Upper Red Hook, New York, and from

DE WITT: EAKIN: EASTBURN FAMILY

1799 to 1809 he was pastor of the churches of Ponds and Wyckoff, Bergen county, New Jersey. He died in 1809.

REV. SAMUEL EAKIN.

Samuel Eakin was graduated from the College of New Jersey in 1763, and received the degree of A. M. in 1766. He studied for the ministry and was ordained by the Second Presbytery of Philadelphia, in 1770. From 1773 until his death, in 1784, he was settled at Penn's Neck Presbyterian church in West Jersey, but rendered himself so obnoxious to the Tories by his zeal in the cause of American liberty that he was sometimes obliged to withdraw. He was the idol of the soldiers. Wherever there was a military training, or an order issued for the soldiers to march, he was, if in his power, always there to address them, and by his eloquence would excite their emotions of patriotism to the highest pitch. It is related of him that he was so warm a Whig that he never entered the pulpit without imploring the Lord "to teach our people to fight and give them courage and perseverance to overcome their enemies." Mr. Eakin was an extraordinary man, and, next to Mr. Whitefield, esteemed the most eloquent preacher who had ever been in the country. See Johnson's History of Salem, 97-98.

EASTBURN FAMILY.

The grandparents of Robert Eastburn, who were Friends, came from England to America in 1714, and probably had several children, as numerous Eastburns appear in the records of Friends' Meetings in and about Philadelphia in the early part of the eighteenth century. Among the children was Robert Eastburn, who was b. in England in 1710. He was m. in 1733 to Agnes Jones, of Germantown, in Friends' Meeting, to which he and his wife belonged. He continued with Friends until on one occasion he heard the celebrated George Whitefield preach, when he became one of his followers. Mr. Whitefield used to call him his "first fruit in America." A congregation was formed—the Second Presbyterian, of Philadelphia—which called the Rev. Gilbert Tennent, of New Brunswick, to be their pastor, and Mr. Eastburn was chosen one of the first deacons. With about thirty tradesmen he marched north in the spring of 1756, toward Oswego, but when the party arrived at Captain Williams' Fort, near Oswego, on March 26, 1756, they were surprised by a party of Indians, and the next day Eastburn was captured by them, and carried a prisoner to Canada, suffering incredible hardships on the way. He was detained a prisoner by the Indians and by the French until July 23, 1757, when he was permitted to sail from Quebec to England, and securing passage thence to the Colonies arrived October 26, 1757, at Philadelphia. (In his account of his capture he gives the date of his arrival at New York as Nov. 21, and at Philadelphia as November 26. But his arrival at New York was chronicled in the New York and Philadelphia newspapers of October 24-28, 1757. See *N. J. Archives*, 20:144.) "The faithful Narrative of the many dangers and sufferings, as well as wonderful deliverance, of Robert Eastburn during his captivity among the Indians," printed at Philadelphia, by William Dunlap, 1758, is one of the rarest accounts of Indian captivities, and owing to its interesting character, has been reprinted several times. He d. Jan. 22, 1778; his wife d. Sept. 27, 1784. Issue:

    i. Sarah, b. 1735; d. 1818.
    ii. Hannah, d. 1773.

EASTBURN FAMILY

     iii. Thomas, prob. m. Rachel Lupton, Dec. 1, 1783.

2. iv. Robert.

     v. John, d. 1806. Children: Sarah Eastburn and Maria Wells.

3. vi. Joseph, b. Aug. 11, 1748, in Philadelphia.

2. Robert[2] (Robert[1]) Eastburn located at New Brunswick before the Revolution, and seems to have been a prominent merchant there. His will made August 10, 1815, when he was "sick and weak," was proved August 29, 1815. The numerous bequests indicate that he owned a considerable estate. He refers to his wife as deceased, and gives legacies to his children as follows: Robert Eastburn, $250; Thomas Eastburn, $775; Joseph Eastburn, $500; Mary Ann, a certain interest yearly during life, the principal to be divided among her children at her death; Abigail Boyer, $104 per year, "if she does not live with her husband, James Boyer"; grandson Robert Boyer, $100. Other legacies were left to Mary Taylor, $50, "for her care during the sickness of Robert Boyer, my grandson"; to Elizabeth Smith, $450, "the faithful nurse of my wife and myself"; William Jobs (son of William Jobs, of South Amboy), $25; to brother John's widow, $100; brother Joseph Eastburn to have the care of about $100 "to hand out as needed"; Susannah Hunt, daughter of Samuel Noe, of New York, $100, "she being a goodly woman, indisposed and poor in estate"; to Elizabeth Evans, $50. He directs that his house on Dennis street shall be rented or sold; to John Vial, $75, to be paid in small sums; to the Humane Society of New Brunswick, the interest of $300; towards building a Friends' Meeting House in New Brunswick, $200; to the City of Philadelphia and to the City of New York, each $200, to be used in providing a school for the education of white and colored children alike; to the New Jersey Bible Society, $50, to be paid John Neilson, Esquire, for the use of the Society; to Joseph Clark of Philadelphia, and Dr. Conover C. Blatchley of New York, each $50, to purchase religious tracts and circulate them; to charities in New Brunswick, $50. Executors—my friends, William P. Deare and Dr. Augustus R. Taylor. Witnesses—Jona. C. Ackerman, Robert Dennis, J. W. Scott. In a codicil dated August 17, 1815, he gives $75 to the corporation for the relief of poor children in the City of New Brunswick; and $25 in addition to his previous legacy to William Jobs, son of William Jobs of South Amboy. The estate was appraised August 25, 1815, by Dower D. Williamson and Asa Runyon. The inventory mentions cash delivered to Executors by T. Eastburn, on sale of oil, $26.31. Among the debtors are William Jobs, on bond; David Allison, due bill for books; note due from John Metcalt, insolvent; note due from John K. Joline; due bill from Lewis Dunn; debt due from Jeremiah Parsell, 5th mo. 3, 1815; Michael Pool, Feb. 11, 1806; Gideon Voorhees (Insolvent), 1807; Garret Nefie, 1808; Jacob Probasco, 1810; Moses Jones; John Dill, 6th mo. 27, 1814. It also mentions household goods, wine, contents of shop, etc., etc. Issue:

     i. Robert, m. ——— ; ch., Joseph.

     ii. Thomas.

     iii. Mary Ann, m. William Jones, Dec. 30, 1800.

     iv. Abigail, m. James Boyer; ch., Robert.

3. Joseph, b. August 11, 1748; he followed his father to northern New York in 1756, and was taken prisoner at the capture of Fort Oswego, by the French and Indians. He had the good fortune to rejoin his father while a prisoner in Canada, and they remained together

thereafter during their captivity. On returning to Philadelphia he resumed his trade as a cabinet-maker; he m. Agnes Owen of that city, June 12, 1771, in the Second Presbyterian Church of that city; she d. June 21, 1811, aged 66 years. He performed two or three tours of duty in the Revolutionary War, and was at the Battle of Princeton, January 3, 1777. At an early age his attention was turned towards religious subjects, and he was very anxious to go into the ministry, but owing to his lack of education was refused a license by the Presbytery. However, he was encouraged to take charge of prayer meetings in the Second Presbyterian Church, and proved so acceptable a speaker, that in 1805 he was granted a qualified license. He preached at New Brunswick frequently, between 1812 and 1815, on which occasions he was a guest of his brother at that place. Toward the close of 1819, he began to preach regularly to the mariners of Philadelphia, and a church was erected for such meetings, in which he officiated until his death, January 30, 1828. He had one son, Thomas, b. about 1772 or 1773. Contrary to the wishes of his parents, he entered upon a seafaring life and became commander of a merchant vessel. Losing his little property by the failure of a mercantile house, by which he was employed, he sailed from the West Indies as a passenger, for Philadelphia, and on the voyage was instantly killed, his head being taken off by a cannon ball, fired from a French man-of-war; he was comparatively young at the time of his tragic death. Having no children, Joseph, in his will, distributed his property among his nephews and nieces and various charitable objects, especially the Mariners' Church, over which he had presided for nine years before his death.

EATON FAMILY.

Thomas Eaton was doubtless a grandson of Thomas Eaton, 1st, who came to America from Goodhurst, Kent, England, and landed in Rhode Island, where he married a widow, Jerusha Wing. About 1670 he located in Monmouth County, N. J., where he built a grist mill on one of the headwaters of South Shrewsbury, in the present village of Eatontown, four miles west of Long Branch. He died November 26, 1688, leaving his mill property to his widow in trust for their unborn child. John Eaton, his son, was born March 26, 1689. He married Joanna, daughter of Joseph Wardell, who lived at the present Monmouth Beach. He was elected to the Assembly in 1727, and was re-elected in 1730, 1738, 1740, 1743, 1744, 1745, 1746, 1749, serving continuously for twenty years. He sold the mill property April 26, 1716, to Gabriel Stelle. He died April 1, 1750. In his will, dated Dec. 2, 1745, proved May 11, 1750, he gives to his son Thomas £600 in money, also his "big Bible big Dicksonary Nelsons Justice and my Sord and Pistils." To his son Joseph his "small gun, small Dicksonary Church history and Conductter generall [Conductor Generalis] and ten shillings in money." —*E. J. Wills*, E, 485. His widow made her will May 25, 1769; it was proved January 15, 1770.—*Ib.*, K, 163. She d. January 1, 1770. Joseph Wardell, of Shrewsbury, in his will, dated May 5, 1733, proved May 30, 1735, speaks of his daughter, Joanna Eaton. John Eaton's children were:

1. Thomas, who lived on the paternal acres. In 1749 he was a merchant in New York. He was baptized in the Old Tennent Church, Monmouth County, in Old Shrewsbury, on profession of faith, August 20, 1749. In 1754 he advertised for sale a lot of thirteen and a quarter acres, about a quarter of a mile from the centre of the township of Shrewsbury. A Thomas Eaton, perhaps his son, was living at Elizabethtown, where his first wife died, and several of his children, 1774-1795.

2. Joseph, a physician, who died April 5, 1761, in his 44th year. The will of Joseph Eaton, of Shrewsbury, "Surgion," dated March 30, 1756, proved May 6, 1751, names his wife Lucy, and sons John and Thomas. Testator "would have them educated by the direction of my brother Thomas Eaton and taught merchants accounts and would have them brought up to College if their part of the personal estate or income or lands should be sufficient but not to encumber said lands with any debts."—*E. J. Wills*, G, 445.

3. Valeria, married Dr. Joseph Le Conte, of Middletown Point. She and her husband joined the Old Tennent Church, May 4, 1744. He subscribed £10, March 16, 1749-50, towards the erection of the present meeting-house. He died January 29, 1768, in his 66th year, and is buried in the Presbyterian cemetery, near Matawan. His widow died in 1788, and is buried at Orange, where she had made her home for several years with her daughter Margaretta, the second wife of the Rev. Jedidiah Chapman, pastor of the Presbyterian Church at that place.

4. Sarah, married Richard Tole, in Christ church, Shrewsbury, June 25, 1761.

5. Lydia, m. John Wanton, of Rhode Island, Aug. 12, 1750.

6. Joanna, married, October 15, 1750, the Rev. Elihu Spencer, a Presbyterian clergyman, who was temporarily supplying Shrewsbury and Middletown. She died at Trenton, November 1, 1791, aged 63 years. He died at Trenton also, December 27, 1784, in his 64th year.

7. Elizabeth. She and her sister Joanna, both being "Young women grown," were "baptized on profession of their own Faith," August 5, 1750, in the Old Tennent church. She m. Thomas Richardson, April 4, 1755.

8. Margaret, married John Berrien, marriage license August 16, 1759. Child—Mary, who. m. Dr. Thomas West Montgomery.—*Hist. Monmouth County*, 876; *N. J. Historical Society Proc.*, V., 36; *N. J. Archives*, XIX., 437; *Hall's Pres. Church in Trenton*, 288; *Wickes's Hist. Medical Men of N. J.*, 242, 310; *Wickes's History of the Oranges*, 198; *Hist. of Old Tennent Church*, Freehold, 1897, 122; *Inscriptions in First Pres. Church Yard, Elizabeth*, 106.

REV. ISAAC EATON.

The Rev. Isaac Eaton was a son of the Rev. Joseph Eaton, minister of the Baptist society at Montgomery, Pa. (about 20 miles northwest of Philadelphia), 1722-1744, and then of the New Britain church, which split from the former in 1744, until his death. Joseph was b. Aug. 25, 1679, in Radnor, Wales, and came to America about 1686. His second wife, Uria Humphreys, was the mother of Isaac Eaton. Joseph attended monthly at Hopewell, during fifteen years of his ministry at Montgomery and New Britain. He d. April 1, 1749, and was buried at New Britain.

Isaac Eaton, son of the Rev. Joseph Eaton and Uria Humphreys, was b. 1726, and studied divinity at Southampton, Bucks county, Pa., with the Rev. Oliver Hart, who was destined to be one of his successors at Hopewell. Mr. Eaton came to this church in April, 1748, and was ordained its pastor on Nov. 29 of that year. He remained in that charge for twenty-four years. The Rev. Dr. Samuel Jones, of Pennepek, Pa., who preached the funeral sermon, said: "The natural endowments of his mind; the improvement of these by the accomplishments of literature; his early and genuine piety; his abilities as a divine and as a preacher; his extensive knowledge of men and books; his catholicism, &c., would afford ample scope to flourish in a funeral oration." Mr. Eaton opened a school at Hopewell in 1756, for the education of youths for the ministry, he being the first among the American Baptists to establish such a school. Many of his students became eminent in the ministry, and many more in other walks in life. The school was closed in 1767. Mr. Eaton m. Rebecca Stout, by whom he had many children, some of whom d. young or unm. Joseph, David and Pamela grew up and married. Mr. Eaton also practiced physic, and was very helpful to the poor. He d. at Hopewell, July 4, 1772, and was buried in the meeting house. At the head of his grave, near the base of the pulpit, the congregation set up a marble slab, suitably inscribed, with the verse appended:

> In him, with Grace and Eminence, did shine
> The Man, the Christian, Scholar and Divine.

Yale College conferred upon him the honorary degree of A. M., and Princeton in 1756 did the same.—*Edwards's Hist. of Baptists in Penna.*, 17, 33, 50-52; *in New Jersey*, 47-50; *Benedict's Hist. of the Baptists*, I., 572.

ELLIS FAMILY.

Rowland Ellis was a schoolmaster at Burlington, by appointment of the Society for the Propagation of the Gospel in Foreign Parts, from September 29, 1711, to March 17, 1738. He drew his passage money, £20, Nov. 13, 1711, and doubtless sailed soon after for America. By the favor of the government for the time being he was able to add to his revenue as school teacher, the fees of Naval Officer for West Jersey, to which post he was appointed Nov. 30, 1731. On Feb. 5, 1733-4, he was commissioned Clerk of the Court of Chancery. His tombstone in St. Mary's Churchyard, Burlington, states the term of his service as schoolmaster as above, and adds this scriptural quotation: "They that be teachers shall shine as the brightness of the firmament." It fails to state the date of his death. He married Sarah Allison, April 17, 1715, in St. Mary's Church. She was buried in that Churchyard July 18, 1760. Issue:

    i. Margaret², b. Sept. 17, 1716; bap. Nov. 1, 1716; m. Fretwell Wright, of Burlington, mar. lic. Aug. 2, 1738. Children: 1. Peter, bap. Jan. —, 1742; also the following, all bap. Sept. 11, 1754, with their father, in St. Mary's Church, Burlington: 2. Jonathan; 3. Ellis; 4. William; 5. Isaack.

    ii. Richard, b. July 18, 1718; bap. Aug. 26, 1718.

    iii. John, b. June 1, 1720; bap. June 19, 1720.

    iv. William, b. Sept. 25, 1722; bap. October, 1722.

    v. Joseph, b. Sept. 23, 1724; bap. Dec. 21, 1724; he d. intestate, and letters of administration were granted on his estate to John How, Oct. 29, 1785.—*N. J. Wills*, Lib. 27, p. 14.

2.   vi. Daniel, b. Feb. 5, 1727-8; bap. March, 1727-8.

    vii. Rowland, b. Aug. 16, 1734; bap. May, 1735; he became insolvent in 1765; letters of administration were granted on his estate, Nov. 3, 1797, to Hannah and James Ellis.—*N. J. Wills*, Lib. 37, p. 68.

    viii. John, b. Sept. 18, 1736; bap. Dec. 26, 1736.

    ix. Thomas, b. January 13, 1738-9; bap. Feb. 1738-9; d. intestate, and letters of administration were granted on his estate, Aug. 12, 1793, to Martha Ellis; Amos Sharp, bondsman, all of Burlington county.—*N. J. Wills*, Lib. 33, p. 50.

2. Daniel² (Rowland¹) Ellis, born February 5, 1727-8; m. Bathsheba ———; d. September 1, 1794; she d. June 8, 1795, in the 65th year of

her age. He was appointed Deputy Surveyor of the Western Division, in 1753, and qualified as follows:

"Daniel Ellis—Being duly sworn on the Holy Evangelists of Almighty God, Declared that he would well and truly Execute the Office of Deputy Surveyor of the Western Division of New Jersey & would observe and keep such Reasonable Instructions as should be by the Suyveyor Generall under his hand Given him to the best of his knowledge.

DANIEL ELLIS.

"Sworn before me this Twenty-sixth day of February, 1753.

"NATHL. THOMAS."

This oath of office is recorded in Book S, of Surveys, page 97, in the Surveyor General's Office at Burlington. In 1762 he was elected a member of the Council of Proprietors of West Jersey, according to the following entry in Book A of Minutes of the Council of Proprietors, page 264, in the Surveyor General's Office, at Burlington:

"May ye 5th, 1762.

"The Council of Proprietors met according to their usual custom & it appearing by the return from the County of Burlington that George Reading Esqr, Abraham Heulings, Jos. Hollinshead, Daniel Ellis and William Heulings was chosen for said County & that John Ladd, John Hinchman, Daniel Cox Esqr & Samuel Clements Junr. for the County of Gloucester.

"And the Persons appearing was
John Ladd Esqr.
Abraham Heulings
John Hinchman
Daniel Coxe Esqr.
George Reading Esqr.
Daniel Ellis
Saml. Clements Junr. &
William Heulings

"Who proceeded to the Choise of their Officers and chose
John Ladd President
Abraham Heulings Vice Prest
and
William Heulings Clk."

He began to buy land at a very early date. John Childs and the rest of the West Jersey Society, by Lewis Johnson, their attorney, conveyed to Charles Read, Esquire, of the City of Burlington, for £48, eight hundred acres of unappropriated land to be taken up and surveyed in West Jersey, said conveyance being dated January 25, 1755. On February 3, 1755, Read, for the consideration of £40, assigned this deed to Joseph Holinshead and Daniel Ellis, both of the City of Burlington.—*West Jersey Deeds*, Liber M., pp. 440-442. By deed dated August 9, 1755, Thomas Gardiner, chairmaker, of the City of Burlington, conveyed to Daniel Ellis, of the same place, for £30, 1128 acres of land in Gloucester County, "beginning at a twin cedar standing by a creek called Attsionk, being the bounds between Burlington and Gloucester counties, and marked T. G.; thence south 41 degrees, W. 85 chains to a cedar marked T. G. E. standing by a branch of the Mullekeys river called Mechescatuckzing thence down sd branch to a Creek called Sleepy Creek," etc.—*West Jersey Deeds*, Liber M, p. 430. On September 10 following, Thomas Gardiner and Daniel Ellis reconveyed said premises to Charles Read, for the nominal consideration of 5s., and a yearly rent of £4. 10s.—*West Jersey Deeds*, Liber Y., p. 113. By deed dated September 6, 1755, Daniel Ellis bought from Filo

Leeds, of Burlington county, for the consideration of £2. 16s., 56 acres
to be surveyed in any part of West Jersey, below the falls of the Delaware.—*Ib.*, Liber P., page 336. On June 9, 1760, William Coxe, of the
City of Philadelphia, Gent., conveyed to Daniel Ellis, John Munroe and
Joseph Hollinshead, all of Burlington County, 1700 acres of unappropriated land to be taken up and surveyed in West Jersey; consideration £95.—*Ib.*, Liber Q., page 318. Thomas Shaw appointed Daniel
Ellis, of the City of Burlington, New Jersey, his attorney, the instrument being dated May 16, 1757.—*Ib.*, Liber N., page 397. By deed
dated May 18, 1767, Joseph Hollinshead and Susannah, his wife;
Abraham Heulings and Rachel, his wife; John Lawrence and Martha,
his wife, and Thomas Rodman, all of the city of Burlington, conveyed
to Daniel Ellis and others, Esquires, Justices of the Peace of Burling
ton county, and Timonty Abbott and others, chosen freeholders of said
county, for the consideration of £106 12s., "all that lot of land in the
City of Burlington situate on Broad Street beginning at a corner to a
street 25 ft wide, then runs along Broad Street N. 83 deg. E. 186 ft to
land late of John Craige's, then S. 15 deg. E. 77 ft to the lot of land
where the Secretary's Office stands," etc., for a goal.—*Ib.*, *Liber Z*, p.
178. John Hoskins and Daniel Ellis were on July 13, 1767, appointed
trustees for the insolvent estate of Levi Murrell, saddler, of the City
of Burlington.—*Ib.*, *Liber X*, p. 395. To complete this transaction,
Sarah Murrell, wife of Levi Murrell, resigned her claim for 5s., on the
same day.—*Ib.*, *Liber X*, p. 397. Joseph Perkins, of Willingborough,
Burlington County, assigned all his real and personal estate, by deed
dated July 14, 1767, to Daniel Ellis, William Smith and Joseph Fennimore, as Trustees for his creditors.—*Ib.*, *Liber X*, p. 328. John Shaw,
an insolvent debtor, made an assignment of his estate on June 8, 1767,
to Abraham Hewlings and Daniel Ellis, both of the City of Burlington, for the benefit of his creditors, his wife Elizabeth Shaw, releas-
ing her claim to her husband's estate the same day.—*Ib.*, *Liber X*, pp.
284-386. Joseph Hollinshead, of the City of Burlington, being about to
"reside out of the Province for sometime," appointed Thomas Rodman
and Daniel Ellis, his attorneys to sell lands, etc., said instrument being dated September 24, 1767.—*Ib.*, *Liber W*, p. 496. On August 10,
1772, Daniel Ellis and his wife, Bathsheba, of the City of Burlington,
for the consideration of £110, conveyed 100 acres of land in Chester
township, Burlington county, to Joseph Worrington, of Chester
township, Burlington county, and Daniel Walton and Thomas Walton, of Philadelphia county, Pa., said tract bounding on lands of
Darling Conaroe, Hudson Middleton, William Fennimore and William
Ivins.—*Ib.*, *Liber Y*, p. 535. He was one of the managers of St.
Mary's Church lottery, in 1762.—*N. J. Archives*, XXIV., 42. Complaint
was made against him, Sept. 22, 1762, by Anthony Woodward, to the
Governor and Council, probably for some act as justice or as sheriff,
but that body, after hearing all the evidence produced, two days later
unanimously decided that the charge, whatever it was, was not supported.—*Ib.*, XVII., 319-320. In 1764 he was sheriff of Burlington
county.—*Ib.*, 379, 412. He was appointed in 1765 to be one of the
managers and commissioners for a proposed road leading from Perth
Amboy to Burlington.—*Ib.*, 590. In 1767 (August 21) Gov. Franklin
appointed him one of the justices of the quorum of Burlington county.
—*Ib.*, XVII., 455. At the beginning of the Revolution, Mr. Ellis' sympathies with the American cause were a matter of question by his
neighbors, and accordingly, at a meeting of the Council of Safety, on
Tuesday, April 8, 1777, he "was summoned to appear before the Board

ELLIS FAMILY

& to take the oaths to Government, did accordingly appear, and refusing to take the Oaths, was indulged at his request until Friday next, in order to provide Sureties for his appearance at the next Court of General Quarter Sessions of the Peace for the County of Burlington." On Friday, April 11, he "entered into recognizance with Abraham Hewlings his surety, in £300 each &c., as above."—*Minutes*, pp. 16, 20. He held the office of township clerk from 1763 to 1779, and from 1782 to 1791.—*Hist. of Burlington and Mercer Counties*, p. 126. His tombstone in St. Mary's churchyard, Burlington, has this elaborate tribute to his memory:

Sacred | to the memory of | Daniel Ellis, Esq. | who departed this life | in full Assurance of Faith | in the great Atonement of | Jesus Christ | the 1st Day of September 1794 | in the 67 Year of his Age | Universally esteemed and as | Universally lamented.

Faithful to his God without ostentation
Upright and just in all his dealings
Benevolent and Compassionate his
Liberality and Charity was Extended
to all
We therefore piously hope he is now
Enjoying the Happiness resserved for
The pure in Heart with his Saviour
In the Realms of unfading Bliss.

His wife's tombstone is more simply inscribed:

To the memory of | Bathsheba Ellis | Widow of Dan'l Ellis, dec'd. who departed this life | June 8th, 1795 | in the 64th year of her age.
Beneath this Stone the dust is plac'd
of her who living was possess'd
of cheerful sympathizing mind
of love to God and all mankind.

The will of Daniel Ellis, dated January 8, 1793, proved September 10, 1794, gives to his wife Bathsheba, £1000 at her own disposal, and the use of the house where he then lived, with its furniture, and a meadow by London Bridge (Burlington), during her natural life. To his children, Samuel, Micajah, Charles and Rowland, each £1200, which they had respectively already received; to his son Daniel, the interest of £1200 for his lifetime, and then to the testator's surviving children; to his son Richard, £1200, on arriving at the age of twenty-one. He provides that his negro woman called Pender, shall be set free and receive £15 and articles in her room; also that his negro woman called Tenah shall be set free when twenty-three; he gives £15 to St. Mary's Church as a fund to pay an Orthodox minister. He provides that Maria Howe, wife of John Howe, shall have a deed made to her for household goods, lands, etc., to fulfil a trust. His executors were also directed to make deeds for lands surveyed by him in Gloucester county; they were also authorized to sell and convey all his lands, proprieties and unlocated lands to any persons. He gave to the Council of Proprietors for their own use, his book that had the account of the General Proprietors stated. Executors—Sons Micajah Ellis and Charles Ellis. Witnesses—Edward Collins, Israel Tomkin and George Sweetman.—*N. J. Wills*, Liber 33, p. 450. His widow did not long survive him. Her will, dated May 26, 1795, was proved June 15, 1795, at Burlington. She gives to her sons Rowland and Ellis "£1,000 I am entitled to under the will of my late husband, Daniel Ellis, and all money due me from my late mother also deceased, which is £60, in hands of my son, Charles Ellis;" to three daughters in law, Nancy Bloomfield, Sarah Ellis and Mary Ellis, all her wearing apparel, to be equally shared; to Agnes Treat, wife of Dr. Samuel Treat, her gold watch. Executors—sons Rowland and Richard Ellis. Witnesses —William Orr, Thomas Adams.—*N. J. Wills*, Liber No. 35, p. 209. Daniel Ellis and Bathsheba his wife had issue:

   i. Joseph[3], bap. May, 1755; d. Oct. 7, 1785, "after a short illness;" he was buried Oct. 9, 1785.

   ii. Micajah, m. Sarah ———; d. March 20, 1813, in his 49th yr.; she d. Dec. 2, 1836, aged 72 yrs. Children—1. Micajah S., d. Sept. 2, 1819, in his 24th yr.; 2. Bertha S., m. Dr. Davidson, and survived him, dying April 5, 1878, aged 84 yrs.

   iii. Charles, b. Feb. 12, 1767; m. Mary ———; d. June 17, 1842; she d. May 27, 1830, aged 63 yrs. Child: Daniel C., d. January 8, 1862, in his 70th year.

   iv. Martha, b. May 27, 1769; bap. July 2, 1769; buried Nov. 13, 1772.

   v. Rowland, "5th child," buried Aug. 15, 1770.

   vi. Rowland, b. July 8, 1771, bap. at Burlington, Aug. 21, 1771.

   vii Richard, b. Aug. 13, 1773; bap. Aug. 22, 1773; twin with Sarah.

   viii. Sarah, b. Aug. 13, 1773; bap. Aug. 22, 1773; buried Aug. 25, 1773.

   ix. Rowland, b. Nov. 5, 1774, at Burlington; m. Hannah ———; d. Feb. 6, 1845.

   x. Daniel, d. Dec. 22, 1859, in his 80th yr.

   xi. Samuel.

There was another Rowland Ellis among Friends in Philadelphia or vicinity. He was from Bryn Mawr, near Dolgelly, North Wales.— *Pa. Mag.*, 4: 324-5. Ellis Ellis, of Haverford, Pa., in his will, dated 1705, names Rowland Ellis as executor.—*Philadelphia Wills*, Book C, p. 28.

There was still another Rowland Ellis, of Boston, in New England, 1776-1807, a descendant of John Ellis, Jr., who came to Plymouth in the Mayflower.

JACOB EOFF.

Jacob Eoff, senior, was one of the German Palatine emigrants who arrived at New York in 1710, when he was aged 32 years. In 1742 he bought from Dr. Lewis and Mary Johnston a tract of 432 acres, at Pluckamin, and built a substantial house, where he kept tavern. He gave the site for the erection of St. Paul's Lutheran church at Pluckamin, in 1756, and £20 in money. He was a member of the vestry of Zion Lutheran church of New Germantown in 1767. The Provincial Council of Safety ordered, July 22, 1777, that he and other citizens of Somerset County should be apprehended and brought before that body to take the oath of allegiance to the State. His will, dated Aug. 12, 1772, was proved Sept. 10, 1780, which would seem to indicate that he was more than 100 years old at the time of his death. His children were: 1. John; 2. Peter, innholder; 3. Garret; 4. Jacob, bap. Jan. 19, 1728; 5. Abraham, bap. Oct. 25, 1730; 6. Robert, bap. May 24, 1741; d. 1814; 7. Cornelis, bap. Dec. 18, 1743; 8. Christian, tavern keeper; 9. Mary Magdalen; 10. Mary; 11. Catharine.—*The Early Germans of New Jersey*, by Theodore Frelinghuysen Chambers, Dover, N. J., 1895, 351; *Story of an Old Farm*; *Hist. Hunterdon and Somerset Counties*; *Minutes Council of Safety*.

CAPTAIN ROBERT ERSKINE.

Robert Erskine, son of the Rev. Ralph Erskine, of Dunfermline, Scotland (who is buried in Dryburgh Abbey), was born September 7th,

ERSKINE: EVANS

1735. In 1771 or 1772 he came to America, to act as manager for the London Company's extensive iron mines at Ringwood, Charlottesburgh, &c., in the upper part of the present Passaic county, in which position he proved to be a man of excellent capacity, and thoroughly devoted to the interests of his employers. But as early as 1774 he was in active sympathy with the colonists in their opposition to the oppressive measures of the British ministry. In the summer of 1775 he organized a military company, composed of men employed at the iron works. This was done, primarily, to keep the men together, and at work, but he tendered their services to the province, whereupon the Provincial Congress commissioned him Captain, and enacted that his men should be exempt from compulsory service in any other company. Subsequently, when Washington passed through the Ringwood valley, on his way from the Hudson river, he made the acquaintance of Erskine, and finding him an accomplished civil engineer, and, moreover, thoroughly acquainted with the country west of the Hudson, he caused him to be commissioned, July 27th, 1777, Geographer and Surveyor-General to the American Army, in which position he made a series of maps, still preserved, showing the topography of the country, and every stream, road and house from the Hudson river, westerly, to Ringwood, and from Jersey City to Cornwall. Erskine died October 2d, 1780, and is buried at Ringwood, his grave being marked by a slab of gray marble, suitably inscribed. In communicating the fact of his death to Congress, Washington spoke of him as "that useful and valuable officer."—*Sparks,* VII., 107. The Marquis de Chastellux, in passing through the Ringwood valley, stopped at Mrs. Erskine's, December 19th, 1780, and found "a very handsome house, where everybody was in mourning.——Mrs. Erskine, his widow, is about forty and does not appear the less fresh or tranquil for her misfortune."—*Travels in North America,* I., 347. Erskine's grave and monument were restored a few years ago by Abram S. Hewitt, they being near his country house at Ringwood. Erskine's letter-books and accounts with the London Company are in the library of the N. J. Historical Society.—*Proceedings N. J. Historical Society,* for May, 1869; *Historical Sketch of Passaic County,* 1877; 2 *N. J. Archives.* I., 114.

REV. NATHANIEL EVANS.

The best sketch of the Rev. Nathaniel Evans is that by the Rev. William Smith, afterwards Provost of the University of Pennsylvania, and which is prefixed to the talented young missionary's poems:

"The author of the following poems was born in the city of Philadelphia, June 8th, 1742; and was sent to the Academy there, soon after it was first opened, and before the Collegiate part of the Institution was begun. Having spent about six years in Grammar Learning, his parents, who were reputable citizens, designing him for Merchandize, put him Apprentice; but not finding either his genius or inclination leading him much to that profession, he devoted more of his time to the service of the Muses, than to the business of the Counting-House. Soon after the expiration of his apprenticeship, he accordingly returned to the College, and applied himself, with great diligence, to the study of Philosophy and the Sciences, till the Commencement, May 30th, 1765; when, on account of his great merit and promising genius, he was, by special Mandate of the Trustees, upon the recommendation of the Provost and Faculty of Professors, complimented with a Diploma for the degree of Master of Arts; although he had not taken the previous degree of Bachelor of Arts, on account of the interruption in his course of studies, during the term of his apprenticeship.

Immediately after the Commencement he embarked for England, carrying with him recommendations to the Society for propagating the Gospel in foreign parts, as a fit person to supply the new Mission, then proposed to be opened for Gloucester county, in New-Jersey. Upon the Society's nomination, he was admitted into holy orders by the present Lord Bishop of London, Dr. Terrick, who expressed great satisfaction in his examination, and particularly in the perusal of an elegant English piece which he composed in a few minutes, upon a Theological question, which he was desired to give his sentiments upon. He returned from England, and landed at Philadelphia, December 26th, 1765; having had for his fellow-passenger (among others) the worthy and ingenious Lady, to whom many of his pieces are addressed. Upon his arrival, he entered immediately upon the business of his Mission; and alas! but just lived long enough to shew, by the goodness of his temper, the purity of his morals, the cheerfulness and affability of his conversation, the sublimity and soundness of his doctrines, and the warmth of his Pulpit Compositions, how well he was qualified for the sacred office, to which he had now wholly devoted himself. He died October 29th, 1767, lamented by all that knew him; and by none more earnestly and affectionately, than by his own Congregations, whom he had not yet served two years."

Mr. Evans is said to have attended a Moravian boarding school at Germantown, which was opened in 1746. While in London he seems to have formed a lasting friendship with William Strahan, the bookseller, who, writing April 7, 1766, to David Hall, the Philadelphia printer, sends his "best compliments to Mr. N. Evans." "Tell him 1 received his letter from Dr. F. for which I thank him, and shall take his advice."—*Penn. Mag. of Hist. and Biog.*, X., 99; XIX., 110. The present writer has found no record of Mr. Evans's baptism or parentage. His poems were published with this title and imprint: Poems | on | several occasions, with | some other compositions. | By Nathaniel Evans, A. M. | Late Missionary (appointed by the Society for Pro- | pagating the Gospel) for Gloucester County, | in New-Jersey; and Chaplain to the Lord Vis- | count Kilmorey, of the Kingdom of Ireland. | Philadelphia: | Printed by John Dunlap, in Market-street. | M.DCC.LXLII. | 8vo. Pp. xxviii, 160, 24. Size of type-page, 3¼x6 inches. Title, 1 leaf. Prefatory sketch, [iii]-x. List of Subscribers, [xi]-xxviii. Poems, 1-160. The Love of the World incompatible with the Love of God: a Discourse on 1 John II., 15, 16, 17. Title, 1 leaf; To the Members of the Congregation of Gloucester, dated Haddonfield, April 18, 1766, pp. 5-6; Discourse, 7-24. It was probably printed separately, with a half title (pp. 1-2). The list of subscribers foots up 970 copies subscribed for, of which 461 were taken by booksellers, 150 going to two dealers in Charleston, S. C., indicating some special influence thereabouts, to secure so large a sale in advance of publication. The list of individual subscribers includes a very large number of prominent people in New York. New Jersey and Pennsylvania, as well as many in the remoter Colonies, so far north as Quebec and Nova Scotia, and south to Barbadoes, and a goodly number abroad, among the latter being Oliver Goldsmith, Esq; London.

It may be added that his father was Edward Evans, who d. near Gloucester, Oct. 21, 1771; "a Gentleman of exemplary Piety and Virtue," says the *Pennsylvania Chronicle*, Oct. 14, 1771. His remains were taken to Philadelphia "and decently interred in Friends' Burying Ground," indicating his religious affiliations during his life.

EWING FAMILY: FAUCONIER

EWING FAMILY.

The Ewing family of New Jersey is descended from Finlay Ewing, a Scotch Presbyterian, who left Scotland, with his wife Jane, during the religious oppressions, and settled in Londonderry, Ireland. For his bravery at the battle of Boyne Water, in 1690, he was presented with a sword by King William III. His son, Thomas Ewing, born in Londonderry, came to America, in 1718, on account of the troubles in Ireland, and settled at Greenwich, now in Cumberland County, N. J. He there married, in 1720, a granddaughter of Thomas Maskell, of England, who had married Bythia Parsons, in Connecticut, in 1658. (Thomas Maskell, 2d, their son, was one of the grantees, in April, 1717, of the site for the Presbyterian Church at Greenwich.) Thomas Ewing's oldest child was Maskell Ewing, born in 1721; he married Mary Paget, of English descent, in 1743. She proved herself a thorough housekeeper, and a helpmeet in every sense of the word. Maskell attained to much prominence in his neighborhood, being appointed to various local offices, and in 1757 was appointed Sheriff of Cumberland County, from which he retired in 1760. He was commissioned, March 12, 1762, one of the Surrogates for West Jersey, holding that office until 1776. He is said to have been County Clerk also, and Judge of the Common Pleas. He died in 1796. He had ten children, among them

1. Maskell, 2d, born January 30, 1758. He was elected Clerk of the Assembly before he was twenty-one, and removed to Trenton for the greater convenience of attending to the duties of the office, which he retained for twenty years. He was Recorder of Trenton for some time. In 1803 he removed to Philadelphia, and in 1805 to Delaware County, Penn., representing the latter county in the State Senate of Pennsylvania for six years. He died August 26, 1825.

2. James, the youngest son, married Martha Boyd, whose father came from the North of Ireland in 1772 and settled at Bridgeton, where he died the year after. James Ewing was a member of the famous "Tea Party" which, on the night of Thursday, December 22, 1774, destroyed a quantity of tea which had been landed at Greenwich, contrary to the Articles of Association of the Continental Congress. He was elected to the Assembly from Cumberland County in 1778, and liked the atmosphere of Trenton so well that he took up his residence there the next year, 1779. He engaged in mercantile business, and for a short time was a partner of Isaac Collins, the printer of the New Jersey Gazette. For several years he was one of the Commissioners of the State Loan Office. He was the author of an ingenious "Columbian Alphabet," an attempt at a reformed system of spelling, which he explained in a pamphlet published at Trenton in 1798. He was Mayor of Trenton, 1797-1803. He died October 23, 1823. His only son, Charles Ewing, born in 1780, was Chief Justice of New Jersey, 1824-1832, dying in office.—*Hall's Hist. Pres. Church in Trenton*, 363; *Genealogy of Early Settlers of Trenton and Ewing*, by Rev. Eli F. Cooley, Trenton, 1883, 64; *Elmer's Cumberland County*; *Elmer's Reminiscences*, 326; *N. J. Archives*, IX., 359; X., 532.

PETER FAUCONIER.

Peter Fauconier was a great favorite with young Lord Cornbury, and when the latter was commissioned Governor of New York and New Jersey, in 1702, he at once arranged with Fauconier to supply the troops with clothing. He came to America in the household of the newly appointed Governor, in 1702, and on that account was immediately made a freeman of the city of New York, by the corporation, June 27, 1702. He is therein designated "Gentleman." The clothing contract had been transferred to one J. Champante, but Fauconier was appointed one of the commissioners to examine the clothing supplied by Champante. It is not surprising to find that his opinion was unfavorable. This led Champante to write to the Lords of Trade, March 22, 1702-3, in self-defence, and in criticism of Lord Cornbury and Fauconier, the latter being characterized as "a Frenchman and a bankrupt here tho' now thought by his Lordship to be the properest manager of Her Majesty's revenue there." Lord Cornbury did indeed regard him as "an excellent accountant," and accordingly selected him, in 1704, to audit Lord Bellomont's accounts as Governor. In 1705 he recommended him for Collector and Receiver General of New York. "He is one of the best accomptants that ever I knew, he is a Man of very great application to and diligent in business, And I have by experience found him a very honest Man, he has been Naval Officer ever since I came into this Province, which he has executed with the utmost diligence, and has taken pains to acquaint himself very well with the Laws of Trade." Fauconier once rejected a bribe of £50 offered to influence his action as Naval Officer. He was regarded as the "Chief Manager of affairs" in New York, in 1707, by his and the Governor's enemies. There was some trouble between him and the Assembly over £500 which had been paid him for the erection of a fort on the Indian frontiers, but he boldly challenged an inquiry into his accounts, and produced vouchers showing that he had disbursed £2,000 on this account. Being Receiver General of New Jersey also, the Assembly demanded his accounts, in 1709, which he promptly presented, from December, 1704, to December, 1708; but he firmly declined to produce his vouchers, on the plea that they were under the control of the Governor. Gov. Robert Hunter did not have the same confidence in his accounts that Cornbury had expressed.—He was largely interested in real estate speculations, and it was charged that he was a patentee in "all the grants for lands that are good and valuable." He was concerned in extensive tracts in Ulster, Albany and Kings Counties. His familiarity with land patents, and his experience as a collector of revenue, led him to recommend in 1709 the survey of the line between New York and New Jersey. In that year he bought of William Davis a tract of 2,424 acres of land on the east of Hackensack River. Peter Sonmans having secured the Indian deed for the Ramapo tract, Nov. 18, 1709, took out a patent therefor, which on Dec. 10, 1709, he conveyed to Peter Fauconier, Lucas Kierstead, Andrew Fresneau, Elias Boudinot and others. On April 25, 1710, they caused the tract to be surveyed, for 42,500 acres, beginning at the "Big Rock," four or five miles northwest of Paterson, and embracing most of the northwestern portion of the present Bergen County. It is probable that Fauconier settled on the "Ramapo Patent," as it was called, within a few years after the date of this deed, and in the neighborhood of Paramus. To encourage the establishment of a church there he made a written offer, Dec. 26, 1730, to give a site for a Reformed Dutch Church. When the people decided to build they voted that "Peter Fauconier shall have seats for himself and wife for a continual possession for themselves and their heirs." His earliest religious affiliations were naturally with the French Church, in New York. . Madelaine Fauconier, his wife, was a witness at a baptism there, Nov. 21, 1703. He had three children (perhaps more), probably all born before his coming to America:

    i.   Madelaine, m. Pierre (or Peter) Valleau, and lived at or near Paramus, Bergen county. (For some account of her children, see Valleau.)

    ii. Theodorus.

    iii. Jeanne Elizabeth, b. 1699; m. 1st, August 12, 1725, in

Christ church, Philadelphia, Robert Assheton, of a
Lancashire (England) family; he was a Supreme
Court Judge and Provincial Councillor of Pennsylvania; he d. suddenly, in 1727. She m. 2d, April 8,
1729, the Rev. Archibald Cummings, Rector of Christ
church, Philadelphia, who d. in April, 1741. She m.
3d, his successor in that Rectorship, the Rev. Robert
Jenny, who d. January 5, 1762, aged 75; she d. six
days later, in her 64th year, and is buried with her
third husband in Christ church.

JOHN FELL.

John Fell was the senior member of the firm of John Fell & Co., merchants in New York, at least as early as 1759, when they had several
armed merchant vessels plying the seas. He continued in New York
for some years thereafter. Subsequently—just when is not known—
he purchased a tract of 220 acres, being 32x69 chains in area, at or
near Paramus, in Bergen county. He called the place Petersfield.
probably in imitation of Colonel Philip Schuyler's Petersboro, opposite
to Belleville. The name Petersfield was doubtless, however, suggested
in honor of some relative of John Fell, perhaps his father. From the
beginning of the Revolution he took a most positive stand in favor of
his country, serving with great energy as Chairman of the Bergen
County Committee, in which capacity he gained the reputation of
being "a great Tory hunter." He was a member of the Provincial
Congress which met at Trenton in May, June and August, 1775, and
of the Council in the first State Legislature, in 1776. On the night of
April 22d, 1777, he was taken prisoner at his house by twenty-five
armed men, who hurried him to Bergen Point, where Colonel Abraham
Van Buskirk was in command of the British forces. The two men had
been well acquainted before the war, and when Fell was brought before Van Buskirk the latter remarked: "Times have changed since
we last met." "So I perceive," replied the prisoner. Van Buskirk,
however, assured him that on account of their previous acquaintance
he would give him a letter to General Robertson, in New York, with
whom he was well acquainted, and this letter would doubtless insure
him proper treatment. Fell was sent to New York and confined in the
provost jail, where he was treated with such severity that the New
Jersey Committee of Safety offered to release James Parker and Walter
Rutherford in exchange for John Fell and Wynant Van Zandt, on October 16th, 1777. This proposition not being acceded to, the committee,
on November 17th, 1777, ordered that Parker and Rutherford be committed to the Morris county jail until Fell and Van Zandt should be
released. General Robertson does not appear to have seen Fell until
December 8th following, when he called upon him at the jail. Fell
gave him the letter of Colonel Van Buskirk, which he read and then
handed back, with a curious smile, to the prisoner, who found that
the purport of the letter was that "John Fell was a great rebel and a
notorious rascal." But it happened that General Robertson and Fell
had made each other's acquaintance years before, after the capture of
Quebec, during the French War. "You must be changed, indeed, John
Fell," said the General, "if you are as great a rascal as this Colonel
Van Buskirk." He assured the prisoner that he would secure him
good treatment, but he afterwards declared that owing to various circumstances he was unable to show him the favor he desired. However, on January 7th, 1778, he secured his release on parole, and in
the following May Fell was allowed to go home. The New Jersey Legislature elected him, November 6th, 1778, one of the State's delegates

to Congress, in which capacity he served two years. He was evidently a man of considerable means and accustomed to live in good style, and was frequently the guest of John Adams and other distinguished members of that notable body. A diary kept by him while in Congress was formerly owned by Gen. Wm. S. Stryker. Fell was elected a member of the Legislative Council from Bergen county in 1782 and 1783. The Legislature appointed him, September 6th, 1776, one of the Common Pleas Judges of Bergen county, and at the expiration of his term he was reappointed, September 28th, 1781. He sold his Petersfield estate, November 1st, 1793 to John H. Thompson, a merchant of New York City, for £2,000. In the deed he is described as "John Fell of Petersfield, Bergen County, Esq." He then removed to New York, Dutchess county, taking up his residence with his son, Peter, and died at Coldenham. He m. Susanna Marschalk, wid. of —— McIntosh.

2. Peter Renaudet[2] (John[1]) Fell raised a regiment of militia, and was elected by the New York Legislature to be Lieutenant Colonel of the First Regiment of Bergen County Militia, March 27, 1778. He devoted himself so zealously to the service, and exposed himself so recklessly that he became hopelessly crippled with rheumatism, and rejoined his command Oct. 5, 1779. He subsequently, however, acted as aid to Gov. Clinton, of New York, during the last two years of the war. Being sent on some duty from West Point, where Gov. Clinton was, he had the good fortune to be present at the taking of Stony Point, where he acted as a volunteer in the assault. After the war he settled in New York, following his father's mercantile pursuits, but on account of failing health withdrew from that occupation, and retired to Coldenham. There he spent his time overseeing his estate, causing himself to be carried about in a chair. He m. in 1781 Margaret, dau. of Cadwallader Colden, 2d, of Coldenham, and granddaughter of Lieutenant-Governor Cadwallader Colden. He d. at Coldenham, Oct. 6, 1789, aged 37, and was buried in the Colden family vault at that place. His wife survived him, and m. 2d, —— Gallatin, by whom she had one son, D. P. Gallatin, who removed to Michigan. Col. Peter R. Fell and Margaret his wife had issue:

    i. Elizabeth, b. in New York; m. her cousin, William Colden, and for many years lived on the old place, built by her father. She became the mother of six children.

    ii. John, b. in New York; m. ——, and left several children. He resided for the last years of his life at the cottage at Coldenham.

    iii. Susan, b. at Paramus; m. at the age of 22 Charles Rhind, of New York, she became the mother of ten children, one of whom was the late Admiral Alexander Colden Rhind, U. S. N.

HENDRICK FISHER.

Hendrick Fisher was b. in 1697, in the Palatinate, and came to this country when young, taking up his residence near Bound Brook. He was received into the Reformed Dutch church of that place in 1721, and held various offices in the church thereafter, being also a lay preacher. By an act of the Legislature, passed ————, 1739, he was naturalized. The next year he was elected to the Assembly from Somerset, but was declared ineligible, on the ground that not enough time had elapsed since his naturalization, which had taken place only the preceding session. He stated that he had been informed he had a right to sit as a member of the Assembly, by virtue of an act of Parliament passed in Queen Anne's reign, which naturalized other Germans, the provisions of the same act being thought to include him. Thomas Leonard, however, was chosen in his place, and took his seat May 28, 1740. Mr. Fisher was again elected in 1745, and qualified without objection. He was re-elected in 1746, 1749, 1751, 1754, 1761, 1769 and 1772, representing his county continuously for thirty years. He was manager of the Bound Brook bridge lottery in 1762, and in 1764 of the lottery for the benefit of the New Jersey College. In 1765 he was designated by act of the Legislature to pay the New Jersey Regiment which had served in 1764. When the Colonies agreed to send delegates to meet in a Continental Congress, in New York, in September, 1765, Hendrick Fisher was one of the three delegates chosen by the Legislature to represent New Jersey, and he signed the resolutions adopted, and the address to the King and Parliament, urging the repeal of the Stamp Act; he also made the report to the Legislature in behalf of his colleagues. In 1775 he was elected a member of the first Provincial Congress of New Jersey, of which body he was chosen President at the sitting in May of that year. At the session in October, 1775, when Samuel Tucker was chosen President, Fisher was elected Vice-President. He was also a member of the Committee of Safety, appointed by the Provincial Congress, Oct. 28, 1775. He proved himself an ardent, able and courageous friend of his country. He died Aug. 16, 1779, and was buried on his farm.—*Messler's Hist. Somerset County*, 56; *Assembly Minutes*, passim; *Raritan Church Records; Session Laws*, etc.; *N. J. Archives*, XIX., 390-391 The fullest sketch of Mr. Fisher that has appeared is by the Rev. Theodore Davis, read before the N. J. Historical Society at the annual meeting in January, 1899, and published in the Proceedings of the Society, Third Series, IV, p. 129.

PHILIP VICARS FITHIAN.

Philip Vicars Fithian was born in Cumberland County, New Jersey. In connection with his classmate, Andrew Hunter, and about forty other young patriots, he assisted in the destruction of a cargo of tea at Greenwich, New Jersey, on the evening of November 22, 1774. Mr. Fithian was licensed to preach by the Presbytery of Philadelphia in 1775. For some time he labored as a missionary under the direction of the Presbytery, and then entered the army as Chaplain. At the battle of White Plains he fought in the ranks. He died in 1776 from disease contracted in camp. Mr. Fithian was never ordained. A volume of his "Journal and Letters, 1767-1774," was published by the Princeton Historical Association in 1900.

JACOB FORD, First and Second.

Col. Jacob Ford, senior, was a son of John Ford (son of William and Sarah Dingley Ford, b. at Duxbury or Marshfield, Mass., 1659; settled at Woodbridge, N. J., in 1700 or earlier; deacon of the Presbyterian church there in 1708, and elder in 1710; removed to Morris county; d. before May, 1724. John Ford m. at Woodbridge, Dec. 13, 1701, Elizabeth Freeman, who was b. in March, 1681, "in the city of Axford, Old England, came to Philadelphia when there was but one house in it— and into this province when she was but one year and a half old: deceased April 21, 1772, aged 91 years and one month." Jacob Ford, senior, the son of John Ford, was born at Woodbridge, April 13, 1704. He was one of the pioneers in the iron business of New Jersey, and for nearly half a century was interested in mines and forges in Morris

county and vicinity. In 1738 he applied for a license to keep an inn at
"New Hanover" (now Morristown). When Morris county was created,
in 1739, the first courts were held at Jacob Ford's house, and in 1740
he was appointed collector of Morris township. In 1748 he located the
land on both sides of the river at Rockaway, and the tract was said
to include Job Allen's iron works, which are believed to have been built
in 1730. He was Judge of the Morris county courts in 1740, and most
of the time for the next forty years; was a ruling elder in the First
Presbyterian church of Morristown from 1747. In 1755 he had command of a detachment of 300 men to protect the frontiers against
threatened invasion of French and Indians. He m., in 1742, Hannah
Baldwin (dau. of Jonathan Baldwin and Susanna Kitchell, b. Nov., 1701;
d. July 31, 1777); he d. Jan. 19, 1777. It is believed that he built (in
1774) the house afterwards occupied by his son, Col. Jacob Ford, junior
(b. Feb. 10, 1738; m. Jan. 27, 1762, Theodosia Johnes, and d. Jan. 11,
1777), and which was occupied by Washington in 1779-80, and is now
owned by the Washington Association.—*Hist. of Morris County, New
Jersey*, New York, 1882, passim; *Centennial Collections of Morris County*,
passim; *The Records of the First Presbyterian Church of Morristown, N. J.*,
I., 19; II., 76; *Woodbridge and Vicinity*, by J. W. Dally, New Brunswick,
1873, 167, 169; *N. J. Archives*, XII., 665-666.

Jacob Ford, junior, was the Colonel of the Eastern Battalion of the
Morris County, New Jersey, Militia. He was also in commission as
Colonel of a battalion of New Jersey State Troops, organized in the
counties of Bergen, Essex and Morris. He died of pneumonia, at Morristown, N. J., Jan. 10, 1777, brought on by exposure in repelling the
incursions of the British the month previous, and was buried with military honors by order of General Washington. His residence in Morristown is now the historic building known as "Washington Headquarters." He built a powder mill for the use of the American Army.—*N. J.
Archives*, 2d Series, I., 121.

EBENEZER FOSTER.

Ebenezer Foster was a prominent citizen of Woodbridge some years
before the Revolution. He was already one of the trustees of the Free
Schools of the Township when Governor Franklin granted a charter
of incorporation to the trustees, June 24, 1769, naming Mr. Foster as
one of them. He was a vestryman of the Church of England of Woodbridge, and was named as such in the charter incorporating the
church, December 6, 1769. He was appointed a justice of the peace of
Middlesex County, June 9, 1770. He was commissioned a Judge of the
Court of Oyer and Terminer of the same county, July 10, 1773, and on
December 14, 1773, was appointed a Judge of the Court of Common
Pleas of that county. His sympathies were evidently with the British,
and perhaps it was because this fact was well understood, that at a
meeting of the freeholders of the county, on January 3, 1775, held pursuant to the recommendations of the Continental Congress, he was
appointed on a committee of observation for Woodbridge, apparently
with the purpose of getting him committed to the American cause. A
few days later, at a meeting of the inhabitants of the town, he was
appointed on the committee of observation, and with two others was
authorized, in case the Assembly failed to appoint delegates to the
Continental Congress in the May following, to meet with the committees from the other counties of the province in Provincial Congress,
and appoint such delegates. On January 16, 1775, at a general meeting
of the committee of observation and inspection, Mr. Foster was
appointed on the committee of correspondence for the County of
Middlesex. Subsequently, just when we have no record, Mr. Foster

was arrested as a sympathizer with the British. At a meeting of the Convention of the State of New Jersey, July 19, 1776, he "asked and was given leave on his parole, and security in the sum of £1000, to remove to the public house of Mr. White, in Barnardstown, in the county of Somerset, and not to go more than six miles from thence, unless with the leave of the Convention, or the future Legislature of this state." His confinement naturally was irksome, and on August 2, he prayed that he might be permitted to return to his farm at Woodbridge, but the petition was ordered to lie on the table. When the British overran New Jersey, in December, 1776, he was released, and returned home. He remained there but a short time, where he was employed, according to his own statement made some years later, "in taking (by virtue of a special commission for that purpose) the Submission of such of the Inhabitants of his Neighbourhood as wished for British Protection," until the surprise and capture of the Hessians at Trenton, when, on January 2, 1777, he "crossed over to Staten Island, where he was frequently hunted by small Parties of Jersey Militia," inquisition was found against him and many other persons of Middlesex county, "who had either joined the army of the King of Great Britain, or had otherwise offended against the form of their allegiance to the State," and he was advertised August 15, 1778. Judgment final was entered against him in due course, and his property was advertised to be sold on March 22, 1779. While on Staten Island he witnessed the will of Oswald Ford, September 22, 1777, another refugee from Woodbridge. His family were sent to him, and after three years he removed to New York, where he remained until April 27, 1783, when he sailed for Nova Scotia. While in the British lines he "attempted every service required of him" by the British commanders. In a communication to the printer of the *Royal Gazette*, of New York, of August 5, 1780, he says he did not join the army, but accompanied it into New Jersey on the occasion of the raid upon Connecticut Farms, and saw the body of Parson Caldwill's wife immediately after she had been shot by a British soldier. In just what capacity he was with the army he does not state, but presumably as a guide. His account of the shooting of Mrs. Caldwell entirely lacks any expression of horror or even regret which the shocking tragedy would naturally excite in any humane breast. He claimed compensation from the British Government for his losses, in a statement dated at St. John, New Brunswick, March 14, 1786, in which he listed a farm of 149 acres, with buildings, &c., in Woodbridge, valued at £1788; and a farm of 52 acres in Bergen county, valued at £156; and personal estate valued at £1500, in New York currency, or £843. 15, or £1937. 5 in all. Of his Woodbridge lands 72 acres came to him by descent from his mother, Margaret Heddon, who died about 1767; 22 acres by deed from Charles Wright, in 1753; 22 acres by deed from David Wright, in 1754; 10 acres from Joseph Shotwell, in 1755; 19 acres from Silas Walker. His Bergen county lands were bought from George Sly, in 1771. Stephen Foster and Lawrence Foster, his sons, made oath in support of their father's claim, as did Joseph Thorne and William Bears, two of his neighbors. He was allowed £906. He resided at Kingston, King county, New Brunswick, Canada.

GEORGE FRASER, JUN.

George Fraser, junior, was commissioned an Ensign in the 60th (Royal American) Regiment, June 23, 1760; and lieutenant in the 78th Regiment, April 24, 1761. The 60th (known as the 62d, prior to 1758) served in America from 1756 to 1773; and the 78th from 1758 to 1763.

FRAZER: FRELINGHUYSEN:
FURGLER (or PHYLE)

REV. WILLIAM FRAZER.

The Rev. William Frazer took charge, in 1768, of St. Thomas' church, at Kingwood, and St. Andrew's church, of Amwell, and a third at Mosconetcong, twenty-eight miles north of Kingwood. He labored in these several charges until the breaking out of the Revolution. "Being supported by a British Missionary Society, he would not omit the prayers for the royal family. This rendered him obnoxious to the patriots. One Sunday, when he entered his church, a rope was hanging over the pulpit. Public sentiment grew so violent that he was compelled to suspend worship in his church. But so prudent was his conduct and so lovely his character, that soon after peace was declared he reopened his church and resumed his ministry, with general acceptance." He died in 1795, aged 52 years. He m., July 13, 1768, Rebecca (bap. March, 1750), dau. of the Rev. Colin Campbell, missionary in St. Mary's church, Burlington, and Mary Martha Bard, his wife. Issue: 1. Colin, b. May 24, 1769; 2. Elizabeth, d. Aug. 21, 1774, aged three months; and perhaps others.

GENERAL FREDERICK FRELINGHUYSEN.

Frederick Frelinghuysen was a son of the Rev. John Frelinghuysen, of New Jersey. He was sent as a delegate to the Continental Congress from New Jersey in 1775, when but twenty-one years of age. He resigned in 1777. He entered the Revolutionary Army as Captain of a corps of artillery, and was at the battles of Trenton and Monmouth. He was afterwards engaged actively as a Colonel of the militia of his native State. He also served in the Western Expedition as Major-General of the New Jersey and Pennsylvania troops. In 1793 he was elected to the Senate of the United States, and continued in that station until domestic bereavements, and the claims of his family, constrained him to resign in 1796. General Frelinghuysen stood also among the first at the Bar of New Jersey. He was the father of the Hon. Theodore Frelinghuysen. He died April 13, 1804.—*N. J. Archives*, XXVII., 266-267.

FRANCIS FURGLER (or PHYLE).

The Pennsylvania Evening Post, of January 31, 1778, announces the death, on the 19th of that month, of this singular character, "Francis Furgler, the hermit," in his 66th year, who had existed alone twenty-five years in a thick wood, about four miles from Burlington, "in a cell made by the side of an old log in the form of a small oven, not high or long enough to stand upright in or lie extended." It was thought he meant by living his secluded life "to do penance for crimes committed in his own country, for he was a man subject to violent passions." From whence he came or who he was nobody could find out, but he appeared to be by his dialect a German, yet he spoke that language imperfectly, either through design or from a defect in his intellects. . . . He was found dead in his cell, with a crucifix and a brass fish by his side; and on the 20th he was decently interred in Friends burying place at Mountholly." In 1811 there was published a small volume, 12mo in form, the type-page only 2¼x3⅜ inches size, and bound in boards, with this title-page: *THE HERMIT*, | or an account of *Francis Adam Joseph Phyle*, | a native of Switzerland, | Who lived without the use of fire for upwards | of twenty-two years, in a small cave, in the | midst of a wood, near Mount-Holly, in | Burlington county, New Jersey; and was found | dead therein, in the year 1780. | In a series of letters, | from | Batlus Hiltzhimer to Melchoir Miller. |

FURGLER (or PHYLE): FURMAN

Interspersed with some | *Observations of the Author, and Senti-* | *ments of celebrated men.* | NEW JERSEY: | Published by John Atkinson ¡ Printed by John Bioren, No. 88, Chestnut- | Street, Philadelphia. | 1811. | Pp. 102. A second edition appeared in the same year, with precisely the same title-page, except that the name "Batlus" was corrected to "Baltus," and the imprint was divided thus: "Printed by John Bioren, No. 88, Chestnut-Street, | Philadelphia," and the line "Second Edition." was inserted above "New Jersey" in the imprint. The two editions are identical down to page 60; beginning with that page the second edition has twenty-one lines to the page, instead of twenty, as in the first edition, but the lines are identical, the same type having been used. The first edition ends with Letter VIII, November, 1780, on p. 102. In the second edition this letter ends on p. 99, and there is added a Letter IX, December 25th, 1780, pp. 100-108. The writer states that in the spring of 1756 Francis appeared in the neighborhood of Mt. Holly, wearing the uniform of a French soldier, and totally ignorant of the English language. He had dug out a hole under a large white oak, prostrated by the storm, in a wood belonging to Joseph Burr, on the road to Burlington, about four miles from the latter place, and two miles from Mt. Holly. This hole or cave was barely large enough for him to stretch himself in it. Six or eight weeks after he settled here he told Col. Charles Read, through an interpreter, that his name was Francis Adam Joseph Phyle; that he was a native of the Canton of Lucern in Switzerland, which he had left on account of some disagreeable circumstances, and went to France; that he came with the French troops to Canada, and soon after, becoming disgusted with the life of a soldier, left them and came to New Jersey. He seemed to be under great distress of mind, occasioned, he said, by a sense of his sins, which appeared to overwhelm him, and there was some hint of his having killed an adversary in a duel. He never used fire, and lived entirely on the charity of the neighbors, until his death, in 1778, and nothing more was ever learned of his history than above related.

MOORE FURMAN.

Moore Furman was, in 1757. Postmaster at Trenton, where he was a highly esteemed merchant, carrying on business in the firm of Read and Furman, with stores kept at Princeton, by Joseph Yard, junior, and at Hopewell, by Josiah Furman, junior. This partnership was dissolved in 1762. In October, of that year, he advertised that the "Shop lately kept by Moore Furman in Trenton,at his House at the Corner, below the Market," was kept by Furman and Hunt, and that he was intending to remove to Philadelphia. Soon after this he removed to Philadelphia. where he was in mercantile business with Andrew Reed, the firm name being Reed & Furman. In 1765 he lived "next Door to the Mayor's, in Water-street." He seems to have retired from his late partnership at this time, as the firm name was Reed & Pettit, in 1765. He appears to have removed thence to Pittstown. N. J., where he was in 1778, but in the spring of 1780 he was at Trenton. He was Deputy Quartermaster General of New Jersey during the war, and General Stryker says "he was a faithful patriot, and greatly entrusted by the government and by Washington during the Revolution." He married Sarah White, eldest daughter of Townsend White, of Philadelphia, March 17, 1767. Mr. Furman was a Trustee of the Presbyterian Church of Trenton, 1760-62. and 1783-1808, and occupied what is now (1897) the hotel known as the State Street House, on State street, having his office in a one-story brick building adjoining. He was the first Mayor of Trenton, under the charter of 1792. He died in that city, March 16, 1808, in his eightieth year.

FRANCIS GERNEAUX.

Francis Gerneaux was a Huguenot on the Isle of Guernsey, in the British Channel, according to family tradition, and was marked out for assassination, getting word of which the night before the day set for his death, he secured a vessel and got out of the harbor with his family before morning. (As Guernsey had long been a stronghold of Protestantism, it is probable that Gerneaux fled to that island, from the French mainland.) He came thence to America, and settled at New Rochelle, New York, where he survived to the great age of 103 years. The family name was transformed in time to its present form. He brought to this country his son Stephen, then a child, who. m. Ann Walton, it is believed, and had nine children who grew up and married. The first was Daniel, who m. Sarah, dau. of Nathaniel Britton, of Staten Island. They had two children b. there, and then removed to Hopewell, N. J., where six more children were born to them, among them John Gano, b. July 22, 1727. He was ordained to the ministry May 29, 1754, at Hopewell, entering immediately upon the charge of the infant Baptist church at Morristown, which he served for two years, with considerable intervals of missionary tours in the South. In 1756 he accepted an urgent call to Yadkin, N. C., where he remained two years and a half, when he returne dto New Jersey, taking up his residence at Elizabethtown. He preached alternately at Philadelphia and New York, but in 1761 accepted a call to the latter place, where he continued until 1776. He now acted as chalpain of a Connecticut regiment, through the battles in and about New York, the retreat across New Jersey, and the battles of Trenton and Princeton. He was subsequently chaplain of Gen. Clinton's brigade, composed of New York, New England and New Jersey regiments. He accompanied Gen. Sullivan's expedition against the Indians, in 1779, and continued in the service until the close of the war. He then gathered his scattered congregation together again, and the church flourished greatly. In 1787 he accepted a call to Kentucky, where he arrived with his family in June. He remained a year at Lexington, and then removed to Frankfort. He preached continually, frequently going on extensive missionary tours, until afflicted with a paralytic stroke, in the latter part of 1798. He d. Aug. 10, 1804, at Frankfort. Mr. Gano m. 1st, Sarah, dau. of John Stites, Mayor of the Borough of Elizabethtown, in 1756; she d. at Frankfort, Ky., about 1788; he m. 2d., about a year later, in North Carolina, a dau. of Jonathan Hunt, and wid. of Capt. Thomas Bryant. Issue: 1. John Stites, b. cir. 1757; d. 1765; 2. Daniel, b. Nov. 11, 1758, at Yadkin, N. C.; 3. Peggy, b. Dec. 23, 1760, at Philadelphia; 4. Stephen, b. Dec. 25, 1762, in New York, afterwards a distinguished Baptist clergyman in Rhode Island; 5. Sarah, b. Feb. 24, 1764, in New York; 6. John Stites, b. July 14, 1766, in New York; 7. A dau., b. Aug. 15, 1768; d. in her 3d yr.; 8. Isaac Eaton, b. 1770; 9. Richard Montgomery, b. 1776, in New York; 10. Susannah, b. Nov. 8, 1777, at New Fairfield, Conn.; 11. William, b. 1781 or 1782; d. cir. 1799.—*Biographical Memoirs of the late Rev. John Gano*, N. Y., 1806; *Edwards's Hist. of the Baptists of N. J.*, 74.

There was also a Gano family in Dutchess county, N. Y., about or prior to the time of the Revolution.

GIBBON FAMILY.

Edmund Gibbon was a merchant in New York, 1673-1682.—*Calendar of N. Y. Hist. MSS.*, II., 34, 100. In 1677, inorder to secure a debt due to him by Edward Duke and Thomas Duke, he took from them a deed for 6,000 acres of land in West Jersey, which had been conveyed to them by John Fenwick, in England. Gibbon, by virtue of this deed, had a tract of 5,500 acres surveyed for him by Richard Hancock, in 1682. It was resurveyed in 1703 by Benjamin Acton, and lay in Cohansey Precinct, now in Greenwich and Hopewell Townships, Cumberland County, including Roadstown, extending southward to Pine Mount Branch, and westward to the Delaware. He devised this tract to his grandson, Edmund, who devised it to Francis Gibbon, of Bennensdere, England. In 1700 Francis devised it to his two kinsmen, Leonard and Nicholas Gibbon, of Gravesend, in Kent, England, describing it as "all that tract of lands called Mount Gibbon, upon the branches of unknown creek, near Cohansey in West Jersey," provided they settled upon it.

Nicholas Gibbon, born in 1702, was a son of Arthur and Jane Gibbon, of Gravesend, Kent, England. Nicholas and his younger brother, Leonard, came to New Jersey and erected one of the first grist-mills near Cohansey. They later built a fulling mill on Mount Gibbon (now Pine Mount) Run. They soon became influential in that neighborhood. In 1730 they divided their tract, Nicholas taking the southern part, including the mill and 2,000 acres of land. Leonard erected a stone house about two miles north of Greenwich. Nicholas built a substantial brick house in Greenwich, which he occupied until about 1740, when he removed to Salem. Both houses were still standing in 1868. The two brothers gave six acres of land in Greenwich for a Presbyterian Church, to be erected by 1729. They were Episcopalians themselves, and erected at their own expense St. Stephen's Church in Greenwich, in 1729, and provided for regular services there. Nicholas was in mercantile business, in partnership with Samuel Fenwick Hedge and Capt. James Gould, the last-named being located in New York, while Gibbon kept store at Greenwich and afterwards at Salem. He was Sheriff of Salem County, 1741-1748, and in the latter year was appointed County Clerk. He was also one of the Commissioners of the Loan Office for Salem County. Hedge dying in 1731, Gibbon married the widow, Anna Grant Hedge. He died 2d of 2d mo. 1758, aged 55 years, 8 months. His widow died 24th of 3d mo. 1760, aged 57 years. They had five children:

i. Nicholas, born 5th of 11th mo. 1732; died 7th of 1st mo. 1748.

ii. Grant, born 28th of 11th mo. 1734. He was a merchant at Salem, and appears to have been a man of superior education and culture. He was one of the Surrogates of West Jersey, was appointed a Justice of the Peace in 1759, a Judge in 1752 and again in 1767, and was Clerk of the County of Salem after his father's death. He was an ardent sympathizer with the American cause, which he evinced in a substantial manner, when, at the solicitation of his fellow citizens, he was appointed, 13th of 10th mo. 1774, to solicit funds for the relief of the people of Boston, when that port was closed to commerce by the British. He collected £157 3s. 2d. for the purpose. He was elected to the Assembly in 1772. He died 27th of 6th mo. 1776.

3. Jane, born 15th of 5th mo. 1736, married Robert Johnson, jun., 3d of 11th mo. 1767, and was the mother of Col. Robert Gibbon Johnson, the historian of Salem; she died 16th of 8th mo. 1815; her husband died 28th of 12th mo. 1796, aged 69 years.

iv. Ann, born 29th of 4th mo. 1741; married Judge Edward Weatherby.

v. Francis, born 14th of 5th mo. 1744; died 11th of 1st mo. 1788.—*History*

GIBBON FAMILY: GOELET

of the Early Settlements of Cumberland County, by Lucius Q. C. Elmer, Bridgeton, 1869, 18; *Historical Account of the First Settlement of Salem,* by Robert G. Johnson, Philadelphia, 1839, 79, 118, 122; *Hist. and Genealogy of Fenwick Colony,* by Thomas Shourds, Bridgeton, 1876, 105-108; *N. J. Archives,* XII., 324; XVII., 205, 342, 455, 517; XVIII., 438; *N. J. Hist. Proc.,* IV., 433-44.

FRANCIS GOELET.

Much interest and importance attached to an act entitled "An Act for the relief of Francis Goelet," passed by the New Jersey Legislature, and which received the Governor's assent April 10, 1761. The act recites: "Whereas *Francis Goelet,* of the City of *Perth Amboy,* hath, by 'his Petition, set forth, that he is under unhappy circumstances, and by misfortunes, rendered incapable of discharging his Creditors just Demands; that he is possessed of sundry Bonds, and other Effects, to a considerable Value, which he is ready and very desirous of assigning and delivering up into the Hands of Trustees justly and fairly, for the Use of his Creditors, or such of them as shall apply for that Purpose, praying the Aid of the Legislature therein." The act then provides that he is to advertise in the *New York Gazette* that he wants to compound with his creditors, vesting 'his estate for that purpose in certain trustees, namely, John Ogden, Andrew Smith, Samuel Kemble, William Bryant and James Neilson. For the benefit of his creditors beyond the sea, said trustees shall "use their utmost Endeavours to notify the foreign Creditors" of having Goelet's estate in their charge, and wait until May 1, 1762, before giving notice in the New York and Pennsylvania *Gazette* and *Mercury* when and where Goelet's property will be sold for the benefit of such creditors as have handed in their claims; after which time no creditor who has not done so shall be entitled to receive anything. The effects of Goelet are not to be taken out of this Province before sale, nor Goelet to be freed from arrest till surety be given. "*Provided* always, That in case it shall thereafter appear, that he the said Francis Goelet, on the Oath to be administered to him by the Trustees aforesaid, respecting his Estate delivered them, hath secreted any Part thereof, he shall not be intituled to any Relief by Virtue of this Act, and every Clause, Article and Thing therein contained, shall be void and of none Effect."

The Lords of Trade advised the King to disapprove this Act, on these grounds: 1. "As this Act is in the nature of a Bankruptcy Act, with respect to the Single Case of one particular person, it appears to Us to be of an Unusual and extraordinary nature, and therefore should have contained a clause suspending its operation until His Majesty's pleasure should be known. 2. The provision for giving notice to foreign creditors is "altogether nugatory and ineffectual." 3. The punishment for his concealing any part of his estate and effects is "much too light and trivial."—*N. J. Archives,* IX., 333-4. The Act was repealed January 14, 1762. Letters of administration were granted, Sept. 4, 1767, to Elizabeth Goelet, widow of Francis Goelet, late of the city of Perth Amboy, deceased. The inventory, signed by the widow, with Jona: Deare and John Griggs as appraisers, amounts to £137, 12s., 7d., all personal property, and mentions: 2 volumes of the "Universal Traveller," 15s.; 2 volumes of Coettegon's Arts and Sciences, 15s.; Sir Phil. Sidney's Arcadia, 5s.; Doctrine of Morality, 7s.; Netleton on Virtue and Comforts, poems, 2s.; Collincby's Memoirs, 4 vols., 4s.; 3 volumes of Shakespeare, 4s.; 2 volumes Telemachus, 1 volume Seneca's Morals and sermons, Geometrical History, 7s.—*E. J. Wills,* Liber I, f. 152.

GORDON

ANDREW GORDON.

Andrew Gordon, of Cranberry (now written Cranbury), in the southern part of Middlesex County, was living there in 1748, when application could be made to him, it was advertised, in reference to the sale of lands in that vicinity.—*N. J. Archives*, XII., 468. He was perhaps the son of Capt. Andrew Gordon (son of Thomas Gordon, one of the most distinguished men in the early annals of New Jersey), who was a Captain in Col. John Parker's regiment on the frontier, in 1721; and who was probably the Andrew Gordon, of Perth Amboy, who had a map of lands for sale in 1733, and who in 1752 was charged with having instigated some contemptuous remarks about Lewis Morris Ashfield.—*N. J. Archives*, XI., 315, 328; VIII., Part I., 42; *Whitehead's Perth Amboy*, 67. The latter, however, in his will, dated Feb. 21, 1777, proved March 26, 1777, in which he describes himself as "Andrew Gordon, of the south ward of Perth Amboy, yeoman," mentions no son, but only his father, Thomas Gordon, his own "grandson, John Von Kirk, jun., son of my daughter, Anne, deceased;" Mary Moore, "now in possession of my tract of land in Windsor, county aforesaid, to have the claim to same." "When the heirs lawfully begotten of the said John Von Kirk jun. shall be extinct, the property bequeathed to him shall become the property of Mary Moore the daughter of Henry Moore deceased and and her heirs." "To Mary Moore, daughter to my late wife Ann Gordon, deceased, a mortgage given by Henry Moore, deceased, to Anthony Hunter, deceased, of New York, which I since paid to the executors of Anthony Hunter." Executors—John Von Kirk, jun., Rescarriah Moore and Mary Moore, daughter of my late wife, Anne Gordon, deceased.—*E. J. Wills*, Liber 18, p. 152.

LEWIS GORDON.

Lewis Gordon was admitted to the New Jersey Bar, May 20, 1755. He advertised, in April, 1756, that he had removed from Easton to Bordentown, "where he may be spoke with by Those who shall be pleased to favour him with their Business."—*N. J. Archives*, XX., 14.

PETER GORDON.

Peter Gordon, of Trenton, merchant, was appointed by Governor Richard Howell to be guardian of one William Voorheis, an infant of fourteen years and upwards, son of Daniel Voorheis, late of Middlesex county, deceased. Elijah H. Gordon, also a merchant of Trenton, went on his bond, which was filed at Burlington, February 9, 1795, and is recorded in Liber 36 of Wills, Secretary of State's Office, page 170.

Peter Gordon married Elizabeth Rhea. The will of this Peter Gordon, who was of Crosswicks, is dated August 20, 1723, and was proved November 1, 1725. He leaves his entire estate to his wife Elizabeth as long as she remains his widow, with remainder to his five children, whose names are not mentioned. As he named no executor, his widow petitioned, Nov. —, 1725, to be made administratrix, and her petition was granted. She speaks of him as of Freehold. His estate was inventoried and appraised at £105. 9. 3.—*N. J. Archives*, XXI., 190, 192. Who were his parents? Who were his children?

Peter Gordon was one of the witnesses to the will of Stephen Cornelious, of Penn's Neck, Salem county, dated April 4, 1726.—*Ib.*, XXI., 110.

Peter Gordon was one of the witnesses to the will of Samuel Reidford, of Freehold, dated Feb. 18, 1709-10.—*Ib.*, XXI., 380.

Peter Gordon was a Captain in the First Regiment, Hunterdon;

GORDON : GRAY : GREEN

Captain, Colonel Forman's Battalion, Heard's Brigade, June 14, 1776; Brigade-Major of same, July 25, 1776.

In the First Presbyterian Churchyard, at Trenton, is the tombstone of Mrs. Susanna Gordon, consort of Major Peter Gordon, died July 18, 1823. No age is given. Adjacent is the tombstone of John Gordon, with no date recorded.

The *Emporium and True American*, published at Trenton, March 7, 1835, contains this obituary notice: "At Geneva, New York, on the 8th ult., in the 88th year of his age. Deacon Peter Gordon, father of Mr. Elijah Gordon."

Peter Gordon, of Middlesex county, set up a lottery, in 1758, for the sale of a tract of 497 acres of land in that county.—*N. J. Archives*, XX., 309 et seqq. The Legislature, in September, 1762, passed an act to render void such lottery, and to relieve the managers from responsibility.—*Ib.*, XVII., 247 et seqq. The act was deemed of sufficient importance to be brought before the Lords of Trade, who advised the King to disallow the act, as being a private matter, in which the Legislature had no concern. The act was accordingly disallowed.—*N. J. Archives*, IX., 443, 446, 458, 487.

CAPTAIN JAMES GRAY.

Captain James Gray located at the Little Falls on the Passaic river (about four miles above the present city of Paterson), where, at least as early as 1763, he carried on iron works, the ore being carted thither on horseback from Ringwood and Charlottenburg. He offered the property for sale, by an advertisement dated December 19, 1770, describing it as "A Plantation of two Hundred and Sixty Acres of Land, great part of which is Meadow with a Forge of three Fires and a Hammer, a grist Mill and saw Mill." He was then living on the premises. He had previously resided on a farm "lying on the banks of the river Passaick, about one mile from the church (Trinity) at Newark. There are on the farm two good dwelling houses, barn, stable and coach-house. It contains 20 acres of excellent land, which if well manag'd and improv'd, will afford bread corn (i. e., wheat) for a small family, besides grass and hay for three horses, and four or five cows, a good orchard and large garden. It commands a most extensive view of the river, and overlooks Capt. Kennedy's farm, garden, and deer park, at Petersborough, to which it is opposite." This property was advertised for sale in 1769. It would seem to have been near the foot of the present Fourth avenue, Newark. For the better utilizing of the water power at Little Falls he raised the dam, extensively flooding the farms up the river. In consequence, the Legislature passed an act in 1772 providing for lowering the dam. Captain Gray (it is not known how or where he acquired the title) joined the British at the beginning of the Revolution, and his property above Newark was confiscated and sold by the State. It is probable that he had previously disposed of the iron works at Little Falls.

REV. ENOCH GREEN.

Enoch Green was born in 1735 and graduated from Princeton College in 1760, being chosen to deliver the valedictory oration. He was probably the first undergraduate to be thus honored, the distinction being awarded with special regard to the qualifications of the student as a valedictorian, as well as on the ground of scholarship. He entered upon the study of theology, and lost no time in putting his knowledge to practical use, for in 1761 he was on a missionary tour on horseback along the New Jersey sea coast for six weeks. He was ordained by New Brunswick Presbytery in 1762, and probably continued in missionary service in West Jersey until 1766, when he was called to the Presbyterian church at Deerfield, being formally installed June 9, 1767, and remaining there until his death. He was much esteemed as a preacher and scholar. For several years he taught a classical school. At the beginning of the Revolution he served as chaplain in the American Army, contracting camp fever, from which he died Dec. 2, 1776. He was buried under the brick-paved aisle of the Deerfield church.—*Pres. Mag.*, 1852, p. 471; *Hist. Pres. Ch. in West Jersey*, by Rev. Allen H. Brown, 29, 69; *Elmer's Cumberland County*, 105; *Johnson's Salem*, 92. He was the author of a sermon entitled: Slothfulness reproved, an example of the Saints proposed for imitation: A Sermon, occasioned by the Death of the Reverend Mr. William Ramsey, M. A., who departed this Life November 5, 1771, in the 39th year of his age. Delivered at Fairfield in Cohansie, December 9, 1771 . . .—Philadelphia: Printed by D. Hall, and W. Sellers, in Market-Street. MDCCLXXII, pp. 32. 8vo.

GUEST FAMILY.

Family tradition says that the Guests of New Brunswick came from Birmingham, England. The earliest mention of the name in the New Jersey records is in a deed from Dirck Schuyler to John Guest, in October, 1741, for a plot of land in the city of New Brunswick. This was probably John Guest, 2d, and the same John Guest who made his will March 26, 1743, proved at Perth Amboy May 24, 1743. His residence is not given. He devises to son John "my house and lot; but my sloop shall be sold and money put out so that the interest may maintain my wife and child." The inference is that he was a young man, with but one child, and that the will was hastily made, during what proved to be a fatal illness. His wife's name is not mentioned. He appointed his father executor, and John Guest, "father of the testator," says the record, qualified as executor. Witnesses—Peter Collas, Lewis Guest, Henry Dally, John Salnave. It is probable that the progenitor of the New Jersey family was John Guest, and that he had children:

- i. John[2], m. ——; d. May, 1743, leaving one child, John, 3d.
- ii. Lewis[2], m. 1st. June 27, 1743, Neeltje Van Cleve, both of New Brunswick; 2d, May 5, 1747, Jane Lawrence, both of Monmouth county.
- iii. Henry[2], m. Ruth Bong, Dec. 19, 1748, both being of Middlesex county. In a communication dated "Brunswick, East-New-Jersey, Sep. 28, 1767," he strongly urged the advantages of leather for roofing purposes.—*N. J. Archives*, 25: 467-8. In 1780 he advertised for "Two experienced Harponiers in the Whaling business."
- iv. Sarah[2], m. William Nixon, of Middlesex, Jan. 27, 1746, she being of New Brunswick.

It is also probable that Henry Guest[2] was the father of Henry[3], whose wife Anne died at New Brunswick January 4, 1772. She is understood to have been a member of the Forman family of Monmouth county.

There was a numerous Guest family of Gloucester county, where the name was known as early as 1735. William Guest, of Woodwich, in that county, schoolmaster, left a will, dated Sept. 4, 1777, proved at

Woodbury, Oct. 28, 1783, in which he mentions wife Christian, and children:

    i. Henry, to whom he devises two lots, one of them with a meadow lying in John Avises field binding on Oldmans creek, two acres; the other binding on the Great road to Swedesborough.
   ii. Joseph, to whom he devises "the plantation where I dwell, 120 acres."
  iii. Catharine Vanneman, to whom he leaves £10.
   iv. Mary Avise, to whom he leaves £10.

He also leaves £15 to granddaughter Hannah Guest, probably dau. of Henry. Executors—wife and sons Henry Guest and Joseph Guest. Witnesses—James Lord, John Ware, Joshua Lord.

Joseph Guest, of Woolwich, Gloucester county, yeoman, made his will June 24, 1792, and it was proved August 29, 1793. His wife was probably dead, as she is not mentioned. He names children as follows: Mary, William, Christenah, John, Elizabeth, Garrit, Rebecca, all unmarried, apparently, and probably under age, as he leaves his property to his sons "when twenty-one," and to his daughters "at their marriage." Executors brother, Henry Guest, and "Cuzen" Matthew Gill, Jun. Witnesses—Jacob Stille, George Katts, John Sharp.

It is possible that William Guest was a son of John[1] Guest, of New Brunswick.

John Guest and Maria Boa his wife had a child Hindrick (Henry) baptized in the Hackensack Dutch church, June 25, 1727. This may have been the Henry[2] John[1], who m. Ruth Bong, Dec. 19, 1748, as above stated.

DR. ROBERT HALSTED.

Robert Halsted was descended from Timothy Halsted, the first of the name in America, who came from England as early as 1660, and settled at Hempstead, L. I. His son, Timothy Halsted, Jr., removed to Elizabethtown early in the eighteenth century, where he d. Feb. 27, 1734-5, in his 77th year. The latter's eldest son, Caleb, of Hemstead and later of Elizabethtown, d. at the latter place in 1721. He left a son, Caleb, b. July 8, 1721; m. Sept. 16, 1744, Rebecca, daughter of Robert Ogden, 1st, and Phebe (Baldwin) Roberts; he d. at his residence, Halsted's Point, Elizabeth, June 4, 1784; she d. March 31, 1806. They had twelve children, the eldest being Robert, b. Sept. 13, 1746. After graduating from Princeton College at the age of nineteen he studied medicine, and practiced his profession in Elizabeth and vicinity for nearly sixty years. He was held in high esteem as a physician. It is said that he was demonstrative, bold, energetic and sometimes brusque in speech and manner. He was strict in his observance of the Sabbath, a regular church-goer, and always in his seat at the hour of worship. Being decided and outspoken in his patriotic sentiments at the beginning of the Revolution, he became obnoxious to the loyalists, and it is said that he was arrested and taken to New York and confined in the old Sugar House. He m., 1st, April 15, 1773, Mary Wiley; 2d, Oct. 1, 1787, Mary Mills, dau. of the Rev. William Mills, a grad. of Princeton, 1756; he d. Nov. 25, 1825; she d. May 20, 1841, aged 78. Dr. Halstead is probably buried in the First Presbyterian Churchyard, Elizabeth, but there is no tombstone to his memory in that burying ground. He had ten children: five by his first wife, and five by his second. Among his brothers were William, Sheriff of Essex County,

HALSTED : HARKER

1790; Caleb, licensed as a physician, 1774, and who practiced until his death in 1827; Matthias, a Brigade Major in the Continental Army. See *Descendants of Rebecca Ogden, 1729-1806, and Caleb Halsted, 1721-1784*, and *Wickes's Medical Men of New Jersey*.

REV. SAMUEL HARKER.

Samuel Harker was brought up to manual labor, and grew to be a man of remarkable size, vigor and strength. He is said to have graduated from the College of New Jersey, but this is probably an error. He may have matriculated there, however. On Dec. 6, 1749, he was taken under the charge of New Brunswick Presbytery, to pursue his studies for the ministry. He was licensed Nov. 6, 1751, and on Oct. 31, 1752, was ordained and installed pastor of the Presbyterian Church at Roxbury, on Black River, Morris County. He was aggressive in his beliefs. On one occasion he challenged the Rev. Abel Morgan, a Baptist preacher, to a public debate on the subject of infant baptism, and they enjoyed two days of discussion at Kingwood, Hunterdon County. A neighbor near Roxbury having offered $20 reward to any one who could produce a scripture text sustaining the doctrine of infant baptism, Mr. Harker rode over, produced a text to his own satisfaction, and when the other was not satisfied sued him for the $20. He finally got into trouble with his own denomination about some abstruse questions of doctrine, and as he persisted in his views with greater pertinacity, even publishing a statement of them without the assent of the Synod, after a controversy extending from 1757 the Synod of New York and Philadelphia, on May 27, 1763, voted, though apparently with great reluctance and by no means with unanimity, to declare him "disqualified for preaching or exercising his ministry in any congregation or vacancy" under their care. In 1758 he went as Captain of a company on the expedition against Canada. He is said to have been lost at sea, by the foundering of a vessel in which he was sailing to England with his son, who was on his way thither to receive Episcopal ordination. This would seem, improbable, however, in view of the fact that his will, dated March 22, 1764, was proved only six weeks later, or on May 2, 1764. If he had been lost at sea on the way to England, the fact would not have been determined within so short a period. It is more probable that he died at his home in Roxbury. It is quite characteristic of his pugnacity that, notwithstanding the action of Synod, he describes himself in his will as "Minister of the Gospel." He speaks of his wife Deborah, his son Ahimaz, his daughters Rachel, Jemima and Massa, and his grandson Daniel, for whom he makes special provision, "for that he is foolish" (feeble-minded). Traditions of the parson's vigorous personality are still preserved in the Black River region. —*Hist. of the Presbyterian Church in America*, by Richard Webster, Philadelphia, 1857, 622; *Hist. Morris County*, 213; *Records of the Presbyterian Church* Philadelphia, 1841, 329; *Materials for a Hist. of the Baptists in New Jersey*, Philadelphia, 1792, 17; *N. J. Archives*, IX., 184; *E. J. Wills*, H., 435. He published "An Appeal from the Synod of New York and Philadelphia, to the Christian World by the Reverend Samuel Harker. Written by himself." Philadelphia: Printed by William Dunlap. M,DCC,LXIII. 8vo. Pp 40. Also: "Predestination Consistent with General Liberty: Or the Scheme of the Covenant of Grace. By Samuel Harker, Minister of the Gospel at Black River, in New-Jersey." Philadelphia: William Dunlap. 1763. A reply was printed with the title: "The Synod of New York and Philadelphia vindicated. In a Reply to Mr. Samuel Harker's Appeal to the Christian World. By a Member of the Synod." [Rev. John Blair.] Philadelphia: William Dunlap. 1764. 12mo. Pp. 50. His son, Ahimaaz, named in his father's will, in 1764, published in 1768 "A Companion for the Young People of North America."—*N. J. Archives,* XXV., 506; XXVI., 127. He subscribed himself "a Candidate for the Ministry." He died in England, in 1768, of small-pox. In announcing the fact the *Pennsylvania Chronicle,* of October 24-26, 1768, said: "He was a Native of New-Jersey, and a young Man of a good natural Genius, and great Urbanity."

HARTSHORNE FAMILY.

The Hartshorne family of Monmouth County trace their ancestry to Richard Hartshorne, the son of William Hartshorne, of Leicestershire, England. Richard was a brother of Hugh Hartshorne, who was a citizen of London, and was admitted to the freedom of the Skinners' Company, Aug. 1, 1654. He was an "upholsterer" of Houndsditch, and is referred to sometimes as a "skinner," an "upholsterer," and as a "merchant." He was one of the Twenty-four Proprietors of East Jersey, named in the confirmatory grant of March 14, 1682-3, from the Duke of York. He died April 25. 1684, aged 55 years. There is no reason to suppose that he ever visited America.—*N. J. Archives,* I., 366, 374, 383, 412, 528; *Whitehead's East Jersey,* 2d ed., 118, 178; *N. Y. Gen. and Biog. Record,* XIV., 95; *Old Times in Old Monmouth,* 12.

Richard Hartshorne was born Oct. 24, 1641, at Hathearne, Leicestershire, England; he married Margaret Carr, Nov. 27, 1670. Coming from London to America, in September, 1669, he located in East Jersey, and took up an extensive tract of land at Middletown and the Highlands of the Navesink (acquiring Sandy Hook in 1677), where he lavished a generous hospitality, as attested by George Fox and others, he being a Friend, and naturally partial to the traveling ministers of that persuasion.—*Smith's Hist. N. J.,* 63, note; *N. J. Archives,* II., 329, note; *Old Times in Old Monmouth,* 12. He was Town Clerk of Middletown in 1675.— *Hist. Monmouth County,* 519. In 1683 he was appointed Sheriff of Monmouth County, an honor he sought to decline.—*N. J. Archives,* XIII., 77. The precedent has not been followed to any extent. In 1683 he also became a member of Gov. Gawen Laurie's Council. In the same year he was elected to the Assembly, and in 1686 was Speaker of that body, holding that position until October, 1693, and again, from February, 1696, to March, 1698, when he became a member of Gov. Jeremiah Basse's Council. He continued in the Assembly also, and held both offices until the surrender of the Province to the Crown, in 1702.— *N. J. Archives,* I., 220, note. He was again elected to the Assembly from the Eastern Division in 1703 and 1704. He died in 1722.—*Old Times in Old Monmouth,* 291; *Hist. Monmouth County,* 534.

His children were: 1. Robert, born 5th 12th mo. 1671; probably died young; 2. Hugh, born 15th 5th mo. 1673; died in infancy; 3. Thomas, born 14th 9th mo. 1674; 4. Mary, born 14th 8th mo. 1676; married ——— Clayton; 5. William, born 22d 1st mo. 1678-9; lived at Portland, on the Highlands; died 1748: had issue: Richard, William, Margaret (wife of Gershom) Mott, Thomas, Mary (wife of John) Lawrence, Hugh, Robert (died in 1801), John Esek (died in 1796 or 1797), Rachel Robinson; 6. Richard, born 17th 2d mo. 1681; died in infancy; 7. Katharine, born 2d 3d mo. 1682; married Nathaniel Fitz Randolph, of Woodbridge; 8. Hugh, born 21st 6th mo. 1685; m. Catharine Tilton (b. 14th 7th mo. 1684), and had ch. Margaret, who m. Robert White, saddler; she d. 10th of 5th mo. 1747; 9. Sarah, born 3d 7th mo. 1687; married ——— Taylor; 10. Richard, born 15th 12th mo. 1689; 11. Mercy, born 12th 5th mo. 1693; married William Lawrence.—*N. Y. Gen. and Biog. Record,*

HARTSHORNE FAMILY: HEARD

XIV., 95. Robert and Esek appear to have carried on business together, in Monmouth county, in 1767.—*N. J. Archives*, XXV., 292.

Hugh, son of Richard, born 1685, as above, was foreman of the Monmouth County Grand Jury in 1711, and lived at Middletown.—*Old Times in Old Monmouth*, 269, 291-2. His plantation of 600 acres at Middletown was advertised for sale in 1744 by his executors—Catharine Hartshorne (presumably his widow), Robert Hartshorne, Joseph Field and William Hartshorne, jun.—*N. J. Archives*, XII., 242. His children were: Margaret White, Rebecca Wright, Catherine Bowne, Richard, Sarah Van Brakle, Robert, Mary Garrison, Eliza, Mercy.—*N. Y. Gen. and Biog. Record*. It was probably the Robert Hartshorne just mentoined who was admitted to the bar in 1739, and who in 1744 was at Burlington, where he died early in 1761.

Hugh Hartshorne, Clerk of the Assembly in 1757, was doubtless the son of William (b. 1678-9, son of Richard); the latter died in 1746, and in 1748 his executors advertised for sale "The High Lands of Navesinks and Sandy-Hook lying in Middletown, East Jersey, consisting of 2800 Acres," including "a good Dwelling-House, 40 Feet Long and 30 Feet broad, with Sash Windows, two good Stone Cellars under it, with three Kitchens adjoining, pleasantly situated upon Navesinks River."—*N. J. Archives*, XII., 325, 467, 523. Hugh Hartshorne married Hannah Pattison in Burlington Monthly Meeting in 1741.—*Friends in Burlington* by Amelia Mott Gummere, Philadelphia, 1884, 93. He was living in Burlington early in 1743, and was still there in 1755.—*N. J. Archives*, XII., 171, 467; XIX., 481. He was one of the signers of the N. J. currency in 1754-56.—*Ib.*, VIII., Part II., 39, 230, 232. On April 18, 1758, he was allowed £26, 15, 2, for "39 Days Attendance as Clerk of the House of Representatives at this and another Sitting of the Assembly and for Copying the Laws and Votes for the Printer During the Said Sessions."—*Ib.*, XVII., 170. This appears to have been the extent of his service as Clerk of the Assembly. In 1766 he was at Bristol, Pa.—*N. J. Archives*, XXV., 21.

GENERAL NATHANIEL HEARD.

Nathaniel Heard was a member of a family long prominent in the annals of Woodbridge, N. J. He was greatly interested in good horses, and entries in races in the vicinity of Woodbridge were usually made with him, as in 1763, 1767, and later. His bay horse was a winner at the Elizabethtown races in 1767.—*N. J. Archives*, XXIV., 128; XXV., 338, 461. On January 7th, 1775, he was chosen one of a "committee of observation" from Woodbridge.—*Minutes of the Provincial Congress and Council of Safety of New Jersey*, Trenton, 1879, pp. 42, 45. He was one of the delegates elected by Middlesex county to the Provincial Congress which met at Trenton in May, June and August, 1775.—*Ib.*, 169. He was appointed Colonel of the First Regiment, Middlesex; Colonel, Battalion "Minute Men," February 12th, 1776; Colonel, Battalion "Heard's Brigade," June 25th, 1776; Brigadier-General Commanding, ditto; Brigadier-General Militia, February 1st, 1777.—*Official Register of Officers and Men of New Jersey in the Revolutionary War*, by William S. Stryker, Trenton, 1872, p. 349. On January 3d, 1776, the Continental Congress ordered Col. Heard, with 500 or 600 Minute Men and three companies from Lord Stirling, to disarm all the Tories in Queens county, Long Island, which he did with great promptness. An officer under him wrote: "He is indefatigable, treats the inhabitants with civility and the utmost humanity." He carried off nearly 1,000 muskets, four colors of Long Island militia, and nineteen of the principal disaffected persons, and made 349 others swear that they had concealed no arms from him. He received the thanks of the local committee for his prudence in the execution of his duty, and the compliment of a bitter attack in doggerel verse by the Tories, of which this is a specimen:

> "Col. Heard has come to town,
> In all his pride and glory;
> And when he dies he'll go to Hell,
> For robbing of the Tory."

—*Documents and Letters Intended to Illustrate the Revolutionary Incidents of Queens County*, by Henry Onderdonk, Jr., New York, 1846, pp. 41-8; *Calendar of N. Y. Revolutionary Manuscripts,* I., 218, 235, 334; *Bancroft,* VIII., 276; *Memoirs L. I. Hist. Soc.*, II., 34-40; III., *Docs.*, 170. On February 12th, 1776, the Provincial Congress ordered him to take 700 troops to Staten Island, to hold it against the enemy.—*Minutes*, 363. When the Provincial Congress decided, June 16th, 1776, to arrest Gov. William Franklin, that delicate task was entrusted to Col. Heard, the Congress "reposing great confidence in (his) zeal and prudence," and he promptly placed the Governor under arrest the next (Sunday) morning.—*Ib.*, 457-8-61; *N. J. Archives*, X., 719-20. The Continental Congress having ordered Franklin to be sent to Connecticut, Heard set out thither with his prisoner, but halted with him at Hackensack, for which he was sharply reproved by Washington.—*Minutes Provincial Congress*, 475; *Sparks's Washington*, III., 446-8. Two or three weeks later Heard was busy, under orders from Washington, picking up suspicious characters at Amboy and on Staten Island.—*Sparks's Washington*, III., 451-2. His brigade was engaged in the disastrous battle of Long Island, in the subsequent retreat to Fort Lee, and thence southerly through New Jersey.—*Force's Archives*, 5th Series, II., passim; *Memoirs N. J. Hist. Soc.*, III., passim; *Sparks's Washington*, IV., 432; *N. Y. Hist. Soc. Collections*, 1878, p. 404. Letters written by him from headquarters, Raritan, March 16th and April 1st, 1777, show his vigilance in detecting and arresting a British spy, and in taking care of British deserters.—*N. J. Revolutionary Correspondence*, 45; *Penna. Archives*, V., 262. On June 17th, 1777, he reports from Pompton the arrest of several persons "charged with taking away in an unlawful manner some tea stored at Paramus, —supposed to be near four hundred weight."—*N. J. Rev. Cor.*, 69. On October 2d, 1778, his command marched from Woodbridge for Hackensack.—*Sparks's Washington*, VI., 75; *Gaines's N. Y. Mercury*, passim. Heard's rigorous punishment of the enemies of American liberty made the British very bitter against him, and during 1776-7 they burned down two dwelling-houses, a bolting-house, a hatter's shop, a weaver's shop, wagon-house and a stable. besides carrying off his cattle, horses and crops, to his damage £2,189, 17, 6, as appears by his affidavit, recorded in a MS. volume in the State Library. His dwelling-houses were two and a half stories high, with four rooms on a floor, well furnished, fifty feet in length. It is needless to say he was never reimbursed for his great sacrifices for his country. Capt. Montresor, of the British army, says sneeringly that he was a tavern-keeper, and unwittingly pays a high compliment to his usefulness to the American cause by saying that it was one of the great blunders of the British that they did not buy him over to their side.—*N. Y. Hist. Soc. Coll.*, 1881, p. 136. Gen. Heard lived in Woodbridge on the southeast corner of the old post-road and the road from Amboy. He had three sons—John, James and William—and four daughters.—*Whitehead's Perth Amboy*, 193, note. John and James also served in the army with distinction. It may be added that Gen. Heard was appointed one of the trustees of the free school of Woodbridge, in the charter given in 1769. In 1776 he was elected town collector, and the people also voted to continue him as school trustee. He died at Woodbridge, October 28th, 1792,

HEARD: HEATON: HENDERSON: HENRY

aged 62 years.—*Dally's Woodbridge*, passim; 2 *N. J. Archives*, I., 9-11. His will, dated July 6, 1776, describes him as "planter." He mentions wife Mary; devises all lands to sons John, James and William, to be divided among them equally, ("requesting them not to have any dispute in the division thereof in case of my decease before William will be of age and he to be maintained out of the estate"); daughters Phebe, Elizabeth, Mary and Sarah to have £400 each (to be paid out of the estate by the three sons), as they come of age. Executors— sons John, James and William Heard. Witnesses—George Herriot, Samuel Heard, Samuel F. Parker. The will was not changed during the sixteen years the testator lived thereafter. It was proved December 6, 1792.—*N. J. Wills*, Liber 31, f. 247.

REV. SAMUEL HEATON.

The Rev. Samuel Heaton was b. at Wrentham, Conn., in 1712, and was brought up a Presbyterian. He removed to New Jersey, with three brothers, about the year 1734, and settled near Black River, in the county of Morris, and there set up iron works. Becoming a Baptist, he began to preach in the vicinity of Schooly's Mountain, the result being a Baptist church there. In 1751 Mr. Heaton was ordained as a preacher, and the next year went to Mill Creek, in Virginia, and from thence to Konoloway, where he founded another church. Being driven from thence by the Indians, he settled, next year, at Cape May. Thence he removed to Dividing Creek to settle a third church, in the care of which he died, in the 66th year of his age, Sept. 26, 1777. His wife was Abby Tuttle, by whom he had children: Samuel (m. Rhoda Terry, May 12, 1783), Abia, Abigail, Eliona, and Sarah. This family he brought up in a decent way notwithstanding his poverty. His children married into families of the Colesons, Reeves, Lores, Garrisons, Clarks, Cooks, Johnsons, Terrys, and Kelsays.—*Hist. of the Baptists in N. J.*, by Morgan Edwards.

DR. THOMAS HENDERSON.

Thomas Henderson was born at Freehold, Monmouth county, in 1743, where his father was a ruling elder in the Presbyterian church, an office he himself afterwards held for forty years. Having graduated at Princeton, he studied medicine with Dr. Nathaniel Scudder, and began practicing in 1765. He took an active part in the Revolution, attaining to the rank of Lieutenant Colonel in Heard's Brigade. In 1779 he was in the Continental Congress, and in 1795-1797 in the Federal Congress. Various local offices were also held by him. In 1793 he was a member of the State Council from Monmouth county, and was Vice President of that body. We owe to him many of the data in the very remarkable Life of the Rev. William Tennent, his manuscript being in the library of the New Jersey Historical Society. He died December 15, 1824.

SAMUEL HENRY.

Samuel Henry was evidently a native of Ireland. He was the owner of large tracts of land in Trenton and elsewhere, including "the old iron works" at that place, at least as early as 1763, when he advertised a runaway servant. In 1765 he was one of the assignees of Jacob Roeters Hooper, of Trenton, who had made an assignment for the benefit of his creditors.—*N. J. Archives*, XXIV., 235, 631. He was one of the subscribers toward the salary of the Rev. Elihu Spencer, of the Presbyterian church in Trenton and vicinity, but was probably an Episcopalian, as in his will he left a contingent legacy to the English Church of Trenton, and was buried in the yard of that church. He died May 10, 1784, aged 67 years.—*Hall's Hist. Pres. Church in Trenton*, 257. Henry's iron foundry and steel works were on the Assunpink creek, where it is crossed by State street.—*Trenton One Hundred Years Ago*, by William S. Stryker, 4. Samuel Henry bought from the trustees for the creditors of Robert Smith, of New Hanover, Burlington county, April 22, 1738, a tract of land in Trenton. He and his wife Mary conveyed to Neal Leviston, of Trenton, May 29, 1759, a part of this tract: beginning at a stone corner of Neal Leviston and Daniel Belerjeau's, thence by the land of Samuel Henry 89 degs. east 90 ft. to Queen's street; along the same one deg. south. Witnesses—James Cummins, Joseph De Cou.—*N. J. Deeds*, Liber AH, f. 336. In the deed he is described as of Trenton, merchant. From the recitals in this deed we learn that he began buying land in Trenton as early as 1738. The deed was acknowledged by Samuel Henry, March 23, 1774. Samuel Henry, who died in 1784, aged 67 years, was evidently his son, or Samuel Henry, 2d. Other purchases by Samuel Henry, 1st or 2d, were as follows: From John Allen, Sheriff, for £21, 10., May 9, 1753, Lot 24, five acres, of the estate of David Martin, in the township of Trenton, in the hands of Theophilus Severns and Joseph Clayton.—*N. J Deeds*, Liber AF, f. 174. Enoch Andrus, of Trenton, late deceased, by his last will did give unto his son Joshua 200 acres in the township of Nottingham, situate on Assunpink Creek, being part of a tract bought of Thomas Cadwalader and Hannah his wife; said Joshua conveyed the same to John Ely, June 11, 1741; Ely, for £600, conveyed to Samuel Henry, May 10, 1760.—*N. J. Deeds*, Liber AT, f. 150. Henry recovered a judgment, in November, 1760, against Nathan Wright, for a debt of £300, in pursuance of which John Barnes, sheriff of Hunterdon county, levied on a house and lot in Trenton, containing one quarter of an acre, bounded north by lands of Joseph Philips, west by Queen street, east by the Presbyterian church. south by Second street, and sold the same for £82 to Samuel Henry.—*N. J. Deeds*, Liber AW, f. 13. He advertised for sale, in 1768, a tract of land, on which he then lived: "There is on the said premises a good new farm house, also new barn, corn cribs and other useful houses to accommodate the plantation. There is also a good grist mill, well built of good stone and lime, etc. The whole premises being about 1½ miles from Trenton, 30 from Philadelphia and 30 from New Brunswick, and thence by water to New York."—*N. J. Archives*, 25: 14. In his will, dated May 8, 1784, two days before his death, he is described as of Trenton, "Gentleman." He sets forth with some particularity his extensive holdings of land. He disposes of his estate as follows: To Arthur, eldest son of my brother Alexander Henry of the Kingdom of Ireland, five shillings. To my son Samuel Henry, son of Mary Oglebee, all the land on the North side of my plantation: Beginning at James Chapman's to the line of Sarah Penyea and Barnt De Cline to land lately purchased from Isaiah Yard, and also a lot of woodland in Nottingham adjoining the plantation of Eliakim Anderson. To my son George Henry, son of the said Mary Oglebee, all of the residue of the plantation whereon I now live, which I purchased from Thomas Cadwalader, Samuel Burge and Peter Hankinson; also 50 acres of land in Nottingham, being land purchased from John Ely; also land on the North side of Maidenhead Road at Shabacunk, purchased from John Barns, late High Sheriff; also 26 acres purchased from George Davis, together with the new house now building on my plantation, with the white house on Maidenhead Road; also to my son George Henry £250 in money and £250 in Quartermasters liquidated certificates, to be paid him at 21. To each of my daughters, Frances and Mary Henry, daughters of the said Mary Oglebee, £500 in gold and silver money and £500 in liquidated certificates when they arrive at 18 years of age. To my son Samuel Henry, son of the said Mary Oglebee, the stone house and lot of land in Trenton at the corner near to the market house in which Jacob Bergen now keeps tavern; also that land known by the name of the old Iron Works, 27½ acres of land adjoining on the creek in the Township of Nottingham, purchased from Robt. L. Hooper and Margaret his wife; also land on the Northwest side of the road leading from Trenton to my plantation, containing 8½ acres, known by the name of Steel's lot; also 11½ acres purchased from George Cottnam, being part of the estate of Abraham Cottnam, deceased, but if any dispute should arise whereby a title for the same should not obtain, then give to him all the debts due to me from the estate of the said Abraham Cottnam in lieu thereof. Also to the said Samuel Henry, all of those several tracts of land and plantations in the township of Alexandrea, which I purchased from Isaac De Cou, late High-Sheriff; also all my share of lands lying on the Leigh High in the State of Pennsylvania, which I hold in partnership with William and George Henry and Col. John Byard; also tract of land at the mouth of Mough Chunk Creek in Pennsylvania; together with the residue of my real and personal estate whatsoever and wheresoever the same may be, to have and to hold. If my son George should die under age, or [not] have issue lawfully begotten, I give and devise all the estate herein given him to my said son Samuel, his heirs forever, subject to the payment of £250 apiece to my daughters Mary and Frances when they are 18. Whereas, I have already an article of agreement and sold to Jacob Philips, Esq., land with a dwelling house and grist mill thereon, I empower my Executors to make conveyance of the same. Executors—Son Samuel, Abraham Hunt and Charles Axford. Witnesses—Obadiah Howell, Jacob Phillips, James Ledden. By a codicil dated the same day he gives unto Mary, daughter of William Yard, that stone house and land in Trenton, wherein Barnard Hanlon lately lived, to hold during the natural life of Nathan Wright; also the use and benefit of that lot of land herein first devised to my son Samuel Henry, beginning at the corner of James Chapman's lot, taking in the bounds as in the said will, to hold until my son Samuel will be 21; also household furniture as my executors see fit, until my son Samuel will be 21, upon the condition that she shall move into the aforesaid house and care for all my said children, to wit: Samuel, George, Frances and Mary, and provide meat, drink, washing, lodging, mending and clothing until Samuel and George be sent to Princeton Colledge for education and to receive them in at all vacancies [vacations], and other times when they may see fit to come. In consideration of which my Executors to pay her £15 a year for each. Mentions a lot of land at the corner of the road near to John Ricky. Witness—Joseph Inslee, jun. By another codicil he provides: If my son Samuel Henry should die under 21 or [not] have issue lawfully begotten, then I give out of his part of the estate before given him, to Alexander, son of my brother George Henry, £300; also to Frederick, son of my brother George, £300. If my son Samuel should die under 21, I give unto the Trustees of the English Church, Trenton, £300, ½ in gold and silver mone·· ½ in liquidated certificates, to be put to interest for the support of an

Orthodox minister, and in case he should die as aforesaid, I then give to George Johnson of Trenton, £200, ½ in gold and silver money, ½ in liquidated certificates, and in case of his death as aforesaid, the residue of all the estate given him shall be equally divided between my son George and my daughters Frances and Mary. Witnesses— Obadiah Howell, JacobPhilips, James Ledden. The will and codicils were proved May 17, 1784.—*N. J. Wills*, Liber 26, f. 208. The peculiar phraseology of the will suggests a query as to his relationship with Mary Oglebee. Was she his wife? Was she the Mary who joined with him as his wife in the deed of 1759? Was she living at the time of his death? He leaves her nothing in his will, and provides for the care of his children by Mary, dau. of William Yard. Issue:

    i. Samuel Henry, 3d, d. January 9, 1795, aged 24 yrs. 6 mos., according to his tombstone in St. Michael's churchyard, Trenton; he was apparently unmarried and at the time of his father's death he was an infant, 14 years, and accordingly chose Abraham Hunt and Charles Axford as his guardians. Witnesses— Maskell Ewing, junior, William Houston. A. Hunt, Charles Axford, junior, and Isaac D. Cou signed the bond. He was of Trenton when he made his will, Sept. 6, 1794, proved Feb. 21, 1795. He gives to his brother George in fee simple all his estate, subject to the payment of legacies as follows: to sisters Frances and Mary Henry £800 in gold and silver money on arriving at the age of 18 years; to Mary, dau. of Dr. Nicholas Belville, "my household goods and furniture"; negro Peter to be set free. Executors—brother George Henry and Charles Axford. Witnesses—Benjamin Smith, Peter Howell and John Bellerjeau.—*N. J. Wills*, Liber 36, p. 144.

    ii. George, m. Mary, dau. of Col. Thomas Lowry, of Hunterdon county; d. Oct. 23, 1846, aged 76 yrs.; she d. Jan. 23, 1804, aged 29 yrs. Says a newspaper of the day: "She was sitting by the fire, no other person in the room but an old helpless domestic, the former was seized with a violent fit and in her convulsion fell into the fire, from which she was not rescued until her clothes were almost entirely consumed and herself so shockingly burned that her life is despaired of." She died the same evening.

    iii. Frances.

    iv. Mary.

ARCHIBALD HOME.

Archibald Home was distinguished in his immediate circle as a man of much literary ability, but modest and retiring, and probably delicate in frame. He was in America as early as 1733, and mingled in the best society in New York. The first official mention of him is his presentation of a bill to the Council of New Jersey, in September, 1736, for "two pounds ten Shillings due to him for his Charges in bringing Down the Commission Seal &c from New York to Amboy after Col: Cosbys Death."—*N. J. Archives*, XIV., 534. The office of Secretary of the Province of New Jersey was held about this time by one Burnet, in England, who farmed it out to a Deputy in New Jersey. Home succeeded Lawrence Smyth, of Perth Amboy, as Deputy Secretary, sometime between June 23, 1738, and March 23, 1739.—*Papers of Lewis Morris*, 132; *N. J. Archives*, XIV., 555; XV., 92. In this capacity he also acted as Secretary of the Council. Under date of October 18, 1740, Governor Morris recommended Home for a seat in the Council, to succeed Robert Lettice Hooper, deceased, although, he says, Home was "not expecting or desiring" such elevation.—*Papers of Lewis Morris*, 122; *N. J. Archives*, VI., 109. The recommendation was approved by the King in Council, April 23. 1741, his commission was dated May 29, 1741, and he took his seat as a member of the New Jersey Council, October 31, 1741.—*Papers of Lewis Morris*, 127, 122, note; *N. J. Archives*, XV., 220-221. The Journal of the Council shows that he was very faithful in his attendance on the sessions of that body. He was one of the earliest members of the American Philosophical Society, at Philadelphia, in 1743-4.—*Sparks's Franklin*, VI., 14, 29. He appears to have resided at Trenton, and died in the latter part of March, 1744, his funeral sermon being preached on Sunday, April 1, 1744. He was buried in a vault under the broad aisle of the First Presbyterian church in that city; this vault was revealed when the church was taken down in 1805. His will was dated February 24, 1743, proved October 5, 1744; the executors were Robert Hunter Morris, Thomas Cadwallader and his brother, James Home, of Charleston, South Carolina, to whom he bequeathed all his property. The testator's device on his seal was an adder holding a rose, the crest of a prominent Home family in Scotland.—*Hall's First Pres. Church in Trenton*, 150-152. A curious and interesting memento of his literary ability turned up in London in June, 1890, when a London bookseller offered for sale a manuscript volume entitled:

POEMS
on
Several Occasions
By
Archibald Home, Esqr.
late Secretary, and One of His
MAJESTIES Council for the province of
New Jersey, North America.

This volume was purchased by the writer of this note, but was lost in the great fire at Paterson in 1902. It was a small quarto volume, neatly bound in old calf, containing 15 pages of preliminary matter, 130 pages of Poems by Home, and 16 pages of Appendix, poems by Home and some of his friends, the whole beautifully engrossed, evidently after the death of Mr. Home, by a professional penman. Various bards emulated each other in singing the praise of their departed friend, but none in more tuneful numbers than a lady, A. Coxe:

> Great Judge of Numbers! when He struck the Lyre,
> 'Twas Attic Harmony, and Roman Fire;
> Anaacreon's Ease; Gay Horace's sprightly Art:
> And Ovid's melting Language of the Heart;
> But (like Roscommon) Chaste; He scorn'd to use
> The pert, low Turn, and prostitute the Muse;
> His happy Thought with Elegance express'd.
> Yet not for Gifts like these, esteem'd alone,
> In social Life the bright Companion shone;
> The candid Friend, Ingenious, Firm and Kind ⎫
> Who polish'd Sense to Faultless manners joined ⎬
> And ev'ry manly Virtue of the Mind. ⎭

Mr. Home's poems consisted of translations from Ovid, Horace, and the French; epigrams from the classics; Latin verses; "Elegy: On the much to be lamented Death of George Fraser of Elizabeth Town," a

HOME: HOOGLANDT: HOPKINSON

humorous bit in Scotch dialect; "Prologue: intended for the second opening of the Theatre at New-York, Anno 1739;" verses addressed to various ladies; "On a Dispute, between two Scotchmen [Dr. Archibald Ramsay and Quinton Malcolm], at a S. Andrews Feast in New-York Anno 1733;" "On killing a Book-Worm"; and occasional verses, of various degrees of merit. In an Imitation of the "First Satyr" of Horace he thus philosophizes:

> Life's Golden Mean who steadily pursues
> Will Fortune's Gift by no Extreme abuse:
> Ten, or Ten Thousand Acres let her give
> In due Proportion still that Man will live;
> And whether Roots or Ragouts are his Diet,
> Alike will dine, alike will sleep in Quiet.
> In Time be wise, & give your Labour o'er
> Enough acquir'd, why should you toil for more?
> Has Heaven been pleased your industry to bless }
> To Heav'n by use your Gratitude express, }
> The more you have, the Risk of Want's the less. }

His Elegy on George Fraser begins:

> Jersey! lament in briny tears,
> Your Dawty's gane to his Forbears:
> Wae worth him! Death has clos'd the Sheers,
> And clip'd his Thread:
> Just in the Prime of a' his Years
> George Fraser's dead.
> Sure Heav'n beheld our Courses thrawn,
> And him in Anger has withdrawn;
> This Tide o' Grief, poor Parson Vaughan
> Can never stem it:
> Nae mair the Blythesome day shall dawn,
> On thee, George Emmott!

The Elegy concludes:

> Weel, since from weeping us he's riv'n
> Just at the Age of Forty Seven,
> May to his Hands the Staff be given
> Which he on Earth
> Refus'd, and Constable in Heav'n
> Be George's Berth!

The Prologue above referred to, on the second opening of the Theatre in New-York, Anno 1739, was printed from this copy, in the Collections of the Dunlap Society, Second Series, New York, 1899.

CHRISTOPHER HOOGLANDT.

Christopher Hooglandt (son of Christoffel Hooglandt, the progenitor of the family in America) was baptised in New York, Nov. 24, 1669; he married 1st, Sarah Tellet or Teller, Feb. 15, 1695; 2d, Helena, daughter of John and Adrianna Middagh, prior to Aug. 6, 1696. He lived at Flatlands, L. I., but in 1711 he bought from Cornelius Powell a tract of land in Piscataway, Middlesex county, on the east side of the Raritan river, and in 1727 bought 250 acres on the Millstone river. He died in 1748, and was interred in the family burying ground, where his remains still repose.—*The Hoagland Family in America*, by Daniel Hoagland Carpenter, 1897, pp. 63-64. A notice for settling the estate of Christopher Hooglandt is advertised in *N. J. Archives*, 24: 233.

FRANCIS HOPKINSON.

Francis Hopkinson, afterwards one of the signers of the Declaration of Independence, was a son of Thomas Hopkinson, an Englishman of brilliant accomplishments, who married, in 1736, Mary Johnson, a niece of the Bishop of Worcester. Thomas was Deputy Clerk of the Orphans' Court of Philadelphia for several years under Charles Read, and on the death of the latter, in 1736, was appointed to fill the vacancy. It was a singular coincidence that thirty-six years later his son, Francis, should have been named to succeed in an important station his own former patron's son, Charles Read, the younger. Francis was baptized in Christ church, Philadelphia, November 12, 1737, being at the time seven weeks old.—*Hist. Burlington and Mercer Counties*, 468; *Records Christ Church*. He was liberally educated, and so far departed from the ordinary curriculum of the time as to familiarize himself with the Dutch language, utilizing his knowledge in making a translation of the Psalms, etc., for the Dutch church at New York, in 1765, for which he received £145. With the money thus earned he sailed for England in 1766, remaining abroad more than a year, being the guest of his relative, the Bishop of Worcester. On September 1, 1768, he became identified with New Jersey thus, in the eloquent language of a Bordentown correspondent of the *Pennsylvania Chronicle* of the day:

"On Thursday last Francis Hopkinson, Esq., of Philadelphia, was joined in the Velvet Bands of HYMEN, to Miss Nancy Borden, of this place, a lady amiable both for her internal as well as external Accomplishments, and in the words of a celebrated poet:

" 'Without all shining, and within all white,
Pure to the sense, and pleasing to the sight.' "

Ann Borden was a daughter of Judge Joseph Borden, the son of the founder of Bordentown. Probably about the time of his marriage, Mr. Hopkinson took up his residence at Bordentown, where he remained for several years.—*Hist. Burlington and Mercer Counties*, 468-9. He still retained his connection with Pennsylvania, however, being a vestryman and acting as organist at times for Christ church, Philadelphia.—*Dorr's Hist. Christ Church*, 298. On May 1, 1772, he was appointed Collector of Customs at New Castle, on the Delaware.—*Penn. Archives*, IV., 451. He was licensed as an attorney and counsellor of New Jersey, May 8, 1775.—*Vroom's Sup. Ct. Rules*, 60, 94. On June 22, 1776, he was appointed by the Provincial Congress as one of the delegates from New Jersey to the Continental Congress.—*Minutes Provincial Congress*, etc., 473. The journals of the latter body show that Mr. Hopkinson presented the instructions under which he and his colleagues were to act. He signed the Declaration of Independence. The Legislature in joint meeting on September 4, 1776, appointed him one of the Associate Justices of the Supreme Court, but he declined the office.—*Vroom's Sup. Ct. Rules*, 47. The Continental Congress appointed him, November 6, 1776, one of three persons to constitute the Continental Navy Board.—*Journals of Congress; Penn. Col. Records*, XI., 260. Some account of a quarrel he had at Bordentown in this capacity, in 1778, will be found in the *Hist. Mag.*, III., 202-3. The Pennsylvania Legislature appointed him, July 16, 1779, Judge of Admiralty, which office he held by successive appointments until the court was superseded in 1789 by the Federal Courts.—*Penn. Col. Records*, XII., 49, 307, 567-73-84; XV., 191; XVI., 99. Mr. Hopkinson's connection with New Jersey, slight as it had been, appears to have ceased from 1779, and he became identified exclusively with his native State. Shortly after the accession of Washington to the Presidency, he appointed Mr. Hopkinson Judge of the United States District Court for Pennsylvania; he continued in that office until his death, May 9, 1791. Mr. Hopkinson was more famous as a clever, ingenious and witty political writer, essayist and poet, than as a statesman or judge. He was something of an artist and musician as well. One of the fullest sketches of his life and varied accomplishments is to be found in the *History of Burlington and Mercer Counties*, 468-9. *Duyckinck's Cyclopedia of American Literature* (I., 209) dwells more upon the literary side of his character.—*N. J. Archives*, X., 426-8.

HORTON: HOUDIN: HOUSTON

AZARIAH HORTON.

Azariah Horton was the son of Rev. Azariah Horton, of South Hanover (Madison), New Jersey. In his will his father gave to him his "whole library of books and pamphlets, except Flavel's works, Henry's and Dickinson's, and several hereinafter named. My two walking canes, and a silver spoon marked I. T. M;" "and my further wish is that my negro wench Phillis, and her two sons Pompey and Pizarro, be sold, the money arising from the sale to be equally divided between my wife and son Foster, and daughter Hannah." Azariah received no share of the sale of the negroes. The son graduated at Princeton College in 1770. In 1779 he entered the American army, and was commissioned Lieutenant Colonel Deputy Commissary-General of Musters, April 6, 1779. He d. in 1793.

REV. MICHAEL HOUDIN.

The Rev. Michael Houdin was born in France in 1705. He was educated for the priesthood, and became Superior of a Franciscan Convent at Montreal. Leaving the Church of Rome, he entered the Church of England in New York in 1747. In June, 1750, he says, "having my residence in New York, I heard of repeated complaints made by gentlemen and principal inhabitants of this place [Trenton], Allen's Town and Borden's Town, it being for many years destitute of a Church of England minister; and without any sort of application of mine, ... some of them were pleased to press me by letter to come amongst them." This led to the organization of St. Michael's Church, of Trenton, in 1755—the name being probably an unintentional compliment to the first Rector. In 1759 he was ordered by Lord Loudon to accompany General Wolfe to Quebec, as his guide, on account of his familiarity with the country, and he was retained in the army some time. From Canada he was sent as missionary to New Rochelle, Westchester county, N. Y., where he died, in October, 1766.

WILLIAM CHURCHILL HOUSTON.

William Churchill Houston was born about 1746 in Sumter county, South Carolina, son of a prominent and wealthy planter, who was a member of the Society of Friends. His father, in deference to the views of the Society, refused to give his son a liberal education, but at last consented to furnish him a horse, equipments, clothes and fifty pounds in money, to do with as he pleased. The young man gladly accepted the compromise and made his way to Princeton, where he entered the College of New Jersy in the freshman year. In order to defray his expenses he also took charge of the grammar school connected with the college, and taught it while keeping up with his classes in college. He graduated in 1768 with distinguished honor, receiving from the authorities a silver medal. On graduating, he was continued as tutor[1] until 1771, when he was appointed the first professor of mathematics and natural philosophy, the duties of which chair he discharged for twelve years with fidelity and signal ability. From his orders on the treasurer of the College, in 1770, and a receipt to that officer in 1773, both in the Dreer Collection, in the Historical Society of Pennsylvania,

---

[1]Writing from Nassau Hall, September 30, 1769, James Madison mentions that the trustees "have chosen for tutors for the ensuing year, for the junior class, Mr. Houston from North Carolina, in the room of Mr. Peream." . . . . —*Letters and Other Writings of James Madison*, New York, 1884, I., 3.

HOUSTON

it would appear that his yearly salary was something like £40 Jersey money, or about $100. Young as he was, the Continental Congress selected him to serve as Deputy Secretary of that body, and he officiated as such during a part of 1775 and 1776. Two documents in his handwriting, and signed by him as Deputy Secretary, one of 22 December, 1775, and another of 1 May (1776 ?), are in the Historical Society of Pennsylvania. He was treasurer of the College, 1779-1783, and acted as librarian also for a time. When the institution was suspended, in 1776, he was appointed by the Provincial Congress, Feb. 28, 1776, Captain in the 2d Regiment of foot militia in the county of Somerset, serving in that capacity until Aug. 17, 1777, when he wrote the Provincial Congress "that, from his connexion with the college in the absence of Dr. Witherspoon, & other circumstances, he cannot pay the due attention to his company, & begging leave to resign his commission." His resignation was accordingly accepted. He was elected to the second Assembly, from Somerset county, taking his seat Oct. 28, 1777, and was re-elected a year later, but vacated his office June 11, 1779, on his election (May 25) as a delegate to the Continental Congress. As just stated, the New Jersey Legislature in joint meeting on May 25, 1779, elected Mr. Houston to be one of the delegates of New Jersey to the Continental Congress. He was re-elected to that body Nov. 17, 1779, Nov. 23, 1780, Nov. 2, 1781, and after an interval of three years was again elected to Congress on Oct. 29, 1784. In the deliberations and measures of that body he took an active and prominent part. Several of his letters, while in Congress, to Governor Livingston, show that he possessed a clear and intelligent perception of the critical situation of the country, and of the measures best calculated to improve its condition. In the meantime he studied law with Richard Stockton, of Princeton, and was admitted to the New Jersey Bar at the April term, 1781. Determined to address himself exclusively to the practice of his chosen profession, he resigned his professorship, and also his office as treasurer of the College, in 1783, and removed to Trenton, where he soon acquired a considerable practice, notwithstanding his rigid determination that he would never undertake a cause which he did not believe to be just. He received the appointment of Clerk of the Supreme Court, Sept. 28, 1781. He resigned this office March 17, 1786, but was re-elected the same day, and continued in that position until his death. He was Receiver of Continental Taxes, 1782-1785. It has been stated that he held the office of Surrogate of Hunterdon county, but no evidence has been found in support of that assertion. He was one of the five commissioners appointed by Congress to adjust the dispute between Pennsylvania and Connecticut, in relation to the Wyoming lands. They met at Trenton, November 12-December 30, 1782, and their award, though acceptable to neither side, did avoid a very threatening situation. The New Jersey Legislature appointed Mr. Houston, on March 21, 1786, to represent New Jersey at the Annapolis Convention, giving the delegates larger powers than those vested in the representatives from other states, thus paving the way for the Federal Convention a year and a half later. On Nov. 23, 1786, the Legislature appointed Mr. Houston, together with David Brearly, William Paterson and John Neilson, to represent New Jersey in the Federal Convention, which met at Philadelphia in 1787, and framed the National Constitution. William Livingston and Abraham Clark were added to the deletion, May 18, 1787, and Jonathan Dayton on June 5, 1787. Mr. Houston had been detained at home by illness, but was present to help form the quorum which was obtained on May 25, 1787. On June 6 he was absent. (Madison to Jefferson, June 6, 1787.) On July 17, 1787, when the Convention had under consideration the clause relating to the Presidency, Mr. Houston moved to strike out the paragraph making the President of the United States ineligible for a second term, and his motion was carried. (Mr. Bancroft, however, says this motion was made by Mr. William Houston, of Georgia. The published reports of the Convention merely mention "Mr. Houston" as taking part in the proceedings that day; but in the indices to Gilpin's ed. of Madison's Papers, II., 1124; Elliot's Debates, V., 325, and to the Documentary History of the Constitution, published by Congress in 1900, the motion in question is attributed to William Churchill Houston.) His name does not appear among those who signed the Constitution, probably because of his absence on account of declining health, which had rendered him unable to remain in the Convention after July 23. He signed the report made to the Legislature by the New Jersey delegates to the Convention. In order, if possible, to regain his former strength, he resolved to go South, but was stricken down suddenly at Frankford, near Philadelphia, and died there on August 12, 1788.[1] The Pennsylvania Packet, and Daily Advertiser, No. 2973, August 13, 1788, contains this brief announcement of his death and of the funeral services: "Yesterday morning died on his way to this city, the Hon. William Churchill Houston, Esq. late of Trenton, formerly one of the Representatives in Congress from the State of New-Jersey.—The citizens are respectfully requested to attend his funeral from the house of Mr. Sergeant, in Arch-street, This Morning, at Eight o'clock." The Pennsylvania Gazette and the Pennsylvania Journal make no mention of Mr. Churchill's decease. He was buried in the yard of the Second Presbyterian church, which then stood at the northwest corner of Arch and Third streets, Philadelphia. Mr. Churchill married Jane, daughter of the Rev. Caleb Smith, pastor of the First Presbyterian church of Orange, New Jersey. His wife's mother was Martha (m. Sept. 7, 1748, d. Aug. 10, 1757), youngest daughter of the Rev. Jonathan Dickinson, the first President of Princeton College. Mrs. Houston died in 1796, aged forty-one, and is buried in Lawrenceville cemetery.

Children:

1. William Churchill, a successful merchant in Philadelphia, who married Susan Somers, of Philadelphia.
2. Louisa Ann, married Dr. John Vancleve, of Princeton.
3. Elizabeth, married Horace G. Phillips, who removed to Dayton, Ohio, about 1804.
4. George S., married Mary Forman.

The foregoing account of William Churchill Houston has been compiled from a biographical notice by William C. Alexander, published in the New York Observer, of March 18, 1858, and reproduced in great part in Hall's Hist. Presbyterian Church in Trenton, p. 308; Cooley's Genealogy of Early Settlers in Trenton and Ewing, N. J., pp. 124-128; Correspondence of the Executive of N. J. during the Revolution; Minutes Provincial Congress of N. J., 395, 541; Minutes of the Legislature, and of the Joint Meeting, passim; Princeton University General Catalogue. Other sources are noticed in the text. Since the foregoing was written there has appeared the fullest sketch of Mr. Houston yet published—by Thomas Allen Glenn, Norristown, Pa., 1903, 8vo, pp. 96.

---

[1]David Evans, cabinet maker, of Philadelphia, enters in his daybook, August 12, 1788: "Made a coffin for William Churchill Houston Esq. of Trenton, who died at Geiss's tavern, on Frankford road."— *Penn. Mag. of Hist. and Biog.*, XXVII., 50.

HOWELY: HUGG

DAVID HOWELL.

David Howell, a native of New Jersey, graduated from Princeton College in 1766. He subsequently removed to Providence, Rhode Island, and was for three years a tutor in the College of Rhode Island (Brown University); for nine years he was Professor of Natural Philosophy; for thirty years Professor of Law; for fifty-two years a member of the Board of Fellows, and for many years Secretary of the Corporation. He represented Rhode Island in the Continental Congress from 1782 to 1785. In 1812 he was appointed United States Judge for the District of Rhode Island, and this office he held until his death, July 9, 1824.

JOSEPH HUGG, 1st.

Joseph Hugg, 1st, a descendant of John Hugg, the founder of the family in Old Gloucester, settled at Gloucester Point in 1722, where he kept the ferry and inn for several years. He d. in 1757, leaving two children—Samuel and Joseph, 2d. The latter was probably the Joseph "Hogg," joiner, in Philadelphia, who advertised land for sale on Little Timber creek, Gloucester, in 1752 and 1753.—*N. J. Archives*, XIX., 183, 268. He was Sheriff of Gloucester county in 1769. The will of Joseph Hugg, Esqr., of Gloucester Town and County, dated March 10, 1795, was proved December 12, 1796, at Woodbury. The testator gives his wife Elizabeth his furniture, carriage, two horses, and £60 half yearly during life; divides "my plantation where I live" between his two sons— Joseph and George Washington; devises to son Isaac "my plantation at Great Egg Harbour, in Galloway township, late Richard Westcoat's;" gives his daughter, Elizabeth Kennard, wife of Samuel Kennard, £400, some silver, etc.; to grandson, John Hampton (apparently son of a deceased daughter), £300, "and I commit him to the care of his uncle Joseph;" also mentions his brother, Samuel Hugg. Executors—sons Joseph and Isaac, and son-in-law, Saml. Kennard, junior. Witnesses— Charles West, Jas. B. Cooper, Saml. Flaningam. In a codicil, dated the same day, he says he has "heard of my son Isaac S. Hugg's death," and divides that son's share between his dau. Elizabeth and his grandson, John Hampton. Witnesses—Edward Lucas, Henry Shevileer, Amos Pearce. In a second codicil, dated Nov. 19, 1796, he says: "Having lately sold my land in Gloucester township near Long Coming to several persons in the Neighborhood, I hereby empower and direct my Executors to make good Conveyances;" and he appoints his son, George Washington Hugg, one of his executors. The inventory of his estate, taken Dec. 6, 1796, by James Hurley and Jno. Brick, footed up £2973, 3, 10¼.—*Lib. No. 36 of Wills*, f. 206.

WILLIAM HUGG.

William Hugg was a great-grandson of John Hugg, who came from the parish of Castle Ellis, in the County of Wexford, Ireland. He was a Friend, and refusing to pay a tax to repair the church at Rosanellis, Queen's County, in 1669, was imprisoned. In 1683 he bought 500 acres of land of Robert Zane, on Little Timber creek, near the Delaware. His house is supposed to have been on the site of Fort Nassau, constructed by the Dutch in 1623.—*Clement's First Settlers of Newton Township*, 284. William was living at Gloucester in 1766.—*N. J. Archives*, XXV., 255, 274. He kept tavern there in 1767.—*Ib.*, 374.

JOHN HUGHES.

John Hughes was a grandson of John Hughes and Jane Evans, of Merionethshire, Wales. In 1680 their son, Hugh, then nine years old, ran away and came to America, whither his parents followed him settling in Upper Merion, now in Montgomery County, Pa. Hugh, their only child, married Martha, only daughter of Hugh and Martha Jones, of Upper Merion. He was a tanner, in Philadelphia. Hugh Hughes had four children, among them John, who m. Sarah Jones in 1738, and died in Charleston, S. C., Feb. 1, 1772, aged 60 years; he was the Stamp Distributor for Philadelphia. His younger brother, Hugh Hughes, was in business in New York at the beginning of the Revolution, was an active "Son of Liberty," was Deputy Quartermaster General of the Continental Army, and Quartermaster General of the State of New York during the Revolution. He died at Tappan, N. Y., March 29, 1802, in his 75th year. Both John and Hugh left descendants in New Jersey. The latter, Col. Hugh Hughes, had a granddaughter, Sydney Maria Stotesbury, who m. Philemon Dickerson, Governor of New Jersey, 1836; member of Congress, 1840-41, and U. S. District Court Judge, 1841-63; she d. in Paterson, N. J., in 1900.

ABRAHAM HUNT.

Abraham Hunt, b. 1740; d. Oct. 27, 1821. He was appointed Postmaster of Trenton, Jan. 10, 1764, for three years, and again, Oct. 13, 1775, for a like term. It was at his house that the Hessian Colonel Rall spent Christmas night. 1776, in such hilarious festivities as to make him neglectful of Washington's approach.

REV. SAMUEL HUNTER, 1st and 2d.

Andrew Hunter, 1st, was a native of Ireland. He was licensed to preach by the Presbytery of New Brunswick, May 28, 1745, and was pastor of the churches at Greenwich and Fairfield, Cumberland county, 1746-60, and of Fairfield alone from 1760 until his death, July 28, 1775. Princeton college conferred on him the honorary degree of A. M. in 1760. He m. Ann, a cousin of Richard Stockton, the signer of the Declaration of Independence; she was buried in the Presbyterian churchyard, in Trenton, in October, 1800.—*Webster's Hist. Presbyterian Church*, 505; *Elmer's Cumberland County*, 103; *Hall's Hist. Pres. Church in Trenton*, 341. His son (?) Andrew S. Hunter, received from Princeton college the honorary degree of A. M. in 1802; at the September term of the New Jersey Supreme Court, in the same year, he was licensed as an attorney, and three years later as a counsellor-at-law. He practised in Trenton.—*Princeton General Catalogues*; *N. J. Supreme Court Rules.* He probably had practised law in some other State before settling in New Jersey.

Andrew Hunter, 2d, was a son of David Hunter, a British officer, and was a nephew of the Rev. Andrew Hunter, of Fairfield. He was born in Virginia, in 1752. He was graduated from Princeton college in 1772, and entered upon the study of divinity wih his uncle, being licensed by the Presbytery of Philadelphia about the middle of June, 1774. He seems to have been master of an academy at Wilmington about this time. Immediately after being licensed he went on a missionary tour in Pennsylvania and Virginia. He was a member of the Greenwich "tea party," Nov. 22, 1774. On the breaking out of active hostilities, at the beginning of the Revolution, he entered the army, being commissioned chaplain of Col. Stephen Van Cortlandt's battalion, Heard's brigade, of the New Jersey militia, June 28, 1776; chaplain Third battalion, second establishment, Continental army, Jersey Line, June 1, 1777; chaplain to General Maxwell's brigade, June 15, 1777; chaplain Third regiment and brigade, Sept. 26, 1780; discharged at the close of the war. He received the personal thanks of Gen. Washington for his conduct at the Battle of Monmouth. He was taken prisoner in the raid by the British to Elizabethtown, but escaped. It is probable that he was somewhat feeble in health, and that his strength was still further impaired by his military experiences. We have no further account of his labors until 1789, when he was pastor of the Presbyterian Church at Woodbury, and represented his Presbytery in the General Assembly of his denomination at Philadelphia. He was again a member of that body in 1794, when he served on an important committee having charge of the revision and printing of a report relating to the Confession of Faith and Form of Government of the Presbyterian Church in the United States. He appears to have occupied the pulpit of the Woodbury church for several years prior to 1800, being succeeded by the Rev. Thomas Picton. In 1791 he and others received from Joseph Bloomfield, afterwards Governor of New Jersey, a deed for a plot of land, for the erection of an academy thereon. He became principal of this academy and conducted a classical school there for some years, until he was obliged to give it up on account of ill health; for the same reason we find him, in 1803, cultivating a farm near Trenton. He was a trustee of Princeton college, 1788-1804, when he resigned to accept the professorship of mathematics and astronomy. This position he retained until 1808, when he relinquished it for the purpose of assuming charge of an academy at Bordentown. Here he remained until 1810, when he was appointed a chaplain in the United States navy, being stationed at the Washington navy yard. On giving up his professorship at Princeton, in 1808, he was again elected a trustee of the college, until 1811. He owned considerable property in and near Princeton, his residence being afterwards occupied by Prof. Arnold Guyot. His wife d. there, after 1807. He maintained close relations with the Rev. James F. Armstrong, pastor of the Presbyterian church in Trenton, frequently preaching for him. Mr. Hunter died in Burlington, Feb. 24, 1823. He m. 1st, Ann Riddell; 2d, Mary Stockton, a dau. of Richard Stockton, signer of the Declaration. Issue:

    i. David, b. in Washington, D. C., July 21, 1802; graduated at West Point in 1822, and served with great distinction in the Civil War as a Major General; d. at Washington, Feb. 2, 1886.

    ii. Lewis Boudinot, b. in Princeton, Oct. 9, 1804; graduated there in 1824, and at the medical department of the University of Pennsylvania in 1828; Surgeon U. S. army in the Mexican War, and during the Civil War as fleet surgeon under Admiral David Forter.

    iii. Mary Manners, m., 1st, Lieut. Samuel Witham Stockton, U. S. A.; 2d, July 8, 1852, the Rev. Charles Hodge, D. D., of Princeton Theological Seminary; she d. Feb. 28, 1880.

—See *Alexander's Princeton College in the Eighteenth Century*, 153; *Gillett's Hist. Pres. Ch. in the U. S. A.*, 1: 287, 311; 2: 16; *Hall's Hist. Pres. Ch. in Trenton*, 341; *Stryker's Officers and Men of N. J. in the Revolution*, 76, 379; *Journal of Philip Vickers Fithian*, 7, 157, 162, 164, 216, &c.;

HUNTER—Second : HUNTER : JACKSON , JELF—First and Second : JONES

Hageman's Hist. of Princeton and its Institutions, 1: 88; 2: 105, 271, 408; *Carter's Woodbury and Vicinity*, cited in *Hist. of Gloucester, Salem and Cape May Counties*, 176; *Life of Charles Hodge, D. D., LL. D.*, 391, 392; *N. J. Archives*, 2d Series, 3: 108.

MICHAEL HUNTER.

Michael Hunter, by will dated June 12, 1758, proved July 8, 1758, in New York, gives "all my hole Estate Wages Sum and sums of money Lands Tenements Goods Chattels and Estate whatsoever . . . unto my loving Eare Phillip Burgin," whom he also appoints sole executor. The will is recorded in Liber 21 of Wills in the Surrogate's office of N. Y. county, p. 56. Hunter was probably a mariner.

REV. WILHELMUS JACKSON.

The Rev. Wilhelmus Jackson studied in Holland four years, and on returning to America was licensed in 1757 to preach, and was pastor of the Reformed Dutch churches of Bergen and Staten Island, 1757-1789. He died in 1813. He was noted as a powerful preacher, with a far-reaching voice, rivaling Whitefield as an open-air speaker.

JOSEPH JELF, 1st and 2d.

Joseph Jelf was a resident of Elizabethtown at least as early as 1738, for on July 5, of that year, his wife Sarah died, aged 37 years, and was buried in the First Presbyterian churchyard.

Joseph Jelf, 2d, made an affidavit in 1757, that he was of full age, and that he had lived for upwards of three years with Samuel Woodruff, as his clerk and bookkeeper. A few years later he was in partnership with his former employer.—*N. J. Archives*, XX., 124; XXIV., 303. He married Susanna Hampton, who d. April 27, 1792, in her 57th year, and is buried in St. John's churchyard, Elizabethtown. Their daughter Sally, b. March 29, 1766, survived to the extraordinary age of 104 years, dying April 23, 1870.—*Tombstone Inscription*. Mr. Jelf d. Sept. 30, 1772.

CHIEF JUSTICE NATHANIEL JONES.

The circumstances attending the appointment of Nathaniel Jones to the office of Chief Justice of New Jersey, and his futile efforts to assume the position, make one of the most interesting episodes in the history of our Supreme Court.

Soon after Gov. Lewis Morris entered upon the duties of his office of Governor of New Jersey, he issued a commission, dated March 12, 1738, appointing his son, Robert Hunter Morris, to the office of Chief Justice of the Province, "for during good behaviour in the same," although his predecessor, Robert Lettice Hooper, had been commissioned by royal warrant dated February 29, 1727-8, only "during the royal pleasure."—*N. J. Archives*, IX., 206-7, 230, 235. In a letter dated Amboy, August 10, 1760, to Gov. Thomas Boone, Morris gives these interesting details:

"In 1738 I was appointed Chief Justice of this Province, *during good behaviour;* and Continued in the Exercise of that Office till 1749, when at the request of His Majesty's Council, I went to England, to lay before the Ministry the state of the Colony, then disturbed by frequent Riots, and thrown into the utmost disorder and Confusion.

"In March 1754, Just before I was named to the Government of Pensilvania, I wrote to the Board of Trade, desiring their Lordships 'would give me Leave to Resign the Office of Chief Justice.' I had no answer to that Letter: And therefore as I passed through New Jersey to Pensilvania, I made the same request of the Governor and Council; But they declined Accepting my Resignation, Saying the Offices were not incompatible, and the Provinces only separated by a River.

"I went on then in the Discharge of the Duties of the Place, as well as the Perplexed Affairs of Pensilvania would permit, till 1756, when having Resigned that Government, I Returned to New Jersey and Remaind in the full Exercise of the Office till October 1757.

"I beg leave to observe that in All this time; a space of near four years, I had not the least Intimation, that the Board of Trade considered my Request of March 1754 as a Resignation.

"In October 1757, I obtained Leave from the President of the Council to go to England; During my stay there, I Received Information from America, that Mr. Ainsley was, Pursuant to his Majesty's Mandamus, Appointed Chief Justice of this Province: I Expressed my surprise thereon to your Predecessor, then in London; And Endeavoured to see the Earl of Halifax, but was so unfortunate as not to have an opportunity of speaking to his Lordship upon the subject."—*N. J. Archives,* IX., 235-6. See also ibid., 206-7.

He had used substantially the same arguments in an interview with Governor Bernard, who in a letter to the Lords of Trade, Feb. 25, 1760, makes these shrewd comments on his position:

"The whole amount of it is that, as he proposed a resignation on account of his taking the government of Pennsylvania & he quitted that government & returned to New Jersey before your Lordships had accepted his resignation, the reasons of it ceasing, the resignation itself was revoked. But I observed to him that in his letter to your Lordships, He did not attribute his desire to resign the office to his taking the Government of Pennsylvania, but to his private affairs not permitting him to attend the duties of it: And therefore your Lordships could not take notice of his quitting that government as a ceasing of his reasons for his resignation; if it were so he should have signified it to your Lordships & prayer leave to withdraw his resignation. As he did not, all this misunderstanding has arose from his own omission."—*Ibid.,* IX., 210-211.

As for Morris's assertion that he "went on in the Discharge of the Duties of the Place, as well as the Perplexed Affairs of Pensilvania would permit, till 1756," this is contradicted by Governor Bernard, who says that after Morris "took upon him the government of Pennsylvania," "he never sat as Chief Justice, till after he had relinquisht that government. After that He sat once in Novr Term 1756, and divers times in each of the Terms in March May & August 1757. Soon after the last he went to England."—*Ibid.,* 212.

The records of the Court fail to show that Chief Justice Morris sat in the Court during 1754, 1755 or 1756. Whatever duty he performed in respect to the office must have been attended to off the bench, possibly in consultations with his associates, or in advising the Governor and Council, or in signing papers.

The Lords of Trade, in an address to the King, June 17, 1760, state that Morris, after residing in England a considerable time, "by his Letters to us dated the 31st of March, 1754, desired Leave to resign his said Office, as his private Affairs would not permit him to attend to the Duties of it."—*Ibid.,* 230. Quietly ignoring the evident fact that Morris's resignation was not accepted, they excuse that omission on the plea that "It was not till the beginning of the year 1757, that we were enabled to recommend to Your Majesty a proper person to supply the Vacancy Occasioned by this Resignation." Referring to the appointment of William Aynsley as Chief Justice, on February 17, 1757, and his subsequent performance of the duties of that office during the March and May terms, 1758, and until his death, they make the very good point: "it is remarkable, that, during this Course of time Mr. Morris neither contested the Appointment of Mr. Aynsley here, nor set up any Claim of prior Right in the province."—*Ibid.*, 231.

Chief Justice Aynsley having died in May, 1758, the Lords of Trade proposed to the King the appointment of Nathaniel Jones for the succession, May 22, 1759, saying he had been "recommended to us as a Person well qualified to serve Your Majesty in that Station."—*Ibid.*, 173. He was appointed May 24, and the appointment was approved in Council, May 31, 1759.—*Ibid.* This selection for so important an office immediately aroused the strongest opposition in the Province, and was viewed with manifest apprehension and alarm, if we may judge from the few guarded criticisms of the King's action that have come down to us, and which suggest much more than is expressed. In a letter dated Perth Amboy, December 16, 1761, published in the *Pennsylvania Journal* of January 7, 1762, Jones is contemptuously described as having been a "Newgate Solicitor" at the time of his appointment. This letter was probably written by Morris. The statement is accepted as true by William Smith, the New York historian.—*Hist. of N. Y.*, 1830, II., 347. According to his own account, Jones was of the Middle Temple, a barrister at law.—*N. J. Archives*, IX., 342. We have no other particulars regarding his standing at the bar.

Mr. Morris's attitude was described in a letter from Gov. Bernard, dated Perth Amboy, August 28, 1759, to the Lords of Trade: "Some few days ago Mr. [Robert Hunter] Morris arrived in this province [from England] & soon after signified to me that he proposed to resume his office of chief justice by virtue of his former patent, which, he said was not surrendered or otherwise determined. . . . I repeated to him the confusion that would be the consequence of his resuming this office against my protestation, and he expressed his earnest desire to do nothing which should embarrass the government upon which we came to the following agreement: that he should suspend his purpose until I could write to your Lordships and receive your commands; and that I would not in the meantime appoint any other Person, unless I received the King's command therefor. . . . I have not seen Mr. Morris since advices arrived of the appointment of Mr. Jones; I imagine that he will contest Mr. Jones' appointment." —*N. J. Archives*, IX., 176-7. In reply, the Lords of Trade wrote to Governor Bernard, December 14, 1759: "Mr. Morris's conduct appears to us to highly reflect upon His Majesty's Honor and Justice, in the subsequent appointments which have been made, founded upon Mr. Morris's resignation."—*N. J. Archives*, IX., 192.

Mr. Jones subsequently stated that upon receiving his appointment he "Relinquished his business in the Law in England, to attend the Duty of his Office, and at a vast Expence, repaired to America, in which he was unhappily obliged to break in on the future Dependance of a most Valuable Wife, and her Children, in Order to Discharge the Trust reposed in him, with Dignity and Fidelity."—*Ibid.*, 342. He arrived in New Jersey in November, 1759, and proceeded to Perth Amboy, where he received a commission under the great seal of the Province, dated November 16, 1759, at the hands of Gov. Francis Bernard.—*N. J. Archives*, IX., 214; XX., 391.

JONES

It was customary to tender so important a representative of the King a series of ovations and addresses on his coming into the Province. The only demonstration of the kind offered to Mr. Jones was by the Mayor, Recorder, Aldermen and Commonalty of the Borough of Elizabeth; he had intimated a purpose to make that town his place of residence, and having gone thither on a visit the Corporation invited him to "a genteel Entertainment," on December 3, and presented him with an address which is singularly guarded and non-committal, and free from the usual adulatory compliments on such occasions. "Your late designation to the first Seat on the Bench," they cautiously say, *"affords a strong presumption* of Abilities adapted to the conspicuous Theatre on which you are destined to Act," and they conclude with a perfunctory declaration of their "Respect due to a Person, whom [the King] hath thought worthy to elevate to the second Post of Power and Influence in the Government of his flourishing Province of New-Jersey."—*Ante,* 396-7. In all this there is a remarkable reserve which is highly significant under all the circumstances. The authorities of Elizabeth were willing to pay the respect due to the King's appointee, but they would not commit themselves to any endorsement of the individual. The dissatisfaction over his appointment, occasioned by his low reputation, was greatly enhanced by his conduct after his arrival in the Province. Even Gov. Bernard, who naturally disliked to reflect upon the new Chief Justice, in a letter to the Lords of Trade declared: "Mr. Jones has been so unfortunate, that there is an universal dissatisfaction at his appointment: so it seems to me it will be difficult for him to hold the office, even if he will serve it for nothing." —*Ibid.,* IX., 210-211. More emphatic were Chief Justice Morris's comments, in a letter to Governor Thomas Boone, August 10, 1760: "The Character of Mr. Jones which came here before him, and the Absurdity, to say no worse, of his behaviour, after his Arrival, greatly alarmed the People of all Ranks; And Occasioned the strongest Solicitations from the most considerate men in the Province, That I would insist on the Tenure of my Commission, and Resume the Bench."—*Ibid.,* IX, 236. As already stated, Mr. Morris had called on Gov. Bernard immediately upon his return from England, in August, 1759, and "signified that he proposed to resume his office of chief justice by virtue of his former patent." As he put the matter himself, in his letter of August 10, 1760, quoted above: "When I returned to New Jersey, Mr. Ainsley was Dead, and tho' I had no doubt of my Right to Resume the Bench, Yet, as Mr. Bernard apprehended it might Embarrass his Administration, I declined it till he should hear from England."—*Ibid.,* 236. That is to say, as stated by the Lords of Trade in a letter to the King, June 17, 1760: "It was at length agreed between them, that Mr. Morris should suspend his purpose and that the Governor should not appoint any other Person to the Office, until further Directions should be received from hence."—*Ibid.,* 232. Mr. Morris says that Gov. Bernard, "being soon after informed of Mr. Jones's Nomination, told me, I was quite at Liberty to take any measures I thought Proper, And that he wish'd nothing more than to see me established upon the Bench."—*Ibid.,* 236. Mr. Jones's manifest unfitness increased the pressure upon Mr. Morris to prevent the induction of the new-comer into office, even by the setting up of his own extraordinary claim that he was still entitled to the position by virtue of his ancient commission. As he had been perfectly open with the Governor in this matter, he wrote him a letter, February 22, 1760, notifying him of his intentions, and setting forth again his reasons for the proposed step.—*Ibid.*, 206-7. When the next term of the Supreme Court was about to open, at Perth Amboy, on Tuesday, March 18, 1760, he called on Gov. Bernard. in the morning, before the opening of the Court, and once more announced his intention of interposing his claim, in order to keep Mr. Jones off the bench. The Governor, in a letter dated March 22, 1760, to the Lords of Trade, thus describes the interview: "Mr. Morris came to me and said that the people in general were so uneasy at Mr. Jones's taking his seat as Chief Justice, that he could not resist their solicitations for him to take the seat and thereby prevent Mr. Jones. I reminded him of his promise to me that he would not interrupt Fr. Jones in taking his seat. He said that he entered into that engagement upon account of his desire not to undertake any business that was like to give me much trouble: but that, as I was removing from the Province & not like to be affected by this contest, He thought he should be remitted of his liberty of prosecuting his right in such manner as he should see occasion. I said that, to be sure, I should release him from this engagement so far as I was concerned: but I thought it was extended much beyond me. It seemed to me that Your Lordships had an intrest in it, as I had acquainted you with it more as a public than a private transaction, and that Mr. Jones was intrested in it, as most probably he had staid in the Country in dependence that Mr. Morris would not obstruct him in taking the office. He replied that his engagement was made only to me and on my account & that, as my intrest in it ceased & I had released him from it, he considered himself as quite free from it."—*Ibid.*, 212. Mr. Morris says of this interview: "Mr. Barnard . . . in Presence of Mr. Ogden and Mr. Read, Acquitted me Again, of any Engagements to him on the Occasion; and at the same time was Pleased to thank me for the tenderness and Regard I had shown to his Administration."—*Ibid.*, 237. David Ogden and Charles Read, here referred to, were two of the ablest and most experienced members of the Governor's Council; Mr. Ogden was one of the leading lawyers in the Province.

When the Supreme Court met the bench was occupied by Chief Justice Morris and Second Justice Samuel Nevill; the Third Justice, Mr. Saltar, was in too infirm health to attend. Mr. Jones presented his commission, and requested to have it read. Then the record of Chief Justice Morris's commission was read, showing that he had been appointed during good behavior. The commission of Nathaniel Jones was next read, from which it appeared that he was appointed "in the room of William Aynsley Esqr. deceased," to hold office "for and during our pleasure and your residence within our said province." Mr. Jones thereupon prayed to have the oath of office administered to him and to be admitted. At his request the commission of Chief Justice Aynsley was also read, and the records of the Court, showing that he sat as Chief Justice at the March term, 1758, and at the term following. Chief Justice Morris, although sitting, with a proper delicacy declined giving any judgment on the application of Mr. Jones, and the opinion of "the Court" was delivered by Second Justice Nevill.—*Ibid.*, 214. But the whole proceeding is so extraordinary that it is worth while to reproduce the exact language of the minutes of the Court, now in the Clerk's office at Trenton:

March 1760
    At a Supreme Court of Judicature held at Perth Amboy in & for the Province of New Jersey, of the Term of March in the thirty third Year of the Reign of Our Sovereign Lord George the Second &c.
3d Tuesday March 18 1760
The Court opened

145

JONES

The Honble Samuel Nevill Esq. 2d Justice
Adjourned to two o.c. p. m.
The Court rret according to Adjournment
Present
The Honble Robert H. Morris, Esqr. Chief Justice
Samuel Nevill Esqr. 2d Justice

Nathaniel Jones Esqr Offered to the Court a Commission under the Great Seal of the Province of New Jersey, bearing date of the Sixteenth of November 1759, appointing him Chief Justice of the said Province & prayed that the Same might be Read.

Whereupon the Record of a Commission Dated March 17th 1738 appointing Robert Hunter Morris Esq. Chief Justice of the Province of N. J. (during his good Behaviour in the same) was read: . . . . . Then the Commission appointing Nathaniel Jones Esqr. was read: . . Whereupon the said Nathaniel Jones Esq. pray'd to have the Oath of Office administered to him and to be Admitted. Then an Entry in the Minutes of this Court of March Term 1758 at the request of Nathaniel Jones was read (in these words) A Commission appointing William Aynsley Esq. Chief Justice of the Province of N. J. was openly read, also other Entrys shewing that Wm Aynsley Esqre Deceas'd sett as Chief Justice for the said Term of March 1758 and the Term next following and that Mr. Nevill Sett as 2d Justice of the said Court.

As the Motion of Mr. Jones might Effect M. Morris he declined giving any Judgment thereon, and Mr. Nevill, Second Justice, delivered the Opinion of the Court as follows, that since the Commission to Mr. Morris grants him a ffreehold in the Office of Chief Justice of this Province of N. J. and Nothing was shown legally to Divest him thereof, this Court therefore Cannot administer the Oath of Office to Mr. Jones nor admitt him to Enter into the Execution of said Office of Chief Justice, but Leave his right to said Office if any he has to be determined by a Due Course of Law.

Mr. Morris requested David Ogden and Charles Read Esqrs to Enter his appearance to and Defend any Action or suit that shall or may be brought against him respecting this matter.

At the request of Nathaniel Jones its ordered that he have a Copy of the foregoing Entrys.

The Court adjourned.

Gov. Bernard was very well satisfied with the action of the Court, there is little doubt. But to relieve himself from culpability he wrote in this strain to the Lords o' Trade, March 22, 1760, after detailing the above proceedings: "It may seem to your Lordships that I ought to have interposed the Copy of Mr. Morris's Resignation. But, besides that there was no time given me to order the Attorney general to intervene for the King, I could not have introduced that copy, because being a copy and no way authenticated, it would not have been permitted to be read in a Court, tho' its authority would be undoubted everywhere else.

"Altho' this business will soon cease to be my concern [referring to his transfer to Massachusetts] yet I must think it my duty to enter a public protest on the behalf of the King against this order of the Supreme Court. The proper method for doing this appears to be, to order the Attorney General to sue out a writ of error & bring this order before the Governor & Council, from whence, if there should be occasion, it may be carried to the privy Council in England either by the Attorney general or by Mr. Morris."—*N. J. Archives*, IX., 214.

Chief Justice Morris put the boldest front on the whole matter. In his letter to Gov. Bernard, of Feb. 22, 1760, he says: "The income of the office is now & ever has been, too inconsiderable to make me in the least anxious about it. I took the office & have held it, rather to Prevent it falling into contempt than expecting any Support from it, and am therefore, as I have more than once assured your Excellency (as to myself) Extremely Indifferent about it, but cannot help wishing, for the sake of the province, that an Office of such Consequence and in which the people are so nearly intrested, May always be in the hands of a Man of independent fortune, & Known Integrity."—*Ibid.*, 206-7.

Again, in his letter to Gov. Thomas Boone (successor to Gov. Bernard), August 10, 1760, after referring to the public uneasiness over the reputation and unbecoming conduct of Mr. Jones, he says:

"Your Excellency will be no Less Surprised at the Earnestness and Apprehensions Expressed on this Occasion, as you are sensible the first seat in the Highest Court of Common Law, in the Province, is of great Importance to the Privileges and Properties of the People, and may Essentially Affect the Rights and Prerogatives of the Crown.

"It may not be improper here to inform your Excellency, that the profits of the Office fall short of one hundred pounds Sterling A Year a sum, by no means adequate to the trouble and Expence attending the Employment.—I was therefore very indifferent as to the benefits arrising from the Office, But could not be so, when the Publick safety was at stake, and the Royal Authority ready to fall into hands that must have brought it into the utmost Contempt. . . . .

"My own and the Conduct of my family, who have been Constantly ingaged in Support of the Royal Authority, in these Colonies, when it stood in need of every aid, Render it unnecessary to vindicate myself, even from the surmise of Opposition to Government; For this I may Appeal to the Minutes And papers of the Board of Trade, and to the Records of this and the Neighbouring Provinces of New York and Pensilvania.—Besides, a People unused to the Necessary Subordinations of Government, are in danger of falling into Levilling and Democratical Principles, And I am too Sensible of the Mischievious Tendency of such a Spirit, to be led into Measures that might encourage it; And which, by weakening the Administration must destroy the Peace and Happiness of the Provinces." He concludes with this manly assurance: "Upon the whole Sir as I know you have nothing so much at Heart as to maintain the Dignity of the Crown and promote the Prosperity of the Province, I beg Leave to Assure your Excellency, That whatever the Issue of this Affair may be, you will find me ever ready to Concur in every measure Conducive to those Salutary Ends."—*Ibid.*, 235-238.

There is little doubt that Mr. Morris was perfectly sincere in his professions of disinterestedness in this proceeding, and that he was actuated by purely patriotic motives.

The Lords of Trade, upon receipt of Gov. Bernard's letter of March 22, 1760, laid the whole matter before the King, in a letter dated June 17, 1760, embodying the Governor's suggestion as to the proper steps to be taken: "We have only further to offer our humble Opinion, that your Majesty should be graciously pleased to referr the whole matter to your Attorney Genl, with Directions to consider and report what Measures are most proper to be taken in Order to support your Majesty's Right of Nomination against the extraordinary and unprecedented Claim of Mr. Morris."—*Ibid.*, 230-235.

All the facts in the case appear to have made it impolitic, if not impossible, for the Ministry to sustain so inferior and so objectionable a person as Mr. Jones in his very natural attempt to vindicate the appointment of the King, and the unfortunate affair was quietly dropped, to the great satisfaction of the authorities of New Jersey. The attitude of Mr. Jones bears out the presumption of his unfitness for the high station to which he had been assigned. Indeed, he seems to have realized the fact himself, for after his claim to the office had been denied by Second Justice Nevill, and notwithstanding the formal backing of Gov. Bernard, he did not have the courage or address to attempt to possess himself of the office. The minutes of the Supreme Court make no further mention of Mr. Jones or his claims, but do show that Chief Justice Morris was on the bench during every sitting of the Court in 1760, except May 16 (when Justice Saltar sat), August 12 (when Justice Nevill sat alone), and November 8 and 10, when Justice Nevill presided. By a letter from Nathaniel Jones, dated January 2, 1761, and addressed to the Earl of Hillsborough, we learn that Jones was then in England. In this letter he sets out his appointment as Chief Justice of New Jersey, the "vast Expence" he had incurred in giving up his law practice in England and in repairing to America, and "Mr. Morris's proceedings, as illegal, and Unwarrantable, as he absolutely prevented your Memorialist in Execution of his Office.

"That through the heavy Expences your Memorialist hath Sustained, his whole Substance is Exhausted, and he was constrained to return to England, in Vain to Attempt the Recovery of his lost business in the Law, through his long absence abroad, which before afforded him a Competent Maintenance, nor has your Memorialist received any Satisfaction, or Compensation whatsoever, for the above Charges, or the injury he has suffered by this disappointment, which has reduced him to Calamitous Circumstances." But instead of praying that the royal authority be vindicated, and that the power of the Crown be exercised in installing him in the office to which he had been appointed, he concludes with this singular prayer:

"That your Memorialist being informed of a Vacancy of the office of Chief Justice of South Carolina, Most humbly supplicates your Lordship, to consider the premises and your Memorialists perseverance and Fidelity, in his Majesty's Service, And that your Lordship will be pleased to Recommend him to his Majesty as an Object Meriting his Royal favour, And that he may be appointed to succeed in the above office now Vacant or have such other relief as in your Lordships benignity, and wisdom shall seem most meet."—*Ibid.*, 342.

The Lords of Trade in a perfunctory address to Lord Halifax likewise tacitly confess the unfitness of Jones for the New Jersey office:

"We should not be so importunate with your Lordship, but the bearer, Mr. Jones, is as great an object of your Compassion, as ever was, he tells us which we believe to be true; that by his Voyage to and from America, and the great Expence he was at in providing necessarys for himself and Servants, suitable to his Station abroad, that he has spent all his substance, and by his absence so long abroad, he says he has lost all his Business, which he had here, which though not great afforded him a Competent Maintenance, so that he is now left destitute of any provision:

"We desire therefore that your Lordship will be so good to recommend him to some of the Offices now Vacant, or that some provision may be made for him, as we think we could not ask it, for one who deserves it so well:

"We hope your Lordship will not consider this as a Letter of Course; for we are really concerned for this Poor Gentleman; and whatever favour you bestow on him, we shall Esteem it an Obligation lain on us."—*Ibid.*, 342-344.

No further mention has been found of Nathaniel Jones. He seems to have sunk again into the obscurity whence he was lifted up to be Chief Justice of New Jersey

When Governor Josiah Hardy arrived in the Province, in 1761, he found the situation and his necessary action in consequence thereof to be as set forth in this letter to the Lords of Trade:

'I found there was a total Stop to the Administration of Justice in the Supreem Courts, by the Judges Commissions not having been renewed since the death of his late Majesty, and a Rumour began to be spread that the Judges were not qualify'd to act. I therefore (for fear of any bad consequence, and to quiet the minds of the people who appeard much dissatisfy'd) thought it best for his Majesty's Service as well as the good of the Province to order the Commissions to be renew'd in the same manner as they have hitherto been granted, which is during good behaviour; I must observe to your Lordships likewise that I found the General Assembly had come to a resolution not to make any provision for the Judges in the bill for Support of Government if they accepted Commissions during pleasure: I therefore hope I shall have his Majesty's & Your Lordships approbation for what I have done. I likewise found it absolutely necessary to renew Mr. Morris's Commission of Chief Justice and I cannot help observing that he is certainly a very proper Person for this Post which ought to be held by a Man of Abilities & character."—*N. J. Archives*, IX., 346-347.

KAIGHN FAMILY.

The Kaighn family of Old Gloucester is descended from John Kaighn, who came from the Isle of Man, and in 1694 was a resident of Byberry, Bucks county, Pa. He was a carpenter by trade. In 1693 he married Ann Albertson, widow of Walter Forrest; she d. July 6, 1694, and in 1696 he m. Sarah Dole, wid. of Andrew Griscom. In the latter year Kaighn bought a tract of 455 acres in Newton township, Old Gloucester, and resided thereon thenceforth; he m., 3d, Elizabeth Hill, of Burlington, in 1710. He d. in 1724, leaving two sons, by his second wife:

i. John, b. Dec. 30, 1700; m. Abigail Hinchman, dau. of John Hinchman, in 1732. He was a blacksmith at Haddonfield. He d. in 1749, leaving issue: 1. Sarah, b. 1733; 2. Elizabeth, b. 1736; 3. Samuel, b. 1737; 4. John, b. 1740; 5. Ann, b. 1744.

ii. Joseph, b. Dec. 4, 1702; m. Mary Estaugh, of Philadelphia, dau. of James and niece of John Estaugh, of Haddonfield. He d. 1749, leaving issue: 1. Joseph, m. Prudence Butcher, a widow; 2. John, a physician, who d. in 1770, unmarried, aged about 40 years; 3. Isaac, d. under age; 4. James, m. Hanna Mason; 5. Elizabeth, m. Arthur Donaldson. —*Clement's First Settlers of Newton*, 149-157; *N. J. Archives*, XXVII., 178.

REV. JOHN WILLIAM KALS.

The Rev. John William Kals came from London in 1756, and labored in Philadelphia for about a year, when he became pastor of the "Calvanistical High Dutch Congregation," of Amwell, organized about 1744 or earlier. The church was visited by the Rev. Michael Schlatter in 1747, and a house of worship was erected in 1749. Mr. Kals preached there, 1757-9, and then removed to New York.

KEARNEY : KEENE : KEMBLE FAMILY

MICHAEL KEARNY.

Michael Kearny was a son of Michael Kearny, an eminent citizen of New Jersey. Michael, 2d, entered the British navy. In 1769 he was recommended by Gov. Franklin for a seat in the Council, as a "Gentleman who has a Commission in His Majesty's Navy, but resides at present on his Paternal Estate in Monmouth County, and is related to some of the principal Families in the Colony." His residence was on the Morris estate. He died unmarried.—*Whitehead's Perth Amboy*, 92; *N. J. Archives*, X., 132. Mr. Whitehead says he was a son of Sarah, dau. of Lewis Morris (and Isabella, his wife); but Mrs. Lewis Morris, in her will, dated Aug. 9, 1746, proved April 20, 1752, does not mention him, although particular to name all her children, and children of her deceased daughters, Kearny and Isabella. It is not unlikely that Michael, 2d, was a son of Michael, 1st, by his second wife, Elizabeth Britz or Britain (who was not known to Mr. Whitehead), who was also the mother of Philip, the eldest son (born at sea) of Michael, 1st.

MOUNCE KEEN.

Mounce (i. e., Moses) Keen, son of Maons and Magdalen (Hoffman) Keen, was b. in West Jersey Aug. 18, 1715; m. Sarah, dau. of Benjamin and Christina Seeley. He lived in Pilesgrove township, Salem county, and afterwards in Woolwich township, Gloucester county. He was for many years a vestryman of the Swedish church at Swedesboro. He was buried in Trinity churchyard, Swedesboro, Oct. 14, 1794; his wife, Feb. 24, 1790.—*Descendants of Joran Kyn*, by Gregory B. Keen, in Penn. Mag., III., 447.

KEMBLE FAMILY.

Peter Kemble's grandfather was Richard Kemble, deputy alderman of Bishopsgate ward, London, a merchant who resided in Bishopsgate many years. He had a son, Richard, who "was bound an apprentice to one Barnardiston, a Turkey merchant with a considerable sum of money, who was by indenture bound to send him the last two years of his service to Smyrna, where he went, and afterwards settled." There he married a Greek lady, named Mavrocordato, a native of the isle of Scio, whose sister married Mr. Edwards, the British consul at Smyrna. Peter Kemble, one of the children, was born at Smyrna, in Asia Minor, December 12, 1704, and remained there until 1712, when he was sent to England to be educated. His father was appointed English consul at Salonica in 1718, and died there in June, 1720. In 1718 Peter Kemble was sent to a wine merchant at Rotterdam to learn mercantile life. In 1720-21 he made a trading voyage to Guinea, and on his return engaged in business in London, where he continued for some years. About 1730 he came to America, and soon after settled at Piscataway Landing, near New Brunswick, where he carried on a successful business.—*N. Y. Hist. Soc. Collections*, 1884, xiii-xiv. He was living there in 1740.—*N. J. Archives*, XII., 20. Writing to the Lords of Trade, Jan. 28, 1744-5, Governor Lewis Morris recommended his appointment as a member of the Council, and said he was "a considerable merchant."—*Papers of Lewis Morris*, 220, 283. His intimacy with the Morris family is indicated by the fact that he was one of the pall-bearers at the Governor's funeral in 1746.—*Ib.*, 314. having been appointed to the Council, Sept. 23, 1745, he was sworn in as a member, Aug. 10, 1747, and remained therein until the Revolution, being Speaker in 1765, and several years thereafter.—*N. J. Archives*, IX., 274; X., 561;

XV., 512-513; XVII., 412. In 1748 he was manager of a lottery for completing the Episcopal church at New Brunswick, and building a parsonage house.—*Ib.*, XII., 471, 518, 520. Charles Read, one of the ablest public men in New Jersey, considered him suitable for Supreme Court Judge, in 1753.—*Ib.*, VIII., Part 1, 188. Some time prior to 1758 he acquired an extensive tract of land near Morristown, where he took up his residence before 1765, his place being known as "Mount Kemble," a name perpetuated in one of the most beautiful avenues in that town to-day.—*Smith's Hist. N. J.*, 499. He was commissioned one of the Justices of the Peace of Morris county, April 30, 1768.—*Hist. Morris County*, 75. During the Revolution he sided with the British, but was not disturbed by the Americans, except as they cantoned on his estate while the army was in winter quarters at Morristown. He died there, Feb. 23, 1789, having passed his eighty-fourth year. Very soon after coming to this country he married Gertrude Bayard, second daughter of Samuel Bayard and Margaret van Cortlandt, and thus became connected with a number of the most influential Colonial families of New York and New Jersey.—*N. Y. Hist. Colls.*, 1884, xiv. He married, 2d, Elizabeth Tuite, of Trenton, Oct. 10, 1749. She was of an old Irish family, settled in Maryland. By his first wife he had five sons and two daughters:

I. Samuel, who entered the British army, but left it in 1773 to accept the post of Collector of the Port of New York. In 1783 he went to London, and thence to the East Indies, where he died in the island of Sumatra about 1796.

II. Richard, born in August, 1733, and died at Mount Kemble, which he inherited, Sept. 13, 1833, unmarried.

III. Peter, born in 1739. He was educated in the "college in Philadelphia," now the University of Pennsylvania, then engaged in business, and later, with his two brothers-in-law—Nicholas and Isaac Gouverneur—established the commercial house of Gouverneur & Kemble, in New York. He died July 6, 1823. He married Gertrude Gouverneur (daughter of Samuel Gouverneur and Experience Johnson), June 5, 1784. Issue: 1. Gouverneur, b. Jan. 25, 1786; d. Dec. 16, 1875, at Cold Spring, N. Y., unmarried. He was the owner of "Cockloft Hall," near the Erie railroad station, in Newark, made famous by Washington Irving and James K. Paulding, in "Salmagundi." 2. Peter, drowned, Nov. 24, 1813, in his 26th year. 3. William. 4. Richard, born in 1800, inherited Mount Kemble from his uncle Richard, but sold it and removed to Cold Spring, where he died in 1888. 5. Gertrude, married James Kirke Paulding; she died in 1841, leaving four sons. 6. Mary, married Robert Parker Parrott, a graduate of West Point Military Academy, in 1824, and later the inventor and manufacturer of the "Parrott gun."

IV. Stephen, born at or near New Brunswick, in 1740. He entered the British army in 1757, and in 1772 became Deputy Adjutant General of the Forces in North America, which position he resigned in 1779. He was commissioned Colonel in 1782, and served in the army in America, the West Indies, the Spanish Main, Nicaragua and England, until 1805, when he sold out, returned to America, and settled at New Brunswick, in the house in which he was born, and there died, Dec. 20, 1822, unmarried.

V. William, died in England, a Captain in the British army.

VI. Margaret, married, Dec. 8, 1758, at Mount Kemble, General Thomas Gage, Commander-in-Chief of the British army in America, and Governor of Massachusetts at the beginning of the Revolution.

KEMBLE FAMILY :
KENNEDY—First and Second

He was the second son of Thomas, eighth Baronet and first Viscount Gage. General Gage died in 1788; she died Feb. 9, 1824. Issue: 1. Henry, born March 4, 1761, and by the death of his uncle without male issue became Viscount Gage; he married, Jan. 11, 1789, his cousin, Susannah Maria, only daughter and heir of Lieut. Col. William Skinner, of Perth Amboy, by his wife Susan, daughter of Admiral Sir Peter Warren. He was succeeded by his son, Henry Hall, fourth Viscount, and he by his grandson, Henry Charles, the fifth Viscount Gage. The other children of General Thomas Gage and his wife Margaret Kemble were: 2. John; 3. Admiral Sir William Hall Gage; 4. Marion, wife of Sir James Crawford; 5. Louisa, wife of Sir James H. Blake; 6. Harriet, died single; 7. Charlotte Margaret, wife of Admiral Sir Charles Ogle; 8. Emily, wife of Montagu Bertie, fifth Earl of Abingdon.

VII. Judith, married Archibald McCall, a Philadelphia merchant, by whom she had eighteen children. She died there, aged 89 years.

By his second wife Peter Kemble had

VIII. Robert, b. April 5, 1755. He served in the British army during the Revolution. He lived at Mount Kemble, where he died, January 1, 1820.

IX. Elizabeth, born Dec. 18, 1753; d. June 16, 1836. X. Ann, b. June 9, 1757; d. Sept. 2, 1820—both at Mount Kemble, where they lived, unmarried.

These genealogical details of the Kemble family have been compiled from the very full and interesting account given by Edward F. de Lancey in connection with the Journals of Col. Stephen Kemble, published by the N. Y. Historical Society in 1883-1884. See also *Whitehead's Perth Amboy*, 114-115; *N. J. Marriage Licenses*, and *N. J. Archives*, passim; *N. Y. Chamber of Commerce Records, Biographical Sketches*, 139; *Family Records and Events (Rutherford Papers)*, 301.

ARCHIBALD KENNEDY, 1st and 2d.

Archibald Kennedy, 1st, was a Scotch gentleman, a lawyer by profession, who was complimented with the freedom of New York, by the corporation of that city, July 25, 1710.—*N. Y. Hist. Soc. Coll.*, 1885, 484. In 1727, on the recommendation of Governor William Burnet, he was appointed a member of the Council of the Province of New York, in which body he served until 1761, when he resigned, on account of his age, and other employments. He was Speaker of that body in 1757.— *Journals of the Legislative Council of New York*, passim. He was Receiver-General of the same Province, 1722-54; Collector of Customs for the port of New York in 1758.—*N. Y. Hist. MSS.*, II., 475, 539, 616, 678, etc. In 1724 he acquired a tract of 383 acres at Bergen, being part of what was formerly called the West India farm.—*Winfield's Land Titles of Hudson County*, 303. Mr. Kennedy died June 14, 1763, after a few days' illness, aged about 78 years. "He was a Gentleman who always sustain'd a fair and amiable Character, and his Death is universally lamented by all his Acquaintance," said the *New York Gazette* of June 20, 1763.—*N. J. Archives*, XXIV., 200. He left two children—Archibald and Catherine—to whom he devised his farm at Bergen, two-thirds to the son and one-third to the daughter. In 1765 Catherine conveyed her interest to her brother. The property was in litigation until 1804, when a compromise was effected.—*Winfield*, ut supra.

Archibald Kennedy, 2d, married Catharine, only daughter of Col. Peter Schuyler, of Petersborough, Second River, opposite Belleville, on the banks of the Passaic, and lived there for some years. By her he acquired large estates in New Jersey and New York. She died at Second River, December 25, 1765, of quinsy, in her 29th year.—*N. J. Archives*, XXV., 263. In April, 1769, he married Anne, daughter of John Watts, of New York, who was very wealthy. The *New York Gazette and Weekly Mercury*, of May 1, 1769, announced the event thus: "Last Thursday Capt. Archibald Kennedy, Esq; was married to Miss Nancy Watts, Daughter of the Hon. John Watts, Esq; of this City, a young Lady of great Merit, with a handsome Fortune."—*N. J. Archives*, XXVI., 429. He became a Captain in the Royal Navy in 1757, commanding the *Coventry* for some time, and won much distinction in the service by his gallantry. In 1765 he refused to take on board his frigate, then at New York, a quantity of stamped paper, as the mob threatened to destroy his many houses in the city. For this he was superseded.—*N. Y. Col. Docs.*, VII., 792, 821. Being suspected of sympathy with the British cause, he was arrested on the order of the Council of Safety of New Jersey, in 1778, and ordered to remove to Sussex, but was subsequently permitted to resume his residence at Petersborough. In 1792 he succeeded his great-grandfather as eleventh Earl of Cassillis, Scotland, and his oldest son became twelfth Earl and Marquis of Ailsa. He died December 29, 1794. His New York residence, No. 1 Broadway, was one of the most noted in that city for its historic associations.—*Winfield's Hudson County*, 312-13; *Mrs. Lamb's Hist. N. Y.*, 655, 671; *Old New York*, by Dr. J. W. Francis, 1858, 15; *N. Y. Col. Docs.*, VII., 822. The Bergen common lands were divided by commissioners appointed by the Legislature in 1765. Their field-book forms the basis of Mr. Winfield's admirable "Land Titles of Hudson County."—*N. J. Archives*, IX., 460.

REV. SAMUEL KENNEDY.

The Rev. Samuel Kennedy was born in Scotland in 1720, and came to this country in early life, settling in New Jersey. By advice of the Presbytery of New Brunswick, he began studying for the ministry, and on December 26, 1749, was received under their care. He was licensed to preach the gospel, May 18, 1750, and on June 25, 1751, was ordained, and installed as pastor of the Presbyterian church at Baskinridge, where he remained for thirty-six years. He conducted a classical school for some years at the same place, which was noted for the character of the men it produced. He advertised in 1764 that he designed "to have the learned Languages, and liberal Arts and Sciences, taught under his Inspection, in a School-House now built on his own Plantation; where Persons may be fitted to enter any Class in College. . . . There are Scholars now learning the Latin and Greek Languages in said School." He also practiced medicine, at least in his own congregation, his skill and judgment in this profession being regarded as uncommonly sound and correct. He was a remarkably evangelical preacher, and under his ministrations his congregation experienced several notable revivals. Although his ministerial brethren from Scotland and the North of Ireland were sticklers for a high grade of education among the candidates for the ministry, he favored a more liberal policy, and allied himself to what was known as the New Side wing of the Church, as distinguished from the more conservative, or Old Side, wing. He received the honorary degree of A. M. from Princeton College in 1760. In 1767 Mr. Kennedy advertised his plantation, on which he then lived, to be sold at public vendue. He described it as containing 300 acres of land, a dwelling house with three rooms and two fireplaces on the lower floor, a good barn, and a stable at each end of it, an apple orchard, 72 acres of plow land cleared, 27 acres of meadow cleared; also his horses, cattle, sheep and utensils of husbandry. He was admitted to the New Jersey Medical Society in 1768, and was an attentive member. He died at Baskinridge, August 31, 1787. In announcing his death, *The Brunswick Gazette and Weekly Monitor*, of Tuesday, September 4, 1787, remarked: "This was a faithful servant of Jesus Christ, and has for a great number of years preached the gospel with success; he also followed the practice of physic, and was one of the Trustees of Princeton College.——It is but too common to ascribe merit to persons after their decease which they do not deserve: we shall only say that Mr. Kennedy was a truly pious, honest, upright, and zealous man; and in him the people have lost an excellent teacher, his wife an affectionate husband, his children an indulgent father, and his servants a kind and benevolent master." The statement that he was a Trustee of Princeton College is not borne out by the General Catalogue, 1746-1896, of that institution.—*Memoirs of the Rev. Robert Finley*, by the Rev. Isaac V. Brown, New Brunswick, 1819, 183-188; *Webster's Hist. Pres. Church*, 604; *Sprague's Annals*; *Wickes's Medical Men of N. J.*, 305; *Transactions N. J. Medical Society*, reprinted in 1866; *N. J. Archives*, XIX., 418, 421, 577-8; XX., 489; XXIV., 407; XXV., 350. He d. intestate, and letters of administration were issued, Dec. 3, 1787, to Samuel Kennedy (his son?) and Henry Southard.—*N. J. Wills*, Lib. 29, f. 439.

REV. NATHAN KER.

Nathan Ker was from Freehold. After graduating from Princeton he was licensed in 1762 as a preacher, and in 1766 became pastor of the Presbyterian church at Goshen, N. Y., where he remained until his death, Dec. 14, 1804. He served as a volunteer Chaplain in the Revolution. He was vigorous and persistent in the prosecution of the Rev. David Barclay for heresy in 1794.

REV. ABRAHAM KETELTAS.

The Rev. Abraham Keteltas, born in New York, Dec. 26, 1732, was ordained pastor of the Presbyterian Church at Elizabethtown, Sept. 14, 1757, and continued there until July, 1760, soon after which he took up his residence at Jamaica, L. I., where he died Sept. 30, 1798. During the Revolution he made himself very obnoxious to the British by his ardent and outspoken patriotism.

CONSTANT KING.

Constant King was among the early settlers of Morris county, from Southold, L. I. His wife was Phebe Horton. Their children were: 1. Joseph, b. Dec. 13, 1735; m. 1st, Prudence Howell, of Southampton; 2d, Rhoda Carter, of Chatham, 1768; d. May 19, 1794; 2. Frederick, b. Oct. 6, 1738, at Southold; m. Mary Ayres, of Morris Plains, Nov. 23, 1762; d. April 4, 1796; he was the first postmaster at Morristown; 3. Catharine, b. Feb. 15, 1740; m. William Walton, who was killed in the British attack on Charleston, S. C.; she d. Oct. 4, 1805; 4. John, b. March 10, 1742; 5. George, b. Sept. 15, 1745; m. Esther Dickerson, Oct. 2, 1774; d. July 3, 1780.—*Registers First Church, Morristown*, 127. He was a Judge of the Morris county common pleas, Feb. 15, 1771, and a Justice of the Peace in 1776.

JOHN LADD, First and Second.

"Of John Ladd, the father, and John Ladd, the son, much appears in the various records and traditions of their times, which proves them to have been conspicuous persons. They were prominent in the political and religious matters that surrounded them, and the subjects of much hard talk, for which some of their defamers appear in no very enviable position."—*First Settlers of Newton Township, Old Gloucester County*, by John Clement, Camden, 1877, 142. The father was a practical surveyor, and assisted in laying out the city of Philadelphia for William Penn, but in compensation preferred £30 cash to a square of land in the embryo city, which moved Penn to say, "Friend John, thou art a Ladd by name, and a Ladd in comprehension. Dost thou not know this will become a great city?"—*Ib.*, 143-5.

John Ladd, second, was a surveyor and man of prominence for many years in Salem and Gloucester counties.—*Clement's First Settlers of Newton Township*, 142-3-5. In 1740 he interested himself in getting evidence against Robert Jenkins, of Salem, arrested for having counterfeit money in his possession.—*Penn. Archives*, I., 623. He was elected a member of the Assembly from Gloucester in 1754.—*N. J. Hist. Proc.*, May, 1850, 31. While still a member of that body, he was recommended by Governor Belcher in 1758 for a seat in the Council.—*N. J. Archives*, IX., 127. In 1762 he was appointed one of the Surrogates for West Jersey.—*Ib.*, 359. In 1763 Governor Franklin recommended him for appointment as Councillor, saying: "Mr. Ladd is a Gentn. of Fortune and unblemished Character, was formerly in the Assembly where he was always on the Side of the Administration, and is now one of the principal Magistrates of Gloucester County, which Office he has long executed with Ability, and Credit to himself."—*Ib.*, 387. Mr. Ladd was appointed August 31, 1763.—*Ib.*, 394-5. He continued in that office until his death, at Woodbury, February —, 1771.—*N. J. Archives*, IX., 395; X., 224; XXVII., 380.

HENRY LANE.

The will of Henry Lane, of Paramus, Bergen county, merchant, dated December 27, 1762, was proved January 29, 1763, so that it was probably a death-bed will. The testator devises to his wife, Elizabeth, one-third of his real estate (not described) in "Bargin" county and in New York, and all his silver-plate; one-third of said real estate to his son, William Henry Lane, and one-third to his daughter, Geesie Lena. He leaves a legacy to his wife's mother, Geesie Lena Rousby. Executors—his wife and William Rousby, of New York, merchant. The West Jersey Society gave a power of attorney, dated May 7, 1752, to Henry Lane and Lewis Johnston, which was revoked August 5, 1761. In the meantime Henry Lane had executed two conveyances as agent and attorney of the Society. One of them recites that Thomas Lane, one of the Committee of the West Jersey Society, was eldest son of John Lane, who was eldest son of Sir Thomas Lane, Knight, and Alderman of London. The executrix advertised, February 28, 1763, "four valuable plantations (pleasantly situated) in Salem county, and a dwelling house and lot in New York." She also advertised for sale certain tracts upon Ancocus brook, in Bergen county, which elicited a warning from the East Jersey Proprietors, who claimed the title to be still in them.

THOMAS LAURIE.

Thomas Laurie was a storekeeper at Allentown. His grandfather, Thomas Laurie, brother of Gawen Laurie, came to America in 1683, with two children, James, who probably married Sarah, dau. of William Redford, of Freehold, and Anna, who married John Hebron. His will, dated March 6, 1712-13, was proved August 2, 1714. His son James bought land near Allentown in 1705, and there spent the remainder of his days. He had two sons, William and Thomas.—*Salter's Hist. Monmouth and Ocean Counties,* Appendix, xxxvi; *N. J. Archives,* XXIII., 286, 377.

LAWRENCE FAMILY.

Elisha Lawrence was one of the earliest and most prominent settlers of Monmouth county. He m. Lucy Stout, and d. at Chestnut Grove, Upper Freehold, May 27, 1724. Issue:

Second Generation.

2.   i.   Elisha[2], m. Elizabeth, dau. of Dr. John Brown. He probably removed to Burlington. In 1764 there was a letter in the Trenton post-office for "Elisha Lawrence, jun., West Jersey."

3.   ii.   John[2], b. 1709; m. Mary, dau. of William Hartshorne; d. 1794. He was a surveyor, and ran the "Lawrence line" between East Jersey and West Jersey. He advertised a plantation at Upper Freehold for sale, in 1767.

Third Generation.

2.   Elisha[2] Elisha[1] Lawrence and Elizabeth Brown had issue:

4.   i.   John[3], b. about 1726; m. Martha ———; prob. d. in Burlington in 1796. She was bap. at Burlington, April 20, 1764, with two infant daughters. He was admitted to the New Jersey Bar either in May, 1747, or at the November term, 1749.—*Vroom's Sup. Ct. Rules,* 58. He was called up to be a sergeant-at-law in 1771.—*Ib.,* 54. He was a prominent lawyer of Burlington county for many years. To distinguish him from his uncle, John Lawrence, the surveyor, and from his cousin, Dr. John Lawrence, as well as from others belonging to the Quaker Lawrences, of Bordentown, he was often spoken of as John Brown Lawrence, after his maternal grandfather. (It was perhaps John Lawrence, who traded at Bordentown, 1751-7, who was admitted to the Bar in 1747 or 1749. —*Hist. Burlington and Mercer Counties,* 1882, p. 456.) John Lawrence (but whether of Burlington or Bordentown is not stated) was appointed one of the commissioners to erect a suitable house at Burlington for the preservation of the public records, by act of the Legislature passed Dec. 5, 1760. By act passed April 7, 1761, he was appointed one of the commissioners to grant relief to townships for the support of soldiers disabled in the French war. He was a manager of the Burlington church lottery in 1762. In 1763 he was interested in a visionary scheme to found a Colony, to be called New Wales, upon "the finest part of the Ohio," which was speedily abandoned by the chief "promoter," Lieutenant T. Webb, of the British army. He was named on a committee in 1765 to receive subscriptions for the erection of a causeway and bridge over Newtown creek, Gloucester county. John Lawrence was elected to represent Burlington county in the Assembly of 1767. It is not

likely that it was the Assemblyman who was one of the Committee of Lawyers to present charges against ex-Sheriff and Assemblyman Samuel Tucker. —*Field's Provincial Courts*, 170. That was probably the Bordentown John Lawrence. Mr. Lawrence was Mayor of Burlington in 1769.—*Hill's Hist. of the Church in Burlington*, 296. Upon the representation of the Board of Trade, June 27, 1771, Mr. Lawrence was appointed by the King in Council, July 19, 1771, to be of the Council of New Jersey. He sat with that body until its dissolution, in November, 1775.—*N. J. Hist. Soc. Coll.*, V., 422-3; *N. J. Archives*, X., 302-3; XVIII., passim. When Col. Donop approached Burlington with his Hessians, December 11, 1776, Mr. Lawrence, with the Rev. Jonathan Odell, Rector of St. Mary's church, and two or three other of the principal citizens, went out to meet the troops, and to intercede with Col. Donop to protect the town from pillage by his soldiers. To this the Colonel graciously agreed, and he and some of his officers dined with Mr. Lawrence. The American gunboats lying in the river fired upon the town to drive the Hessians out, compelling their retreat to Bordentown, whither Mr. Lawrence, Dr. Odell and others were obliged to accompany them, in order to avoid arrest by the Americans for harboring the enemy.— *Hill's*, ut supra, 315; *The Burlington Smiths*, 170. Mr. Lawrence subsequently returned to Burlington. On March 31, 1777, he was "desired" by the Governor and Council of Safety to "attend" them at Bordentown. He did so on April 3, when he was examined, but it is not stated that anything came of this.— *Minutes Council of Safety*, 1777, 11, 12. He was for many years a leading member and officer of St. Mary's church in Burlington, his name appearing repeatedly in the church records from 1765 to 1795.— *Hill's*, 286, 305, 324, 341. He was also one of the first Trustees of Burlington Academy, founded in 1792.— *Ib.*, 328-9, 332-3-4-5.

ii. Anne, m. Raynold Keen, of Philadelphia (his third wife), and d. August 1, 1823, in her 72d year.

iii. Elizabeth, m Dr. James Newell, of Upper Freehold; d. Feb. 22, 1791, aged 60 years.—*Penn. Hist. Mag.*, V., 97-98; *Wickes's Hist. Medicine in N. J.*, 431.

3. John[2] Elisha[1] Lawrence and Mary Hartshorne had issue:

i. John[3], b. 1747.

Having graduated at Princeton in 1764, young Lawrence studied medicine and graduated from the Medical College of Philadelphia in 1768, being one of the first ten who received literary honors from that institution. His was the first medical degree conferred in America. He began his practice in Monmouth county. Early in the Revolution he was suspected of disloyalty to the American cause, and by order of Gen. Washington he was arrested at Perth Amboy, with a number of other prominent citizens of that place, by Major Duyckmck, July 6, 1777, and removed to Trenton. A committee of the Provincial Congress reported, July 9, 1777, that they had waited on Dr. Lawrence and others, "apprehended and removed to this place, pursuant to an order of Gen. Washington," and had taken "their parole, not to depart the town of Trenton, unless with leave of Congress." On Saturday, July 13, 1777, it was "ordered, that Dr. John Lawrence have leave to remove, on his parole, to Morristown, and not to depart from thence, more than six miles, without leave of Congress." A remarkable tribute to his ability and popularity appears in the proceedings of the Provincial Congress of Wednesday, July 17, 1777, when

"A petition from sundry ladies at Perth Amboy, setting forth, that they apprehend fatal and melancholy consequences to themselves and families, and to the inhabitants in general, if they should be deprived of the assistance of Dr. Lawrence's skill in his profession, as his attendance is hourly necessary to several patients now much indisposed, who will be left helpless if he be removed, as no other practitioner resides in that place, praying that he may be permitted to remain in Amboy; was read, and ordered a second reading.

"The petition from sundry ladies at Perth Amboy was read a second time, and ordered that a copy of the following letter, addressed to Mrs. Franklin, one of the subscribers, be signed by the President and sent:

"Madam:—

"I am ordered by Congress to acquaint you, and through you the other ladies of Amboy, that their petition in favour of Dr. John Lawrence has been received and considered.

"Could any application have procured a greater indulgence to Dr. Lawrence, you may be assured yours could not have failed of success. But, unhappily, madam, we are placed in such a situation, that motives of consideration to individuals must give place to the safety of the publick.

"As Dr. John Lawrence therefore has fallen under the suspicion of our generals, we are under the necessity of abiding by the steps which are taken; And are, &c."

He was subsequently permitted to leave the State, and located in New York city, where he practiced medicine until 1783, and was also in command of a local Company of volunteers for the defence of the city. At the close of the War he returned to New Jersey, residing at Upper Freehold, but did not resume practice, having abundant means. His patients were among the most prominent families of New Jersey and New York, Long Island and Westchester county. He was never married. He died April 29, 1830, at Trenton, while away from home. His remains were brought back and interred in the grave yard of the Old Yellow Church (Baptist) at Upper Freehold.—*N. J. Archives*, X., 302, note; *Wickes's Hist. Medicine in New Jersey*, 307-310; *Old Times in Old Monmouth*, 48, 150; *Lawrence Genealogy*, 1858; *Sabine's Loyalists*, II., 2; *Whitehead's History of Perth Amboy*, 330; *Minutes of Provincial Congress*, passim. His will, dated Feb. 1, 1816, proved May 21, 1830, describes him as "of Monmouth county." He gives to his sisters Elizabeth Le Conte and Sarah Lawrence all his estate, equally, and mentions nephew Henry Waddell. Executors—the two sisters named above. Witnesses—Samuel Newell, William Thompson, Elizabeth Hartshorne. Letters testamentary were granted to Elizabeth Le Conte, surviving executrix. The "inventory of the personal estate of Dr. John Lawrence, late of the city of Trenton, was filed May 21, 1830. It mentions "Articles at Trenton"—purse, apparel, carriage and harness, carriage horses, covered wagon, etc. "Articles at the Farm"—horses, oxen, etc. The total was appraised at $2,127.20. Appraisers—Samuel C. Newell, David Fischer.—*Originals*, Hunterdon Wills, 1828-30.

Fourth Generation.

4. John³ Elisha² Elisha¹ Lawrence and Martha ——— had issue:

      i.   John⁴, 5th child, b. Sept. 27, 1768; licensed as an attorney in 1789, and settled at Woodbury, N. J., where he enjoyed a large practice, and where he died; he was buried Nov. 7, 1806.

      ii. James⁴, b. at Burlington, October 1, 1781; bap. in St. Mary's church there, November 14, 1781; studied law, 1796-8, with his brother John at Woodbury, in deference to his father's wishes, but on the latter's decease entered the American Navy, September 4, 1798, winning in his chosen sphere an imperishable renown as one of the most gallant of heroes, even though cut off at the early age of 32 in his daring but disastrous fight with the *Chesapeake* against the British frigate *Shannon.—Mickle's Old Gloucester*, 71; *Hist. Collections of New Jersey*, 96; *Alden's Epitaphs*, No. 583; *Hill's*, 319; *Mag. Am. Hist.*, XXV., 283.

     iii. Elizabeth², m., June 30, 1774, Michael³ Kearny, son of Philip² Michael¹ Kearny, by his wife Isabella, dau. of Chief Justice Robert Lettis Hooper, of Trenton.— *Whitehead's Perth Amboy*, 91.

     iv. Martha, b. Feb. 24, 1773; buried Sept. 14, 1773.

      v. Sarah, bap. April 20, 1764.

     vi. Catherine, bap. April 20, 1764.

    vii. Elisha Talman, b. Feb. 13, 1775.

   viii. Lucy, bap. Nov. 24, 1771.

BRYAN LEFFERTY.

Bryan Lefferty, Esq., is mentioned in 1755 in the record of a road near Lamington, Somerset county. He subscribed, in 1756, £1, 15s. toward the erection of St. Paul's Lutheran Church at Pluckamin. In the same year he built his house, at Pluckamin, south of the village, north of Chambers's or Lefferty's brook, and east of the road running from Pluckamin to Somerville. He was appointed one of the Common Pleas Judges of Somerset County, March 19, 1759, and again in 1768. He loaned money, June 3, 1767, to Peter Eoff, innholder, of Pluckamin, on a mortgage on the latter's house. On July 20, 1769, administration was granted to "Mary Leferty, widow of Bryan Leferty Esq late of Somerset county deceased." His tombstone in the Lamington churchyard says he was 64 years old. His children probably were: 1. Bryan; 2. Priscilla, married William Steward, of Somerset County, April 11, 1748; 3. Catharine, married Asher Herriott, Jan. 6, 1755; 4. John, who removed to Sussex county; administration on his estate was granted to Moses Van Campen, July 14, 1781; 5. Ruth, said to have been one of the most beautiful and most wayward girls in the county; her son's half-brother, William McDonald, made a runaway match with a sister of Jennie McCrea, who was murdered by Indians near Fort Edward, during the Revolution. Bryan Lefferty, second, is said to have been a noted Tory in the Revolution. His prominence in the community is indicated by the fact that the War Office of the Continental Congress wrote, July 20, 1776, to the Provincial Congress of New Jersey, suggesting "the propriety of Bryan Lefferty, Esquire, his residing in New

LEFFERTY: LEONARD: LIVINGSTON: LONGWORTH

Jersey, and to take his parole and security," whereupon the Provincial Congress "*Ordered*, That Mr. Lefferty do sign his parole as settled by Congress. and give security in the sum of one thousand Pounds, to depart hence to the house or the widow Lefferty, in the Township of Bedminster, Somerset County, and there to remain, or within a circle of four miles thereof, until he have leave to the contrary." After the war it would seem that he was still a Justice of the Peace as late as 1786, about which time he probably died, as in 1787 his property, 174 acres, is assessed to Mrs. Lefferty, the tax being $4, 15s., 8d. About 1800 the property passed into the hands of John Davenport, who came from Connecticut, and built a tannery on the place. The Lefferty house was torn down in 1879. The name is written Lafferty, Lefferty and Leferty in the records.—*Hist. Hunterdon and Somerset Counties*, 703, 711, 713; "*Our Home,*' Somerville, 1873, 481-6, *Minutes of Provincial Congress*, 1775-1776, 518; *Records of Wills and of Marriages*, in Secretary of State's Office, at Trenton.

THOMAS LEONARD.

Thomas Leonard was a prominent citizen of Freehold, residing on Lahaway creek, near its junction with Crosswicks creek, on the place where his father, Capt. John Leonard, was murdered by Wequalia, an Indian, in 1727. Thomas was a Loyalist during the Revolution, and so early as April 3, 1775, the Committee of Inspection for the Township of Freehold decided that he had "in a number of instances been guilty of a breach of the Continental Association, and that, pursuant to the tenour of said Association, every friend of true freedom ought immediately to break off all connexion and dealings with him, the said Leonard, and treat him as a foe to the rights of British America." He narrowly escaped arrest once by disguising himself as a negro, and so passed out from his home forever. He was a Major in the First Battalion of New Jersey Loyalists in 1778. He went to New York, and after the war removed with his family to St. John, New Brunswick, where he was granted Lot No. 1 in Parr Town (afterwards incorporated in St. John), in 1783. His property in Monmouth County was confiscated, and in 1779 was sold to Gen. David Forman, of Revolutionary fame.

COLONEL WILLIAM SMITH LIVINGSTON.

William Smith Livingston, a son of Robert James Livingston, was commissioned Major of Lasher's Regiment, New York Militia, July, 1776; Aide-de-camp to Gen. Greene, 12th August, 1776, to 14th January, 1777; Lieutenant Colonel of Webb's Additional Continental Regiment, 1st January, 1777; retired 10th October, 1778.—*Heitman's Register*. He then studied law and was admitted an attorney of the Supreme Court of New Jersey at the April Term, 1780. Afterwards he practised law in the City of New York.

ISAAC and THOMAS LONGWORTH.

Isaac Longworth was a son of Thomas Longworth, of Newark, who died September 4th, 1748, aged 56 years. Isaac was probably born about 1730. He advertised for sale the property of Col. Josiah Ogden, deceased, in Newark, in 1763 and 1764. He was elected one of the chosen freeholders for Newark in 1765, 1766, 1769 (election contested, but decided in his favor by the Court of Quarter Sessions) and 1774; town clerk in 1772 (and surveyor of the highways), 1773, 1774, 1775 ("and to be exempt from working on the highway for his service") and 1776. He was county collector, 1772-1776. He married, first, Sarah ————, who died January 19th, 1754, aged 23 years; second, Catherine, daughter of Col. Josiah Ogden, and widow of David Ogden, Esquire (who died January 28th, 1750, aged 40 years), marriage license dated February 19th, 1761. Isaac Longworth was appointed a member of the Committee of Correspondence of Newark, May 4th, 1775. He soon after went over to the enemy, and in June, 1777, his wife was sent from Newark to join him. Steps were taken for the confiscation of his property in due course. He was advertised, December 8th, 1778, as "a fugitive now with the enemy;" an inquisition was returned against him, January 19th, 1779, and he was again advertised as "a fugitive now with the enemy," April 29th, 1779, and April 26th, 1784. The board of justices and freeholders of the county informed the Legislature, December 20th, 1780, that Longworth, who was one of the commissioners of the loan office for Essex county, had taken with him the books and papers and some of the money entrusted to his care, by which means he had forfeited his bond. He was one of the fifty-five civilian Loyalists who, in July, 1783, petitioned for lands in Nova Scotia, as consideration of their services to the King. He appears to have returned to Newark after the war, where he made his will, in 1790, in which he names his wife Catherine and grandson David Johnson. His brother, Thomas Longworth, a leading member of Trinity Church, Newark, was also advertised as "a fugitive now with the enemy," at the same time as Isaac, and his wife, Mary Bruen, and was deported from Newark in June, 1777. He returned to Newark after the war, and died July 23d, 1790, aged 72 years. He was the father of David Longworth, who published the first New York directory, in 1786, and was the grandfather of Nicholas Longworth, one of Cincinnati's prominent citizens for many years.—*Collections N. J. Hist. Soc.*, VI., and Supplement, passim; 1 *N. J. Archives*, XXII; *Minutes Provincial Congress*; *Revolutionary Correspondence N. J. Executive Sabine's Loyalists*, II., 546.— *N. J. Archives*, 2d Series, page 419.

REV. JAMES LYON.

James Lyon was licensed to preach by the Presbytery of New Brunswick in 1762, and was ordained by the same body, December 5, 1764, to go to Nova Scotia, where he labored in the ministry for several years. In 1771 he removed to Machias, Me., preaching there under great difficulties, especially during the Revolution. He supplied the pulpit of Newtown, L. I., for two or three years until the spring of 1785. He died October 12, 1794. He is said to have been of Irish birth. In the *New American Magazine* (published at Woodbridge, N. J.), for September, 1759, appears an original ode, "Louisburg Taken," introduced by a note, signed "Al - - - - s" (i. e., Alumnus), in which the writer asks his readers to "impute any impropriety in the Performance, or Incorrectness in Measure, to the Unskilfulness of a Lyre, touch'd by unexperienced Youth." The ode is two pages in length, and is signed "Nassovian," with the date, "E. Jersey, Aug. 1, 1759." It is probably from the pen of Mr Lyon.

CAPTAIN JOSEPH LYON.

Joseph Lyon was a descendant of Henry Lyon, one of the first settlers of Newark, in 1667, but who was of Elizabethtown in 1673. Capt. Joseph Lyon was an Elder in the Presbyterian Church at Elizabethtown as early as 1759. He died at Lyons Farms, August 26, 1772, in his

LYON: MOELICH: MAXWELL

61st year. His son, Joseph Lyon, born 1741, and who graduated at Princeton in 1763, was an Elder in the same church for thirty-five years before his death, which occurred May 14, 1821.

JOHN MOELICH.

Johannes Moelich (Melick, Mellick) was born Feb. 26, 1702, at Bendorf on the Rhine, Germany, son of Johan Wilhelm Moelich and Anna Catharine, his wife. He married Maria Cathrina (born Jan. 8, 1698, daughter of Burgomaster Gottfried) Kirberger, at Bendorf, Nov. 1, 1723. He emigrated with his wife, his four children born at Bendorf, and his youngest brother, Johan Gottfried, and arrived at Philadelphia May 29, 1735, in the ship "Mercury." In December, 1747, he bought a tract of 409 acres in Greenwich township, now in Warren county. In 1750 he was living on a farm of 400 acres in Readington township, Hunterdon county, where he established a tannery. He bought from George Leslie, in November, 1751, a tract of 367 acres in Bedminster township, on the road now running from Pluckamin to Peapack. Here he built a substantial stone house, which he occupied thereafter, and also established an extensive tannery and bark mill, which continued in successful operation for more than a century. He was an officer and active in the affairs of Zion Lutheran church at New Germantown for several years before his death, but when St. Paul's church was projected at Pluckamin, in 1756, he gave £1, 15s. towards its erection, and on his death, Nov. 16, 1763, he was buried in the new churchyard at that place. He had children: 1. Georg Wilhelm, b. Aug. 12, 1724; d. Aug. 20, 1724; 2. Aaron (bap. Ehrenreich), b. Oct. 17, 1725; d. at Bedminster, April 7, 1809; 3. Veronica Gerdrutta, bap. Nov. 21, 1727; m. Johan Jacob Klein; d. Oct. 9, 1801; 4. Andrew, bap. Dec. 17, 1729; d. June 29, 1820, near Phillipsburg, N. J.; 5. Georg Anthon, bap. April 6, 1732; d. June 25, 1732; 6. Marie Cathrine, b. Dec. 5, 1733; m. Simon Ludewig Himroth, who came to America in 1752, settling at Bedminster, but in 1772 removed to Milton, Penn.; 7. Philip, b. Oct. 9, 1736; settled near Pluckamin; 8. Peter, b. Dec. 5, 1739. From Aaron (3) are descended the Mellicks of Plainfield.—*The Story of an Old Farm*, by Andrew D. Mellick, jun., 1889, 631; *Hist. Hunterdon and Somerset Counties*, 716.

GENERAL WILLIAM MAXWELL.

William Maxwell was a native of Greenwich township, Sussex county. At a meeting of the people of that county, July 16th, 1774, he was appointed on a committee to co-operate with the other counties, and subsequently was elected a Deputy to the Provincial Congress which met at Trenton in May, June and August, 1775.—*Minutes of Provincial Congress*, 19, 169, 184. On October 28th, 1775, the Provincial Congress recommended him for appointment as Colonel of the Western Battalion of New Jersey, and on November 7th the Continental Congress appointed him, accordingly, Colonel of the Second Battalion, First Establishment.—*Ib.*, 245; *Officers and Men of New Jersey in the Revolutionary Army*, by William S. Stryker, 12, 16. The Continental Congress appointed him, October 23d, 1776, Brigadier-General, and placed under him the four battalions raised on the Second Establishment, called "Maxwell's Brigade."—*Stryker*, ut supra, 41-2. On May 11th, 1779, Maxwell's Brigade was ordered to the Susquehanna, on Sullivan's expedition. He resigned July 25th, 1780. "He commanded the Jersey line, during his entire term of service, as a general officer, and took an active part in every battle in which his brigade distinguished itself." —*Stryker*, ut supra, 64. "He served in the French War of 1755 as an officer of Provincial troops; was with Braddock when that officer was

defeated, and fought under Wolfe at the taking of Quebec. He was afterwards attached to the Commissary Department, and was posted at Mackinaw, holding the rank of Colonel. As soon as he heard that the Colonies which bordered on the Atlantic had resolved to resist the Crown to the death rather than be enslaved, he resigned his commission in the British army, marched on foot to Trenton, and tendered his services to the Provincial Congress, then in session. They were accepted and a Colonel's commission bestowed upon him, with others, to raise a battalion to march for Quebec. He succeeded in enlisting a fine body of men, and was engaged in recruiting when the meeting of the Sussex County Committee of Safety was held, August 10th and 11th, 1775, of which he was chosen Chairman. He took up his line of march, according to orders, but the defeat of Montgomery occurred before he could possibly reach Quebec, and nothing remained but to return to headquarters. He was soon after raised to the rank of Brigadier-General, and served with distinction in the battles of Germantown, Monmouth, Brandywine, Springfield, Wyoming and elsewhere. His personal frankness and the absence of all haughtiness in his manners made him a great favorite with the soldiers; but his merits, as is too often the case, excited envy; some of the officers who boasted a more aristocratic lineage than he could claim showed much jealousy of his advancement, and (in 1780), when one of this class succeeded in obtaining promotion over his head, he resigned his commission. He enjoyed to the last the special regard of Gen. Washington, who visited him. Gen. Maxwell's house took fire just after the close of the Revolution and all his valuable papers and correspondence were destroyed."
—*The First Sussex Centenary,* Newark, 1853, p. 60. An eloquent inscription, written by his friend and compatriot, Gov. Richard Howell, is placed over his remains, in the graveyard of the First Presbyterian Church of Greenwich township, setting forth that he was the oldest son of John and Anne Maxwell, and that he died November 4th, 1796, in the 63d year of his age (he never married):

In The Revolutionary War Which Established The Independence
of the
UNITED STATES,
He took an early, an active part;
A DISTINGUISHED MILITARY PARTISAN,
He arose, through different grades of the American Army,
to the rank of Brigadier-General;
A GENUINE PATRIOT,
He was a warm and decided friend
To the Constitution and Government of his Country;
In private life he was equally devoted to its service, and to the
good of the community of which he was a member,
An honorable and charitable man,
A warm and affectionate friend,
A zealous advocate of the institutions and
An active promoter of the
interests of the Christian Religion.
—*Ib.,* 60, note.

After the foregoing was put in type, the following additional particulars were furnished the writer by George Maxwell Robeson, ex-Attorney General of New Jersey and ex-Secretary of the Navy, since deceased:

General William Maxwell was born near Newtown Stewart, in county Tyrone, Ireland. He was of Scotch-Irish descent and was the son of John and Anne Maxwell. He came to this country with his father when nearly a man grown. His father settled at Greenwich, in the then county of Sussex, now Warren county.

William entered the Provincial army as an officer. He was at the taking of Quebec by Wolfe, and was one of Washington's Provincials in the Braddock Expedition against Fort Duquesne, and he was at the defeat of that unfortunate General. For his military services at that period he received from the British crown a grant of land near where Tarrytown is now located. The papers with regard to this grant were, however, lost in the burning of his house just before the close of the Revolutionary War.

At the time of the breaking out of the Revolution he was in the Provincial army, holding the rank of Colonel, and was stationed at Mackinaw. Upon receiving news of the first hostilities, he resigned his commission and started for home on horseback. His horse dropped dead in New York State somewhere near the New Jersey line, but he pushed on on foot until he reached Sussex county, where he immediately began to raise troops for the patriot cause.

No portrait of General Maxwell is known to exist, but according to family tradition he was a tall, stalwart man, with large bones. He had a florid complexion, large grey eyes, and his hair was dark brown, almost black—iron grey during the Revolutionary War. His manner was bluff but hearty, and, from his Scotch descent and accent, his soldiers called him "Scotch Willie."

His father lived in Greenwich with his wife, a young son, Robert, and two daughters. On one occasion the house was raided by a party of Tories. They ransacked the house, beat the old gentleman, and gave Robert a violent blow on the head, which injured him severely. The wife and daughters were forced to flee to the woods for safety. General Maxwell, as soon as he was able, got leave of absence from the army and, with a party of soldiers, pursued the Tories. He captured them and hanged them promptly, it is said, without judge or jury.

His brother John, who was next to him in age, was a Lieutenant in the First Jersey Establishment and afterwards a Captain in the service. He served at one time on General Maxwell's staff with the rank of Major. It is related that he one day rode into camp at Morristown with a full company of one hundred stalwart soldiers from Sussex, to the surprise and delight of Washington.

Captain John Maxwell's eldest son was George Clifford Maxwell, Jefferson's United States District Attorney, and member of Congress from New Jersey in 1811-13, elected as a Democrat. He married Miss Rachel Bryant and they had two children:

i. A son, John Paterson Bryant Maxwell, who was a member of Congress from New Jersey from 1836 to 1840, and died at Belvidere, November 14th, 1845.

ii. A daughter, Anna Maria, who married William P. Robeson, of Oxford Furnace, and their eldest son is the George Maxwell Robeson from whom the above information was derived, who was also a member of Congress from New Jersey from 1878 to 1892.

Captain John Maxwell had also a younger son, William, and two daughters.

McCAIN (McKEAN) FAMILY.

Susan McCain (probably widow of William McKean), of New London, Chester County, Penn., in her will, dated December 28, 1730, devised her lands to two sons—William McCain and Thomas McCain. William, her oldest son, was born in Ireland in 1707. He kept a tavern

McCAIN (McKEAN) FAMILY : McEOWEN

in what is now known as Chatham, New London, until 1741, when he removed to Londongrove, an adjoining township, where he kept tavern, and in 1745 removed to Londonderry, where he followed the same business. He married, 1st, Letitia Finney, who died in 1742; 2d, Anne Logan, widow of James Logan, who had preceded him as tavern keeper at Londonderry; she died in 1751. He died November 18, 1769. He left issue (among others) by his first wife:

i. Robert, born July 13, 1732. He studied medicine, and was missionary at New Brunswick for several years, and at Perth Amboy, from February, 1763, until his death, October 17, 1767.

ii. Thomas, born March 19, 1734, in New London, Penn. After receiving a preparatory education under the Rev. Francis Allison, D. D., he entered the office of a relative, David Finney, at Newcastle, Del., as a law student, and was admitted to the bar in 1754 (before he was twenty-one), so superior was his reputation as a student. In 1756 he was appointed prosecutor of the pleas in Sussex County, Del. He was admitted to the bar of the Pennsylvania Supreme Court, April 17, 1758. He then went to England, and entered the Middle Temple, May 9, 1758, to pursue his law studies. June 20, 1765, he was licensed to practice in the New Jersey Courts. He was a member of the Legislature from Newcastle, 1762-1779; was a delegate to the Stamp Act Congress of 1765, and was elected to the Continental Congress in 1774, and served in that body several years, being one of the Signers of the Declaration of Independence, and President in 1781. He was Chief Justice of Pennsylvania, 1777-1799. In 1799 he was elected Governor of Pennsylvania, by the Republicans, and immediately began a wholesale system of removals of his politcal opponents from office. He was re-elected in 1802 and 1805, serving nine years of most turbulent experience as Governor. He married, 1st, July 21, 1763, Mary Borden, oldest child of Col. Joseph Borden, of Bordentown, N. J.; she died March 12, 1773, in her 29th year. He married, 2d, September 3, 1774, Sarah Armitage, of Newcastle. He died June 24, 1817. His widow died May 6, 1820.—*McKean Genealogy*, by Roberdeau Buchanan, Lancaster, Pa., 1890; *Lives of the Governors of Pennsylvania*, by William C. Armor, Philadelphia, 1873, 289, 307.

DANIEL McEOWEN.

Daniel McEowen came to this country from Argyleshire, Scotland, with his brothers Duncan and Alexander, and his sister Mary, in the spring of 1736, in the same ship with Alexander Kirkpatrick and his family. The Kirkpatricks located at Mine Brook, Somerset county, and the McEowens not far away, in Bedminster township, in the same county. The latter were accompanied by their mother, and perhaps by their father, and were all young, Mary being only eight years of age. Daniel married Ann Graham, of Somerset county, Dec. 4, 1744. He subscribed £1, 16s. in 1756 towards the erection of St. Paul's Lutheran Church at Pluckemin. No record has been found of his appointment as Judge or Justice of the Peace. His will, dated May 8, 1762, was proved June 15, 1762. In it he refers to his "honored mother Ann McEoen," and to his six children—Hugh, George, Daniel, Alexander, William and Mary. It was witnessed by Peter Penier, George Remer and John Castner, jun. His brother Duncan married Jennet, daughter of Alexander Kirkpatrick. His sister Mary, born in Argyleshire, Scotland, Aug. 1, 1728, married David, son of Alexander Kirkpatrick, March 31, 1748; she died at Mine Brook, Nov. 2, 1795; her husband died March 19, 1814. One of their children was Andrew Kirkpatrick, born Feb. 17, 1756, who was Chief Justice of New Jersey, 1803-1824. William McEowen, son of Daniel, was a merchant at Pluckemin during the Revolution, and bought flour for the American army. He died at Pluckemin, March 10, 1817, aged sixty-one years.

McKEAN

REV. ROBERT McKEAN.

The Rev. Robert McKean was b. July 13, 1732, the son of William McCain and Letitia Finney, his wife. William McCain was b. in Ireland in 1707, and coming to America in early life with his mother, Susan McCain, settled with her at Chatham, New London, Chester county, Penn., where he kept tavern until 1741, thereafter for four years at Londongrove, and later at Londonderry, in the same region. He d. Nov. 18, 1769.

Robert McKean (as he wrote his name) studied for the ministry, probably under the Rev. Francis Allison, D. D., and having been ordained in England, in 1757 was appointed by the Society for the Propagation of the Gospel in Foreign Parts to be a missionery of the Church of England, at New Brunswick, his labors, however, often extending so far afield as Piscataway, Spotswood, Woodbridge, and more distant settlements in Central New Jersey. On taking charge of his mission he wrote home to the Society, January 8, 1758, that he "arrived at New Brunswick on the 16th of Dec., and was kindly received by his congregation, and had officiated regularly to them from that time." Writing again from New Brunswick, Feb. 5, 1758, to the Rev. Dr. Peter Bearcroft, Secretary of the Society, he says: "Since my arrival here I have wrote to you by two different Conveyances, one by the Pacquet, and another by means of a friend via Ireland. In them I have troubled you with a particular account of my Voyage and other proper occurrences, as also the kind reception I have met with and the happy prospect I have as yet in my mission." Young as he was, his indefatigable zeal and marked ability were speedily recognized. The College in Philadelphia (now the University of Pennsylvania) conferred upon him the honorary degree of A. M., in 1760. When Gov. Thomas Boone arrived in New Jersey, in July, 1760, the clergy of the Church of England waited upon him with an address, presented by a committee of three, of whom Mr. McKean was one. He served on a similar committee to address Gov. Josiah Hardy in November, 1761. He was regular and faithful in his attendance upon the convention of clergy which met in Philadelphia, April 30-May 5, 1760, to discuss the affairs of the church in Pennsylvania and the Lower Counties; he and Mr. Samuel Cook, "two of the Society's worthy Missionaries of New Jersey, [attending] with the kind intention of giving their best advice and assistance in promoting the designs of the Convention." When the pulpit of St. Peter's church at Perth Amboy became vacant, in 1761, the people of that congregation "had so much their hearts set on Mr. McKean" that they were "utterly averse" to the Society's selection, and were correspondingly glad when the appointee declined to leave Litchfield, Conn., and in the course of a year Mr. McKean was transferred to Perth Amboy, where he arrived in February, 1763, with a notification of his appointment as Missionary, his services being restricted to that parish exclusively, at the request of the vestry. In 1764 Woodbridge was placed in his care, he visiting it once every three weeks. In these charges he labored with indefatigable zeal and assiduity, and manifestly had the confidence of the older clergy. His own experience of the hardship laid upon young Americans who were obliged to go to England for ordination made him an ardent and perhaps intemperate advocate of the plan of appointing American Bishops—a cause so ably urged by Dr. Chandler. Mr. McKean studied medicine, and was a successful practitioner in that profession, and so much esteemed among his fellow medical men that he was one of the seventeen who organized the New Jersey Medical Society, in July, 1766, and was elected its first

President. His parishioners did not object to his practicing, but they —at least some of them—did find fault when he sent in his bills. He also seems to have taught school at Perth Amboy.

Mr. McKean m. Isabel Graham Antill, Feb. 19, 1766, at Christ church, Shrewsbury. She was a dau. of Edward Antill, 2d, of New Brunswick, and Anne Morris, his wife, dau. of Gov. Lewis Morris. She is said to have been "a young lady of very gay and independent spirit, not calculated to enhance the domestic happiness of the missionary." In his will, dated Sept. 13, 1767, he describes himself as "Clerk, Missionary from the Society for the Propagation of the Gospel in Foreign Parts, at Perth Amboy." He mentions his wife, but no children. He died at Raritan Landing, near New Brunswick, at the residence of his father-in-law, Edward Antill, 2d, October 17, 1767, after a long and wasting illness. Writing to the Society, October 12, 1767, the Rev. Dr. Thomas Bradbury Chandler, of Elizabethtown, says: "Wasted away with a tedious disorder, the worthy, the eminently useful and amiable Mr. McKean is judged by his physicians to be at present at the point of death." He adds: "A better man was never in the Society's service." The lamented young clergyman was buried in St. Peter's churchyard, Perth Amboy, where a monument erected by his brother, Thomas McKean—a Signer of the Declaration of Independence, Chief Justice and afterwards Governor of Pennsylvania— bears this inscription: "In Memory of The Rev. Robert McKean, M. A., Practitioner in Physic, &c., and Missionary from the Society for the Propagation of the Gospel in Foreign Parts, to the City of Perth Amboy:—who was born July 13th, 1732, N. S., and died Oct. 17th, 1767, An unshaken Friend, an agreeable Companion, a rational Divine, a skillful Physician, and in every relation in life a truly benevolent and honest man, Fraternal love hath erected this monument." —*Genealogy of the McKean Family*, by Roberdeau Buchanan, Lancaster, Pa., 1890, 8-9, 13; *A Record of Christ Church*, New Brunswick, by the Rev. Alfred Stubbs, New York, 1850, 9; *Historical Collections relating to the American Colonial Church*, edited by William Stevens Perry, D. D., Volume II., Pennsylvania, 1871, 270-273, 295-305, 380, 381, 410; *History of St. John's Church, Elizabeth Town*, by Samuel A. Clark, Philadelphia, 1857, 85, 96, 110, 118-119; *Contributions to the Early History of Perth Amboy*, by William A. Whitehead, New York, 1856, 225, 228-9, 291, 391, 392, 409; *N. J. Archives*, 1st Series, IX., 338, 340; XX., 262, 434, 468, 636; XXIV., 457; XXV., 472-3; *N. Y. Colonial Documents*, VI., 610; VII., 497; *Woodbridge and Vicinity*, by Rev. Joseph W. Dally, New Brunswick, 1873, 130-132; *A Collection of American Epitaphs*, by Rev. Timothy Alden. A. M., New York, 1814. No. 1045; *Historical Collections of the State of New Jersey*, by John W. Barber and Henry Howe, Newark [1844], 309; *Edward Antill and His Descendants*, by William Nelson, 1899, 24-25; *History of Medicine in New Jersey, and of Its Medical Men*, by Stephen Wickes, A. M., M. D., Newark, 1879, 329-330; *Transactions of the New Jersey Medical Society*, 1766-1800, Newark, 1866. passim.

PETER MERSELLIS.

Peter Mersellis—so the name appears on his tombstone—died at Trenton, June 25, 1764, aged 43 years. He was a carpenter at that time. His brother, Henry Marselis, was a brewer in Trenton until his death, in 1753. Peter and Henry had a brother John and a sister Catharine.

EBENEZER MILLER.

For a sketch of Ebenezer Miller, see N. J. Archives, XIX., 392, note. Some account of his descendants is given in Shourds's "History and Genealogy of Fenwick's Colony," 153-160. He is frequently mentioned

MILLER: MORRIS

in Elmer's "Cumberland County." An interesting memorial of his oldest son, Ebenezer Miller, jun., born in 1728, died 11th of 7th mo. 1800, will be found in "Memorials of Deceased Friends," Philadelphia, 1821, 106-109. He had been a minister among Friends about thirty-five years before his decease.

PAUL MILLER.

Paul Miller was one of the petitioners for the charter of New Brunswick, granted Dec. 7, 1730. He is mentioned in various records as being of New Brunswick, in 1743 to 1749. In the latter year he lived in French street, opposite Burnet street. He was appointed one of the Common Pleas Judges of Somerset County, March 19, 1759.

CHIEF JUSTICE ROBERT HUNTER MORRIS.

Robert Hunter Morris, born at Morrisania, N. Y., about 1700, was the second son of Governor Lewis Morris, who appointed him Chief Justice of New Jersey on the unanimous recommendation of the Council, to succeed Col. Robert Lettice Hooper, deceased. His commission, dated March 17, 1738 (1739 N. S.), was during *good behaviour.* It is published in N. J. Archives, IX., 207-9. (For a note on the significance of this provision in the commission of Judges, see N. J. Archives, IX., 323-6.) Chief Justice Morris was also named as a member of his father's Council, in the commission (1738) appointing the Governor, and sturdily defended the doughty Chief Magistrate on all occasions. In 1748 he was one of the three commissioners to run the northern boundary line of New Jersey. He had accompanied his father to England in 1735, and revisited that country in 1749, when he lodged with a Mrs. Stuart, a widow, in St. James's Place, the result being a child. When he returned to assume the government of Pennsylvania he left the child with Will Shirley, who paid out £70 or £80 subsequently for its support. Writing in 1763, Morris asked his friend, John Penn, to make some inquiries about the child, of whom he had lost all trace, and whom he was anxious to have in America. He spent several years in England on his second visit, and was treated with respect and consideration. He sought an appointment as Lieutenant Governor of New York. Instead, John and Thomas Penn made him Governor of Pennsylvania, and he returned in 1754 to assume that office. For two years he enjoyed a continual disagreement with the Assembly of that Province, and then resigned. He had tendered his resignation of Chief Justice of New Jersey in 1754, but as it was not accepted he resumed the duties of the office in 1756. In 1757 he revisited England once more, and during his absence William Aynsley was appointed to succeed him, taking his seat on the bench at the March Term, 1758, but died July 6 of the same year. Nathaniel Jones was commissioned to fill the assumed vacancy, and presented himself at the March Term, 1760. But Chief Justice Morris was on the bench. His commission was during *good behaviour.* True, he had resigned, but his resignation had not been accepted, and he had concluded to resume the position. His right to do this was sustained by his associate, Justice Samuel Nevill, in an opinion from the bench. Morris died suddenly on the night of January 27, 1764, at a party at Shrewsbury. He led out the parson's wife in a dance, opened the ball, danced down six couples, and then fell dead on the floor, in an apoplectic fit. He was buried at Morrisania, Westchester county, N. Y. Chief Justice Morris was a very remarkable man, and filled a large place in the public affairs of New Jersey, New York and Pennsylvania. Samuel Smith, the historian, speaks very highly of his abilities as a judge and as a speaker. He never married.—*N. J. Archives*, XI., 562-3; XXIV., 305. (See, also, under ' Nathaniel Jones," supra).

REV. ANDREW MORTON.

The Rev. Andrew Morton was an itinerant missionary in New Jersey as early as 1760, having been sent out by the Society for the Propagation of the Gospel in Foreign Parts. He was commended for his shrewdness in persuading "the people to obligate themselves to do such and such things for him so that he has a legal demand on them for ye same when he discharges his duty." In 1764 he had some difficulty with a Mr. Garrison, who claimed that Mr. Morton had wronged his daughter; but having been confronted by Mr. Morton and a Mr. Steuart at Trenton, Mr. Garrison withdrew his charge. However, the affair apparently impaired Mr. Morton's usefulness. His field of service seems to have been in the western part of New Jersey.

WILLIAM MOTT.

William Mott was a descendant of Adam Mott, of Essex, England, who married, at New Amsterdam, July 28, 1647, Jane Hulet, of Buckingham, England. He was in New Amsterdam as early as 1644, and received a grant of twenty-five acres of land on Mespath Kill (Newtown Creek, Long Island), April 23, 1646, from the Dutch Government of New Netherland. On March 17, 1657, he was chosen one of the townsmen of Hempstead, L. I. His wife, Jane Hulet, died, after bearing eight sons, the youngest of whom was Gershom. Adam married, 2d, Elizabeth Richbell, daughter of John Richbell, of Mamaroneck. She bore him five children, one of whom was baptized Adam, although his father's eldest son, Adam, was still living. In his will, proved in 1689, Adam Mott speaks of his eldest son Adam, and his youngest son Adam.

Gershom Mott, the youngest son of Adam Mott and Jane Hulet, was born about 1663. In early manhood he removed to Monmouth County, N. J., where he is mentioned in the records in 1685. He was Sheriff of the county, 1697-8, and a member of the Assembly, 1708-16. He married, in 1695, Catherine Bowne, daughter of Captain John Bowne. His will, dated Feb. 15, 1730, was proved March 30, 1733. In it he describes himself as "Gershom Mott, Gentleman, of Middletown, Monmouth County." His second child was William, born November 9, 1699. He was elected to the Assembly in 1743, and when the Governor repeatedly dissolved that body, in hopes of securing one more favorable to himself, William Mott was re-elected each time—in 1744, 1745, 1746, 1749 and 1751—sitting in that body until its dissolution in June, 1754. He is mentioned in the newspapers of the day as one of those who would receive subscriptions for Nevill's Laws, Vol. I., and for Leaming and Spicer's compilation of the Grants and Concessions, etc. He married Margaret Hartshorne, daughter of William Hartshorne (born January 22, 1679). His will is dated Middletown, May 14, 1742. His oldest son was John, born January 18, 1734; married Eleanor Johnston, June 17, 1784. He served in the French and Indian War, and in the Revolution, attaining the rank of Captain. He was the grandfather of General Gershom Mott, of New Jersey, who commanded a Brigade of Jerseymen in the War of the Rebellion.—For the genealogical data above, the writer is indebted to a well written article by Miss Kate A. Mott, in the *N. Y. Genealogical and Biographical Record*, XXV., 49-56. See also *N. J. Hist. Soc. Proc.*, V., 25-26; *N. J. Archives*, II., 363; III., 212; IV., 125; VI., 202; VIII., Part II., 151; XII., 690; XVI., passim; XXV., 18.

MOUNTERE: NEILSON: NEWELL: OGDEN

WILLIAM MOUNTERE.

William Mountere or Mountier was living in Princeton in the summer of 1748, in a house which he rented from Judge Thomas Leonard, at £20 per annum, and was building a house in Middlesex county, on a lot of his own, on the other side of the street, which he was occupying in February, 1750-51. He advertised the place for sale in September, 1753, describing the lot as "containing three acres, subject to Five Pounds a year, ground rent. the house is new and well finished, and very convenient for a tavern (one being kept in it now), or any other public business, being well situated, and near where the college is to be built." He was then living in Trenton. He was probably a tavern keeper. He seems to have been again occupying the premises in 1761, and as late as 1767. —*N. J. Archives*, XIII., 465; XIX., 218, 219, 290; XXV., 432.

JAMES NEILSON.

James Neilson and his brother, John Neilson, M. D., came from Belfast, Ireland, in 1730 or earlier, and settled at New Brunswick, where the former became a shipping merchant and ship owner, his vessels trading with Belfast, Lisbon, Madeira and the West India Islands. He was appointed one of the Judges of the Middlesex county courts, in 1749, and again in 1768. In 1749 he was talked of as a candidate for the Assembly, but was never elected to that body. He was prominent in the early days of the Revolution. His partner in the shipping business was Richard Gibbs. James Neilson was manifestly one of the leading men of his day in Middlesex county, occupying numerous positions of trust, and his store was the centre of a large trade and was a public resort for a wide region. He was the uncle of Col. John Neilson, who was distinguished in the Revolution, and who had the honor to be counted a friend and acquaintance of Washington.

DR. JAMES NEWELL.

James Newell, son of Robert Newell, of Upper Freehold, was born in 1725, and was sent to Edinburgh to receive his medical education, receiving his diploma at London in 1746. Returning to America, he practiced his profession through a wide region in and about Monmouth county. In 1764 he was living at Allen Town, Monmouth county. He was elected President of the New Jersey Medical Society in 1772. During the Revolution he acted as Surgeon of the Second Regiment of the Monmouth County Militia. He married, Dec. 14, 1749. Elizabeth, daughter of Elizha Lawrence. He died Feb. 20 and his wife died Feb. 21, 1791, of malignant fever. Both were buried on the same day.

REV. JOHN COSINS OGDEN.

John Cosins Ogden, a native of New Jersey, resided in New Haven for fifteen years after graduating at Princeton College in 1770. Having been ordained by Bishop Seabury, in 1786, he became Rector of an Episcopal church in Portsmouth, New Hampshire, where he remained until 1793. He died in Chestertown, Maryland, in 1800.—*N. J. Archives*, XXVII., 267.

JONATHAN OGDEN.

Jonathan Ogden was from Elizabethtown, probably a cousin of Robert Ogden, 3d. He returned to that place after graduating. He never entered a profession.

ROBERT OGDEN, Third.

Robert Ogden, 3d, son of Robert and Phebe (Hatfield) Ogden, was born at Elizabeth Town, March 23, 1746, in the house afterwards occupied by General Matthias Ogden, and subsequently by Joel Davis. After graduating from Princeton College, in 1765, he studied law with Richard Stockton. He was admitted to the New Jersey bar, June 21, 1770, and began the practice of law at Elizabethtown. To him, in connection with William Paterson, Luther Martin, Oliver Ellsworth and Tapping Reeve, is ascribed the founding of the American Cliosophic Society, which dates its origin back to 1765. He was a fine scholar, and kept up his classical reading after entering upon his profession. Being a warm and earnest patriot, he was obliged to move with his family to Morristown in 1776 for safety from British raids. In this year he was commissioned surrogate by Gov. Livingston. In 1777 he removed again to Turkey, now New Providence, in what is now Union County. In 1780 (May term) he was called up as one of the twelve sergeants-at-law of New Jersey. After the war he was compelled to leave the seaboard on account of the asthma, and in the spring of 1786 he removed to Sussex county, where he resided during the remainder of his life, his homestead being about two miles north of the village of Sparta. The house was built by Cornelius Hoagland near the close of the Revolutionary War, and was conveyed with ten acres of land to Robert Ogden, Jun. (3d), by his father, Robert Ogden (2d), in 1786. Here his children were brought up and his youngest were born. This house witnessed great hospitality and many distinguished visitors were entertained there. It now forms a part of the Fowler estate. In 1787 he was one of the members of the convention called to approve the Constitution of the United States. He was married by Rev. John Close, May 19, 1772, to Sarah Platt, daughter of Dr. Zopher Platt and Rebecca Wood; she was born at Huntington, L. I., Sept. 27, 1750; she d. Jan. 21, 1782; she had five children. He was married, (2), by Rev. Nathan Woodhull to Hannah Platt, sister of his first wife, Mar. 12, 1786. She was b. Dec. 17, 1756, and d. on Thursday, May 7, 1812, of a cancer in the breast. She had three children. "She endured much pain with great fortitude and Christian resignation." He d. Feb. 14, 1826, in his 80th year, at the residence of his grandson, the Hon. Daniel Haines, at Hamburgh, Sussex county, and was buried at Sparta, beside his 2d wife, Hannah Platt. His first wife (Sarah Platt) is buried at Elizabeth.—See sketch of Robert Ogden, written for the *History of the Cliosophic Society*, by Gov. Daniel Haines; the Rev. A. A. Haines's *Hardyston Memorial*; "*Descendants of Robert Ogden*, 2d, 1716-1787," by Edmund Drake Halsey, 1896.

UZAL OGDEN.

Uzal Ogden was a son of Capt. David Ogden, who died July 1, 1734, aged 56 years; the latter was the eldest son of David Ogden, who removed from Elizabethtown to Newark about 1676, he having been one of the first settlers of the former town, in 1664. Uzal Ogden was a leading merchant in Newark many years. In 1748 he was one of the managers of the lottery to raise money to complete Trinity Church, Newark. He was appointed one of the Common Pleas Judges for Essex County in 1749, and again in 1768; one of the Surrogates of the Prerogative Court in the Eastern Division of New Jersey, in March, 1759 (Lewis Ogden being appointed to the like office at the same time), and again, March 22, 1762, and was High Sheriff of Essex County, 1763-5. He and his brother John invested heavily in mining properties in Morris County and the upper part of the present Passaic County—at Bloomingdale, Ringwood, Long Pond, Charlottenburg, and that region, they being known as the "American Company." There they had mines, forges, etc. At Newark they conducted the "Vesuvius Furnace," for the manufacture of hollow iron ware, etc. Their general mercantile business in Newark was also extensive, they carrying on a general country store. All this required a large outlay of capital, with slow and uncertain returns. They were obliged to mortgage their mining property to Messrs. Thomas and Ferdinand Pennington, of Bristol, England. Other debts accumulated, and in 1769 they became insolvent, with imprisonment for debt facing them. With a bitter heart Uzal Ogden gives notice to his creditors, Feb. 24, 1770, of his intention to apply to the Legislature at its next sitting, in the ensuing March, for an act to save him from imprisonment for debt. There is a deep touch of pathos in his declaration, "having spent near sixty years of life, in the most unwearied industry, (the latter part of which has been singularly unfortunate) and being willing and desirous, so far as in my power to do justice to all men, and to deliver up all my effects to the use and benefit of my creditors." The firm made an assignment of all their property to Joseph Riggs, jun., and Thomas Longworth, who advertised the mining properties to be sold on March 2, 1771, at the dwelling-house of Mr. James Banks, Innholder in Newark. The property passed into the hands of London capitalists, known as the "London Company," who operated the mines until the beginning of the Revolution. Uzal Ogden died July 25, 1780. He is spoken of as "a gentleman of undissembled goodness and universal esteem." He was the father of the Rev. Uzal Ogden, a prominent clergyman of New Jersey, who was born in Newark about 1744, and died in that town, Nov. 4, 1822.

WILLIAM OUKE.

William Ouke was a prominent merchant at New Brunswick, where he had been engaged in trade prior to 1740. He was active in the Reformed Dutch Church of that place. He was baptized Aug. 4, 1708, being the son of Aucke Janse, who removed from Flatlands, L. I., to the Raritan. The latter was the son of Jan Auckersz, sometimes called Jan Auckers Van Nuyse. Ouke was a Justice of the Peace in 1740, and in 1744 was elected to the Assembly from Middlesex, serving one year. He was one of the managers of a lottery in 1748 to raise money to pay the debts of Peter Cochran, of New Brunswick.—*N. J. Archives*, XII., 485. He had tickets for sale in the Connecticut lottery for the College of New Jersey (Princeton), in 1754.—*Ib.*, XIX., 376. In 1762 he was one of the managers of the Bound-Brook bridge lottery.—*Ib.*, XXIV., 36. He was a Judge of the Mayor's court of common pleas of the city of New Brunswick, in 1763-1766.—*Ib.*, 609; XXV., 38. At the beginning of the Revolution he was one of the prominent patriots of Middlesex County.—*N. J. Archives*, X., 471, 588. In his will, dated Nov. 6, 1778, proved Jan. 23, 1779, he names a son, Abraham Oake, "grandson Abraham Oake, son of my brother Abraham Oake, deceased;" Mary Vorhize, "daughter of my beloved brother, Jacob Oake." His signature to the will is undecipherable, but with a fine and tender regard for his educational reputation the note is made in the margin: "The reason that Mr. Oaks name is not signed fully is that his hand is crampd with the palsy."—*W. J. Wills*, Liber No. 21, f. 81. He seems to have written his name *Oake*. The confidence with which Mr. Ouke was regarded by his neighbors is attested by his selection as executor for numerous estates. There are many references to him in Vols. XII and XIX., N. J. Archives.

JAMES PARKER.

James Parker, son of Elisha Parker, was born in 1725. He married Gertrude, daughter of the Rev. William Skinner. He was a member of Governor Franklin's Council, 1764-1755, and was one of the most influential men in the Province. He was a large landholder, was in mercantile business in New York and New Jersey, and was prominent in the control of the East Jersey Board of Proprietors for many years. His official associations and his pecuniary interests naturally inclined him to the Royal cause, at the beginning of the Revolution, but there were also strong ties binding him to those who were among the first to take up arms against the King. Under the circumstances, having repeatedly been called upon to swear allegiance to the King, and being unwilling to take an active part in the new struggle, he was neutral, and sought to avoid any part in the war by retiring to a country place in Hunterdon county. But the Council of Safety, on July 21st, 1777, ordered him and Walter Rutherfurd to appear before that body and take the oath of allegiance to the new independent State of New Jersey. They appeared two days later, but refused to take the oaths, and were thereupon held to bail to appear at the next Court of General Quarter Sessions of the Peace for Hunterdon county. When the Court met they again refused to take the oaths before the Court, and the Council of Safety ordered (August 15th, 177) them to be brought before the Governor and Council as persons disaffected to the State. They came before the Council August 20th, pursuant to citation, and after being examined it was resolved that they be "confined as disaffected to the State, until an Equal number of our subjects captivated by the Enemy be released or other order taken therein." The next day they appeared before the Council and gave bond in £2,000, conditioned to "remain at the Court House in Morris county, or within a mile and a half, until further order be taken therein." The Council agreed, on October 16th, 1777, to release Parker and Rutherfurd from their confinement in exchange for John Fell, Esq., and Wynant Van Zandt, captured by the Tories in Bergen county, and confined in New York, and shortly after admitted the two gentlemen to their parole at Morristown, in order to induce the Britisn to make the proposed exchange; but this proving ineffective, it was ordered, November 17th, 1777, that Parker and Rutherfurd be "forthwith committed to the Common Gaol in Morristown until the Honorable John Fell, Esq. and Wynant Van Zandt are exchanged for them or released from their confinement in New York." Four days later the Council directed the Sheriff of Morris county to confine the two prisoners in "a private room nearest the Court House, for a space of three weeks from the date hereof; and then to execute the precept lately delivered to him for their imprisonment, unless he shall receive orders to the contrary." On December 13th, 1777, the Council agreed, that "In consideration of Mr. Rutherfurd's & Mr. Parker's indisposition, they be Enlarged from their present Confinement until the 1st day of February next, upon the terms of their obligation of having the District of one Mile from the Court House in Morristown, & that they be then committed to Jail unless the Council of Safety shall order to the contrary." This order was still further modified December 31st, 1777, when it was agreed that they be discharged from their confinement in Morristown and suffered to return to their respective places of abode, "there to continue & within one mile of the same respectively until the first day of February next. & then to be confined in prison until the Hon. John Fell Esq. shall be released from his confinement in New York, on condition of liberating the said Walter Rutherfurd." The two men were finally released in the following February, upon the release of Mr. Fell. James Parker after this resided in peace on his country place until the close of the war, when he returned to Perth Amboy. He was honored in the community, and throughout the State, as a man of ability and distinguished probity, and died, full of years and honors, October 4th, 1797. His wife died February 10th, 1811, aged 71 years. A very full sketch of James Parker may be found in the *New York Genealogical and Biographical Record*, XXX., 31-36.

WILLIAM PATERSON.

William Paterson was famous for his influence in the Federal Convention of 1787. He was chosen United States Senator in 1789, but resigned in 1790 to accept the office of Governor of New Jersey, which in turn he relinquished, March 4, 1793, on his appointment by Washington to a seat on the Bench of the Supreme Court of the United States. He held this high office until the end of his life. Judge Paterson received the honorary degree of Doctor of Laws from Dartmouth, in 1805, and from Harvard, in 1806. He died at Albany, September 9, 1806. The fullest account of his life appeared in the *Somerset Co. Hist. Quarterly*, Vol. I, pp. 161, 241.

EBENEZER PEMBERTON.

Ebenezer Pemberton was probably born in Boston. He pronounced the Valedictory at Princeton College on Commencement day, 1765, on "Patriotism." He was appointed a tutor in the college in 1769. On one of the public occasions, while he was a tutor, he was addressed by Madison, then a student, in a Latin address, valedictory and complimentary, on the part of the class, to the teacher. His life was devoted to teaching, and at one time in Phillips' Academy. In 1766 he became associated with Tappin Reeve in the management of the grammar school at Elizabethtown. He was admitted to an ad eundem Master's degree at Harvard in 1787, at Yale in 1781, and at Dartmouth in 1782. In 1817 he received the honorary degree of Doctor of Laws from Allegheny College. He died June 25, 1835.

CHARLES PETTIT.

For a sketch of Charles Pettit, see *N. J. Archives*, X., 133. To that it may be added that Mr. Pettit was one of the owners of Batsto furnace in 1781. He resigned from the Continental Army June 20, 1781. He d. Sept. 4, 1806. His eldest dau. m. Jared Ingersoli, in 1781; he was a famous lawyer, b. in New Haven, 1750, d. Oct. 31, 1822.

EPHRAIM PHILLIPS.

In a petition to the Legislature, dated April 20, 1771, Ephraim Phillips states that he has been Goal-keeper for thirteen years past, and asks for an increase in his daily allowance of sixpence per day for provisions furnished criminals, &c.—*N. J. Hist. Soc. Proceedings*, 2d Series, XIII., 74.

WILLIAM PIDGEON.

William Pidgeon was admitted to the New Jersey bar in 1750. He resided in Trenton, on King (now Warren) street, near the present State street, and was a man of some substance. He advertised land for sale at Trenton in 1758 and 1760, as acting executor of Daniel

Coxe, and also advertised land from 1751 to 1761. Gov. Franklin appointed him, March 31, 1774, a justice of the peace in the counties of Burlington and Monmouth. In 1756 he was one of the managers of the Trenton lottery for finishing and completing the church in that place. He died at Stafford, Monmouth county, January 5, 1780, from burns in getting out of his house when it was on fire. He left £50 to the Methodist Society of Trenton, for the repair of their meeting house, and £3,000 to his executors, to be used for charitable purposes.

ROBERT FRIEND PRICE.

The earliest mention that has been found of Robert Friend Price in the public records of New Jersey is in a deed dated July 14, 1755, where by Hannah Roe and Abraham Roe. executors of the estate of Henry Roe, late of the township and county of Gloucester, convey to Edward Hollingshead, of Greenwich township, and Robert Friend Price, of Newton township, Gloucester county, yeomen, for £500, a tract of 300 acres in New Whippany, Morris county.—*Liber O of Deeds, Secretary of State's office*, f. 441. This deed appears to have been in trust, to enable the grantees as trustees to pay the debts of Henry Roe, deceased, and Abraham Roe.—*N. J. Archives*, XX., 193. In 1758, Robert Friend Price, Esq., at Haddonfield, was to receive subscriptions for the laws of New Jersey, which appeared in 1761, as the second volume of Nevill's Laws.—*Ib.*, 295. By an act of the Legislature, passed March 25, 1760, Price was appointed one of the commissioners to see that the soldiers disabled in the war with Canada were properly provided for.—*Nevill's Laws*, II., 264. He was appointed a justice of the peace for Gloucester county in 1761.—*N. J. Archives*, XVII., 274. He was Sheriff of that county in 1757. and 1764-65, and advertised many sales of land in that capacity.—*Ib.*, XX., 145; XXIV., 383, 471, 515, 530, 531; *Lib. R of Deeds, in Secretary of State's office*, f. 307. The Governor commissioned him a judge of the Gloucester court of oyer and terminer, April 31 (sic), 1768, and again April 20, 1769; September 21, 1770; April 2, 1771; April 6, 1772, and May 16, 1774; also justice of the peace, December 7, 1769.—*Books of Commissions, Secretary of State's office*, Trenton, sub nom. In 1761 he was elected one of the two Assemblymen from Gloucester, and was re-elected in 1769, serving as a member of the Legislature for fourteen consecutive years, and until the end of the Royal government. On Feb. 8, 1774, he was appointed by the Assembly on a Standing Committee of Correspondence and Inquiry, to keep New Jersey in touch with the other Colonies in the great movement which culminated in the Revolution. In 1774 he was appointed by Gloucester county a member of the Committee—representing the several counties—which on July 23, 1774, nominated the Deputies to represent New Jersey in the Continental Congress, chosen to meet on September 5, 1774, at Philadelphia. —*Minutes Provincial Congress*, 31. He does not appear to have sat in the Assembly in 1775, and on November 17 of that year the sergeant-at-arms was ordered to give notice forthwith to him and five other members that their absence retarded the business of that body.—*Ib.*, 282. He still failed to appear, however. That he retained the public confidence, nevertheless, is shown by his reappointment, by the Legislature, on May 18, 1775, and again on May 21, 1778, to the office of judge of the Gloucester county court of oyer and terminer, and as judge of the court of common pleas, and justice of the peace, May 28, 1779. In January, 1776, he was living at Gloucester town, where, he advertised, he would settle the accounts of Blanch Roberdes, late of Philadelphia, shopkeeper, deceased.—2 *N. J. Archives* I., 28. Mr. Price married, 1st, Mary Thorne, of Gloucester county, marriage license dated March 7, 1761;

PRICE: PROVOOST FAMILY

he m. 2d, Lizzie, dau. of John Collins, of Haddonfield (who d. 1761), and
wid. of Samuel Hugg (whom she had m. in 1752), marriage license dated
August 6, 1766; she survived him, and m. 3d, Daniel Smith. Mr.
Price's acquaintance with his second wife was of some years' standing,
as in 1757 he had gone on the marriage bond of Dr. James Mulock, who
was about to marry Priscilla Collins, sister of Elizabeth, or Lizzie.—
Clement's First Settlers of Newton Township, 81, 187, 397; *N. J. Archives*,
XXII., 305. The will of Robert Friend Price, of Deptford township
Gloucester county, bears date July 31, 1782, he being then "sick and
weak," and was proved Oct. 29, 1782. In it he mentions wife Liza, and
children Margery, son-in-law Samuel Mickle, Blanche, Hannah, Polly
and Robert Friend Price; also brother, Thomas Price. Executors—
friends John Est. Hopkins and James Wilkins. Witnesses—William
Harrison, Danl. Wills, Jeremiah Paul.—*Liber* 23 *of Wills, in Secretary
of State's office*, f. 506. Hannah Price (prob. his dau.) m. John Baker,
of Burlington county, by marriage license dated Feb. 10, 1779. His son,
Robert Friend Price, 2d, m. Mary Brian, mar. lic. dated Jan. 14, 1784.
Thomas Price, prob. his brother, of Hanover, Burlington county, m.
Edith Hart, of the same county, mar. lic. dated March 4, 1747.

PROVOOST FAMILY.

The progenitor of this family in America was David Provoost, who
came from Holland to New Amsterdam before April 28, 1639. In that
year he was granted a lot of land in Pearl street, near Fulton, where he
resided for some time. In April, 1642, he was placed in charge of Fort
Good Hope, at Hartford, Conn., to resist the aggressions of the English,
where he remained until June, 1647, when he returned to New Amsterdam, and taught school for a time. He died in January, 1656. His wife
was Grietje Gillis, daughter of Gillis Jansen Verbrugge and Barbara
Schut. She was still living July 29, 1701. They had nine children, the
second, David, born in Connecticut, and baptized Sept. 31 (sic), 1645.
In partnership with Johannis Van Inburgh, of Hackensack, surgeon,
David Provoost, of New York City, bought of Peter Johnson, of Hackensack, by deed dated April 7, 1698, half of a tract of 500 acres of land
on Hochas brook, where it joins Saddle River—being at or near Paramus or Hohokus, Bergen county. This property appears to have remained in the family many years. David Provoost married July 29,
1668, Tryntje Laurens, from Amsterdam. They had eleven children,
among them:

William Provoost, baptized Oct. 8, 1679; married Nov. 20, 1700, Aefje
Van Exveen, baptized Dec. 19, 1683, daughter of Gerrit Corneliszen Van
Echtsveen and Wyntje Stoutenburg. William Provoost was Assistant Alderman from the North Ward of New York City, 1708-9,
1709-10. He was already identified with New Jersey, probably occupying the paternal acres near Paramus or Hohokus. He was a witness at the baptism of children of Paramus families in the Hackensack Reformed Dutch Church in 1705, 1710 and 1714. In 1722 he was
elected a member of the Assembly from Bergen County. He appears
to have been prominent in that body until 1725, serving frequently on
Committees to wait on the Council. In 1725 he is referred to as "Col."
Provoost. In the mean time he was recommended by Gov. Burnet,
June 17, 1722, as "an eminent merchant" of New York city, for a seat
in the Provincial Council of New York, and was appointed by the
King, in July, 1723, serving until August, 1732. By deed dated Dec. 3,
1725, Jurya Westervelt, of Bergen county, and wife Cornelia, conveyed
to William Provoost, of New York City, merchant, a tract of four and
a quarter acres on the west side of the Hackensack river, in the pre-

cinct of New Barbadoes, between John Wright, Gerrit Van Dien and the highway, for £68, New Jersey money. Here he took up his abode, and in 1726 his family were living there. He joined the Hackensack Dutch Church on confession of faith, July 13, 1727, being styled "Col. W. Provoost." His wife was probably dead before this. In 1728 he was appointed one of the N. Y. Commissioners to try pirates. It would seem that he took up his residence permanently at Hackensack about that time or shortly after. On May 6, 1734, he was sworn in as a member of the Provincial Council of New Jersey, in which he continued until 1740. On Dec. 1, 1739, he was appointed one of the Common Pleas Judges of Bergen County, and Colonel of the Bergen County militia, Dec. 4, 1739. For some reason Provoost attended no meetings of the Council after the last mentioned date. That body met on Dec. 29, 1739, and began a new session on March 26, 1740, at Perth Amboy. They sent a letter to Provoost, "in a pressing manner requiring his Attendance and afterwards they sent for him by the Serjeant at Arms attending the Council, which Serjeant at Arms reported that Mr. Provoost had promised him to Set out from his House in order to attend ye Council on Monday the Nineteenth day of May last [1740], since which they have not heard anything from the said William Provoost." Thus they reported to the Governor on June 9, 1740, and gave it as their advice that the delinquent Councillor should be suspended, which was done July 7, 1740. Gov. Lewis Morris wrote to the Lords of Trade that it was not from any prejudice to him that Provoost did not attend, nor was it to gratify any resentment of his that the Councillor was suspended, he being indeed a good friend of the Governor. The will of William Provoost, of New Barbadoes, Bergen county, dated April 22, 1745, was proved August 26, 1746. He left issue:

     i. Wyntje, baptized April 27, 1701; d. s. p.

2. ii. David, baptized Nov. 8, 1702.

     iii. Catharine, baptized Oct. 8, 1704; married Gerard Beekman, "merchant of the City of New York."

     iv. Maria, baptized July 21, 1706; married May 22, 1726, Rev. Reinhart Erichzon, minister of the Reformed Dutch Churches of Hackensack, Schraalenburgh and Paramus, 1725-1728; Schenectady, N. Y., 1728-1736, and later of Freehold and Middletown, N. J. Issue: 1. Anna, baptized at Schenectady, July 13, 1729; 2. William, baptized 1737; 3. David, b. 1740.

     v. Cornelia, baptized Oct. 20, 1711; she joined the Hackensack Church June 17, 1729, upon confession of faith. She married Perregrin Van Imburgh (who joined the church the same day she did), probably after Nov. 18, 1733, when she was a witness at the baptism of Maria Pettet. Issue: 1. Eefjin, baptized January 39, 1737; 2. Catrina, baptized Nov. 5, 1738. She is not mentioned in her father's will, and probably died before it was made.

     vi. Wyntje, baptized May 13, 1722; died young.

     vii. Anneke, baptized March 11, 1724; joined the Hackensack church Feb. 7, 1743, upon confession of faith. She was living at Hackensack in 1746, with her brother David.

2. David Provoost, frequently called David W. or David William Provoost, baptized Nov. 8, 1702. He joined the Hackensack church, Dec 8, 1726, on confession of faith. He married 1st, Feb. 8, 1729, Anneke, daughter of Evert and Catharine (Provoost) Vandewater. They joined the Hackensack church Feb. 19, 1733, on certificate from the New York church. He married 2d, Oct 14, 1741, Geertruyt Reinder,

(Rynders), widow of Nicholas Gouverneur and daughter of Barent Reinders and Hester, daughter of Jacob and Elsje (Tymens) Lester. She joined the Hackensack church, Nov. 26, 1741, by letter from the New York church. He advertises land for sale at Hackensack and in New York, in 1746 and 1750, being himself then of Hackensack.—*N. J. Archives*, XII., 287, 620. He was probably a merchant, near the Hackensack church, living on the tract bought by his father in 1725. He was appointed one of the Justices of the Quorum of Bergen county, Dec. 1, 1739. By proclamation of April 18, 1740, Gov. Lewis Morris urged the enlistment of patriotic Jerseymen to join in an expedition in behalf of His British Majesty against the Spanish West Indies, and appointed David Provoost, of Bergen county, as one of the persons to enlist volunteers for this service. He died at Hackensack early in 1765, leaving a will dated Feb. 21, 1760, proved March 15, 1765. He describes himself as of New Barbadoes, Bergen county. He names wife Geertruyd, and children—William, David Rynders, Catharine and Affie, all under age, who with his wife are his heirs and executors of "all my estate whatsoever." Witnesses—Abraham Westervelt, Nicasie Kip and Sarah Gutridge. Issue:

By his first wife:

i. Wilhelmus, bap. March 4, 1730; d. in inf.

ii. Willem, bap. Nov. 10, 1731; m. May 31, 1758, Elisabet Van Wyck. He and his wife were living in the bounds of the Hackensack church in 1777.

iii. David, bap. Nov. 18, 1733; d. in inf.

iv. Catharina, bap. July 20, 1735. In the jurat to her father's will, March 15, 1765, she is named Catharine Leydack.

v. Samuel, bap. July 9, 1738; m. Henne Eerl (Earle). He was perhaps the Samuel Provoost who in August, 1765, took the benefit of the insolvency act. Children: 1. David, bap. Dec. 7, 1760; 2. Wellem, bap. Sept. 31, 1764; 3. Willem, bap. Oct. 19, 1766.

vi. Effie. She was received into the Schraalenburgh church on confession of her faith, April 5, 1759; she was still living and unm. in 1765. Efye Provoost (prob. the same) and Abraham Lefferts had a child, Jenneke, b. Aug. 15, 1771, bap. in this church.

By his second wife:

vii. David Rynders, bap. between July 7 and Aug. 11, 1745.

COLONEL NATHANIEL RAMSAY.

Nathaniel Ramsay, a brother of David Ramsay, the Historian, after graduating, studied law and became eminent in his profession. When the war of the Revolution began, he joined the Maryland Line as a Major, and soon rose to the rank of Colonel. At the battle of Monmouth he particularly distinguished himself. From 1785 to 1787 Colonel Ramsay represented Maryland in the Continental Congress. He resumed and continued his practice of law in Baltimore until his death, which occurred October 24, 1817.

GARRET RAPALYE.

Garret Rapalye, son of George Rapalye and Dinah (dau. of Gerrit) Middagh, was born in Brooklyn, May 31, 1730. He seems to have entered mercantile life in New York at an early age, for he was admitted as a freeman of that city, July 17, 1753, being recorded as a merchant by occupation. He engaged in the importation of iron-mongery and drygoods, his store being opposite the Fly Market, at the foot of Maiden Lane. In 1757 he offered for sale a new house on the Jamaica road, on Long Island, about a mile from Brooklyn ferry, with forty acres of land. His family owned the Wallabout. When James De Peyster, treasurer of the Province of New York, became financially involved, in 1768, Rapalye presented an account of moneys advanced him, and petitioned the Assembly for an amendment, for his benefit, to the bill pending in that body for vesting the late treasurer's estate in trustees for the payment of the public debt. In partnership with William Faulkner he opened a brew-house in 1768 at the Brooklyn ferry. Garret Rapalye and others received from the Province of New York, Aug. 16, 1774, a grant of 24,000 acres of land on the east side of Lake Champlain, subsequently located in Vermont. When the Chamber of Commerce of New York in 1772 resolved that its members would not receive New Jersey currency in payment of merchandise, Garret Rapalye was one of a large number of merchants of the town who advertised that they would continue to receive the currency of their neighbor Province as formerly. On June 3, 1775, John Rapalye and Garret Rapalye petitioned for a grant of 30,000 acres of land formerly granted to them and their associates, between the Susquehanna and Delaware rivers.—*Riker's Annals of Newtown*, 270; *N. Y. Hist. Soc. Coll.*, 1885, p. 178; *Colonial Records N. Y. Chamber of Commerce*, Part II., 158; *N. Y. Hist. MSS.*, II., 771, 778, 789; *Stiles's Hist. Brooklyn*, II., 318; *Calendar Land Papers, N. Y.*, 625, 984; *N. J. Archives*, 28:——. His business as an importer of iron ware naturally turned his attention toward the iron industry in America. On June 5, 1764, Benjamin and Thomas Coe deeded to Garret Rapalye "all one half of a certain forge with one fire, and one equal undivided half part of five acres of land which was surveyed for the use of s'd forge, with half of the stream of water (only excepting what the saw mill now standing upon the same premises draws), standing, lying and being upon the Musconetcong river in the Province of New Jersey aforesaid, near the uppermost falls below the mouth of the Great Pond" (Lake Hopatcong). January 1, 1768, Rapalye leased to Joseph and John Tuttle, who were brothers, and then living in Hanover, his iron works for five years at £300 a year, reserving the right to build a furnace on one end of the dam. The Tuttles were to deliver all the iron they made to Rapalye in New York for £28 per ton for refined iron, and £24 per ton for Whippany or bloomed iron, but the prices to vary with changes in the market. This lease was so onerous that it caused the failure of the Tuttles. In *The New Jersey Gazette*, 1778, is noticed the sale of a large tract of land "at the head of the Musconetcong River, about 35 miles from Elizabethtown and 4 from Succasunny Plains, containing about 3,000 acres, having on it a large forge with four fires and two hammers . . . which is now under lease for eight and a half tons of bar iron per annum. Rapalye mortgaged this forge to a London merchant, and on foreclosure of this mortgage it was sold in 1809 by the Sheriff to Thomas Cadwallader, a lawyer of Philadelphia. September 25, 1811, Cadwallader sold it to James and John R. Hinchman, for $1,000."—*Hist. Morris County*, 46-47. The forge established by Rapalye at the outlet of Lake Hopatcong had four fires for the making of bar-iron, and was called—after his native place—the "Brooklyn (or Brookland) Forge," and gave its name to the Great Pond, which was long known as "Brooklyn Pond." Here he took up his residence about the beginning of the Revolution, or perhaps before. In June, 1776, he advertises for sale five plantations at Squire's Point (doubtless at Brooklyn, as above), in Sussex County, containing 1,800 acres of land, with a very good grist-mill. He was then living on the premises. He also offered 9,000 acres of land about 60 miles back of Esopus, in the Delaware valley. "Also, a Shop to be Let, opposite the Fly-Market," probably the place where he had formerly carried on his importing business. Not having sold his mill he advertised in August, 1776, for a good miller and a good fuller. On May 20, 1777, he advertised another "Valuable Plantation & Iron Works situate in Morris & Sussex County," describing it as "containing 2000 acres of good land, on which is erected a good grist mill, saw-mill, and a large forge with four fires, two hammers, one large stone coal-house, one large dwelling-house, and five small blacksmith's shops, all in good order, where 300 tons of bar iron can be made a year, as it never wants water."—*N. J. Archives*, 2d Series, 1: 133, 161, 380. By an unfortunate coincidence, the very day this advertisement appeared, in *The Pennsylvania Packet*, he and his son George were haled before the New Jersey Council of Safety, and "had the oaths of Abjuration and Allegiance tendered to them, which they declined taking and desired until the following morning to consider them, which was granted." The next day Garret Rapalye appeared and entered into recognizance with Jacob Drake as his surety in the sum of £300 for his appearance at the next session of the Court of Quarter Sessions of the Peace for Sussex County. George Rapalje's case was taken up the same day, and the Council finding by his own confession that he had some time in January previously, "voluntarily gone over to the Enemy at New Brunswick, where he had taken an Oath of Allegiance to the King of Great Britain, whence he went to Staten Island, New York and Long Island, and has continued with the Enemy ever since, till within a few days & is now come back into this State, without Flag or Passport, of any kind whatever; The Board after mature Deliberation, Ordered, That a Warrant of Commitment directed to the Sheriff of the County of Gloucester, do issue against the s'd George Rapalje for advisedly & wittingly by Speech, Writing, Open Deed and Act, maintaining and defending the Authority, Jurisdiction & Power of the King of Great Britain as heretofore claimed within this State."—*Minutes Council of Safety*, sub ann. George must have been a truculent youngster to disturb the Council of Safety to this extent, considering that he was under 18 years of age at this time! Garret continued to reside, unmolested, at Squire's Point, for at least another year. Under date of March 4, 1778, he again advertises for sale the premises last above described (now expanded, however, to 3000 acres, instead of 2000), "which is now under lease for eight and a half tons of bar iron per annum." Also the other tract on Musconetcong river, known as Squire's Point, containing about 1800 acres, "having on it an old forge and a very good grist mill, a dwelling house and barn, all in good order." Also the tract of 9000 acres, fifty miles from Esopus; also another tract of 4000 acres, on Otter creek. He also advertises cattle, sheep, hogs and farming utensils. A glimpse of the style in which he lived is afforded us by the mention of "a phaeton and a pair of neat horses, chair and sulky, a fine English stallion and several breeding mares." The occasion of this proposed sale is frankly advertised: "I intend to remove to West Florida, chief of my family being now there." He accordingly requests his debtors to settle up at once, and agrees to accept Continental money or credit, "with bonds and good security."—*N. J. Archives*, 2d Series, 2: 91, 263. Riker says (*Annals of Newtown, L. I.*) Rapalye removed to New Orleans. Garret Rapalye m. Helen Denys, of New Utrecht, by whom he had issue, all baptized in the Reformèd Dutch Church, New York, on the dates mentioned: 1. Joris, bap. March 12, 1755; d. in inf.; 2. Gerrit, Feb. 22, 1757; 3. Joris, Aug. 19, 1759; 4. Anna, May 26, 1762; m. 1st, Jacob Wilkins; 2d, Charles Smith; 5. Johannes, May 20, 1764; 6. Denys, June 15, 1766; 7. Dina, Dec. 27, 1767; 8. Isaac, July 16, 1769; 9. Cornelia, Jan. 13, 1771. Dina is said to have been quite a favorite in Presidential circles in New York, in her early days, but later developed many eccentricities; in 1824 she m. John Fisher; after his death she m. 2d, in June, 1827, Lemuel Sawyer, member of Congress from North Carolina; she d. Jan. 30, 1849, in her 82d year. She lived on the old Rapalye homestead, on Fulton street, opposite Hicks street, Brooklyn.

GEORGE READING.

George Reading, b. in Amwell, N. J., Feb. 26, 1725, was a son of John Reading (sometime President of the Council and acting Governor of New Jersey) and Mary Ryerson, his wife, dau. of Joris (i. e., George) Ryerson, of Pacquanac, in the present Passaic county. He inherited from his father extensive tracts of land. He was a member of the Assembly, 1761-5, and was appointed Surrogate in 1774. Early in the Revolution he removed to Westmoreland county, Pa., where he was commissioned Sub-Lieutenant, with rank as Lieutenant-Colonel, and was recommissioned June 2, 1780. In this year he removed to what was afterwards Bourbon county, Ky., where he died, Aug. 12, 1792.

THOMAS READING.

Captain Thomas Reading was b. in Amwell township, Hunterdon county, Sept. 27, 1734, being a son of John Reading, some time President of the Governor's Council, and acting Governor on two occasions. The Provincial Congress appointed him, Feb. 9, 1776, Captain of the sixth company, third New Jersey regiment, First Establishment, and he was in service with his command in northern New York and Canada until his regiment was discharged, March 23, 1777. By act of the Legislature, June 22, 1778, he was appointed one of the agents of the State for procuring provisions for the use of the army, and other supplies for carrying on the war. He was commissioned a justice of the peace for Hunterdon county, Dec. 18, 1782; Sept. 14, 1788; Oct. 25, 1793; and Nov. 1, 1798; and was appointed judge of the common pleas for said county Nov. 26, 1794, and Oct. 30, 1799. Each of said appointments was for the term of five years. He was one of the founders of the Presbyterian church in Flemington, was a member of the board of trustees, and on July 6, 1797, was ordained an elder of the church, with power to "conduct divine worship and read a sermon when the pastor was absent." He occupied the homestead farm of four hundred acres, near Flemington Junction, devised by his father to his executors in trust for the use of Thomas and his wife for life, with remainder to his two sons, Joseph and Thomas, in fee simple. He probably engaged in the iron industry with his cousins, the Ryersons, and the vicissitudes of the Revolutionary war brought about his ruin. He m. Rebecca Ellis, dau. of Jonathan Ellis, of Waterford, Gloucester county; he d. Dec. 14, 1814, in Amwell township.—*The Reading Family*, by J. Granville Leach, Philadelphia, 1898, pp. 52, 125; *Stryker's Officers and Men of New Jersey in the Revolution*; *First Century of Hunterdon County*, by the Rev.

READING: REED: REEMER: REYNOLDS

George S. Mott, D. D.; *Hist. Presbyterian Church of Flemington*, by the Rev. George S. Mott, D. D.; *Records of Commissions, Secretary of State's Office.*

ANDREW REED.

Andrew Reed was a well-known merchant in Trenton during the Colonial period. He was the father of the distinguished General Joseph Reed, at one time Adjutant-General of the Continental Army. He had lived many years in Philadelphia and was a Trustee of the Third Presbyterian church on Arch street in that city. In 1734 he was appointed the first Postmaster of Trenton, and in 1746 he was made one of the Burgesses and Treasurer of the Borough of Trenton under its new charter. From 1756 to 1759 he was Trustee of the Presbyterian church of Trenton. After residing in Trenton many years, he removed about 1759 to Amwell, Hunterdon county, New Jersey, where he owned extensive tracts of land, and died there December 16, 1769.

GEORGE REEMER.

George Reemer was living, in 1744, in the lower part of Bedminster township, Somerset county, south of Kline's Mills. He subscribed £20 in 1756 toward the erection of St. Paul's Lutheran church at Pluckamin, and it was but natural that he should have been one of the managers of the lottery for the benefit of that church in 1758.

JOHN REYNOLDS.

A petition was presented to the Provincial Congress of New Jersey, June 21, 1776, "from John Reynolds and George Riche, paper makers in Germantown, Pennsylvania, setting forth, that they design to carry on their trade in this Colony, and praying that this Congress would encourage the same." The petition was read, and ordered to have a second reading, which it received on July 4, when action was deferred for further consideration."—*Minutes*, 469, 490. The subject is not mentioned again in the minutes. However, Reynolds, at least, located in Trenton, for the records of conveyances show that John Reynolds, paper maker, of Trenton, bought from Israel Morris, of the same place, gentleman, son and heir of William Morris, late of Trenton, Esq., deceased, by deed dated June 1, 1778, for £350, a lot situate on the east side of King street, Trenton, touching the late Thomas Smith's land, and land of Israel Morris, being part of a larger tract granted to William Morris by William Trent, April 16, 1745. On September 23, 1778, he bought from Israel Morris, for £1400, three lots in Trenton, as follows: 1st lot. Beginning at the southwest corner of Friends' Burying Ground, running thence north to William Tucker's land, thence along Tucker's land west to lot of the Presbyterian congregation, along that south to the street leading to the Quaker Meeting house, thence along said street east to the beginning, containing one acre. 2d lot. Beginning at a corner of the street opposite to said Meeting house and running along the street leading thereto west to the Abraham Cottnam estate, thence along his line south to the Presbyterian Burying Ground, thence along the same to Samuel Tucker's garden lot east and then south to the road leading to Samuel Henry's Mill, then along said road east to the back street and along said street north to the beginning, containing two acres. 3d lot. Beginning at the southwest corner of Joseph Higbee's land on Meeting-house lane or back street, thence along his line east to other land of Samuel Tucker, then along Tucker's line to a corner of another lot of said Tucker, then west by the same and Elihu Spencer and Samuel Henry to said Meeting house lane, then along the same north to the beginning, containing seventeen acres. He sold these three lots, his wife Catharine joining in the deed, May 28, 1779, to Joseph Milnor, of Trenton, merchant, for £2325. No will of John Reynolds has been found on record in New Jersey. It is not unlikely that after he sold these lands in Trenton, he removed from the State.

The records of the Adjutant General's office show that one John Reynolds was a private of the Hunterdon county militia, during the Revolutionary war, and that he received, in 1784, a certificate for the depreciation of his Continental pay, which amounted to £8:5. It is not at all likely that this was the paper-maker of Trenton.

JOHN RICHMAN.

John Richman is said to have been a German (in which case the name was doubtless Reichmann), who located in Pilesgrove township, and followed the milling business during his lifetime, acquiring a large property, which he left to his two sons, Isaac and Abraham, who added to the wealth derived from their father. Richman's mills, erected in 1833, were for many years a centre of industry in Pilesgrove. The family is still numerous and influential in the northern part of Salem county.

JONATHAN RICHMOND.

Jonathan Richmond, of Nottingham Township, Burlington County, bought from Ilisha Lawrence, of Upper Freehold, Monmouth County, by deed dated October 1st, 1774, for the consideration of £250, a messuage and lot of land situate in Kingsbury (now in the southern part of Trenton, immediately south of the Assunpink), Burlington County, "called Lott 3 in plan of the town: Beginning at a post at the east side of the Broad Street that leads from the Mills towards Crosswicks and corner to Lott 2; thence along that Lott north fifty-six degrees east one hundred and eighty-one and one-half feet to another post for a corner, being also a corner of Lott No. 2; thence south thirty-four degrees east sixty feet to a post, corner of Lott 4; then along said Lott south fifty-six degrees west one hundred and eighty-one and one-half feet to a post at the east side of the Broad Street and is also another corner to Lott 4; thence along the east side of said Street north thirty-four degrees west sixty feet to the beginning; being one-quarter of an acre." Witnesses—Benjamin Yard, Thos. Yard.—*N. J. Deeds, Liber AM.*, p. 21. "Across the Queen Street bridge on the east side was the site of Mahlon Stacy's flour mill, built in 1680, of hewn logs. In 1714 Wm. Trent purchased the property and built a two story stone building, a mill. Geo. Bright had a bakery next to it and lived opposite. Next to this bakery was Jonathan Richmond's True American Inn, built in 1760, the headquarters of Gen. Washington for the first two days of 1777, but which he was obliged to abandon on the afternoon of January 2d. This building was destroyed by fire in 1843."—*Stryker's "Trenton 100 Years Ago,"* p. 20. Jonathan Richmond was a barrack master at Trenton during the Revolutionary War, in 1779; it is not known how long he held that office. On October 27, 1788, being "weak," Jonathan Richmond, of Nottingham Township, Burlington County, made his will, which was proved at Burlington, April 8, 1789. He gave to his wife Emmy one-third of his estate, and to his niece Sally James, daughter of his sister Mary Watley, 20s; to his nephew, Samuel Wooley, son of his sister Catherine Wooley, the rest of his estate. Executor—nephew, Samuel Wooley. Witnesses— C. Higbie, Abraham Woglaam and Rensellr Williams.

REV. DIRCK ROMEYN.

Dirck Romeyn is said to have been descended from Claes or Klaese (Nicholas) Jansen Romeyn, who, according to family tradition, migrated from Amsterdam to Brazil, between 1650 and 1660, and came thence to New Netherland about 1653. It is more probable that it was his father, Jan Romeyn, who was the emigrant, and that Claes was but an infant, if he was here as early as 1653, for it was not until May 2, 1680, that he m. Styntje Albertse Terhune. He bought a plantation, March 3, 1679, at Gravesend, L. I., where he resided several years. In 1696 he bought a tract of 300 acres of land between the Hackensack and Saddle rivers, to which he added 600 acres in 1697. He was a cooper by trade. He lived near Hackensack about ten years, removing thence to Shappekenike, or Greenwich, now in New York city, where he died. Kristyna Ter Heune, wid. of Klaes Jansen Romeyn, Minades Island (i. e., from Manhattan Island), was received into the Hackensack church by letter, May 18, 1732.—*History of Paterson, by William Nelson*, I., 210. In the work just quoted details are given of the children and grandchildren of Claes Jansen Romeyn, which indicate this line of descent for Dirck: Jan, son Claes Jansen, m. Lammetie Bongaert, May 20, 1699, and was the father of Klaes, bap. Feb. 25, 1700, m. 1st, Elizabeth Outwater, May 20, 1726; she d. Sept. —, 1732, leaving one son, Thomas, b. March 9, 1729; he graduated at Princeton College in 1762, and became a noted preacher in the Reformed Dutch Church. Nicholas Romeyn in April, 1733, "trod again in the honorable state of matrimony with Rachel Vreelandt," according to his Dutch family bible. (The Hackensack Dutch church records, in chronicling the baptisms of their children, in at least one instance, 1744, gives her name as Marretje.) They had Dirk, bap. at Hackensack Aug. 1, 1736, who d. in inf. On Jan. 12, 1744, was b. another son, who was bap. at Hackensack Jan. 29, 1744, Dirk. This was used by the Dutch in Northern New Jersey generally as the equivalent of Richard, but sometimes for Theodorick. The latter interpretation was assumed by the boy born in 1714. Upon graduating at Princeton in 1765 he received, besides his small parchment diploma, a certificate of his religious conduct and standing, signed by President Finley, at Princeton, Sept. 28, 1765. After leaving College he studied theology, part of the time under the Rev. J. M. Goetschius, of Hackensack and Schraalenburgh, who preached his ordination sermon, in May, 1766, when he was called to the pastorate of the Dutch churches of Marbletown, Rochester and Wawarsing, Ulster county, N. Y. He became pastor of the churches of Hackensack and Schraalenburgh in May, 1776, just at the beginning of the Revolution. When the British pursued Washington through Hackensack in November, 1776, they plundered Dominie Romeyn's house and destroyed all his furniture, books and papers. He then removed his family to New Paltz, and thence to his mother-in-law's at Marbletown, where they remained nearly two years. He made frequent but brief visits to his congregation, often at great personal risk, he being obnoxious to the British and their tory sympathizers. He received many calls to other and better charges, but it was not until 1784 that he concluded to change, and accepted a call to Schenectady. Here he was largely instrumental in establishing an academy, which subsequently developed into Union College. He received the degree of D. D.

in 1789, from Queen's College, and in 1797 was appointed a Professor of Theology by the General Synod. He d. April 16, 1804. He m. June 11, 1767, Elizabeth, dau. of Wessels and Catherine (Dubois) Brodhead; she d. July 27, 1815. One of their children was the Rev. John Brodhead Romeyn

REV. JOHN ROSBROUCK.

John Rosbrough, born in 1714, came from Ireland in 1735, learned a trade, and married, but losing his wife his thoughts were turned towards the ministry, and as a preparation therefor he entered Princeton, and having graduated in 1761 he was licensed by the Presbytery of New Brunswick, August 18, 1762. He was ordained, and installed as pastor of Greenwich, Oxford and Mansfield churches, in Sussex and Warren counties, December 11, 1764. In 1769 he removed to the Forks of the Delaware, where he was pastor, until his death, of the Presbyterian church of Allen's Township, Penn. As Chaplain of the Northampton county militia he was at the battle of Trenton, and was cruelly murdered at Trenton by the Hessians, January 2, 1777.

ROBERT RUTHERFORD.

Robert Rutherford was of a family living in the North of Ireland. Having quarreled with an elder brother, the father took the latter's part, and chastised Robert, who thereupon ran away from home, and shortly after enlisted in Ligonier's troop of Black Horse, a famous regiment in the British regular army. Subsequently he went to England, but he soon left that country and came to America, settling at Trenton, where he opened a tavern, at the northwest corner of Broad and Front streets, which he called "The Ligonier or Black Horse," after his old regiment. He is first mentioned as of Trenton in March, 1756. Having married, he became the father of four daughters— Margaret, Sarah, Nancy and Frances Mary—who were all grown up in 1770, or thereabout. In or about that year there one day drove up to the tavern, in a coach and four, Colonel Fortescue, an English officer. He dined at the tavern, and after dinner had a conversation in private with the youngest of the girls, Frances Mary. Less than two hours later she, notwithstanding her sisters' entreaties, quit the house in company with Colonel Fortescue. They went to Paris together, where they lived several years, when he died, leaving her, it was supposed, a considerable sum of money. On his death she left Paris and went to England, where she married a well-to-do gentleman, named Shard. In 1799 she conceived a great desire to ascertain what had become of her father's family, and through her confidential solicitor inquiries were made of the Rev. James F. Armstrong, a Presbyterian clergyman at Trenton. He advertised in the *New Jersey State Gazette*, of Trenton, July 9, 1799, asking for information as to what had become of Robert Rutherford and his three eldest daughters, named above, "who were, previous to the American Revolution, living at or in the neighborhood of Trenton, whether they are yet living . . . This information is most earnestly entreated by a gentleman of respectability and fortune in England." The inquiries were fruitless. The family had removed from Trenton soon after the disgrace brought upon them by the youngest daughter, and were supposed to have died. It is understood, however, that some of them returned to Trenton early in the present century, and asserted certain rights in the old tavern property. Mr. Shard died in 1806, and in 1819 his widow died, childless and intestate. Her property went to the Crown. In 1846 it was claimed by a distant relative of Mrs. Shard, and in 1856 the matter was still pending in the English Court of Chancery.

RUTHERFURD

MAJOR WALTER RUTHERFURD.

Walter Rutherfurd, born December 29th, 1723, was the sixth son of Sir John Rutherfurd, of Edgerston, Roxburgshire, Scotland, and Elizabeth Cairncross, his wife. Sir John was knighted by Queen Anne in 1706. He had twenty-two children, and at one time eighteen of his sons and grandsons were in the army, navy and East India service. Walter entered the army when but fifteen years old, and served on ships-of-war off the coasts of America, Spain and Portugal until the spring of 1746. During the next eight years he served in the army as Lieutenant of the Royal Scots. At the outbreak of the French and Indian War of 1756 he was ordered to America, holding the positions of Battalion Paymaster and Judge-Advocate of the army, with the rank of Captain (commissioned December 30th, 1755), and subsequently as Major of the Sixty-second or Royal American Regiment. After twenty years of active service, he resigned at the close of the successful campaign of 1760. In the meantime—December 21st, 1758—he had married Mrs. Catherine Alexander Parker, widow of Elisha Parker, of Perth Amboy, and daughter of James Alexander, one of the most eminent lawyers of the day. Her brother was William Alexander, known as Lord Stirling, who served under Washington during the Revolution as Major-General Stirling. After retiring from the army, Major Rutherfurd lived on Broadway, New York, and later built a handsome residence on the corner of Broadway and Vesey street, opposite St. Paul's Church, where the AstorHouse now stands. He had ample means of his own, and his wife had a large estate in her own right. He and James Parker served on the commission which, in 1769, established the northern boundary of New Jersey. In 1775 he received for his military services a patent for five thousand acres of land in Tryon (now Montgomery) county, N. Y. After twenty years of honorable service in the army of his King, which had just been so generously recognized, it was not easy for Major Rutherfurd to take an active part in the revolution against his sovereign. On the other hand, many of his nearest connections were outspoken in the American cause. Accordingly, he retired to his extensive summer estate in Hunterdon county, which he called Edgerston, after his father's place in Scotland. John Stevens, his brother-in-law, and James Parker also retired to the same neighborhood, where they hoped they might keep out of the turmoil of the struggle then waging in New Jersey. The capture of Judge John Fell and Wynant Van Zandt by Tories, and their subsequent imprisonment with barbarous severity, as reported, aroused the indignation of Governor Livingston and the Council of Safety of New Jersey, and they ordered the arrest of Walter Rutherfurd and James Parker, and their imprisonment, as hostages for the proper treatment and safe delivery of Messrs. Fell and Van Zandt. The families of Livingston, Rutherfurd and Parker were on closest terms of friendship, and Mrs. Rutherfurd personally appealed to the Governor for leniency toward her husband. The Governor submitted her letter to the Council of Safety, September 22d, 1777, and it was thereupon agreed that Mr. Rutherfurd "be permitted to go home and remain there for ten days, at the expiration of which he must return to his present place of confinement in Morristown." The biographer of the Rutherfurds erroneously says that the Governor was inflexible in resisting Mrs. Rutherfurd's appeals for kind treatment for her husband. Whatever alienation was occasioned between the Livingston and Rutherfurd families at the time was healed in later years, when Peter Augustus Jay, grandson of the Governor, married Mary Rutherfurd Clarkson, granddaughter of Mr. Rutherfurd. Walter Rutherfurd lived after the war in his Broadway house, New York, where he died January 10th, 1804. His son, John Rutherfurd, born September 20th, 1760, resided near the present Rutherford, on the Erie railroad in Bergen county, New Jersey. He was United States Senator from New Jersey from 1792 to 1798, when he resigned. He died in 1840. The latter's grandson, John Rutherfurd, born in 1810, was one of the benefactors of the New Jersey Historical Society in its early years; he was one of its Vice-Presidents, 1865-1871, and President from January, 1871, until his death, November 21st, 1871. He was President of the East Jersey Board of Proprietors for many years.

MARTEN RYERSON.

Marten Ryerson was baptized Oct. 9, 1698, son of Joris (George) Ryerson and Anneken Schouten. They removed from the Walle Bocht (Wallabout), N. Y., about 1719, to Pacquanac, near the present Mountain View, Passaic County. Marten settled at Readington, Hunterdon county, where he was a surveyor—doubtless through the influence of John Reading, one of the Deputy Surveyors of New Jersey, who visited Pacquanac in 1715, and five years later married a sister of Marten Ryerson. The later died in 1790.

SACKETT FAMILY.

This family of Sacketts descended from Simon Sackett, who, about 1628-29, came from the Isle of Ely, Cambridgeshire, England, and settled at Cambridge, Mass., where he died in 1635. His grandson, Joseph Sackett, born at Springfield, Mass., Feb. 23, 1656, was brought by his maternal grandfather, William Bloomfield, to Newtown, L. I., in 1662, where he died in 1719. His grandson, Joseph Sackett, was a merchant in New York for some years, subsequently removing to Orange county, where he held a large tract of land. His son Joseph was born Feb. 16, 1733-4, became a physician, and practiced in Newtown, L. I., before the Revolution. According to *N. J. Archives*, XX., 578, it would seem that he was practicing in Somerset county in 1761. During the Revolution, it is said that he lived at Paramus, N. J. He died in New York, July 27, 1799.—*Riker's Newtown*, 344-7.

SAYRE FAMILY.

The Sayre family, in the person of two brothers, Thomas and Ananias, sons of Jonas Sayre, settled about 1716 in Cumberland county, at the place now or lately known as Maskell's Mill, where Thomas bought a large tract of land. Ananias was one of the contributors towards the erection of the Presbyterian church at Greenwich, about 1730. He married Mary, daughter of Richard Gibbon. His children were: 1. Hannah, m. Job Remington, of Greenwich; 2. Rachel, m. Job Tyler, of Greenwich; 3. Mary, m. David Mulford; 4. Sarah, m. Richard Cole; 5. Leonard G., removed to Cincinnati, Ohio. Ananias Sayre was Sheriff of Cumberland county, 1748-1751, and 1754-1757. He was appointed a Justice of the Peace for the same county in February, 1751.—*Shourds's Fenwick's Colony*, 227-232; *Elmer's Cumberland County*, 34; *N. J. Archives*, XII., 516; XVI., 267; XIX., 380.

JOSEPH SCATTERGOOD.

Joseph Scattergood was admitted to the New Jersey Bar at the May Term, 1748. In March, 1756, Rebecca Scattergood, executrix, and Hugh

SCATTERGOOD: SCHENCK:
SHARP SHINN

Hartshorne, executor, living in the city of Burlington, advertised requesting accounts to be presented and settled, "the executrix intending shortly to leave the province." They offered for sale "sundry valuable law books," and some small tracts of land.—*N. J. Archives*, XX., 13.

REV. WILLIAM SCHENCK.

William Schenck was a native of Allentown, New Jersey. He was licensed by the Presbytery of New Brunswick in 1771 and ordained in 1772. After preaching at various places in New York and New Jersey, he was finally settled, in 1780, at Pittsgrove and Cape May, where he remained until 1787, when he removed to Ballston, New York. Toward the close of 1793 he removed to Huntingdon, Long Island, and was installed pastor of the Presbyterian Church, December 27th of that year. In 1817 he left Huntingdon and removed to Franklin, Ohio, where he was pastor for several years, and died September 1, 1822. Mr. Schenck was the grandfather of the Hon. Robert C. Schenck, Minister to Great Britain.

ISAAC SHARP.

Isaac Sharp was a son of Isaac, son of Anthony Sharp, born about 1630, of a family holding a large estate in Tillbury, near Bristol, England. In the time of Cromwell he removed to Ireland, where he purchased a large country seat called Roundwood, in Queens county, and carried on an extensive mercantile business in Dublin. On the 22d of 4th mo., 1681, he bought one-tenth of a one-hundredth share of West Jersey, and by several later purchases he acquired further interests in West Jersey and East Jersey. Isaac Sharp, his grandson, came to America about 1730, and settled at Blessington, now Sharpstown, Salem county. He brought the frame of his house with him. He was appointed a Judge of Salem county in 1739, and again in 1741 and 1767. He was a member of the Society of Friends. He established the "Sharpsborough Iron Works" about a mile south of Hamburgh, Sussex county, perhaps about 1765, which proved a losing venture. He was elected to the Assembly in 1769, dying in office about 1770.—*Shourds's History and Genealogy of Fenwick's Colony*, 244-6; *N. J. Archives*, XV., 97; *Ibid.*, XVII., 455; XXVII., 72; *First Sussex Centenary*, 21; *N. J. Hist. Soc. Proceedings*, 1st Series, V., 32.

JOHN SHINN.

John Shinn was among the early English settlers of Burlington, coming over about 1678, or within a few years thereafter.—*Smith's N. J.*, 109. His name is appended to a Testimony of the Burlington Monthly Meeting, 7th of 12th mo. 1680 (March 7, 1681).—*Friends in Burlington*, by Amelia Mott Gummere, 21. He appears to have been a man of considerable substance, and was probably one of the colonists and proprietors of the Yorkshire Tenth, in Burlington. John Shinn was among the signers to a petition to Lord Cornbury praying for the removal of his prohibition of Nov. 14, 1706, against the granting of any warrants for laying out lands. —*N. J. Archives*, III., 165. He was a wheelwright by trade. The following conveyances indicate his prominence and the extent of his possessions in West Jersey:

1687, May 25: John Shinn, senior, and 23 others, proprietors of several undivided shares of land in West Jersey, to Thomas Budd, for 15,000 acres, to be bought from the Indians; grantee to pay the debts of the Province of West Jersey, according to Act of General Assembly of 1687.—

Liber B, ff. 150, 231. 1687, Dec. 14: John Shinn, senior, of Springfield Lodge, Burlington Co., wheelwright, to John Crosby of the same place, millwright, and wife Mary, daughter of said Shinn, for 150 acres, near Bearch Creek.—*Liber B*, f. 168. 1686, Oct. 8: John Skene of Peach-field, West Jersey, gentleman, to John Shinn, senior, of near As-siscunk Creek, for 100 acres in the First or Yorkshire Tenth, to John Skene of Peachfield, West Jersey, gentleman, to John Shinn, senior, of near Assicunk Creek, for 100 acres in the First or Yorkshire Tenth, to be surveyed.—*Liber B*, f. 196. 1686, Oct. 10: Same to same, for a wharf, and a town lot in Burlington.—*Liber B*, f. 197. 1688-9, Feb. 12: John Shinn and other Proprietors consent to the agreement, made by Dr. Daniel Coxe with East Jersey concerning the partition line.—*Liber B*, f. 233. 1686, Sept. 6: Eleazer Fenton to John Shinn, senior, both of Birch Creek, yeomen, for his share (1-16) in the First Tenth.—*Liber B*, f. 247. 1690-1, Feb. 2: John Shinn of Springfield, Burlington Co., wheelwright, to Will-iam Bustill, of said county, carpenter, for 50 acres at Oneanickon, for-merly laid out to Peter Harvey.—*Liber B*, f. 267. 1690-1, Jan. 11: John Shinn, senior, of Burlington County, carpenter, to Edward Bolton of said county, husbandman, for 100 acres near Mount Pisgah.—*Liber B*, f. —. 1695, June 11: John Shinn, of Springfield Lodge, wheelwright, to John Crosby and wife Mary, daughter of grantor, for 150 acres on Birch Creek [apparently the same as above, p. 163].—*Liber B*, f. 443. 1693, April 10: Same to his son-in-law, Thomas Atkinson, and wife Sarah, for 195 acres in Burlington County.—*Liber B*, f. 582. 1697, July 17: John Shinn, of Springfield, Burlington County, wheelwright, to his son, James Shinn, for 120 acres on Birch Creek.—*Liber B*, f. 619. 1711, July 15: John Shinn, of Springfield Township, wheelwright, to John Shinn, junior, of the same place, for 1-15 of one of the 100 shares of West Jersey bought by William Einley of Nottingham, West Jersey, Sept. 18, 1680.—*Liber AAA*, f. 368. The will of John Shinn, senior, of Springfield, names son (sic) Thomas Atkeson and wife Sarah, son-in-law Richard Fenimore and wife Mary, grandchild Mary Crosby, an idiot, sons John, James, son-in-law Joshua Owein and wife Martha, grandson Thomas Shinn; wife mentioned, but not by name. Dated Jan. 11, 1711-12. Proved Feb. 20, 1711-12.—*W. J. Wills, Liber 1*, f. 337.

Second Generation.

John Shinn, senior, had issue, doubtless all born in England:

2. i. John, m. Ellen Stacy, 1686. The following conveyances to and from him are recorded: 1685, May 13: John Renshawe of Burlington, butcher, to John Shinn, Junior, of Birch Creek, West Jersey, husbandman, for 200 acres, to be surveyed in the First Tenth as part of 1-16 of a share, bought by Renshawe of John Haslehurst, Dec. 19-20, 1683.—*Liber BB*, f. 87. 1706-7, Jan. 6: John and Mary Crosby to John Shinn, junior, all of Spring-field Township, for the land, given them by John Shinn, senior.—*Liber BBB* f. 215. 1716, May 17: Joseph Ambler, of Philadelphia, to John Shinn, of Springfield, for 100 acres adjoining Peter Harvey, et al.—*Ib.*, f. 298. 1718, Aug. 27: John Shinn, of Springfield, to John Ogborne, junior, of the same place, for 30 acres there.—*Ib.*, f. 348. 1713-14, Jan. 11: Same to Abra-ham Bickely, of Philadelphia, for 100 acres in Springfield Township.—*Ib.*, f. 421. 1722, June 30: John Shinn, of Springfield, yeoman, to Thomas Budd, of Northhampton, for a meadow in Springfield.—*Liber BB*, f. 379. 1726, June 1: John Shinn, of Springfield, to Widow Sarah Dimsdale, of Hattonfield, Gloucester County, for 618 acres on a branch of Raritan River, in Hunterdon County.—*Liber D*, f. 189. 1736, Oct. 21: John Shinn, of Springfield, to David Lues of Lebanon, Hunterdon County, for 210 acres in Lebanon.—*Liber E*, f. 203. 1736, Oct. 21: Same to his son, William Shinn, for 426 acres in Lebanon.—*Liber E*, f. 205. John Shinn, junior, died

between the date of the deed just cited, and Dec. 12, 1739.

3. ii. Thomas, m. 1st, Sarah Shawthorne, in Burlington Monthly Meeting, 1688; 2d, in 1693, Mary Stockton, daughter of Richard Stockton, whose son, Richard, was the founder of that family in New Jersey. Thomas Shinn and the Stocktons lived in Springfield township, Burlington county. He died in December, 1694. The will of Thomas Shinn, of Springfield, Burlington county (not recorded), dated Nov. 4, 1694, leaves to son Thomas 80 acres; to an unborn child another share of the plantation; "unto my now wife Mary Shinn" the other half of the plantation, to go to the two children, if she should marry again. Witnesses—John Shinn, senior, Isaac Horner, Matthew Champion. Executors—Francis Davenport and John Wilston. Proved Dec. 15, 1694. Widow Mary made administratrix same day. Inventory, taken same day, amounts to £273, 9s., 6d. By deed dated Dec. 14, 1687, Benjamin Wheate, of Burlington county, shoemaker, conveys to Thomas Shinn, of same county, 200 acres of the 500 bought of Benjamin Antrobus, July 23, 1683.—*Liber B*, f. 186. Dec. 28, 1697, Mary, widow of Thomas Shinn, of Burlington county, yeoman, conveys to Richard Stockton, junior, her brother, and John Shinn, junior, her brother-in-law, feoffees in trust to and for her children, Thomas and Samuel Shinn, she intending to become the wife of Silas Crispin, of Pennsylvania, for the plantation in Burlington, bequeathed to her by the last will of her late husband, dated Nov. 4, 1694.—*Liber B*, f. 612. Crispin was of Dublin township, northeast of Pennepach creek, Penn.; he d. May 31, 1711.—*Friends in Burlington*, 83, 84; *Penn. Mag.*, XX., 253.

iii. Mary, m. John Crosby, 1686; 2d, Richard Fenimore, in 1711.

iv. George, m. Mary Thomson, 1691. The will of George Shinn (not recorded), dated Jan. 27, 1694-5, makes his wife Mary sole heiress and executrix, mentioning children, but not by name. Proved March 2, 1694-5. As none of the children are mentioned in the will of their grandfather, John Shinn, Jan. 11, 1711-12, it is probable that they were then deceased.

v. Martha, m. Joshua Owen, 1697.

vi. James, m. Abigail Lippincott, 1697.

vii. Sarah, m. Thomas Atkinson.

Third Generation.

2. John Shinn, junior, had issue:

i. William, who received by deed from his father, in 1736, a tract of 426 acres in Lebanon, as above mentioned.

ii. Clement; he seems to have died without issue. William Shinn, his "brother and heir-at-law," conveyed to their father, John Shinn, all of Springfield, by deed dated Oct. 20, 1736, a tract of 300 acres in Hunterdon county.—*Liber E*, f. 202. This tract was probably given to Clement by his father.

iii. Caleb. By deed dated Dec. 12, 1739, Caleb Shinn, of Springfield, son of John, conveyed to his brother Jacob 100 acres, inherited from their father.—*Liber EF*, f. 147.

3. Thomas Shinn, 1st, had children:

i. Thomas, 2d; he m. Martha Earl, 1718. By deed dated Sept. 7, 1720, he bought from Jennet, the widow, and John, the son, of Alexander Steward (all the parties being of Springfield township, Burlington county), a plantation of 350 acres in that township, on the south side of Barker's creek, between John Ogborn and John Shinn (his brother).— *W. J. Deeds*, Liber DD, f. 79. In 1739 he was living on "the back street" in Bridge-Town (Mt. Holly).—*N. J. Archives*, XI., 582. He was appointed one of the Justices of the Quorum and Assistant Judge of the Burlington common pleas, Aug. 19, 1732; Dec. 1, 1739, and again April 3, 1741; also Judge of that court, July 10, 1746, and on March 28, 1749.—*Ib.*, XV., 98, 197;

XVI., 89; *Liber AAA* of Commissions, 211, 212, 262. He was elected to the Assembly from Burlington county, in 1743, and again in 1744, being classed as "a professed Quaker" in that body, a reputation which he maintained by voting against a militia act.—*Ib.*, VI., 202. At a meeting of the Justices and Freeholders of Burlington county, August 1, 1749, a resolution was adopted ordering the payment of a bill of £10 15s.; there were present fourteen Freeholders and five Justices, Shinn being among the latter. Five Freeholders and all the Justices voted for the bill; five Freeholders voted in the negative, and two did not vote. Complaint was made to the Assembly in the following February, that the bill had been illegally ordered paid, on the ground that a majority vote of all the Freeholders was requisite. The Justices were summoned to appear and answer for their illegal conduct. Two of them promised not to do so again; two refused to make any promises. Shinn was too ill to appear. —*Ib.*, XVI., 222-239. His will, dated 10th of 8th mo., 1751, devises to his children property on Elbo Alley, Burlington, and "plantations, parcels of land, lots and houses not before mentioned." Executors—son-in-law, Henry Paxson, and John Woolman. Witnesses—Benjamin Bispham, Jos⁴ Humphries, John Clark. This will was proved March 10, 1753.—*Ib.*, XIX., 267; *W. J. Wills*, Liber 7, f. 318.

ii. Samuel; probably died young, as he is not mentioned in the will of his grandfather, John Shinn, in 1712.

Fourth Generation.
Thomas Shinn, 2d, and Martha Earl had children:

i. Susannah Atkinson, b. 3 mo. 10, 1721.

ii. Martha, b. 1 mo. 22, 1722-3; m. Henry Paxson.

iii. Thomas 3d, b. 6 mo. 7, 1725; he was Sheriff of Burlington county in 1761. He was appointed guardian of the person and estate of John Hollinshead, Feb. 17, 1776.—*W. J. Wills*, Liber 16, f. 496. Letters of administration were granted on his estate, on March 8. 1777, to Buddell [Biddle ?] Shinn.—*Ib.*, Liber 18. f. 141.

iv. Mary, b. 10 mo. 22 or 23, 1727; m. 4 mo. 3, 1745, Thomas Allin son; he d. 1754, and she m. 2d, James Clothier.

v. Elizabeth, b. 7 mo. 20, 1732; m. Earll.

vi. Earl, b. 10 mo. 27, 1736; m. Rebecca Monrow.

vii. Gamaliel, b. 5 mo. 10, 1738.

viii. Aquila, b. 1 mo. 8, 1739-40.

ix. Postreme, b. 1 mo. 6, 1744; m. John Ridgway, of Mount Holly; she d. 9 mo. 23, 1813 (the record says 1831). Children: 1. Thomas, b. 8 mo. 17, 1761; d. 9 mo. 14, 1761; 2. John, b. 12 mo. 20, 1762; d. 3 mo. 4, 1809; 3. William, b. 11 mo. 6, 1765; 4. Aquilla, b. 10 mo. 16, 1767; d. 9 mo. 1799; 5. Anna, b. 9 mo. 24, 1769; 6. De la plaine, b. 10 mo. 9, 1772; 7. Mary, b. 11 mo. 24, 1774; 8. Martha, b. 8 mo. 5, 1777; 9. Thomas Shinn, b. 11 mo. 4, 1779; m. Mary, dau. of Captain Daniel Joy; d. 4 mo. 1, 1857; 10. Elizabeth, b. 7 mo. 21, 1782; 11. Edmund, b. 2 mo. 13, 1785; d. 9 mo. 15, 1805 (the Meeting records give the name as Edward).

PETER SIMMONS.

Peter Simmons was b. May 29, 1728, and is understood to have been a native of England. About the middle of the eighteenth century he settled at Flushing, Long Island, opposite to Kip's Bay, and there he married Rachel Kip (b. Jan. 12, 1737-8), July 30, 1756; she died Sept. 17, 1804, aged 67 years, 8 months and five days; one of her sisters, Sally, married Abraham Cadmus, and lived at Belleville; another, Leah, married Richard Leaycraft. Peter Simmons was a seafaring man, captain of the ship Henri IV. Being away most of the time

SIMMONS: SIMPSON: SINCLAIR: SKILLMAN

he established his wife with her uncle, Stephen Bassett, who had a tannery on a small run of spring water flowing into the Passaic river, a short distance above the site of the present Dundee dam. Bassett was of French Huguenot descent; he formerly had a tannery and a tap-room in New York. On his farm, at Wesel, were born the children of Peter Simmons. In a storm in the English channel, Peter was washed overboard and drowned, July 5, 1787. He left fourteen children, one of whom, Peter, Jr., married Margaret Westervelt; he was the father of Henry P. Simmons, born July 8, 1815, who was a very prominent character of Passaic for many years, and d. 1896.— *Hisotry of Paterson*, by William Nelson, p. 177.

REV. JOHN SIMPSON.

John Simpson, a native of New Jersey, was licensed by the Presbytery of New Brunswick, in 1770, and for the two following years he preached at Easton, Pa. In 1772 he was appointed by the Synod of New York and Philadelphia to visit Virginia and North Carolina. He spent seven months in this missionary work, and in 1774 was ordained and settled as pastor of Fishing Creek Church, South Carolina. He was a bold and ardent advocate of Independence, and was in many conflicts and skirmishes, in some of which he was regarded as the leader and adviser. He had many narrow escapes, and in the course of the war his house, his library, his sermons, and indeed all that he possessed, were destroyed by the enemy. After the war he gathered his scattered flock, and for ten years prached to them. In 1790 Mr. Simpson became pastor of Roberts and Good Hope Congregations, in Pendleton County, South Carolina, where he continued his labors until his death, February 15, 1808.

COL. SIR JOHN SINCLAIR, Bart.

M. at Elizabethtown, March —, 1769, Col. Templer, of the 26th Regt., to Lady Sinclair, Relict of Sir John Sinclair, Bart.—*N. J. Archives*, XXVI., 401.

REV. ISAAC SKILLMAN.

Isaac Skillman was a native of New Jersey, and was probably a near relative of Thomas Skillman, senior, of Somerset county, whose son Thomas died in 1796. Isaac was born in 1740, and studied in the Rev. Isaac Eaton's school at Hopewell, the first Baptist school in America for the education of young men for the ministry. Having graduated at Princeton in 1766 he pursued his theological studies for some time, and in 1773 was chosen pastor of the Second Baptist Church in Boston, succeeding the Rev. John Davis. Here he remained until 1787, when he returned to New Jersey. In that year the Salem Baptists erected a new church edifice, and it is probable that Mr. Skillman preached for that congregation from that time, but he was not formally installed as pastor until September 18, 1790, succeeding the Rev. Peter P. Vanhorn. He continued in that charge until his death, June 7, 1799. Rhode Island College conferred upon him the degree of A. M. in 1774, and of D. D. in 1798. He died intestate, and administration on his estate was granted, September 18, 1799, to Abraham and Cornelius Skillman.—*Sprague's Annals of the American Pulpit (Baptist)*, 453; *Benedict's Hist. of the Baptists in America*, ed. 1848, p. 587; *Johnson's Hist. of Salem*, p. 88; *West Jersey Wills*, Liber No. 35, p. 526; *Ibid.*, Liber No. 38. p. 412; *Edward's Hist. N. J. Baptists*, 82.

MAJOR JOHN SKINNER.

John Skinner, fourth son of the Rev. William Skinner, of Perth Amboy, was a Lieutenant in the Company of his older brother, Captain William Skinner, in Col. Peter Schuyler's New Jersey Regiment, in the French and Indian war of 1755 and 1756, and was taken prisoner at Oswego in the latter year. He served in Lord Loudon's Regiment in a secret expedition in the Mediterranean, and in the latter part of 1757 received a commission as Ensign in that Regiment. In 1759 he was a Lieutenant in the Regiment of Colonel Grey, and on June 10, 1768, was commissioned Captain. He was afterwards Major of the 70th Regiment, which during the Revolution was stationed in England. Later he sold his commission and returned to America, and engaged in mercantile business at Perth Amboy, where he died in December, 1797.— *Whitehead's Perth Amboy*, 119.

JOHN SMITH.

John Smith was the second son of Richard Smith, of Green Hill, Burlington, and was a brother of Samuel Smith, the historian, and of William Lovett Smith and Richard Smith. He was born "1st mo. 20th, 1722"—March 20, 1722. In 1741 he sailed in one of his father's ships to the West Indies, returning the next year, and in 1743 engaged in the West India trade, in Philadelphia, where he resided for the next twelve or fifteen years, carrying on a flourishing business, and enjoying the company of a delightful society. He occupied a handsome house on Second street, and in 1746 bought a fine country estate at Point-no-Point, on the Delaware, above the town. At these houses he entertained handsomely a wide circle of friends and acquaintances, including the leading men and women of his day. He and some of his young Quaker friends organized a sort of club, devoted to social converse and mutual improvement; and the cares of business, and even the occasional loss of a ship, captured by Spanish cruisers, did not interrupt his quiet pleasures, nor divert his attention from the best authors of the day Fielding's "Joseph Andrews" and Thomas Story's "Journal" being read with apparently equal interest as they came from over the water. In 1747 he wrote for gratuitous distribution a pamphlet, "The doctrines of Christianity, as held by the people called Quakers, vindicated, in answer to G. Tennent's Sermon on the Lawfulness of War." Withal, he found time to promote the organization of the Philadelphia Contributionship, one of the first fire insurance companies in the country, and helped found the Pennsylvania Hospital (1751). He was also prominent in Friends' councils, being chosen a representative to the Quarterly and Yearly Meeting, and held some minor offices not inconsistent with his professions. In 1750, and again in 1751, he was elected a member of the Pennsylvania Assembly. Meantime (1746-7) he had become smitten with the charms of a fair young Friend, Hannah, daughter of ex-Chief Justice James Logan and Sarah Read (daughter of the Hon. Charles Read, of Pennsylvania). She was thus described, in 1744, by an impressionable young gentleman from Virginia: "She was tall and slender, but Exactly well Shap'd; her Eyes Express'd a very great Softness, denoting a Compos'd Temper and Serenity of Mind, Her Manner was Grave and Reserv'd, and, to be Short, She had a sort of Majesty in her person, and Agreeableness in her Behaviour, which at once Suprized and Charmed the Beholder." After this glowing description of the fair Hannah's charms, Mr. Smith's predilection is not to be wondered at. She was a delicate creature, and having accepted his invitation to accompany him and his sister to Evesham Meeting, he with a lover's solicitude for her comfort borrowed Governor Belcher's four-wheeled chaise, said to be the only vehicle of the kind in New Jersey, to carry the party. He returned the compliment in October, 1748, when he brought over by one of his own ships the Governor's intended bride, and on her arrival at Philadelphia procured a four-oared barge and transported her up the river to Burlington. James Logan favored his daughter's suitor, and told him the girl owned 500 acres of land, that he would give her husband £750, that she should have £2,000 on her father's death, and £1,000 more on the death of her mother. Having duly "passed meeting," they were married "10th mo. 7th, 1748" —December 7, 1748—and after spending a day or two at her father's place, Stenton, he took her to his own home in his chaise. She bore him several children, but six weeks after the birth of her last she died —December 18, 1761. He appears to have taken up a residence in Burlington some years before this, occupying the house built by his father in 1720.—*The Burlington Smiths*, passim. In 1757 he was a subscriber to "The New Jersey Association for Helping the Indians."—*N. J. Hist. Soc. Proc.*, January, 1875. He was appointed, December 12, 1758, a member of the Council, on recommendation of Governor Belcher.—*N. J. Archives*, IX., 127, 151, 153. In June, 1761, he was named as one of the commissioners to try pirates.—*Ib.*, 284. On the death of his wife he retired altogether from business, and spent the rest of his days at Burlington, occupying himself in quiet works of benevolence, and in the faithful discharge of his public and private duties. It is related that Governor Franklin having put up for sale his country place at Burlington, with its herd of an hundred deer, the bellman going about the streets of Burlington very early in the morning disturbed Mr. Smith, whose health had been impaired so that sleep was a rare pleasure to him. Putting his head out of the window, he asked what was for sale. "The Governor's Park," was the reply. "Put up your bell and go home, and I will buy the property at the owner's price," exclaimed the Councillor, as he closed his window and tried to resume his disturbed slumbers. Such is the story of his purchase of this fine estate.—*The Burlington Smiths*. Mr. Smith died March 26, 1771, in his forty-ninth year. Proud says of him: "He was engaging, open, friendly and undesigning, in his address and behaviour; of a cheerful and benevolent disposition of mind; well skilled in the laws of his country; and very ready, generous and serviceable, in giving his advice and assistance. In his religious character, he exhibited an excellent example of true practical Christianity, free from all affectation and narrowness of mind. He was, in several relations, one of the best of neighbours and of men."—*Hist. Penn.*, II., 233. Samuel Smith sums up a characterization of him thus eloquently and feelingly: "He was, in every conjugal relation, affectionately tender; a fond father, an indulgent master; he was more. But I must stop— he was—my brother, my most intimate friend and companion! I lost all that could be lost in those relations."—*The Burlington Smiths*, 165; *N. J. Archives*, X., 231-232.

REV. SAMUEL STANHOPE SMITH.

Samuel Stanhope Smith, a son of the Rev. Robert Smith, a distinguished clergyman of the Presbyterian church, was born in Lancaster county, Pa., March 16, 1750. After graduating from Princeton College, in 1769, he returned to his father's house, assisting him in a school, and giving special attention to belles-lettres and moral and intellectual philosophy. In 1770 he was appointed tutor at Princeton, where he remained three years. In 1773 he was licensed by the Presbytery of New Castle, Del., and went as a missionary to Virginia, where he soon became a universal favorite. In order to keep him in Virginia, funds were collected, and Hampden Sidney College was founded, of which he became President. In 1779 he was invited to the chair of moral philosophy at Princeton, which he accepted. On arriving at Princeton, he found the affairs of the College in a deplorable condition, occasioned by the war, and the occupation of Dr. Witherspoon in the higher affairs of the nation. Mainly by the energy, wisdom and self-devotion of Dr. Smith, the College was speedily reorganized, and its usual exercises resumed. In 1794 Dr. Witherspoon died, and Dr. Smith succeeded him in the Presidential chair. His reputation as a pulpit orator at this time was very great. Visitors from Philadelphia and New York were accustomed to go to Princeton to hear his baccalaureate discourses, which were always of the highest order. In 1802, when the institution was at the full-tide of its prosperity, the College edifice was destroyed by fire, with the libraries, furniture, etc. Dr. Smith assumed the labor of collecting money to rebuild; and he was successful in raising, during the year, about $100,000 from the Southern States, and much more from other parts of the Union. In 1812, through repeated strokes of palsy, he became too much enfeebled to discharge the duties of his office, and at the Commencement he sent in to the Trustees his resignation. He died August 21, 1819, in the seventieth year of his age. He was a voluminous and able writer.

SARAH LOGAN SMITH.

Sarah Logan Smith, dau. of the Hon. John Smith, of Franklin Park, Burlington, and Hannah Logan (dau. of James Logan, of Stenton, Chief Justice of Pennsylvania), was b. Aug. 29, 1749; m. William Dillwyn, of Philadelphia, May 19, 1768; d. April 23, 1769. He removed to Higham Lodge, Middlesex, England. Issue: Susannah Dillwyn, b. March 3, 1769; m. Samuel Emlen, of West Hill, April 16, 1795; d. s. p. Nov. 24, 1819. William Dillwyn was a brother of the famous Quaker preacher and philosopher, George Dillwyn, who was b. in Philadelphia, 26th of 2d mo., 1738, entered the ministry in his 28th year, traveled extensively in his work, spending the years 1784 to 1791 in Europe, and again, 1793 to 1802, in Great Britain, and residing in Burlington, N. J., from 1802 until his death, 23d of 6th mo., 1820.

THOMAS SPICER.

Thomas Spicer was a son of Samuel Spicer and Esther, daughter of John and Mary Tilton, of Gravesend, L. I. Samuel Spicer removed from Gravesend in 1686 to Gloucester, near Cooper's creek, opposite the present city of Camden, N. J. Thomas Spicer, his son, was born prior to 1686. He lived on his father's homestead, on Cooper's creek, to which he added large tracts, occupying his time in business affairs. He married Abigail, daughter of Francis and Sarah Davenport, who in 1691 came from Willington, Derbyshire, England, and settled in Burlington county. The will of Thomas Spicer is dated January 4, 1759, and was probated November 7, 1759. He left children:

i. Thomas, married October 1, 1744, Rebecca, daughter of Humphrey and Jane Day; his will is dated May 4, 1760, and was probated October, 1760.

ii. Jacob, married Mary Lippincott; died October 31, 1779, without issue.

iii. Samuel, born October 29, 1720; married 1st, Nov. 16, 1743, Abigail Willard; she died April 24, 1752, he married 2d, Sarah Potter, of Shrewsbury; he died in 1777.

STELLE: STOCKTON

BENJAMIN STELLE.

Benjamin Stelle was a son of the Rev. Isaac Stelle, pastor of the Baptist church at Piscataway, New Jersey. Through the influence of President Manning, of Brown University, he went to Providence, Rhode Island, after leaving college, and established a Latin school. Here he met with encouraging success, giving great satisfaction to his patrons, and being highly esteemed throughout the community. In 1774 Mr. Stelle was admitted to a Master's degree at Rhode Island College.

PONTIUS STELLE.

Pontius Stelle was a son of Gabriel Stelle, a prominent citizen of Perth Amboy, and was the grandson of Poncet Stelle, who is styled in the records of the French Huguenot church of New York, "sieur des Loriers," and is sometimes referred to as "dit desloriers," whence it is inferred that he was from the little village of Lorieres, near Limoge, in the southwest of France. Elizabeth, the first wife of Gabriel Stelle, died July 29, 1723, aged 38 years, 2 mos., 1 day. She and her infant son Benjamin (died November 14, 1719, in his third year) are buried in Christ church burying ground, Shrewsbury. She was the mother of Pontius Stelle. The latter was a member of the Assembly from Perth Amboy, 1745-49. He is mentioned as of Amboy in 1740. In 1747 he was appointed one of the commissioners to disburse the funds for the expedition against Canada. Administration on the estate of Pontius Stelle was granted, November 12, 1770, to Benjamin Biles.

JOHN STOCKTON.

John Stockton was the fourth son of Richard Stockton, the first settler of that family at Princeton, and received by his father's will five hundred acres of land, "part of his dwelling plantation," known as "Morven." He was appointed a Judge of the Somerset County Common Pleas, March 28, 1749, and was probably reappointed in 1754. He was a warm friend of the College of New Jersey (now Princeton University), and is understood to have been largely instrumental in securing the removal of the College from Newark to Princeton. While it was still at Newark, he was appointed one of the committee to receive subscriptions in its behalf, in January, 1748-9. In 1754 he had for sale tickets in the Connecticut lottery for the benefit of the College. When the corner stone of Nassau Hall was laid, at Princeton, in September, 1754, he was one of the gentlemen who officiated at that important function. He was a Trustee of the College, 1748-58. He died at Princeton, on Saturday, May 20, 1758. His will, dated May 9, 1758, was probated June 9, 1758. He does not mention his wife, she having probably predeceased him, but names children: 1. John; 2. Richard (the Signer of the Declaration of Independence), 3. Phillip (a well-known clergyman); 4. Hannah; 5. Susanna; 6. Rebecca; 7. Abigail. In Hageman's "Princeton and its Institutions" it is stated that he also had Samuel Witham, who was entrusted with many important positions.

The *New York Mercury* of June 5, 1758, publishes the following obituary notice of John Stockton:

"Prince-Town, (in New-Jersey) May 23. Saturday last, after a painful Illness, departed this Life, John Stockton, Esq; of this Place, in the 57th year of his Age. As his Life has been so generally useful, his Death apparently diffuses an universal Sorrow. For about twenty-five years past, he has, with great Acceptance, executed the Office of a Magistrate, and about half the Time, that of a Judge of the Court of

Common Pleas: His Judiciousness, Moderation, and Integrity, in his various Decisions as a Magistrate, rendered him peculiarly dear to the Place and Country in which he lived; where his Merit acquired him a great Influence. As his Situation in Life made it unnecessary for him to regard lucrative Motives, in the Discharge of his public Offices, so his unaffected and steady Piety to God, and universal benevolence to Mankind made him indefatigable in his Endeavours to compose Differences, promote Peace and Harmony, suppress Immorality, and encourage Virtue and true Religion. In the social Duties of Life, he distinguished himself as a tender Husband, an affectionate Father, a kind Master, and a faithful Friend: His last Sickness he supported with great Patience and Composure, and received the Evidences of his approaching Dissolution, with that Magnanimity which true Religion inspires. It pleased God to give him strong Confidence in the Truth of the Gospel, and the Merits of his Lord and Saviour; and when he found his *'Flesh and his Heart to fail,'* he doubted not, and has left his Acquaintances not the least Room to doubt, but that *'God was the Strength of his Heart and his Portion for ever.'* "

RICHARD STOCKTON.

Richard Stockton was descended from an English family of Stockton, in Durham, on the river Tees, England. The first of the family to immigrate to America, Richard Stockton, settled at Flushing, L. I., whence he removed to Burlington county, N. J., where he bought 2,000 acres, March 10, 1692. He died in 1707, leaving children Richard, John, Job, Abigail (Ridgeway), Sarah (Jones), Mary, Hannah and Elizabeth. His son Richard removed from Flushing to Piscataway, and thence (in 1696) to Princeton, buying 400 acres, and in 1701 bought of William Penn 4,450 acres more, in and about the present Princeton. He died in 1709, leaving six sons—Richard, Samuel, Joseph, Robert, John, Thomas. His estate being divided soon after, the homestead, now known as "Morven," fell to John, who became an influential man in the community. He was a Judge of the Somerset Common Pleas, and was a warm friend of Princeton College.—*Princeton and its Institutions*, by John F. Hageman, I., 33-9. Richard Stockton, son of John, was born at Princeton, October 1, 1730, was one of the first class graduates from the College of New Jersey, in 1748, studied law under David Ogden, was licensed in 1754 as an attorney, in 1758 as a counsellor, and in 1764 as sergeant, his practice meantime becoming co-extensive with the Province, and even reaching beyond its limits.—*Ib.*, 78; *Provincial Courts of New Jersey*, by Richard S. Field, 192; *Life of Com. Robert F. Stockton*, 9-10; *Sketch of Life of Richard Stockton*, by William A. Whitehead, N. J. Hist Soc. Proc., January, 1877; *Rules of Supreme Court, N. J.*, 1885, Appendix, by G. D. W. Vroom, 54, 59. In 1764, writing to his former law student, Joseph Read, he suggested as the readiest solution of the troubles between England and her Colonies the election of some bright Americans to Parliament (Reed's Reed, I., 30); but a year later, during the controversy over the Stamp Act, he took the positive ground that Parliament had no authority over the American Colonists; so rapidly did public sentiment develop in those times.—*N. J. Hist. Proc.*, 149. In 1766 he went to England, where he spent a year, mingling in the highest circles, and had much to do with persuading Dr. Witherspoon to accept the Presidency of Princeton College.—*Hist. of College of N. J.*, by John MacLean, I., 297, 385; *Provincial Courts*, 192-6. Appointed to the Council in 1768 (see ante, page 59), on the recommendation of Governor Franklin, he stood so well with the Governor that six years later he was commissioned one of the Justices of the Supreme Court, as above, to succeed Judge Reed, removed to the West Indies. The affairs of his country were evidently on his heart and mind during these trouble-some times, and under date of December 12, 1774, he drafted and sent to Lord Dartmouth "An Expedient for the Settlement of the American Disputes, humbly submitted to the consideration of his Majesty's Min-isters," in which he suggested substantially a plan of self-government for America, independent of Parliament, without renouncing allegiance to the Crown.—*Historical Magazine*, November, 1868, 228. He retained his position in the Council until the end of royal government in New Jersey, and attended the meetings of that body as late as November 24, 1775.—*Minutes Provincial Congress*, etc., 323. He was elected to the Continental Congress, June 22, 1776.—*Ib.*, 473. Six days later the New Jersey delegates took their seats in Congress, in time to hear the clos-ing debate on the Declaration of Independenc, and Mr. Stockton is said to have made a "short but energetic speech" in favor of the measure.—*Works of John Adams*, III., 53-8; *Field's Provincial Courts*, 197. While he was still attending to his duties in Congress, a large number of his friends and admirers at home favored him for Governor, and on the first ballot in the Legislature (August 30, 1776) the votes were equally divided between him and William Livingston, who was chosen the next day.—*Minutes Joint Meeting*, passim; *Sedgwick's Livingston*, 205-6. Gordon alleges this whimsical reason for the preference: "Mr. Stockton having just at the moment (of the ballot) refused to furnish his team of horses for the service of the public, and the Legislature coming to the knowledge of it, the choice of Mr. Livingston took place immediately." —*History of Revolution*, ed. 1789, II., 108. The true reason doubtless was that it was thought best to have a man of some military instincts in the Governor's chair, and Livingston was then in camp. Be that as it may, the Legislature the same day (August 31) elected Mr. Stockton to be the first Chief Justice of the new State, but he declined, prefer-ring just then the more active career of a Congressman.—*Minutes Joint Meeting*, passim; *Sedgwick's Livingston*, 206. On September 25, 1776, Congress appointed him on a committee of two to visit the Northern army, and he set out immediately. He was greatly affected at the un-fortunate condition of the patriot soldiers. Writing from Saratoga, October 28, to Abraham Clark, he says the New Jersey soldiers were "marching with cheerfulness, but great part of the men barefooted and barelegged. My heart melts with compassion for my brave country-men who are thus venturing their lives in the public service, and yet are so distressed. There is not a single shoe nor stocking to be had in this part of the world, or I would ride a hundred miles through the woods and purchase them with my own money."—*American Archives*, 5th Series, II., 561, 1256, 1274. He left Albany on his homeward journey November 21. Two days later he was appointed by Congress on a com-mittee "with full power to devise and execute measures for effectually re-enforcing Gen. Washington, and obstructing the progress of Gen-Howe's army."—*Ib.*, III., 784, 828. During the ensuing week he was ap-pointed on other committees, but it is doubtful if he ever resumed his seat in Congress after setting out from Albany, for by the time he could reach Princeton the British were marching triumphantly through New Jersey, and he was compelled to seek shelter for his family with a friend, John Covenhoven, in Monmouth county. There he was surprised and captured by a party of Tories, who shamefully treated him, and dragged him by night to Perth Amboy, where he was temporarily con-fined in the jail in bitterly cold weather, until he could be removed safely to New York, where he was locked up in a foul prison, and treated with such indignity that Congress was impelled (January 3, 1777) to for-mally remonstrate against his treatment, and took measures to secure his exchange. When released his health was hopelessly shattered, and he was an invalid until relieved by death, February 28, 1781, at Princeton. The date of his arrest is generally given as November 30, 1776, being the very day on which the New Jersey Legislature re-elected him to Congress for another year. He resigned February 10, 1777.—*Hageman,* ut supra, I., 86; *Provincial Courts,* 198-9; *Lossing's Field Book of the Revolution,* ed. 1789, II., 175; *Raum's Hist. N. J.,* I., 423; *Whitehead,* ut supra; *Whitehead's Perth Amboy,* 254; *Gordon's N. J.,* 324. Mr. Stockton married Annis Boudinot, daughter of Elias Boudinot, of Elizabethtown, and sister of Elias Boudinot, LL. D., President of Congress, 1782-3, and first President of the American Bible Society. Dr. Boudinot married (1762) Mr. Stockton's sister.—*Hatfield's Elizabethtown,* 588-9; *Helen Boudinot Stryker, in Penn. Hist. Mag.,* III., 191. Mrs. Stockton frequently wrote verses for the periodicals of the day, and one of her compositions, addressed to Washington, on the surrender of Cornwallis, elicited from him a most gallant and courtly acknowledgment.—*Mag. American Hist.,* V., 118; VII., 66. Mr. Stockton left children: Richard (the "Duke"), Lucius Horatio, Julia (married Dr. Benjamin Rush), Susan (married Alexander Cuthbert), Mary (married the Rev. Dr. Andrew Hunter), Abby (married Robert Field).—*Provincial Courts,* 199. The fullest and most accurate sketch of the family, and especially of the Signer, is given by John F. Hageman, Esq., in his admirable and deeply interesting history of "Princeton and Its Institutions," I., 86-88.—*N. J. Archives,* X., 427-430.

RICHARD V. STOCKTON.

Richard V. Stockton, known as "Stockton the Land Pilot," was Major of the Sixth Battalion, New Jersey Volunteers (Loyalists). He was surprised, with sixty-three privates of his battalion, and taken prisoner, February 18th, 1777, by Colonel John Neilson, of New Brunswick, and was sent in irons to Philadelphia, by order of General Putnam. To this course General Washington objected, he considering that Major Stockton should be treated as a prisoner of war and not as a felon. He was tried by court-martial at Philadelphia, August 15th, 1780, for the murder of Derrick Amberman, of Long Island, found guilty and sentenced to death. The sentence was not carried out. He accompanied the Tory refugees to teh province of New Brunswick. Four sons and a daughter accompanied him in exile.—*Sabine's Loyalists,* II., pp. 334, 335; *New Jersey Volunteers (Loyalists),* by W. S. Stryker, 34. Richard V. Stockton was probably the son of Samuel Stockton (son of Richard Stockton, 2d, the first of the family to settle at Princeton, 1696, who died in 1709), born 1694-1695, died 1739. Major Stockton married a daughter of Joseph Hatfield, of Elizabeth, N. J.—*Ancestry of the Children of Jas. William White, M. D.,* by William Francis Cregar, 1888, p. 108; *Hatfield's Elizabeth,* p. 462; *Hageman's History of Princeton,* I., pp. 38, 39. Richard Stockton, of Somerset county, was advertised August 24th, 1779, as "a fugitive now with the enemy."—probably the same person.

SAMUEL WITHAM STOCKTON.

Samuel Witham Stockton was a brother of the elder Richard Stockton. In 1774 he went to Europe as Secretary of the American Commission to the Courts of Austria and Prussia. While abroad he negotiated a treaty with Holland. He returned to New Jersey in 1779, where he held various public offices. In 1794 he was Secretary of State of New Jersey. Mr. Stockton lost his life by being thrown from a carriage in the streets of Trenton, June 27th, 1795.

STREYDT: STRUYT: TAYLOR

CHRISTIAN STREYDT.

Christian Streydt and Ursula, his wife, came to America from Germany before 1720. Christian Streight, who graduated from the Philadelphia College in 1768, was pastor of the Lutheran churches at Easton, Pa., 1769-1779, and Greenwich, N. J., 1773-1777.

CHRISTIAN STRUYT.

Christian Struyt and Maria Etsels (or Orseltie) doubtless lived in the Saddle River Valley, in the northwestern part of Bergen county, probably in the vicinity of Masonicus, where there was a Lutheran church established in the middle of the eighteenth century. They had children, baptized in the Hackensack Reformed Dutch church: 1. Margrita, Nov. 14, 1714; 2. Anne Catherine, b. at Ramapough, July 13, 1717; 3. Elisabeth, b. at Ramapough, Feb., 1718; 4. Johan Leonhard, b. July 28, 1720. The last-named was doubtless the Leonard Streit who signed a call to the Rev. John Albert Weygand to become rector of Zion Lutheran church at New Germantown, and who, in 1758, was one of the managers of the lottery for the benefit of the newly erected St. Paul's Lutheran church at Pluckamin. In 1756 he lived on the property owned in 1880 by Jacob V. D. Powelson. He sold, May 29, 1766, a tract of 260 acres to Jacob Van Derveer. In the petition, 1767, of the rector, wardens and vestrymen of Zion and St. Paul churches for a charter, his name appears. He was still living in Bedminster township, Somerset County, in 1774.

MATTHEW TAYLOR.

Matthew Taylor, said to have been a distant connection of Sir George Carteret, came to New Jersey to speculate in lands, and dying in New York in 1687 without issue devised his lands to his brother Edward, then living in London. The latter came to America in 1692, and bought an additional tract of about 1,000 acres at Garret's Hill, Middletown, and settled on it. He died in 1710, leaving four sons and one daughter. George, one of his sons, resided at Garret's Hill, and died there, leaving three sons—George, Edward and John.—*Hist. Monmouth Co.*, by Franklin Ellis, Philadelphia, 1885, 524. The John Taylor just mentioned, son of George, son of Richard, was born in 1716, and was known as 'Squire John. He lived at Upper Freehold. There was a John Taylor High Sheriff of Monmouth County in 1753, doubtless the same man, although the writer just quoted says the Sheriff was the son of Edward, and nephew of 'Squire John, which is obviously improbable. In 1754 he was an unsuccessful candidate for the Assembly.—*N. J. Archives*, XIX., 382. Being a man of large wealth, and presumably of influence in the community, he was selected by Lord Howe, when he came to America to offer terms to those in arms, to be "His Majesty's Lord High Commissioner of New Jersey." This arrayed his patriotic neighbors against him, and he was compelled to join his British friends in New York, while his property was applied to the uses of the Continental forces. His lands in Monmouth County were advertised to be sold in 1779. After the war he returned to New Jersey. He died at Perth Amboy, aged 82 years. His daughter Mary married Dr. Absalom Bainbridge, and two of her sons distinguished themselves in the War of 1812, in the United States Navy—Commodore William Bainbridge, and Post-Captain Joseph Bainbridge. The early education of the future Commodore was superintended by his maternal grandfather, John Taylor.—*Old Times in Old Monmouth*, 48; *Life of Commodore Bainbridge*, 3.

REV. WILLIAM TENNENT.

William Tennent was born at Antrim, in the North of Ireland, June 3, 1705, the son of the Rev. William Tennent, who married, May 15, 1702, a daughter of the Rev. Gilbert Kennedy. The Rev. William Tennent came to America in September, 1716, with his wife, four sons and a daughter. He was the founder of the famous "Log College," that celebrated training school for Presbyterian ministers, among whom his own four sons were justly distinguished. He died May 6, 1746.

William Tennent, 2d, is most widely known from the story that has been told of his falling into a trance for three days, during which time "he felt himself wafted along under the guidance of a superior being, till at a distance he beheld an unutterable glory; he saw an innumerable host of happy beings, and heard their songs of praise with rapture. He thought, 'Well, blessed be God, I am safe at last, notwithstanding all my fears.' He was about to join the happy company, when someone came to him and said, 'You must go back.' It was like a sword through his heart; with the shock he awoke." Having studied divinity with his brother Gilbert, he was ordained October 25, 1733. He married the widow of John Noble, of New York. He took a deep interest in the mission of David and John Brainerd among the Indians of New Jersey. A notorious horse thief, Tom Bell, having impersonated the Rev. John Rowland, and in that guise ridden off with a fine animal, Mr. Rowland was indicted for the theft, in 1741. Mr. Tennent and two of his elders testified on the trial that at the time of the theft they were in company with Mr. Rowland in Maryland, one hundred miles or more from the scene of Tom Bell's exploit. Rowland was thereupon acquitted, but by a curious perversion of justice Tennent was indicted for perjury. The story handed down by tradition is that on the day appointed for trial a man and a woman arrived from Maryland, having been miraculously warned in a dream that they must come to Trenton to avert impending danger to Mr. Tennent; they knew that his account was true. Thereupon the prosecution was abandoned. These extraordinary occurrences were narrated in a manuscript addressed to Elias Boudinot, LL. D., by Dr. Thomas Henderson, a physician of Freehold, who was not born until more than ten years after the time laid for the trance, and a year or two after the horse-stealing episode. He received the stories from his father, an elder in Mr. Tennent's church, who died in 1771. Dr. Henderson's MS. is in the library of the N. J. Historical Society. It was communicated by Dr. Boudinot to the *Evangelical Intelligencer*, and published in 1806, under the title "Memoirs of the Rev. William Tennent, late pastor of the Presbyterian Church at Freehold, New-Jersey," and thence transferred to book form, running through numerous editions. Many publishers subjoined the attractive addendum to the title: "In which is contained, among other interesting particulars, An Account of his being THREE DAYS in a TRANCE, and apparently lifeless." An edition printed at Salem, Mass., in 1814, is a very small 12mo, 3x5 inches, pp. 129. A Wilmington edition, 1819, contains 72 pp., in much smaller type, and is 3½x5½ inches. In a paper read before the N. J. Historical Society, September 11, 1851, the late Judge Richard S. Field gave some interesting details regarding the defence of Mr. Tennent on the indictment for perjury, in 1742, and expressed the belief that the two miraculous witnesses had been hunted up and brought forward through the well-directed intelligence and energy of his counsel, three of the ablest lawyers in the country.—*N. J. Hist. Soc. Proc.*, VI., 30. Mr. Tennent's manner "was remarkably impressive, and his sermons, though seldom polished, were generally delivered with indescribable power; what he said seldom failed to instruct and please. He was remarkable for a pointed attention to the particular circumstances of the afflicted in body and mind. Eminent as a peacemaker, all were charmed with his converse. His hospitality and domestic enjoyments were proverbial. More than six feet high, of a spare, thin visage, erect carriage, with bright, piercing eyes, his countenance was grave and solemn, yet at all times cheerful. He lived above the world, with such clear views of heavenly things as seemed to give him a foretaste of them."—*Memoir.* He died March 8, 1777.

REV. WILLIAM MACKAY TENNENT.

William Mackay Tennant was a son of Rev. Charles Tennent, of Delaware, and a nephew of William and Gilbert Tennent. He was ordained, June 17, 1772, as pastor of the Congregational Church in Greenfield, Conn. In December, 1781, he resigned his charge and accepted a call to the Presbyterian Church at Abington, Pennsylvania, where he continued till his death, December, 1810. Dr. Tennent married a daughter of the Rev. Dr. Rodgers, of New York. In 1797 he was Moderator of the General Assembly of the Presbyterian Church.

EPHRAIM TERRILL.

Ephraim Terrill was born in 1714; he was appointed Justice of the Peace in 1768; Deputy Mayor of Elizabethtown in 1774; took a pronounced stand in favor of the Colonies at the beginning of the Revolution; died Aug. 13, 1786, in his 73d year. He was a son of Ephraim Terrill, who died June 18, 1761, in his 72d year. Thomas Terrill, a blacksmith, who in 1675 had a considerable estate in Southold, L. I., bought of William Cramer, Aug. 19, 1696, a plot of land in Elizabethtown, and soon after removed thither. He died in 1725. He was the ancestor of the Terrill family of that town.—*Hatfield's Elizabeth*, 272, 285, 410; *Tombstone Inscriptions, Elizabeth,* 318-319; *N. J. Archives*, XVII., 503.

JAMES THOMPSON.

James Thompson was a tutor in Princeton College, 1762-1770, and in 1767 occasionally supplied the pulpit of the Presbyterian church in Trenton.

WILLIAM THOMSON.

William Thomson was admitted as an attorney and counsellor of New Jersey, May 11, 1758. His will is dated September 14, 1765. In it he speaks of his wife Margaret, and children, whom he does not name. He devises real and personal estate, and names as executors his father, Benjamin Thomson, and his brother-in-law, Edmund Leslie, and Peter Schank. The will is witnessed by James Leslie, William Millan and Hugh Thomson. It was proved October 2, 1765.—*E. J. Wills*, Liber H, page 551.

TOOKER: TUTHILL: TUTTLE

CHARLES TOOKER.

[1]Charles Tooker d. Jan. 15, 1810, in his 66th year, and is buried in the old Presbyterian churchyard in Elizabeth. His widow, Mary, d. Oct. 14, 1814, aged 63 yrs. Their dau. Ann, wife of Benjamin Marsh, is also buried in the same ground, having d. April 8, 1789, in her 19th year.

SAMUEL TUTHILL.

Samuel Tuthill, son of John Tuthill, was born Sept. 22, 1724. He was graduated at Yale College, and appears to have studied medicine, as there are references to him as "Doctor" Tuthill. He is mentioned so often in the local annals of Morristown that he evidently was a leading man in the community. Gov. Bernard appointed him a judge for Morris county, March 19, 1759, and he was again appointed April 21, 1768. In 1773 Lord Stirling complained that Samuel Tuthill and Colonel Samuel Ogden had acted in an unfair and partial manner in "taking the examinations and depositions of several witnesses of and concerning several criminal matters" inquired into by them as judges of the Morris county court of oyer and terminer; he also charged that they had "suppressed the testimony of some material witnesses for bringing certain criminals to justice." These charges being made to the Council of the Province, Col. Ogden in behalf of himself and Judge Tuthill demanded an inquiry. But Lord Stirling withdrew the charges, and the matter was dropped. When Princeton College appealed to the Morristown church (among others) for aid, in 1769, he subscribed £3. He was one of the trustees of the Morristown "Green" in 1771. He was among the first to take a decided stand on the American side in the Revolution, being appointed a member of the Morris County Committee of Correspondence, June 27, 1774, and again on January 9, 1775. The Provincial Congress, on Oct. 27, 1775, appointed him Lieutenant Colonel of the Regiment of Light Horse in the eastern division of the Colony, which he resigned February 3, 1776. He was chairman of a meeting held Sept. 25, 1792, at which was organized the Morris County Society for the Promotion of Agricultural and Domestic Manufactures, which was merged in 1812 in the Morris Library Association, and he was the first President of that society. He was chosen first moderator of the Fire Association of Morristown, organized July 26, 1797. He married, November 3, 1751, Sarah Kenny, daughter of Jacob Ford, senior, and widow of John Kenny. He renewed his covenant with the Presbyterian church of Morristown, April 1, 1754. He died May 31, 1814, in his ninetieth year. His wife joined the church on confession, August 29, 1771. She died November 12, 1811, aged 80 years.

REV. JAMES TUTTLE.

James Tuttle was born May 7, 1742, the son of Col. Joseph Tuttle and his second wife, Abigail Nutman, sister of the Rev. John Nutman. Col. Tuttle was an Elder in the Hanover (Morris County) Presbyterian church for many years. Young Tuttle was fitted for College in the school of his pastor, the Rev. Jacob Green, and having graduated at Nassau Hall in 1764 studied theology with Mr. Green. In 1767 he was licensed to preach, by the Presbytery of New York. On Feb. 2, 1767, he married Anna, daughter of the Rev. Jacob Green. In April he became pastor of the Rockaway Presbyterian church. Before the end of 1769 he became too ill to preach, and so continued until his death, at Hanover, Dec. 25, 1770. He had but one child, Benajah, who died a few weeks before him. Mr. Tuttle was also pastor of the Parsippany

TUTTLE: VALLEAU: VANARTSDALEN: VAN BOSKERCK

church. He lived at Rockaway, in a parsonage built expressly for him. His tombstone (at Hanover) says: "This man of God had a short race but swift, he ran far in littel time. Few exceeded him in sweetness of Temper, Tenderness of conscience and fidelity In his ministerial work and the End of this man was Peace."—*Annals of Morris County*, by the Rev. Joseph F. Tuttle, 1876, p. 80.

PETER VALLEAU.

P. Valleau was a witness at the marriage, in the French Church in New York, September 29, 1689, of Susanne Valleau to Aman Bonin. He married Madelaine Fauconier, daughter of Peter Fauconier. They had children: 1. Peter Theodorus, born April 28, 1716, baptized in the Reformed Dutch Church at Hackensack; 2. Magdelaine, born August 21, 1718, baptized in the French Church in New York; 3. Susanne, born October 14, 1720, baptized in the French Church, "daughter of Pierre Valleau and of Mdlle Magdelaine his wife." She m. Dr. John Bard, of Philadelphia, in 1741. Magdelaine Valleau gave a deed, April 13, 1750, to the Paramus Church, for forty-five acres for a burying-ground, part of the consideration being "three places or seats in the Paramus church that is to say one womans place and two mens places." This burying-ground is known as the "Valleau Cemetery," and is still admirably kept, after a lapse of a century and a half. Theodorus Valleau doubtless lived at Paramus. He married Elizabeth Anthony, and had children (baptized at Schraalenburgh or Hackensack): 1. Jan, bap. July 2, 1738; 2. Andries, bap. April 20, 1740; 3. Steven Cummins, b. September 22, 1742; 4. Samuel, bap. December 15, 1745; 5. Jacobus, bap. January 3, 1748; 6. Marytie, bap. August 20, 1749; 7. Magdalene, b. August 12, 1750; 8. Theodorus, bap. January 19, 1751.

REV. JACOB VANARTSDALEN.

Jacob Vanartsdalen, a native of Somerset County, New Jersey, was b. Feb. 8, 1745, the sixth son of Philip Van Artsdalen, who was b. Feb. 12, 1701, and d. June 17, 1797, at Somerset. He was ordained by the Presbytery of New Brunswick, June 19, 1771; in which connection he remained until the latter part of 1774, when he was received by the Presbytery of New York and put in charge of the Church of Springfield, New Jersey. He continued in the orderly and faithful performance of the duties of the office, as far as his health permitted, for more than a quarter of a century. In the spring of 1797, and again three years later, he was, by reason of long continued illness, disqualified for preaching. He was at length compelled to relinquish the pastoral office, and was dismissed from the charge, May 6, 1801. From 1793 to 1802 Mr. Vanartsdalen was a Trustee of Princeton College. He died at Springfield, N. J., October 24, 1803. His wife was Mary Sutphen, of Somerset, who survived him. They had three daughters and one son, Elias Van Arsdale, a prominent lawyer, of Newark.—*Hatfield's Elizabeth*, 570.

LOURENS ANDRIESSEN VAN BOSKERCK.

Lourens Andriessen Van Boskerck came from Holstein, Denmark, in the summer of 1655, and with others bought, January 6th, 1676, a large tract of land at "New Hackensack," on which he resided as early as 1688. The family have been numerous in the English Neighborhood, Bergen county, ever since. John Jacobus Van Buskirk was probably the John (son of Jacobus, son of Peter, son of Lourens Andriessen)

VAN BOSKERCK: VAN BUNSCHOOTEN: VAN CLEVE

who was born November 28th, 1739. He was charged with holding communication with the enemy on Staten Island, July 8th, 1776, but on being tried was acquitted. Abraham, son of Laurence, was a Captain in the Rangers (Loyalists); at the close of the war he sailed for Nova Scotia, in 1783, but died on the voyage, at the age of thirty-three years. Dr. Abraham Van Buskirk was appointed Surgeon of the Bergen Regiment, February 17th, 1776, but did not serve long.

REV. ELIAS VAN BUNSCHOOTEN.

Elias Van Bunschooten was born Oct. 26, 1738, at New Hackensack. Dutchess county, N. Y., son of Teunis Van Bunschoten. After graduating from Princeton College in 1768 he studied for the ministry with the Rev. Dr. Myer, was licensed in 1773, and in the same year was settled over the Reformed Dutch church at Schaghticoke, on the Hudson, where he labored until 1785, when he resignd. On the 29th of August of the same year he was installed over three churches—Minisink, Magaghamack (near the persent Port Jervis), and Walpack, covering fifty miles of territory—in Orange county, New York. In 1792 he gathered an additional church at the Clove, now Port Jervis, where he resided until 1812, when, on account of the infirmities of age, he withdrew from active duties. He died Jan. 10, 1815. He was in person about six feet in height, erect and stately in his carriage, and was a man of great sternness of character. His manner in the pulpit was earnest and impressive, and his sermons highly evangelical. He preached both in Dutch and English. In his intercourse with his neighbors he seems to have displayed a parsimony that was harsh and miserly, dealing justice rather than mercy. That his object in accumulating money was not selfish was shown when he attended the General Synod in 1814, and emptied pocket after pocket on the Moderator's desk, until he had turned over $800 in cash, and $13,840 in securities, which he gave to Rutgers College, in trust, the income to be used to aid young men to prepare for the ministry. By his will he increased the fund to $17,000. It was allowed to accumulate to $20,000, at which it still stands. The interest has assisted nearly two hundred young men in their studies.

BENJAMIN VAN CLEVE.

Benjamin Van Cleve resided at Maidenhead (now Lawrenceville), near Princeton. He was a son of John Van Cleve, who took up his residence at Maidenhead, where he died in 1772, aged 72 years, and is buried there, in the old cemetery. Benjamin Van Cleve was elected chosen freeholder from Maidenhead in 1775, and a member of the township committee, 1774-76, and 1802. He was commissioned First Lieutenant, First Regiment, Hunterdon county militia, at the beginning of the Revolution; Captain of the same; Captain, Colonel Johnson's battalion, Heard's brigade, June 14, 1776; Second Major, First Regiment, Hunterdon, March 15, 1777; resigned Nov. 13, 1777, on his election to the Assembly. He was again elected to that body in 1779, taking his seat Sept. 16, as the successor of John Hart, deceased. He was elected in the fall of 1779 for the full term of one year, and again in 1780, 1781, 1783, 1784, 1785, 1786 1787, 1788, 1791, 1792, 1793, 1795, 1796, 1797, 1798, 1800, 1801, 1802, 1803, 1804, 1805. He was elected Speaker of the Assembly, Nov. 19, 1784, to fill a vacancy, and was again chosen in 1785, 1786, and 1788. He was appointed a justice of

VAN CLEVE: VANDERVEER: VANHORN

the peace for Hunterdon county, Sept. 7, 1776, Sept. 29, 1781, Nov. 7, 1786, Nov. 9, 1791. Nov. 4, 1796, Jan. 28, 1797. On Dec. 18, 1782, he was appointed one of the judges of the Hunterdon county court of common pleas, which probably accounts for his non-election to the Assembly in that year. When "the Presbyterian Church in the township of Maidenhead" was incorporated, in 1787, Benjamin Van Cleve was one of the trustees named in the certificate of incorporation. The board of. justices and freeholders of the county chose him to be clerk of that body in 1791. Benjamin Van Cleve m. 1st, Mary, dau. of Joseph Wright; she d. 1784, aged 38 yrs.; he m. 2d, Sept. 20, 1786, Anna, dau. of the Rev. Caleb Smith, of Orange, and wid. of George Green, of Maidenhead; she d. 1789, aged 40 yrs. Issue (by his first wife):

    i. John Wright, graduated at Princeton College, 1786; licensed as an attorney, September term, 1791; as a counsellor, November term, 1796; m. Elizabeth, dau. of Isaac Coates, of Philadelphia; d. 1802. Children: 1. Mary, m. Dr. Garbett, of Georgia; 2. Elizabeth; 3. Cornelia, m. Daniel Barnes, of New York.

    ii. Phebe, m. John Stevens; d. s. p.

    iii. Cornelia, m. Thomas Stevens.

    iv. Elizabeth, m. Dr. Israel Clarke, of Clarkesville. Children: 1. Mary, m. Dr. Alexander Hart, of Philadelphia; 2. Elizabeth.

    v. Joseph W., b. 1777; m. Charity Pitney, of Morristown (prob. b. Mar. 31, 1782, dau. of James Pitney and Elizabeth Carmichael); d. 1864, aged 87 yrs. Children: 1. Mary, m. Stacy Paxon, of Trenton; she d. May 26, 1847, aged 49 yrs.; 2. Phebe; 3. Benjamin Franklin, m. Phebe, dau. of Joshua Anderson and Jemima Broadhurst, both of Trenton; 4. Elizabeth, d. young.

Issue by his second wife, Anna (Smith) Green:

    vi. A son, d. in inf.

DR. LAWRENCE VAN DERVEER.

Lawrence Van Derveer was from Somerset county. He was an original member of the New Jersey Medical Society, in 1766. Later he removed to Shepardstown, Va., but soon returned to Somerset county, and practiced at Roycefield. He exploited the value of the *Scutellaria Lateriflora* in the prevention and cure of hydrophobia, and claimed to have used it successfully in four hundred cases. His method was kept secret. He was highly regarded by his neighbors, as a generous friend of the poor. He died in 1815.

REV. PETER PETERSON VANHORN.

The Rev. Peter Peterson Vanhorn (son of Dr. Peter Vanhorn) was born August 24th, 1719, at Middletown, Bucks county, Pennsylvania. and was bred a Lutheran, but joined the Baptists, September 6th, 1741, and was ordained to the ministry June 18th, 1747, and installed pastor of the church at Pennepek, near Philadelphia. He resigned this charge in 1762, and removed to Newmills, in Northampton township, Burlington county, N. J., where a Baptist church was organized on June 23d, 1764, of which he was one of the constituent members, and became pastor. He resigned April 2d, 1768, and returned to Pennepek. Two years later (April 7th, 1770) he was called to the pastorate of the Baptist church at Cape May, which he resigned in 1775. He was also

VANHORN: VAN HORNE: VAN METERS
VIERSELIUS

pastor of the Baptist churches at Dividing Creek and Salem at various times. One of his sons, William Vanhorn, was pastor of the Scotch Plains Baptist church, 1785-1807. See *Morgan Edwards's History of the Baptists*, passim; *Johnson's History of Salem*; *Hatfield's Elizabeth*, etc. Peter Vanhorne and Sarah Mode, both of Bucks county, Pa., were married Sept. 4, 1771, by the Rector of St. Mary's Church, Burlington. Was this the Rev. Peter Peterson Vanhorn, mentioned above? It seems improbable.

JACOBUS (or James) VAN HORNE.

Jacobus (or James) Van Horne, baptized in New York, June 29, 1712, was a son of Johannes Cornelissen Van Hoorn, of New York, and Catharina Meyer, his wife, daughter of Andries Jansen Meyer and Vrouwtje Iden van der Vorst; Johannes Van Hoorn and Catharina Meyer were married March 20, 1693. Jacobus, or James, was their tenth child. He married, Dec. 16, 1742, Margareta, daughter of Samuel Bayard, of New York. His father was a New York merchant, who began buying land in New Jersey in 1706, adding steadily to his purchases during the next sixteen years, acquiring extensive tracts in Somerset and Middlesex counties especially, as well as in Monmouth county. In his will, dated June 23, 1733, he devises to his sons James and Abraham the Rocky Hill tracts. James repeatedly offered for sale his place at Rocky Hill; in 1755 he was living on a farm of 1,668 acres at Dover, near Cheesequakes creek, Middlesex county, and advertised that for sale, also. His will, dated Oct. 29, 1760, was proved April 20, 1761. He gives all his estate to his sons John and James, "James to be given the best education the Province of Pennsylvania affords, either at the Academy or Mr. Dove's English school, then to study physic or law and complete his studies in Scotland." He mentions his late wife Margaret. His brother, Cornelius Van Horne, was for several years a member of the Council of New Jersey.

THE VAN METERS.

The Van Meters were among the early settlers of Ulster county, N. Y. About 1714 a number of the Reformed Dutch people of Esopus and vicinity removed to Pilesgrove, now Upper Pittsgrove, Salem county. Among the newcomers were John and Isaac Van Meter, who, in company with the Dubois family, bought from Daniel Coxe, of Burlington, a tract of 3,000 acres. The Van Meters subsequently added to their purchase, until they owned about 6,000 acres in Upper Pittsgrove. The new colony does not appear to have organized a church for many years, the people worshiping in the schoolhouse or in private residences; but on April 30, 1741, they signed a covenant organizing the Presbyterian church of Pittsgrove, and built a log house of worship. Among those who signed the covenant were Isaac Van Meter and Henry Van Meter, the latter being the son of John, then deceased. Isaac had a son Garret, who married a daughter of Judge John Holme, in 1774. Henry Van Meter was married four times. In his will he names children Joseph, Ephraim, John, David, Elizabeth, Rebecca, Jacob (removed to the Genessee country, N. Y.), and Benjamin, who died 15th of 10th mo., 1826, aged 82 years.—*Shourds's Fenwick Colony*, 301-305.

DR. GEORGE ANDREW VIERSELIUS.

George Andrew Vierselius emigrated from Germany about 1749, or earlier, and settled on the Old York Road, half a mile from Three

Bridges, in Amwell township, Hunterdon county. He was naturalized by act of the Legislature, Nov. 28, 1760. He was an energetic and
successful physician, traversing a wide region of country. He died
in 1767. His descendants generally write the name Vescelius.

REV. STEPHEN VOORHEES.

Stephen Voorhees was b. in 1740, being a son of Isaac Voorhees (b.
March 16, 1716), whose father, Jan Lucasse Van Voorhis, was b. at
Flatlands, L. I., but removed to Six Mile Run, Somerset county, with
three of his brothers—all sons of Lucas Stevense Van Voorhees—and
all four of them were among the founders of the Six Mile-Run Dutch
church in 1717. After graduating at Princeton College in 1765, Stephen
studied theology and taught a classical school at Hackensack, from
1766 until the fall of 1769, part of the time in association with Francis
Barber. In November, 1769, he started a grammar school in New York
city. He was licensed by the General Meeting of Ministers and Elders
of the Reformed Dutch Church, in 1772, and was ordained and settled at
Poughkeepsie, New York, in 1773, where he remained until 1776. From
1776 to 1784 he was pastor of the Reformed Dutch Church at Rhinebeck
Flats, N. Y.; and from 1785 to 1788 at Philipsburg (Tarrytown) and
Cortlandtown, New York. In 1792 he joined the Presbytery of New
Brunswick, and preached as a supply at Kingston and Assunpink, New
Jersey, until his death, November 23, 1796. He m. Elizabeth Clausen,
b. 1749, d. Feb. 23, 1805. See *The Van Voorhees Family*, 358; *Corwin's
Manuel of the Reformed Dutch Church*; *Our Home* (Magazine), etc.

PETER WARD.

Peter Ward was the son of Thomas Ward, an Irishman who settled
near Long Pond (now Greenwood Lake) in the early part of the eighteenth century, where he was probably connected with the Iron Works,
perhaps as manager of the store of the American Company. Peter, born
in 1756, having married Nancy Mead, of Pompton. removed thither.—
Hist. Bergen and Passaic Counties, 1882, 190. During the Revolution he
served as Captain of light horse, Bergen County.—*Stryker's Records of
Officers and Men in the Revolutionary War*, 1876, 416. Under an act of the
Legislature, June 25, 1781, he was appointed recruiting officer for Bergen
County.—*Ib.*, 47. Under a call for troops, Dec. 29, 1781, he was appointed
Captain for Bergen County.—*Ib.*, 328. After the Revolution he bought, by
deed dated July 2, 1784, from the Commissioners of Forfeited Estates, in
Bergen County, a tract of one hundred acres of land, confiscated from
Christian Pullisfelt, who had been adjudged guilty of treason.—*Bergen
County Deeds*, F., 198. By deed dated July 16, 1784, he bought in the same
manner the forfeited estate of Robert Drummond, of Acquackanonk,
sixty-three acres in extent.—*Bergen County Deeds*, H., 43. These two
farms lay at Campgaw, Franklin Township, Bergen County, and he
occupied them thenceforth until his death.—*History of Bergen and Passaic Counties*, 190. He held many offices after the war: Chosen Freeholder from Franklin Township, 1788, 1792, 1793, 1796, 1797.—*Ib.*, 83. Judge
of the Common Pleas, 1808.—*Ib.*, 83. He was a member of the Assembly from Bergen in 1792-3-4-6-7-8-9, 1800, 1801-2-4-5-9-10-11, and represented
the county in the Council in 1807.—*Legislative Journals*, passim. He died
in 1812, aged fifty-six years. He left children: Peter (who was a
Brigade-Major in the War of 1812), John, Jane, Catharine, Thomas.
James, William and Mary.—*Hist. Bergen and Passaic Counties*, 190.

WARDELL : WARRELL

JOHN WARDELL.

John Wardell, of Shrewsbury, was a Coroner of Monmouth County in 1762, and in the same year was appointed one of the Common Pleas Judges of that county. At the beginning of the Revolution he arrayed himself on the British side, and was sent to New York. His lands were confiscated, and were advertised to be sold on March 29, 1779.

JOSEPH WARRELL.

Joseph Warrell was recommended, December 18, 1732, by Governor William Cosby, for a seat in the Council of New Jersey. "He was so well recommended to me by Lord Malpas, before I left England, that there is little more for me to say in his behalf that since my acquaintance with him his behaviour has in every particular confirmed the character given by his Lordship, and one that I can answer for."—*N. J. Archives*, V., 324; *N. Y. Col. Docs.*, V., 939-40. This appointment was not made, but he received the office of Attorney General of New Jersey, which was probably more to his liking, August 28, 1733.—*Book AAA of Commissions*. The Lords of Trade again, Aug. 28 and Sept. 5, 1735, recommended Warrell's appointment to the Council in place of James Alexander, he having been reported as "every way qualified to serve His Majesty in that station."—*N. J. Archives*, V., 410; *N. Y. Col. Docs.*, VI., 35-36. He was actually appointed, it seems, but apparently did not care enough for the unremunerative honor to go to the expense of taking out the warrant, which elicited an expression of annoyance from the authorities a year later.—*N. J. Archives*, XI., 441; V., 454. On December 17, 1733, the Council of New York wrote to the Duke of Newcastle that Lewis Morris had sent to represent him, "Joseph Warrell, Esq., a gentleman of the law and of very fair character."—*N. Y. Col. Docs.*, V., 981. He and William Cosby, of Amboy, and a number of others, petitioned the New York authorities, July 13, 1734, for 20,000 acres of land in the Mohawk country, and on October 4, 1734, a tract of 22,000 acres was surveyed to them, known as "Cosby's Manor," in Herkimer and Oneida Counties.—*Cal. N. Y. Land Papers*, 210, 212, 1003. No record has been found of his origin, nor of his admission to the New Jersey bar, but in 1737 he was residing at Trenton.—*N. J. Archives*, XI., 518. He was appointed, August 13, 1746, one of the quorum Justices of the Peace for Middlesex County.—*Ib.*, XIV., 464. In 1751 he was living at Bellville, near Trenton, and stated that he had lived there many years, and consequently could give a good character of Samuel Tucker, his neighbor, having known him since Tucker was a boy.—*Ib.*, VII., 613. He asked leave to resign, July 5, 1754, in order "to make his declining part of life comfortable." "The long Fatigue of upwards of twenty Years Service without any just Imputation of Failure in my Duty under the Disadvantage of too small a Support from the Assembly (& no likely hood of its increase) will plead for the Reasonableness of my Request to Your Excellency for a Quietus at my age."—*Ib.*, VIII., Part I., 293. As an officer of the Crown the Assembly was naturally averse to increasing his compensation, which stood at the not extravagant figure of £30 a year, payable quarterly. Besides, he prosecuted the pleas in the various counties, as far as practicable, for which he was paid the usual fees. His resignation was promptly accepted by Governor Belcher, and Courtlandt Skinner, whom he had recommended as his successor, was appointed ten days later. Joseph Warrell died in the summer of 1758. Nevertheless, when George III. ascended the throne, a warrant was ordered, by the King in Council, for continuing in office the appointees of the late King, including Joseph Warrell as Attorney General. This warrant was dated, appropriately enough, March 17 (St. Patrick's day), 1761. The fact had been overlooked that Skinner was still in the office, which he retained until the Revolution. Mr. Warrell's wife was of the Bradshaw family, in England. He left two children:

i. Joseph, who was manager of a lottery for the Trenton English and Grammar School, in 1753; was licensed as an attorney, May 13, 1758; was Clerk of the Circuits, 1765-8, and died at Trenton, March 6, 1775. His tombstone, in the First Presbyterian churchyard, is thus inscribed:

"In the Memory of Joseph Warrell, Esq., who departed this life March 6th, 1775; aged 36 years. This stone is erected, not from pomp, or pageantry, but from true affection.

> "For other thoughts employ the widowed wife;
> The best of husbands, loved in private life,
> Bids her with tears to raise this humble stone,
> That holds his ashes, and expects her own."

ii. A daughter, who married Abraham Cottnam, a leading lawyer of Trenton. She had children: 1. Warrell Cottnam; 2. George Cottnam, licensed as an attorney, May, 1780; 3. Martha, m. Robert Hoops, who was a Major in the American Army in the Revolution.

JOHN WATSON.

John Watson, the first painter known to have settled in America, came from Scotland about 1715, and took up his residence at Perth Amboy. He returned to Europe, and brought thence to America a considerable collection of pictures, some of his own composition. So that "the first painter, and the first collection of paintings [in America] of which we have any knowledge, were planted at Perth Amboy." Mr. Watson was so penurious that he was styled "the Miser of Perth Amboy," and besides was extremely irascible. He was unmarried, his family consisting of himself, a nephew, and a niece, for whom he had sent to Scotland soon after his establishment here. He died August 22, 1768, aged 83 years, and is buried in the rear of St. Peter's church. What became of his paintings is not known.—*Whitehead's Perth Amboy*, 125.

REV. JAMES WATT.

James Watt was in 1770 ordained and installed pastor of the Presbyterian Church at Cape May, N. J., by the First Presbytery of Philadelphia. He died November 19, 1798. Upon his tombstone we read, "If disinterested kindness, integrity, justice and truth deserve the tributary tear, here it is claimed."

BENJAMIN WILLIAMS.

Benjamin Williams was a descendant of Matthew Williams, who was of Weathersfield, Conn., in 1636, and whose son, Matthew, was born in 1652 or 1653. The latter was among the Branford colonists who agreed to settle in Newark, but he went to Long Island, and thence to Barbadoes, whence he was granted a ticket of migration to the Colonies, Jan. 14, 1678. He was admitted to Newark as a planter in 1680. In 1686 he took up land near the mountain—now Orange—and there he died, Nov. 12, 1732, in his eighty-first year. His oldest son, Amos Williams, lived on his father's place, and died there in 1754, aged 63 years. The oldest son of Amos was Benjamin, who is said to have been fourteen years old at his father's death. This must be an error, if he was the Benjamin

WILLIAMS : WILLIAMSON :
WITHERSPOON

Williams who in 1758 advertised a runaway negro servant. Benjamin, son of Amos, had a saw-mill, a cider mill and distillery, a tannery, currying shop and shoe shop. He took a protection from the British when they marched through Newark in December, 1776, and on Feb. 27, 1777, took the oath of allegiance to the King and joined the Royal militia in New York. He soon became dissatisfied, or was persuaded by his patriot cousin, Captain Thomas Williams, to forsake his new allies, for on August 4, 1777, he renounced allegiance to the King, and took the oath of fidelity to the State of New Jersey. Thereafter he was quiescent during the war, his sympathies with the British, while prudence bade him be loyal to the country. So many of his relatives were of his mind that their neighborhood is to this day known as "Tory Corner." He died in 1826.—*Wickes's History of the Oranges*, 50, 274, 308.

GENERAL MATTHIAS WILLIAMSON.

Matthias Williamson was born about 1716, being the son of William Williamson, of Elizabethtown, who died Jan. 10, 1735. His mother was Margaret, daughter of Capt. Matthias DeHart; she married, second, William Chetwood, who kept a famous inn, known by "The Sign of the Nag's Head," in that ancient town. which she continued some years after his death, and as late as 1759. In that year Matthias lived near the tavern. He was Lieutenant of a company of cadets at Elizabethtown in 1740, and was High Sheriff of Essex County in 1757. In 1759 he was designated an alternate Paymaster of the New Jersey expedition against Canada. On Dec. 6, 1774, he was selected by his fellow citizens to serve on the Committee of Correspondence for Elizabethtown. He was commissioned Colonel of a regiment of light horse, Oct. 27, 1775; Brigadier General of the New Jersey Militia, Sept. 6, 1776: Brigadier General commanding a brigade, State troops, Nov. 27, 1776, which last named commission he resigned, Feb. 6, 1777. He also served as Assistant Deputy Quartermaster General, as Assistant Quartermaster General, and as Quartermaster General. In all these various positions he rendered good service to the patriot cause during the Revolution. He was a vestryman of St. John's Episcopal Church in 1749, and was an active and liberal supporter of that church for many years. He married Susanna Halsted. His residence was some years ago occupied as the Union Hotel. He died at Elizabeth, Nov. 8, 1807, aged 91 years. He was the father of Isaac H. Williamson, who was Governor and Chancellor of New Jersey, 1817-1829, and who died July 10, 1844; the latter was the father of the late ex-Chancellor Benjamin Williamson.

Mathias Williamson was a native of Elizabethtown, New Jersey. After graduating at Princeton College in 1770, he studied law, and was admitted to the Bar in November, 1774; but the war commencing, he became an officer in the Commissary department. He died in Elizabethtown in 1836, aged 84.—*N. J. Archives*, XXVII., 268.

JAMES WITHERSPOON.

James Witherspoon, a son of President Witherspoon, was a young man of great promise, who graduated at Princeton College in 1770. He joined the American army as aide to General Nash, and was killed at the battle of Germantown, October 4, 1777.—*N. J. Archives*, XXVII., 268.

WOODHULL: YOUNGLOVE

REV. JOHN WOODHULL.

John Woodhull was born in Suffolk County, Long Island. He studied theology with the Rev. John Blair, and was licensed by the Presbytery of New Castle in 1768. He settled at Leacock, Lancaster County, Pennsylvania, where he was installed, August 1, 1770. Mr. Woodhull was a strenuous Whig, and while in this charge advocated the cause so eloquently from the pulpit that he succeeded in enlisting as soldiers every male member of his congregation capable of bearing arms, he going with them as chaplain. In 1778 he succeeded the Rev. William Tennent at Freehold, New Jersey. During many years of his ministry he conducted a grammar school, and superintended the studies of young men preparing for the ministry. He was a Trustee of Princeton College for forty-four years. Mr. Woodhull received the degree of Doctor of Divinity from Yale in 1798. He died Nov. 22, 1824.—*Hist. of Old Tennent Church*, by Rev. F. R. Symmes, 1897; *Funeral Sermon.*

YOUNGLOVE.

Younglove is an unusual name in Morris county. Israel (perhaps an error for Isaiah) Younglove is mentioned among the common pleas judges in 1760. Ezekiel Younglove, of Reddis Town, married Mary Lyon, May 16, 1746, and on presenting his child, Dorcas, for baptism, in the Morristown church, Sept. 27, 1747, renewed his covenant as a member of the church.

Index to Names

[The following index is to surnames only, except where Christian names appear in the titles to biographies. The bold face type indicates the classified biographies, of which there are 224].